BRITISH EMPIRE
1837
...ssessions shown in Solid Black
...d underlined in Black

HEROES FOR
VICTORIA

Heroes for Victoria

JOHN DUNCAN & JOHN WALTON

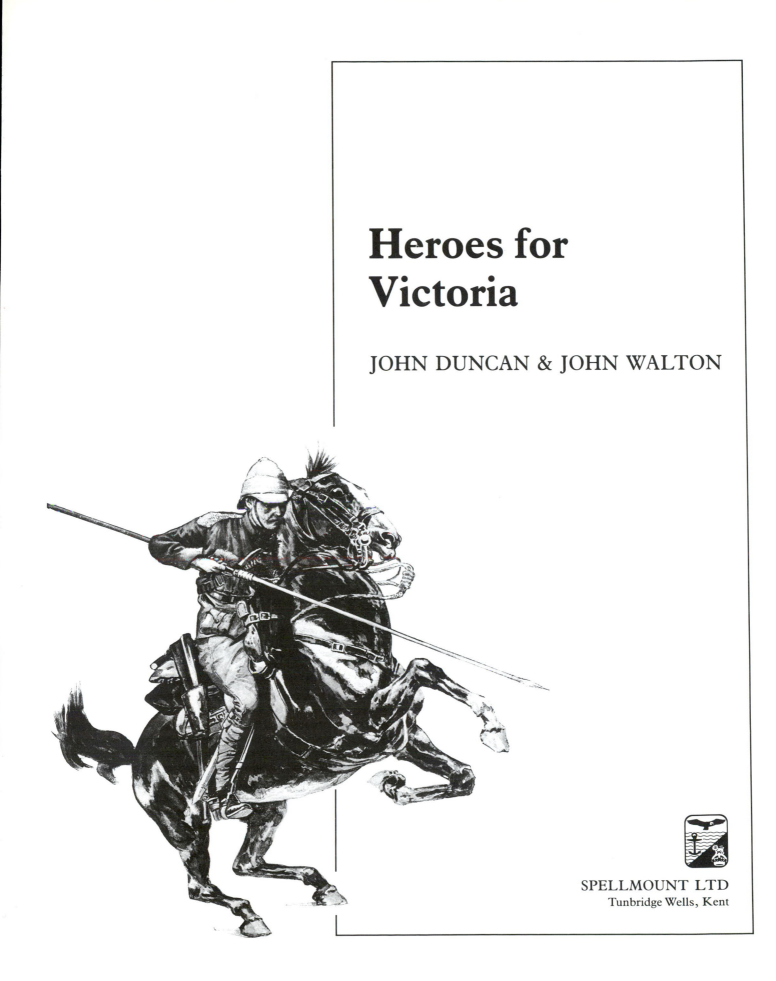

SPELLMOUNT LTD
Tunbridge Wells, Kent

First published in the UK in 1991 by
Spellmount Ltd
12 Dene Way, Speldhurst
Tunbridge Wells, Kent TN3 0NX
ISBN 0-946771-38-3

© John Duncan & John Walton 1991

British Library Cataloguing in Publication Data
Duncan, John
   Heroes for Victoria 1837-1901: Queen Victoria's fighting
   forces. – (Military pictorial histories)
   1.   Great Britain. Military forces. History
   I. Title   II. Walton, John   III. Series
   355.00941

ISBN 0-946771-38-3

Design by Discourses Ltd
Typeset by Vitaset, Paddock Wood, Kent
Printed and bound in Great Britain by
Mackays of Chatham PLC, Chatham, Kent

Contents

Acknowledgements

We wish to thank the following organisations for permission to use the illustrations and quoted extracts in this book:

Army Museums Ogilby Trust
Illustrated London News
India Office Library
National Army Museum
National Maritime Museum
Portsmouth Publishing and Printing Limited
Spellmount Archive

Every effort has been made to trace the copyright holders, but if there has been an inadvertent omission the publishers will be pleased to insert an appropriate acknowledgement in all subsequent editions.

The authors particularly wish to thank Major John Tamplin TD and Major Alan Harfield BEM of The Army Museums Ogilby Trust for their invaluable assistance in providing illustrative material and details of the Indian Army. Our thanks are also due to the Librarians and staff of The National Army Museum, the National Maritime Museum, and the India Office Library; to Marilyn Clarke and her colleagues at Vitaset, to Diane Drummond of Words and Images, and to John Morley-Clarke.

All the maps were specially drawn by Graham Payne.

Authors' Notes

To late 20th century eyes the way the Victorians spelt the names of Asian and African places and people may appear confusing, insensitive and – in some cases – even a touch patronising. The Amirs of Baluchistan appear as *Ameers*, *Meers* or *Mirs*, and are sometimes described as *Baloochees*, *Baluchees* or *Baluchis*. But *Cabool*, *Cabul* and *Kabul* clearly all refer to the same place, as do *Umballa*, *Amballah*, *Ambala*, *Ambeyla* and *Ambela*. Consistency is an admirable goal, but one rarely capable of achievement.

Part of the difficulty lies in the fact that we are concerned with transliteration, not merely translation, from languages whose scripts we do not share, and that conventions in these matters vary over the years. In modern times, for example, Cawnpore (in its English form) has been changed to Kanpur – and so the process continues. It seemed to us that the only sensible course was to follow the source wherever possible. So in this book names are given as they appeared in the diaries, journals, despatches, letters, campaign medals and regimental honours referred to. In the main text modern spellings are used for the most part, but these may also vary from one source to another, as may distances, dates and other statistics, even some of those taken from official documents.

☐ ☐ ☐

Throughout the book lists of battle honours appear, as close as possible to the relevant sections in the main text. These details are taken from official sources, but some care is needed in their interpretation. For example, the dates shown are those on which the honours were awarded, and do not always correspond with the actual dates of the battles or campaigns to which they refer. As already mentioned above, the spelling of place names follows the form in which they originally appeared, and may introduce a further degree of inconsistency. Despite these limitations it is hoped that readers may find it helpful to see at a glance which regiments were involved in each of the many actions mentioned in the main text.

Introduction

VICTORIA'S long reign was a great age for heroes and for heroines although, with few exceptions, women and their achievements largely went unhonoured and unsung. For it was men who dominated Victorian society and set the expansionist mood during the latter part of the nineteenth century.

The reasons for this were twofold. In gaining an empire almost by accident the British, as other imperialists before and since have discovered to their cost, found it necessary to expand in order to defend what they had previously acquired. This 'forward policy' brought regular employment to the Queen's armed forces, as the chronology near the end of this book shows, but little peace or security to tribes and small nations living on imperial borders.

The other driving force behind Britain's expansion in many parts of the world was the need to secure raw materials for her industries, and markets for the goods they manufactured. 'Trade follows the flag' was a popular saying at the time, but the exact opposite is much nearer the truth: the flag was often very reluctant to follow traders and entrepreneurs. The Admiralty, for example, discouraged junior naval officers from planting the Union Jack on islands, occupied or otherwise, they chanced upon during their long voyages.

But the imperial imperative could not be restrained so easily, and as a seafaring race the British knew all about the strategic importance of islands. Furthermore, the steady replacement of sail by steam made it necessary to establish coaling stations along the sea routes of the Empire. Inevitably, as the Victorian age blossomed so did the number of pink dots and patches on maps of the world, most of them drawn to Mercator's projection, exaggerating the already huge land masses of Canada and the Northwest Territories to the north, and Australasia to the south.

While the Royal Navy kept up its ceaseless patrols, protecting Britain's trade routes, supporting her armies, fighting slave traders and pirates, exploring unknown seas and charting the oceans and coasts of much of the world, it was Queen Victoria's soldiers who were called upon, year after year, to fight in small wars or engage in 'punitive' expeditions and campaigns. These were often undertaken in the most difficult and hostile of terrains, and gruelling climatic conditions. The lives of the soldiers and the sailors who were Heroes for Victoria and the hardships they endured are evidence enough that her reign was not, as is so often imagined, a long period of peace and tranquillity interrupted only by the Crimean and Boer Wars.

Heroes for Victoria they certainly were, for she not only instituted the highest award for valour, but to the end of her days she insisted on presenting personally, whenever possible, medals and honours for gallantry and outstanding service. Although we may no longer share Victorian values, it is difficult not to share the admiration expressed by the Queen and the great majority of her subjects for the courage and leadership of such men as John Nicholson, Colin Campbell, Charles Gordon, 'Bobs' Roberts, and even the impossible Lord Cardigan. And as we can see from the extracts quoted from letters and diaries written by privates, NCOs and junior officers, such as private Pearman, RSM Loy Smith, Captain Charles Ewart and 14-year-old Trumpeter Frank Wilde, courage and leadership were not qualities found, as Wellington assumed, only among those born to high rank and command.

The many messages of congratulation or of sympathy that the Queen always sent so promptly to her forces in action throughout the world reveal, in their wording, how deep and sincere was her interest in her fighting men and in their welfare. Hers was a real emotional involvement, which found its response in the affection displayed for the 'widow of Windsor', much warmer and stronger than simple loyalty to the Crown would have required. Victoria had her critics among politicians and others, then as now, but to her soldiers and her sailors she was always 'The Queen, God bless her'.

It was Victoria's instinctive understanding of the men and women who served her that made the monarchy an element of stability against a background of social and technological change, greater than during any previous reign. Sail gave way to steam, as already noted, iron and steel replaced wooden hulls, professionally-trained officers were replacing gentlemen who purchased their commissions, and an increasingly literate public was able to read for itself reports in newspapers and magazines about the ordeals and the triumphs of those who fought for Queen and country.

When the young Victoria came to the throne her Army's 'thin red line' was a proven battle-winner; by the end of her reign it had become a death-trap. In place of the 'Brown Bess' musket, her soldiers went into battle with long-range, highly accurate rifles and deadly machine guns. The Royal Navy had exchanged square-rigged sailing ships for armour-plated battleships with turret-mounted guns of immense range. Telegraphy was rapidly taking over from flag-signalling and heliographs. But perhaps the most significant change of all was that ordinary soldiers and seamen were no longer pressed or flogged into service, but were recruited willingly into forces that offered them adequate training for a respectable career, decent conditions, reasonable pay and a pension on retirement.

It is to the memory of men such as these, and those who went before them, named and unnamed, that with admiration and respect we dedicate this book.

Royal Tunbridge Wells

John Duncan
John Walton

7

*Heroes for Victoria throughout her
long reign were her soldiers and sailors,
beginning with veterans of
Waterloo and Trafalgar . . .*

The Young Queen's Army

Virtually unknown when she
came to the throne, Queen
Victoria performed her royal
duties with 'extraordinary
facility' and soon laid the
foundations of the
remarkable age that bears
her name.

IN THE FIRST years of her reign, Queen Victoria's Army numbered some 5000 officers and 124,000 NCOs and men; in all, about 1% of the total male population of the United Kingdom. All of them owed allegiance to the Queen as their sovereign – an allegiance which meant a great deal to Her Majesty as well as to her soldiers. She herself firmly believed that the Army was her personal property – not without reason, since in English law the Monarch always was, and still is, head of the armed services. But at the time, not even those most concerned with military matters could say with any certainty who controlled, organised, deployed, supplied, financed and paid the Queen's Army, or even who was in command at any one time.

The British Army was not a standing national army as were Continental armies. Indeed, authority for its very existence depended on the passage of the annual Army Act. The Commander-in-Chief since 1828 was Lord Hill who was little more than the Duke of Wellington's shadow, and whose ill-defined powers were derived from the Crown and not from Parliament. A kind of Chief of the General Staff with a bureaucracy rather than a General Staff, he had his office at the Horse Guards in Whitehall. He was, in theory at least, in command of all British troops – but not when they were overseas. Authority to employ the Army in Great Britain, and even to issue arms, lay with the Home Secretary, who also controlled the Yeomanry and the Militia. Almost all other military matters came under the Secretary of State for War and the Colonies, who was responsible not only for the employment of troops in the colonies but for the size and cost of the army.

Financial administration, including pay and pensions, was the responsibility of yet another minister – the Secretary-at-War, who accordingly possessed the greatest power of all in military affairs. But there was also the Master-General of the Ordnance, who was in charge of all fortifications, barracks and equipment, and probably of the Royal Artillery and the Royal Engineers as well. The Commissariat a civilian body controlled by the Treasury, which had ultimate control of army finances was in charge of supplies and transport. The Board of General Officers looked after clothing, the Purveyors Department supplied some, but not all, of the Commissariat's needs, and the Medical Department, though financed by the Secretary-at-War, was very independent in practice. To add to the confusion, many Commanding Officers tended to ignore anything coming from Whitehall, since they regarded their regiments as their own private property.

The young Queen's Army consisted of her Household Cavalry and Foot Guards, twenty-four cavalry regiments and just over a hundred numbered infantry regiments of the line. There were three regiments of Household Cavalry –

The 1st and 2nd Life Guards
(later The Life Guards)
The Royal Horse Guards (The Blues)
and three regiments of Foot Guards –
The 1st or Grenadier Regiment
The 2nd or Coldstream Regiment
The 3rd or Scots Fusilier Guards
(later The Scots Guards)

The Guards were socially prestigious regiments and were very rarely called upon to serve overseas, which caused some bitterness in the rest of the Queen's army.

The cavalry regiments were usually brigaded into Heavy and Light Brigades, as in the Crimean War. A Heavy Brigade of Dragoon Guards and Dragoons rode stronger, heavier horses than a Light Brigade of Hussars, Lancers and Light Dragoons. The cavalry always thought themselves superior to the infantry, and in Victoria's day most cavalry officers were 'tremendous swells', aristocratic horsemen who rode with great vigour and dash but knew little or nothing of the real business of war. The Old Duke grumbled that European cavalry won battle for their commanders, but *his* cavalry invariably got him into scrapes.

It was the infantry of the Queen's Army that won battles for her all over the world. Infantry regiments had been numbered since 1751, but almost all of them were also known by a regional, county or other title, e.g. The 1st or Royal Scots, the 3rd or East Kent (The Buffs), and the 60th or The King's Royal Rifle Corps. Their training consisted of endless drilling and marching, cleaning and polishing, to fit them to stand steadily in line to shoot and be shot at, and then to advance silently on the enemy until close enough to charge with fixed bayonets and blood-curdling yells. Their standard weapons at this period were a smooth-bore musket ('Brown Bess') and a bayonet.

The gunners of the Queen's Army were embodied in The Royal Regiment of Artillery founded in 1716 as a supporting arm for the infantry, and in the Royal Horse Artillery founded in 1793 to provide 'galloper guns' for the cavalry. Other supporting corps were the Corps of Royal Sappers and Miners, later The Corps of Royal Engineers, which produced a number of Heroes for Victoria, including Gordon and Kitchener, and the unloved Commissariat, a civilian body which was responsible for supplies and transport.

The regiment was the characteristic feature of the British Army, which made it quite

The Duke of Wellington: Commander-in-Chief of the British Army, 1827-8 and 1842-1852

The Iron Duke

It is difficult for us now to appreciate how great was the Duke of Wellington's prestige and authority after Waterloo – the victorious commanders of two later World Wars never enjoyed such enormous respect, even adulation, nor such vast rewards.

As a politician Wellington enjoyed limited success, the British being deeply suspicious of generals turned politicians; they could never forget Cromwell's Major-Generals. The Duke of Wellington was too rigidly conservative even for the Tories of his day – although he could take credit for supporting Catholic Emancipation in 1829. As Commander-in-Chief of the Army he opposed almost all change.

Arthur Wellesley (1769-1852) was the fourth son of an Irish peer. He was educated at Eton and the French Military College at Angers. When he was 16 his family bought him a commission in the Army, and at the age of 24 he was lieutenant-colonel of the 33rd Regiment (later the Duke of Wellington's). He made his reputation as a military commander in India where his many victories included defeating Tippu Sultan at Seringapatam (1799) and the Marathas at Assaye (1803) – which he considered the greatest of all his victories.

Appointed to command the British forces in the Iberian peninsula, he fought a succession of bloody battles with the invading armies of Napoleon, including Vimiero (1808), Talavera (1809), Albuera (1811), Salamanca (1812), and Vitoria (1812), driving the French from Spain and forcing Napoleon to concede defeat. But his greatest victory was, of course, Waterloo (18 June, 1815), which he described as 'a damn close-run thing'.

For the rest of his life he was a national hero, the man who saved his country and Europe. It was natural that he should be regarded as an oracle in all military affairs, but his influence on senior army commanders and the War Office was almost entirely negative and conservative, opposing practically all change in the army. On military education, he preferred 'the education usually given to English gentlemen. French military academies (he had attended one!) produced 'pedants and cox-combs'. 'An officer in the British army is not a mere fighting machine.' The only good officers, in his view, were men learned in their military duties by service and practical experience within their regiments; gentlemen fitted for command by their breeding and education, who could purchase their commissions and were willing to serve the Crown for honour and not for material reward.

At Waterloo he described his troops as 'the scum of the earth', and he stuck to this view. Recruits, he said, were the most drunken and worst specimens of humanity. 'In ninety-nine instances out of one hundred soldiers enlist on account of some idle or irregular, or even vicious motive.' Only iron discipline could 'remove those irregular or vicious habits or propensities.' Having relied on the lash throughout his military career, he saw the move to abolish flogging as 'one of the morbid symptoms of the times.' Discipline had to be brutal because soldiers were brutal.

In his old age Wellington became Commander-in-Chief again until his death in 1852. In his hands, 'the army remained preserved like a garment in a bottom drawer, sentimentally loved, but rotted and rendered quaint by the passage of time.' (Corelli Barnett) By 1852 there was a widespread feeling, in the words of one Guards officer, 'that all was not right with our Army', but all proposals for reform were unrecognised or rejected, so that for at least one officer the death of the Iron Duke was 'a happy release for the Army.'

1839

ADEN
Royal Dublin Fusiliers
(then 1st Bombay
Europeans)
AFGHANISTAN:
First Afghan War
4th Hussars
16th Lancers
Queen's
Somerset L.I.
Royal Leicestershire
Royal Munster Fusiliers
(then 1st Bengal Europeans)
GHUZNEE: First Afghan War
4th Hussars
16th Lancers
Somerset L.I.
Royal Leicestershire
Royal Munster Fusiliers
(then 1st Bengal Europeans)
KHELAT: First Afghan War
Queen's
Royal Leicestershire

different in structure from all other European armies. In Britain each regiment of the infantry or cavalry was virtually a separate army, with its own colours, uniforms, practices, customs and traditions. It enlisted its own officers and men, whose greatest loyalty was then given to the regiment (and the Queen) rather than to the Army or nation. For them the regiment was a clan, a club, a family, united against all outsiders – not merely against the enemy in the field, but also against other regiments, the War Office, and most politicians.

Officers in the young Queen's army came almost exclusively from the gentry, aristocracy, and the professional middle class, including army families. Three-quarters of them came from a rural background. Except for a tiny minority of promotions from the ranks, and commissions awarded to cadets of the Royal Military Colleges at Sandhurst and Woolwich, most regimental officers bought not only their commissions but also their subsequent promotion to higher ranks.

The 'other ranks' were recruited largely from the unemployed and the least-skilled and poorest of the labouring classes. The army was traditionally an escape from debt, a nagging wife, a vengeful father of a 'wronged' girl, and even from the gallows. 'Some men enlisted on impulse; they admitted leaving their civilian occupations on a mere whim or fancy, either to travel abroad, or to join family and friends in the ranks, or to embark on a life more glamorous and exciting than the one they currently endured. Gentlemen joined the ranks in small but conspicuous numbers . . . Mainly (failed) students or professional men . . . in the hope of promotion . . . There were also boy recruits from the military schools in Dublin and Chelsea and pauper children from the workhouses. Over half of all recruits came from Ireland and Scotland.

Promotion for officers was painfully slow, and by the time a man achieved the rank of general he was likely to be an elderly veteran of the Peninsular War – as were the Commander-in-Chief, Lord Hill, and the Duke of Wellington himself. And so the Army held on to the ideas and practices which had led to victory at Waterloo, even to the uniforms and weapons. The Horse Guards were dominated by Wellingtonian ideas, which were invariably conservative. There was no General Staff or staff planning, and little or no professional training for officers. Official thinking on military matters was dominated by penny-pinching.

After Waterloo the British believed that they no longer needed an army to fight continental wars, and that their homeland was unassailable behind the shield of the world's most powerful navy. A few soldiers were needed at home to deal with any threat of civil disorder, but for the most part it was the Army's job to protect Britain's interests abroad. During the whole of Victoria's long reign hardly a year was to pass without a military action of some kind being mounted in one or more of her overseas territories. There were punitive expeditions to mount, insurrections to crush, sieges to relieve – operations of every kind to show the British flag in all corners of the world. The young Queen's Army was a colonial Army, and her heroes were to be found scattered throughout a growing Empire on which, it was said, that the sun would never set.

Six thousand miles away in India the Queen could boast another army – the army of the East India Company (popularly known as 'John Company'), raised and controlled by the three 'Presidencies' into which British India was then divided – Bengal, Bombay and Madras. John Company's army consisted of Indian troops commanded by British officers, and although the Company was a private concern it was by this time controlled in fact by the British Government. There was at the same time an army of nearly 20,000 soldiers of the Crown stationed in India.

Lord Hill: Commander-in-Chief of the British Army, 1828-42

The Iron Duke's Shadow

Rowland Hill (no relation to the man who originated the Penny Post in 1840), first Viscount Hill, was born in 1772, fourth son and one of sixteen children of Sir John Hill, of an old Shropshire family. He was bought a commission in the Army in 1790, and soon won promotion, serving with courage and distinction in Egypt, Holland and the Peninsular War.

Like his contemporaries, Sir Arthur Wellesley (later Lord Wellington) and Sir John Moore, he was a strict disciplinarian but treated his men with imagination and understanding, and is said to have started the first Sergeants' Mess. He also founded a school for his regiment – the 90th Foot – later the 2nd Bn The Cameronians (Scottish Rifles).

He commanded a division in all the major actions in the Peninsular War, and eventually led an army corps in the final advance into France in 1813-14, and gave the French, in Wellington's words, 'the soundest thrashing they ever had.'

At Waterloo, Hill – by then a General and a Viscount – commanded the brigade that made the final charge to rout Napoleon's Imperial Guard. As Commander-in-Chief of the Army, for 14 years, he had the habit of seeking Wellington's advice on most matters, and treating that advice as a command.

10

The Iron Duke called him Thomas Atkins

WHETHER there was ever a Tommy Atkins in real life will probably never be known, but he was certainly a figure real enough to Queen Victoria's serving soldiers. And, as Kipling's bitter refrain tells us, he was treated with ill-concealed contempt by most of his fellow-countrymen in times of peace, but hailed as a hero when danger threatened from a foreign foe, or from enemies within.

There was nothing new about this double standard. In 1783 Edmund Burke reflected a widely-held view when he talked about 'a rapacious and licentious soldiery', during his attack on Warren Hastings in the House of Commons. More than a hundred years earlier the royalist chronicler Francis Quarles wrote the following epigram:

Our God and soldiers we alike adore
E'en at the brink of danger; not before
After deliverance, both alike are requited,
Our God's forgotten, and our soldiers slighted.

With their libertarian traditions, the British have always viewed standing armies with healthy suspicion, especially since Cromwellian times. And because of low pay and appalling conditions only the 'scum of the earth' would normally be attracted to the life of a common soldier.

Social class also played a crucial part in shaping British attitudes. Soldiering was a perfectly honourable profession for officers and gentlemen, but most respectable Victorian folk looked down their noses at the ordinary 'Tommy'. All too many pubs and theatres had notices saying 'Men In Uniform Not Admitted'. The mother of William Robertson, who enlisted as a trooper and rose through the ranks to become a Field-Marshal, was not alone when she said that she would rather see her son buried than wearing a red coat.

These many-sided prejudices against the ordinary soldier were certainly not shared by Queen Victoria herself, who was always greatly concerned for 'her' serving men and showed genuine interest in their well-being. Like Kipling in the later years of her reign, she was determined that their heroism and loyalty should be properly recognised, and it was no accident that one in five of the Victoria Crosses she presented went to other ranks – the 'Tommy Atkins' of their day.

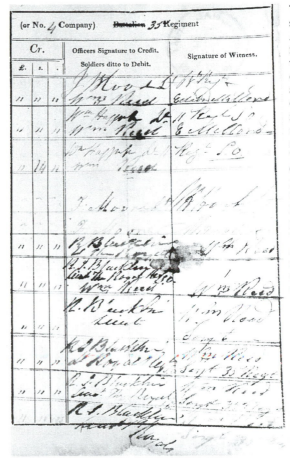

The story goes that when a specimen copy of a new Army Pay Book – a forerunner of the AB 64 – was submitted to the Duke of Wellington for his approval, he used the name of a veteran of his old regiment, the 33rd Foot, and filled in the blank spaces with details of Pte Thomas Atkins, No 6 Company, 1st Battalion, 23rd Regiment of Foot, born at Odiham in Hampshire. The approved pay book was then circulated throughout the Army, and Atkins unwittingly gave his name to future generations of ordinary British soldiers, or 'Tommies'.

These opening pages are reproduced from an actual sample pay book, dating back to about 1820, now in the RAMC Historical Museum at Aldershot.

CLOTHING ACCOUNT of THOMAS ATKINS PRIVATE, No. 6 Comp. 1st Batt. 23rd Regt.				
ARTICLES.	When received.	For the Year.	SIGNATURE.	Signature of Quarter Master or Witness to Delivery.
Suit complete	1814 3d June	1814	Thomas Atkins, his ✕ mark.	Witness, A. B. Serjt. 23d Regt.
Regimental Jacket .. Felt Cap	1815 14th January	1815	Thomas Atkins, his ✕ mark.	Witness, C. D. Corpl. 23d Regt
Waistcoat .... Breeches .... Shoes	9th May	ditto	Thomas Atkins, his ✕ mark.	Witness, E. F. Serjt. 23d Regt.
Regimental Coat .... Shoes	1816 6th March	1816	Thomas Atkins, his ✕ mark.	Witness, G. H. Serjt. 23d Regt.

The Nelson Touch

Horatio Nelson was admired as a national hero throughout the Queen's reign, and many a young Victorian tried to follow his example by 'running away to sea'. When HMS *Victory* was due for the breaker's yard public outcry was so great that the Admiralty had to reverse its decision and provide a permanent mooring for the flagship at Portsmouth Harbour, where she can be seem – much restored – to this day.

WITH THE END of the wars against Napoleon, Britain reduced the number of ships in commission from 713 to 134, a figure which came to be regarded as the normal peacetime complement. This drastic cut had a disastrous effect on the number of officers on the active list, even greater than the figures themselves might suggest. By 1818 only one in ten officers in the Royal Navy was actually employed. Those not on active service were kept on half-pay and promotion became a matter of 'dead men's shoes', for there was at that time no proper system of retirement.

At the start of the decade that saw the accession of the young Princess Victoria to the British throne, fourteen ships of the line – or battleships as we would describe them today – were in active service. Of these, four had been built during Nelson's lifetime and one of them, HMS *Renown*, had actually taken part in the Battle of Trafalgar. His own flagship HMS *Victory* had been listed for demolition, but when the news leaked out the public outcry was so great that she was re-designated as the Port Admiral's flagship at Portsmouth, where of course she can be seen to this day.

As Colin White has pointed out, despite the drastic reduction in the number of serving officers many of Nelson's contemporaries remained on the active list:

Sir Henry Blackwood was in command at the Nore; Sir James Saumarez at Plymouth; and Sir Thomas Foley at Portsmouth. Sir Richard Keats was Governor of Greenwich Hospital and under him, as Chief Physician, was Dr William Beatty, the man who had nursed Nelson on his death-bed. And the professional head of the service, the First Sea Lord, was none other than Sir Thomas Masterman Hardy.

Conditions for ordinary seamen and midshipmen had also changed little since Nelson's day, although some reforms had been introduced and others were on the way. The much-feared Press Gangs, who roamed the streets of Britain's ports and harbours searching for experienced seamen to conscript into the Navy, ceased to operate after 1815 since there was no longer any need for enforcement. Volunteers now formed a nucleus of serving men, and with the establishment of HMS *Excellent* as a naval gunnery school in 1830, a growing number of seamen gunners also became available. The rum ration of half-a-pint a man a day was halved in 1825 in an attempt

The Industrial Revolution might never have occurred so far as Britain's admirals were concerned. When Queen Victoria came to the throne the Navy was much as it had been at the time of the Battle of Trafalgar. But even as the Nelson tradition continued to flourish, the seeds of future change were being quietly sown . . .

cut down drunkenness, and by the late 1830s there was a growing recognition that improvements to diet, accommodation, medical facilities and other amenities, and to the basic terms and conditions under which sailors were engaged, were all long overdue.

For in most respects the life of the serving man, at sea or on shore, was as harsh and as unrewarding as it always had been. Living quarters were extremely cramped and uncomfortable, 'like iceboxes in northern waters and foetid ovens in the tropics'; food on board ship was extremely variable in both quality and quantity; pay was derisory even by the standards of the day; the enforcement of discipline was arbitrary and harsh; and very little was done to cater for the well-being of serving men and their families on shore. Under his bluff and cheerful exterior, many a British sailor might readily have agreed with Dr Johnson that 'being in a ship is being in a jail, with the chance of being drowned'.

NELSON'S STATUE UNVEILED
as reported in the *Illustrated London News* on 10 September 1842 and 4 November 1843

The statue of Nelson—the hero of Trafalgar—having been completed, has been for a short space made visible to the public from a nearer point of view than many of them are destined to have of it in future. It has been exhibited on the surface of *terra firma*, previous to its elevation to the summit of the column, henceforth Nelson's Column, in Trafalgar Square—a locality which, were it not for the common-place character of the front of the National Gallery would become the finest open space in the metropolis. The exhibition is not only a well-advised concession to public curiosity, but an advantage to the artist, being a means of making familiar to the people the talent of one of our best sculptors. Those who have seen his "Nelson" —colossal in size—the features true to nature—a portrait in stone, not an idealism of a hero—the costume, that of an English Admiral, a costume which no skill can

elevate to dignity, or transform to the graceful—will have received, probably, a mingled impression. Unless they remembered they were looking at an object intended to be seen only at a great elevation, they may have been surprised at a sort of coarseness in the workmanship. Yet it has all the finish that can be required, and it has the great merit of likeness and character—one perhaps inseparable from the other in the countenance of such a man as Nelson. It has the sharp, angular features, the expression of great activity of mind, but of little mental grandeur; of quickness of perception and decision; and withal, that sad air, so perceptible in the best portraits of the warrior, of long-continued physical pain and suffering, the consequence of his many wounds, which accompanied him throughout his brightest triumphs, though it never abated his ardour or weakened his energies. The expression is a peculiar one; it is more afflicting to the eye than the expression of deep thought, and though as mournful, it is less abstracted than that of meditation.

If ever man earned his greatness, both by action and suffering, it was the hero of Trafalgar. While we feel a satisfaction that a

public memorial to him is now completed, we cannot help regretting that more than thirty years should have elapsed before so obvious a duty to his renown was accomplished. His monument can hardly be considered as a national tribute to his fame: it is a funeral record, it is raised in a sacred spot, and is consecrated by religion; the interest it possesses is of a higher and more sacred kind. This statue is the public and secular memorial— the tribute of the citizen to the warrior—and till now, in the metropolis of the nation he fought and died for, that tribute has remained unpaid! However, this colossal statue is now completely finished, and the separate pieces of stone, of which it is composed, put together. The figure of the great naval commander measures seventeen feet from the base or plinth on which it stands, to the top of the hat. The whole is cut of stone brought from Scotland, from the Granton quarry of the Duke of Buccleuch. It weighs nearly eighteen tons, and will be taken to pieces in order to be put up. The statue was thrown open to the public last Friday and Saturday, October 27 and 28 [1843], and was visited by a hundred thousand persons.

So, had he not been killed at Trafalgar and had he – like his near contemporary, Wellington – lived to a ripe old age, Nelson would have felt quite at home in the young Queen's Navy. But by 1837, to use an agricultural rather than a marine metaphor, the seeds of dramatic change had already been planted. The first steam-powered vessel, HMS *Lightning* (later *Royal Sovereign*) had appeared in the Navy List as early as 1828. She was built at Deptford, completed in December 1823, fitted with a nominal 100 hp engine and displaced 212 tons. Two years later, in 1829, the first steam fighting ship, HMS *Dee* was laid down at Woolwich. Behind the scenes other rapid advances were being made in the engineering field at a time when, apart from improvements in hull design and construction, sailing ship technology had reached a virtual standstill.

New boilers, paddle wheels and propellers were being designed. Metal fittings had been in use for some time, but now iron hulls were being built and, to the great disgust of the traditional mariner, paddle wheel steamships were introduced, although not yet as fighting units. Her Majesty's Dockyards, at home and abroad, were being equipped to construct and repair these new-fangled monsters, and in the year of the Queen's Accession an Engineering Branch was set up.

This was an important move, because hitherto the maintenance and repair of engines had been carried out by 'labourers' from those manufacturers who had supplied the equipment in the first place. For the most part their status was distinctly 'lower deck', although a handful of civilian engineers who spent their lives developing marine engines and equipment did manage to reach high positions in the Admiralty. But when a separate Branch came into being, engineering officers became part of the establishment and were able to exercise increasing power within the naval hierarchy, although not without considerable difficulty and against great opposition.

Resistance to change was not entirely due to reactionary admirals, although there were plenty of them, nor to the innate conservatism of the British Navy. In the early years there were good reasons for restricting the use of steam power to smaller warships and auxiliary vessels. Paddle wheels were still the only form of propulsion, and it was reasonably held that they took up far too much space amidships, restricting firepower and offering too tempting a target to enemy guns. The engines needed to drive them also occupied much valuable space and protruded well above the water line, offering more vulnerable target areas. The use of sail presented none of these disadvantages, which is one of the reasons why battleship designers stuck with traditional methods until well on into the 19th century.

It was also thought unwise to risk Britain's command of the seas by introducing new inventions too quickly. In a famous minute written in 1828 the First Lord of the Admiralty, Lord Melville, said:

Their Lordships . . . feel it their bounden duty to discourage to the utmost of their ability the employment of steam vessels, as they consider the introduction of steam is calculated to strike a fatal blow to the Naval Supremacy of the Empire . . .

There were financial and political considerations to take into account also. Although the industrial revolution was already a *fait accompli* by the time Victoria came to the throne, there were few people who believed that steam had any part to play in the maintenance of seapower. Even fewer people in positions of authority were prepared to sanction the expenditure of large sums of money on what was still considered to be a largely unproven innovation.

It has also to be said that Britain's industrial power at that time was so much greater than that of her rivals, that she could have mounted a naval rebuilding programme at any time to meet threats posed by a potential enemy. Furthermore, the entrenched attitude adopted by senior naval officers and their civilian masters on the question of steam power did not extent to the other major innovation of the period, the use of iron in ship construction. On the contrary, the Admiralty was quick to recognize the advantages of iron hulled ships. The raw material was inexpensive and readily available, unlike shipbuilding timber which became an increasingly scarce commodity during the Napoleonic Wars and remained so. Iron also provided bette

Rebellion in Canada!

When the 18-year-old Princess Victoria became Queen in June 1837 the whole of her world-wide realm was at peace, but by December there was a rebellion in one of her largest colonies – Canada. Led by a radical newspaperman and ex-Mayor of Toronto named William Lyon Mackenzie in English-speaking Upper Canada and by a French-Canadian lawyer named Louis Papineau in French-speaking Lower Canada, the rebels in both provinces were in effect demanding a Canadian republic to replace British authority, but they failed to unite. The Royal Scots and the Montreal Rifles, commanded by Sir John Colbourne (a veteran who led the final charge at Waterloo) quickly subdued the 'Patriotes' near Montreal, and Loyalist forces soon dispersed Mackenzie's rebels at Toronto. The first of Victoria's little wars was over, and in 1840 an Act of Union made Upper and Lower Canada one province with an elected assembly.

protection against enemy fire, which meant that hulls could be made lighter and less cumbersome.

For all these reasons, the orthodox view in naval circles when Queen Victoria came to the throne was that while the use of iron might be encouraged for ship construction, wind and sail should remain the preferred means of motive power for sea-going vessels.

Ironically, it was the old enemy on the other side of the English Channel who forced their Lordships to take a fresh look at the new technology. The French realised that they could not curb British naval power by conventional means, so they started to build small and highly manoeuvrable vessels equipped with the latest weapons and powered by steam engines. One French admiral, the Prince de Joinville, went so far as to claim that steam had made British sailing ships 'obsolete' and that a lightning invasion across the Channel was now entirely possible. Such sabre-rattling did not go unnoticed in Whitehall and, not for the first time, the views of the ageing Duke of Wellington were anxiously sought. After giving the matter due consideration, and in a remarkable foreshadowing of the conclusions reached by another, even more powerful, enemy of the British a century later, he declared that there was no place along the south coast between Dover and Portsmouth where infantry could not land 'at any state of the tide or weather'.

How Queen Victoria's heroes in the Royal Navy responded to this challenge, and how they kept open the sea lanes of the world to further the expansion of Britain's mercantile trade, form later parts of our story.

This contemporary illustration shows the Duke of Wellington and Prince Albert meeting Louis Philippe at Portsmouth in October 1844. The design and construction of the steam frigate *Gomer*, in which the French king crossed the Channel, aroused much interest in British naval circles.

*There were high hopes of success when
Sir John Franklin's expedition set sail
in 1845 to find the North-West Passage.
It was manned and equipped to standards
unmatched by previous expeditions, all
of which had returned safely, but
without success.*

The Quest for the North-West Passage

Under the command of Sir
John Franklin, HMS *Erebus*
and HMS *Terror* sailed from
Greenhithe, near London,
in May 1845, to 'penetrate
the icy fastnesses of the
north and to circumnavigate
America.'

IN QUEST of the fabled wealth of the Orient,
navigators in Europe had dreamed for nearly
400 years of finding a North-West Passage
through inhospitable Arctic seas to the Bering
Strait, and then south into the Pacific Ocean. In
1773, when he was no more than fifteen years
old, Horatio Nelson himself had served in an
expedition instructed to sail as near as possible
to the North Pole, but on no account 'to go
beyond it'!

The Napoleonic Wars interrupted such
voyages of exploration, but after 1815, with her
naval supremacy beyond challenge, Britain was
able to resume the quest with redoubled energy
and determination. In 1818 an Act was passed in
Parliament offering substantial rewards for the
discovery of a North-West Passage or 'for the
farthest passage north towards the Pole if a route
westward to the Bering Strait cannot be found'.
Among the many explorers were Sir Edward

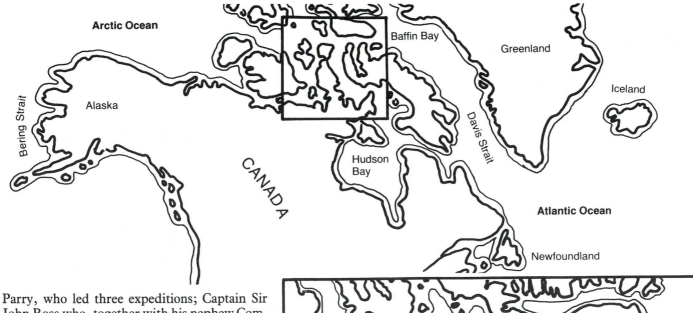

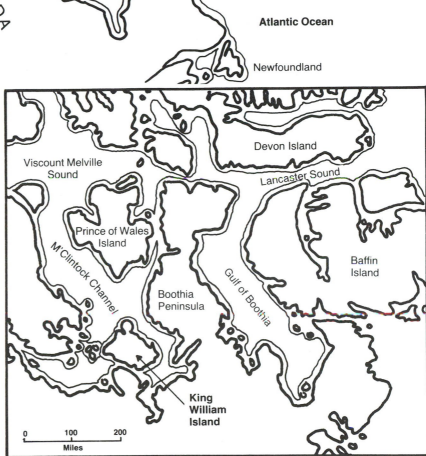

Parry, who led three expeditions; Captain Sir John Ross who, together with his nephew Commander James Clark Ross, undertook a hair-raising journey in the paddle steamer *Victory* and was credited with the discovery of the Magnetic North Pole, and Sir John Franklin, whose amphibian parties succeeded in mapping hundreds of miles of the Canadian coastline.

According to one naval historian, Laird Clowes, the 'objects of the Arctic voyages . . . were not the discovery of routes for commerce, but the attainment of valuable scientific results'. That such results were obtained, and that they provided much of the impetus behind the many expeditions, cannot be denied. But the quest for knowledge went hand-in-hand with enlightened self-interest from Britain's point of view, for her declared policy of international free trade demanded complete freedom of the seas – a freedom which her Navy was in an unrivalled position to impose. Nor did the motives stop at trade, for British suspicions were aroused by Russia who, from her secure base in Alaska, had extended trading posts down the Pacific seaboard of the American continent as far south as the harbour on which San Francisco now stands.

Although Sir Edward Parry had successfully claimed the reward for his voyage of Polar exploration, the actual route of the North West Passage had still not been traced by the early 1840s. So in the *Erebus* and *Terror* Sir John Franklin mounted another expedition and in May 1845 set sail for the northern waters he knew so well. Hopes ran high for, in spite of the many hazards, no previous expedition had failed to return safely. Furthermore, Franklin's new expedition was better manned, equipped and supplied than any of its predecessors. There was every reason for success: none for failure.

It is known that the two ships, sailing in fine weather and good sea conditions, crossed the Arctic Circle at the end of June and made their way northwards, keeping close to the west coast of Greenland. Four weeks later Captain Martin, skipper of the whaling ship *Enterprise*, actually spoke to Franklin and some of his men. This was their last contact with the outside world: from that moment on nothing more was heard of them.

What became of the ships, and of the officers and men who sailed in them with such confidence and optimism, has been pieced together from evidence discovered by later expeditions. The two ships sailed through Lancaster Sound and Barrow Strait and, in the following year, turned south, almost reaching King William Island. They were by then trapped in heavy ice, but a

Later expeditions confirmed that Sir John Franklin and his men reached King William Island, the key to the North-West Passage. But the route was not successfully navigated until 1905, under the Norwegian explorer Amundsen.

Captain Sir John Franklin RN, the object of one of the longest and most expensive manhunts of the 19th century.

IT WAS not force of personality that endeared Sir John Franklin to the British public in the early years of Queen Victoria's reign – indeed, he was shy, awkward and rather pompous in manner – but his brilliant past career and seemingly charmed life. He learned his seamanship on the coast of Australia, surviving a shipwreck which left him marooned on the Great Barrier Reef for several weeks. After returning to England to fight in the Napoleonic wars he served with distinction at the battles of Copenhagen, Trafalgar and New Orleans. He went on to chart, almost single-handedly at the outset, vast stretches of Arctic wasteland, travelling by canoe or on foot and enduring extreme hardship and privation.

He came close to starvation on a number of occasions, not only in the frozen north but also on a tramping expedition into the interior of Tasmania, of which he became colonial governor in his early fifties. His sense of adventure never left him, and when the opportunity arose of going back to the Arctic in yet another attempt to trace the North-West Passage he seized it with both hands.

Sir John Franklin once said of himself that he had no purpose in life but to do his duty. He was a deeply religious man and, beneath his modest manner, very generous in spirit, always ready to give credit where credit was due as well as to admonish when necessary. These were among the qualities that won the admiration and affection of those who served under his command.

One of his fellow serving officers and a man of his own generation was Sir John Ross, who many regarded as an 'eccentric but adventurous old sailor'. His reputation rested more on strength of character than on actual achievements in the field of Arctic exploration, which were considerably less than those of Franklin. Nevertheless, Ross had taken part in at least five expeditions, including one which he had helped to finance himself, and in 1828 he had written a treatise on steam navigation which gave a remarkably accurate forecast of things to come.

At the age of 70 he wrote to the Admiralty about a promise he had made to Sir John Franklin to lead a relief expedition if nothing had been heard by 1847. His letter was ignored, but plans for a search and rescue operation became the subject of a lengthy bureaucratic exchange between the Secretary of State for the Colonies and the Admiralty, at whose door the responsibility was finally laid.

It was not until 1848 that an expedition was sent, led not by Sir John Ross, but by his nephew, Captain Sir James Clark Ross. The enterprise was dogged by ill luck from the outset. The short sailing season was reduced further by abnormally low temperatures at an early stage,

landing party reached the island and set up camp there.

From that point on disaster struck. Sir John Franklin died in June 1847. The ice held, and the expedition's new commander, Captain Francis Crozier, decided to remain with his ships. By this time HMS *Plover* and others were on their way to search for survivors. As hopes of rescue faded and faced with dwindling supplies Crozier had no choice but to abandon the ships. On 22 April 1847 he and his crew set out on foot, probably with the intention of heading west and then south along the coast of King William Island to reach an outpost of the Hudson Bay Company at Fort Resolution.

Of the original complement of 129 officers and men, 105 set out on this last desperate journey. Some may have abandoned the attempt at an early stage, returning to the ships for what little shelter and food remained, but the majority pushed on through the snow and ice. Skeletons discovered along the route many years later suggest that the men, weakened by hunger and scurvy, dropped in their tracks one by one and died where they fell.

and ships were soon ice-bound, unable to reach the various vantage points from which land-based search parties could set out. After months of inactivity, the frustrated Ross decided to avoid a second winter in the Arctic and made for home; his crews, ships and equipment all very much the worse for wear.

By this time Franklin had been missing for four years, and further expeditions were mounted both by the British authorities and by those of the USA, following a personal plea for help to President Zachary Taylor from Lady Franklin, who also funded her own ship, the brig *Prince Albert*. Despite his advanced years, Sir John Ross decided to join the search, and by public subscription fitted out the yacht *Felix*, of which he took command. But these joint endeavours were no more successful than those that had gone before, and eventually Ross and his fellow-commanders had to return to their bases in England and America with little to show for their efforts, other than a handful of new details to add to the incomplete maps of the region.

While these various expeditions were being carried out other voyages of exploration were undertaken, including one by the *Investigator* under the command of Captain Robert McClure RN. He set sail from London on 10 January 1850, was forced into Plymouth Harbour four days later by raging storms in the English Channel, went on to cross the Equator in March, and rounded Cape Horn in a fearsome storm in May. Early in July he reached Honolulu where he had been ordered to await the arrival of his superior officer, Captain Richard Collinson, commander of the *Enterprise*.

Captain Sir John Ross RN, although in his seventies, kept his promise to search for Franklin if he failed to return from the Arctic.

These orders McClure completely disregarded and set out without delay on a northerly course in the direction of the Aleutian Islands, which at that time were still largely uncharted. He then made his way through the Bering Straits and embarked upon his attempt to trace the North-West Passage from west to east, edging along the inhospitable coastline of northern Canada.

Lieutenant W. H. Brown RN, of HMS *Enterprise*, was granted special permission to dedicate his drawing of ships 'boring and warping in the pack' to their Lordships of the Admiralty.

An early portrait of Lady Franklin, who appealed to the President of the USA for help in finding her husband's lost expedition.

After buying the steam yacht *Fox* Lady Franklin placed Captain Francis M'Clintock in command. It was his expedition that discovered the first traces of Sir John Franklin and his crewmen in 1859.

Secrets in the Ice

The fate of Sir John Franklin and his men continues to fascinate scientists and historians to this day. A report published in 1984 by a research team led by Walter Kowal, of the University of Alberta, identifies lead poisoning as the primary cause of death among members of the expedition. Examination of the livers, kidneys and bone samples taken from bodies recovered from the permafrost reveal lead deposits 20 times higher than normal. The lead came from tinned food specially prepared for the expedition, at a time when the new technique was in its infancy and the danger of contamination from the use of lead solder not fully understood.

The *Investigator* reached the Princess Royal Islands before she was locked in an ice floe. Capt McClure's sailing master, Mr Court, was convinced that his ship was trapped not in a bay, but in a strait which would eventually lead first to Viscount Melville Sound, and then to Lancaster Sound, Baffin Bay and the open North Atlantic beyond. The last piece of the puzzle was now in position: all that remained was for McClure to confirm his exploit, which he did by taking Mr Court and chosen members of his crew on an arduous sledging expedition across the frozen sea. The North-West Passage was a reality at last.

But there is a final twist to the story, for by the time McClure had completed his controversial venture and had made a successful bid for an award, papers from Sir John Franklin's party had been found showing that he had actually identified a way through the intricate network of channels and islands without realising that he had done so. Thus the honours and rewards went to the slightly disreputable McClure, but history tells us that the true pioneers were Franklin and his heroic team.

The Thin Red Line and the Square

FOR SOME forty years after Waterloo the British Army was ruled by the axiom that what was good enough for the Duke must be good enough for his successors. Waterloo had been won not by manoeuvre and skirmishing, but by what Wellington called 'hard pounding'. Success came because the solid British lines and squares had stood firm against the French cavalry and skirmishers, who had then been mown down by concentrated British volleys.

Battle tactics in the British infantry were based on three principal formations: the line for firing volleys, the column for movement and manoeuvre, and the square for defence against cavalry charges. All these called for great precision in drill movements and an unbending discipline. So a British soldier's training consisted almost entirely of drill, in which he learned to march, turn and wheel in step with his fellows. All the movements required for a battalion to deploy in battle were practised endlessly so that they could be carried out as perfectly in action as on parade.

In an attack a British battalion would advance in column until close to the moment for the final assault, when it would form a two-deep line on a 200-yard (180 metre) front. The line would then advance on the enemy position, steadily and silently, as if on parade, fire a deadly volley at point-blank range, and then charge with fixed bayonets and blood-curdling yells. In defence, the volley was the standard method of fire, but British infantrymen at this time were also trained in file firing, in which the men in the front and rear ranks fired in succession down the line. This system gave each man time to reload and aim his musket and thus enabled a continuous fire to be maintained.

The square was formed to deal with cavalry charges and also, as in Africa later, the onrush of great numbers of native warriors. Battalions learned a drill in which pairs of companies wheeled and dressed in order to form a square with four-deep faces, the officers, NCOs, guns and auxiliary services being inside the square. The front ranks in each face would kneel to give the rear ranks a clear line of fire. For all regiments the unbroken square was a matter of honour, and to allow a square to be broken was the deepest disgrace.

Boy Soldiers of the Queen

BRITAIN'S WARS of the Victorian Age, and earlier, were largely fought 'not by grizzled veterans of 20 years and up, but by 14 to 20 year olds' – indeed, even younger boys were often found in the forefront of the hottest battles. Officially, there were 957 boy soldiers in Wellington's army at the battle of Waterloo in 1815, but the evidence indicates that at least 4,000 'likely lads' aged 10 to 18 fought on that memorable June 18. The practice of boy soldiering was an age-old tradition; the ancient Greeks, Romans and Celts all used boy soldiers, and in the wars of medieval Europe apprentice boy soldiers played an important role, particularly for producing martial music to rally the troops.

> *The minstrel boy to the war has gone,*
> *In the ranks of death you will find him;*
> *His father's sword he has girded on,*
> *His own true harp slung behind him.*

A drum or trumpet might have been of more practical use in battle. Throughout history boy soldiers were used not only as drummers and trumpeters, but as messengers, look-outs, stretcher-bearers and general aides to commanding officers. In such roles they would be frequently under fire, and right down to the end of Victoria's reign there were many hundreds of 'under-age' soldiers in the fighting ranks of her armies – the 'army brats' who fought and died for the Queen in long-forgotten wars throughout the world. Not until the 1880s was it considered desirable to impose a lower age limit on boys going into action – and even then it was set at 14 years.

Where did they come from – all those fresh, innocent young faces in the regiments, whose service seemed likely to be disagreeable, brutish and short, ending probably in a painful death or the loss of one or more limbs? Probably most of them came from Ireland and, except for young officer cadets – ensigns – from the poorer and less privileged sections of British society. For such, the army offered boys a standard of living which was almost luxurious in comparison with that to be found in the poverty-stricken villages and miserable industrial towns from which they came. From the moment he signed on the young recruit could be sure of food, clothing and shelter. The food and shelter might be basic by today's standards, but still better than any he might have known before. As for the uniform and clothing, there could have been no comparison. A boy soldier in the Royal Artillery, for example, would have in his knapsack four white shirts, a check shirt, a pair of canvas trousers, two pairs of shoes, three pairs of worsted stockings, amongst many other useful items. Undoubtedly most attractive of all to boy recruits would be the uniform – an outfit smarter and more prestigious than anything he could have hoped to boast as a poor town or village lad.

For a young hopeful in Britain there were three routes into the army. He could be entered into one of the two military schools – the Royal Hibernian Military School (RHMS) in Dublin or the Royal Military Asylum (better known as the Duke of York's School) in Chelsea. He could be 'born in the regiment', that is, the son of a serving soldier who would be taken on the strength as soon as he was old enough (the youngest to enlist in this way was Drummer James Wade who joined the 95th Foot on 10 July 1800 – his seventh birthday!). Or he could succumb to the sales talk and wiles of a recruiting sergeant visiting his town or village. If, of course, he had the good fortune to be born into a higher station in life, and his family could afford to buy him a commission, he could enlist as an Ensign – traditionally the standard-bearer in battle – the most junior officer rank. The sons of fallen officers were sometimes awarded such commissions without payment. During the Napoleonic Wars and earlier, many an Ensign began his career at the tender age of 13.

The Military Schools provided a little light in the otherwise dark educational scene of early Victorian Britain. First to be founded was the Hibernian Institute, which was opened in Dublin in 1770 and renamed the Royal Hibernian Military School in 1789. George III contributed £1,000 a year to its upkeep. This was in an age when army commanders (notably the Commander-in-Chief of the British Army, the 'Grand Old Duke of York', second son of the king) were realising that blind obedience and precision in mind-deadening drill were not enough, even for the rank and file; at the very least, soldiers, especially NCOs, should be able to read and write. The same Duke of York established two other military schools. At Marlow, Bucks, in 1799, he founded a school for cadets between the ages of 13 and 16, who were given four years' training before being commissioned into the cavalry and infantry. This school later became the Royal Military College, Sandhurst. A few years later he founded the Royal Military Asylum in Chelsea. Later named the Duke of York's Military School, and more popularly known as 'Dukies', this school was intended primarily 'for the orphaned children of fallen soldiers'. Both the Military Schools contributed thousands of basically trained soldiers to the Queen's armies, and at the end of her reign it was reckoned that some 3,000 of their Old Boys were serving soldiers, of whom only 400 were privates. Three major-generals, a number of lieutenant-colonels, and many junior officers and NCOs were ex-military school lads.

The Military Schools set out to provide a sound basic education by the standards of the day and of the army. However, a confidential report made in 1846 to the Privy Council on 'the Royal Military Asylum at Chelsea' listed Scripture, England, Colonies, India, Greece, Rome, France, Arithmetic, Geography and Natural History, among subjects taught in addition to Reading and Writing, but it was far from impressed by the standards achieved. It noted 'a remarkable deficiency in general knowledge', as well as 'bad reading, writing and cyphering'. In theory, all entrants to these Military Schools were allowed a choice of training in a trade or calling, but not surprisingly they usually gave their 'free consent' in favour of the army.

The Victorian army had a never-ending need for drummers and buglers, and as commanding officers tended to complain bitterly about split notes and erratic drumming, both military schools gave special attention to giving suitable pupils a thorough musical education. Of the 330 boys at the Duke of York's School in 1846, 70 were being given a thorough musical education, and such boys were regularly 'channelled' into army bands. The two schools produced between them many hundreds of fine bandsmen, including over 30 bandmasters, as well as the famed 19th century clarinettist Henry Lazarus and

Thomas Sullivan who rose from very humble beginnings to become a professor at the Royal School of Military Music, Kneller Hall, and who was father of Sir Arthur Sullivan of 'Gilbert and Sullivan' fame.

But all too often a harsher note was struck in these schools, for they were above all *military* and regimental in character and atmosphere, with regular parades, colours, companies, NCOs and the other trappings of army life. Discipline was strict and punishments were frequent and

Many a young head was turned by the splendour of army uniform. This detail, from *Sketches of British Soldiers* by G. H. Thomas [1861], shows a piper and a corporal of the 78th Highlanders, Ross-shire Buffs.

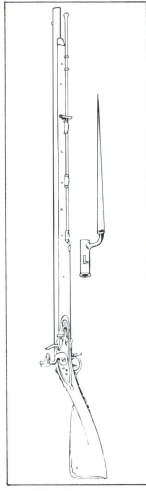

BROWN BESS

The standard infantry weapon until the Crimean War was the flintlock musket, generally known as 'Brown Bess'. This was a muzzle-loading weapon with a smooth-bore barrel. It fired a round lead bullet, and its effective range was about 40 yards, but lucky shot might hit a man at several hundred yards. Brown Bess was most deadly when fired in volleys. The musketeer carried a supply of paper cartridges containing powder and bullet, and loaded his musket with the aid of a ramrod. In 1839 the percussion cap was adopted (24 years after it had been invented and rejected by the War Office), replacing the old method of firing by flint and steel. Brown Bess was also equipped with a bayonet, which usually had to be fixed in battle.

severe. Pupils found not paying attention would be shut in an iron cage and hoisted by means of a rope and pulley high in the school hall. For 'minor offences' the sergeants could and did use the cane freely, in and out of class. 'Offences of a graver character,' said the 1846 Report, 'are punished by flogging, by confinement in a cage or a black hole, by carrying a log chained to the person or by the drill.' In one month, the Report added, 10 floggings of 12 stripes each were inflicted and 2 of 24 stripes, and in the preceding month there were inflicted 17 floggings each of 12 stripes. This dismal record was unfavourably compared with that of the Nautical Upper and Lower Schools at Greenwich. 'The number of floggings (51) inflicted on 800 boys (at Greenwich) in a year is one fourth of the number inflicted in the same time on 350 boys at Chelsea.' Even at Greenwich an average of one flogging a week hardly indicates a mild regime! At the RHMS in Dublin, discipline was just as brutal as in Chelsea, and one observer noted that 'It was left to every subordinate, however irascible his disposition, to punish promiscuously any boy in the School.' Small wonder that in 1882 the pupils mutinied, rioted, and took to the hills. Although it needed the Scots Guards to restore order, the teaching staff of the school was replaced – and the children had won. Flogging, however, continued in the Military Schools for many years after it had been prohibited in the regular army.

Boy soldiers of the Queen were recruited into her armies wherever they were fighting and extending her empire – notably in India and Canada. In India, there was a large European community of army pensioners and their families, as well as traders and employees of the Honourable East India Company. These naturally provided a regular source of Junior recruits for both the Company's army and for the Queen's service. There were also four military asylums which provided homes and education for military orphans, who would usually wish to join their father's regiment on reaching the age of 14. As in Britain, the sons of serving soldiers could be enlisted direct into their father's regiment. Such a one was Boy H. W. Bancroft, the son of a serving soldier, who enlisted in the Royal Artillery as a bugler at the age of nine, and later transferred to the Bengal Horse Artillery and fought in the First Sikh War of 1845-6. Boy soldiers of Indian birth seem to have been as common in the native regiments of John Company's army as in the British Army. The East India Company also had its own Artillery Cadet College, near Calcutta, where the cadets were very young – aged 11 to 14 – and as at the Royal Military College, Woolwich, discipline seems to have been a major problem.

Throughout the 19th century Canada slowly built up its own army as the British force was gradually withdrawn, but in this so-called 'Permanent Force' boy soldiers as young as 10 years of age were often to be found.

Sadly, when boy soldiers went into action as drummers or buglers, and were killed or wounded, no-one took much notice, but in the Indian Mutiny of 1857 they were in the forefront of the fighting and several of them won VCs. It was a boy telegraphist in Delhi who sent out a warning message when sepoys starting killing Europeans and burning their bungalows – and was himself killed as he did so. Bugler Robert Hawthorne aged 16, who was with the explosion party under the walls of Lucknow, won the VC when he dragged his wounded officer to safety under heavy fire. Bandboy George Monger, who was a mere 'Acting Drummer' of the 23rd Foot, also won the VC at Lucknow. When a corporal fell wounded and was left exposed to heavy cross-fire, Bandboy Monger ran out and lay on top of the wounded man to protect him and stayed with him until all was clear. Another VC was won by Drummer Thomas Flynn, aged about 15, of the 64th Foot. Although wounded, Flynn charged the sepoys' guns and fought two of their artillerymen hand to hand – and won.

How many boy soldiers actually served in the Boer War it is impossible to say but, according to the Duke of York school records, in 1900 there were 1610 ex-Dukies in uniform, and almost certainly a similar number from the RHMS. Many died or were killed, and extracts from their letters home give the feel of that bitter conflict.

Trumpeter Frank Wilde, for example, of the 66th Field Artillery, who was aged 14 and recommended for his bravery, wrote:

We went through the Battle of Colenso where, I am sorry to say, my Battery lost four guns . . . It was an awful fight, and we were within 300 yards of the enemy's rifles; our men were getting mown down. It was an awful sight. All our officers got shot down, and the gunners stood to their guns till all our ammunition was gone . . . (*Trumpeter Wilde galloped away under a hail of bullets to get more ammunition, but this he does not mention in his letters.*) I had a few narrow escapes, but I never got wounded . . . This war should have been over three months ago, only the Boers have been a bit smarter than we thought.

Never again were boy soldiers exposed to action of this kind. Maybe by the end of Victoria's reign her people could no longer stomach such scenes as that described by Lord Roberts at the siege of Lucknow. A drummer of the 93rd was in the first rush through the wall: 'when I got in I found him just inside the breach, lying on his back, quite dead, a pretty, innocent-looking fair-haired lad, not more than fourteen years old.'

'Mother, Sister and Mistress'

'WHAT CAN BE FINER than his love for his regiment . . .!' asked Lord Wolseley, a hero for Victoria who was, in fact, not much liked by his monarch. He was speaking of the private soldier, but his question could just as well have been asked about regimental officers. 'To him,' he went on, 'the Regiment is mother, sister and mistress . . . That its fame may live and flourish he is prepared to risk all and die without a murmur. To the soldier, the Regiment is his country.'

The regiment was (and is) a peculiar, indeed a unique, feature of the British Army. For officers and other ranks alike, the regiment was their club, their tribe, their clan, an extended family, giving life meaning and purpose, and even an opportunity for glory. In Victoria's day, and since, a man did not so much enlist in the army as join a regiment. And it was for 'the honour of the regiment' that so many Victorian soldiers of all ranks fought against impossible odds in impossible climates and conditions, and so often won. In the face of the enemy, 'the soldier feels the Regiment solid about him.'

Unlike regiments in other armies, the British regiment had no fixed size or composition. It could be as small as one battalion or consist of several dozen battalions or, as with the Royal Regiment of Artillery, it could be an entire branch of the army. Particularly in Victoria's time, each regiment was like a separate army with its own colours, uniforms, badges, customs, mottoes, marching songs and even marching pace. It recruited its own officers and other ranks.

Regiments varied in size, but normally consisted of two Battalions of 700-900 men, one at home and the other overseas. The home regiments were scattered throughout the country according to the needs of public order; the total strength of the Army in the United Kingdom was just over 50,000 men. Regiments were allotted numbers based on seniority – for example, the 1st was the King's Dragoon Guards and

the 95th, comparatively recently-formed Rifle Brigade. Supporting the regiments were two virtually separate armies run by the Board of Ordnance – the Royal Artillery and the Royal Engineers.

The names and numbers of the regiments are no real guide to their true function at any time in

Pride in the regimental uniform is one of the British Army traditions that survives to this day.

MASCOTS, MEMENTOES AND NICKNAMES

Many regiments boasted their own mascot – often a pet animal. Perhaps the most famous, the Welch Fusiliers' goat, came from a herd of goats presented to Queen Victoria by the Shah of Persia on her accession. In 1844 she gave one of them to the regiment. Thereafter the goat marched on parade with the regiment, and even attended church parades, presumably having been designated C of E on enlistment. When he died he was given a military funeral – and was promptly replaced by another goat from the royal herd. The Queen also presented the Rifle Brigade with a red deer.

Other regiments with animal mascots included the Light Brigade with a horse named Bob (who charged with them at Balaclava); the Irish Guards had an Irish wolfhound; the Coldstream Guards once had a cat named Pinkie, and the Grenadier Guards a goose called Jacob.

The Black Watch (formerly the 42nd or The Royal Highlanders) wear a red hackle on their bonnets in recognition of their conduct at the battle of Guildermalson in 1794. The South Wales Borderers (formerly the 24th Foot) have a silver wreath of immortelles on their colour staff in memory of their losses at Isandhlwana in 1879.

Most regiments had much-prized mementoes and trophies of battles long ago, many of them being captured drums and colours. Some boasted eagle standards from Napoleon's regiments. The 34th (later the Border Regiment) had the French army's drums and drum-major's staff captured during the Peninsular War; the 14th Light Dragoons (later the 14th Hussars) had a silver chamber pot found in the baggage of Joseph Bonaparte, King of Spain, during the same war, and the 17th Lancers had the bugle that sounded the charge of the Light Brigade.

Almost every regiment had a nickname. The Northamptonshire Regiment was christened 'The Steelbacks' for their ability to endure floggings without a murmur. The 17th Lancers were the 'Death or Glory Boys' from their cap badge with a death's head and the words 'or glory'. The Middlesex Regiment were the 'Diehards' because their colonel at the battle of Albuera in 1811 had called out 'Die hard, my men, die hard!' Some other nicknames were less flattering.

their history; they have changed so much over the centuries. Even in 1837 the Grenadiers no longer hurled grenades; the Fusiliers carried no fusils; the Dragoons were light cavalry rather than mounted infantry; the Hussars' only connection with Hungary was seen in their romantic uniform, and the only Lancers who ever used their lances in battle seem to have been the 16th Lancers at Aliwal in the Sikh War in 1846.

The most senior regiments of the British Army are the 1st and 2nd Life Guards, cavalry regiments descended from the troops brought to England by Charles II on his Restoration in 1660. But the Grenadier Guards and the Coldstream Guards claim at least equal historical precedence. The oldest by far, however, are The Buffs (The Royal East Kent Regiment), known until 1708 as 'The Holland Regiment', first raised by Queen Elizabeth I in 1572 for service in the Netherlands. The colonelcy of a regiment was a largely honorary appointment, which was awarded to a distinguished general or, in the most prestigious regiments, to a British or European royal figure. The colonel-in-chief of the 1st Dragoon Guards, for example, was the Emperor of Austria.

Regimental establishments varied enormously, but a typical two-battalion regiment of infantry would be commanded by two lieutenant-colonels, each assisted by a major, half a dozen captains, a dozen subalterns, a surgeon or medical officer, and four staff sergeants. Battalions usually consisted of ten companies, six being service (or overseas) and four depot (or at home) companies. A service company would consist of about 500 private soldiers and a depot company about 200, with a due proportion of colour-sergeants, sergeants, corporals and drummers. Cavalry regiments were generally smaller in number than infantry regiments.

Rivalry between regiments seems to have been an essential part of the system. Often it was harmless enough, producing a spirit of competitiveness which was healthy and good for morale. But there was always a danger that, carried too far, loyalty to any one regiment could produce animosity towards others. When men endure hardship together, train and fight together, tribal attitudes are never far below the surface. Units garrisoned in 'safe' stations in the UK and overseas, without a real enemy to fight, sometimes turned on each other with bloody results. 'We and the Highland Light Infantry were bitter enemies,' wrote Frank Richards, a private who served in the Royal Welch Fusiliers, 'I don't know why – it was something handed down from bygone days.'

No less enduring than the hatreds were the friendships between different regiments, especially those forged in the heat of battle. Men of the Worcestershire Regiment and of the Lincolnshire Regiment were true comrades-in-arms, having fought side-by-side at Ramillies under Marlborough and at Sobraon during the 1st Sikh War. There were many bonds between Scottish and Gurkha regiments as, for example, between the Seaforth Highlanders and the 5th Gurkhas, who saw much active service together on the North-West Frontier. The Gordon Highlanders and the 2nd Gurkhas were also on very friendly terms: officers from the two regiments shared the other's mess facilities as honorary members.

But there was a reverse side to the *espirit de corps* fostered by the system. In some regiments new recruits were forced to undergo brutal and degrading initiation ceremonies. Cruelty in other, more insidious, forms was exercised against junior officers if their social background or behaviour was thought to be unsuitable. Even the most minor infringements of an accepted code could result in ostracism, or worse.

Double standards were also applied in matters of discipline. If the men misbehaved, harsh sentences were usually imposed. Even afer flogging was done away with, there remained solitary confinement, pack drill and other forms of punishment, including loss of rank, of pay, of leave and other privileges.

However, if junior subalterns went wild on mess night, they might expect a severe wigging from the adjutant the following morning, and a bill even larger than usual at the end of the month to pay for damage – but nothing more.

The young officer was expected to let off steam from time to time. Indeed, in many regiments it was considered bad form not to join in the occasional drinking bout and the boisterous mess games that ensued. To turn out smartly on parade at dawn next morning, nursing a monumental hangover or a cracked rib, was regarded as one of the hallmarks of a good officer and true gentleman. As Belloc later observed:

Like many of the upper class,
He loved the sound of broken glass.

Most people believed that the abuses and absurdities of the system were a small price to pay for the way in which it worked in practice, enhancing the honour of the British soldier and giving him so formidable a reputation among friend and foe alike. In *For Queen and Country*, Byron Farwell offers the following view:

The British regimental system was eccentric and . . . expensive; but it did create that spirit in its combatant services which won wars. The attitudes, beliefs and prejudices of the officer corps appear arrogant and ridiculous; yet these British officers were among the bravest of the brave, and they won wars.

It is a judgement with which many serving men of all ranks, then as now, would have agreed most wholeheartedly.

REGIMENTAL COLOURS

Every infantry regiment carried two colours (or flags): the Queen's Colours and the regimental Colour. Until 1858 the Colours were too large flags just over six feet square fastened to ten-foot pikes; after that date the size was halved for easier handling. The Queen's Colour was the Union Flag with the regimental number, name and badge; the regimental Colour until 1881 had a small Union Jack in the top right corner.

Carried into battle by Ensigns, escorted by Colour Sergeants, the Colours symbolised the spirit of the Regiment; where they stood the Regiment stood. To lose them was the greatest disgrace, and so officers and men often fought to the end to keep the Colours from the enemy. When, as at Waterloo, armies fought in close order, the Colours provided a practical and conspicuous rallying-point.

It was in Victoria's time that 'the colours' became deeply reverenced regimental totems, but, with the looser tactics and quicker-firing weapons of the age, the colour party became an easy target and a death trap, as was shown by the loss of some 550 officers and men trying to save the colours at Isandhlwana in 1879. The last British regiment to go into battle with colours flying was the 58th Foot (later the 2nd Battalion The Northamptonshire Regiment) at the battle of Laings Nek, in 1881, during the First Boer War.

REGIMENTAL HONOURS

Battle honours gave a regiment the privilege of inscribing on its colours or its drums the names of battles or campaigns in which it had fought with distinction. The oldest, 'Tangier 1662-1680', was awarded to five regiments –

The Regimental Colour of the 3rd Battalion, Scots Guards, 1900-01.

the lastest, The Queen's, receiving it as late as 1909. Honours were awarded with some reluctance and often long after they had been earned. Honours for Marlborough's victories at Blenheim (1704), Ramillies (1706), Oudenarde (1708), and Malplaquet (1709) were not awarded until 1882, and the Scots Guards received battle honours for 'Namur 1695' in 1910. Honours were almost never awarded for defeats, no matter how well a regiment had fought. Regiments took great pride in these honours, which were generally presented by a royal or other distinguished personage, and when old and tattered they were laid up in a cathedral or church associated with the regiment.

Other regimental honours included the right to use the title 'Royal', as the Royal Fusiliers and The Royal Scots, or to be named some royal personage's 'Own'. The 13th Foot (later The Somerset Light Infantry) were given the title 'Prince Albert's Own' for their heroic defence of Jellalabad in 1841, and kept the title after the Prince died in 1861. The 11th Hussars were also 'Prince Albert's Own', four regiments were 'The Queen's Own', and several others simply 'The Queen's'.

An honour much prized by regiments was the right to march through a city's streets 'with bayonets bared, drums beating and colours flying.' The Grenadier Guards, the Royal Fusiliers, the Royal Marines, the Honourable Artillery Company and the Buffs all enjoy this privilege in the City of London, and occasionally exercise it with great panache.

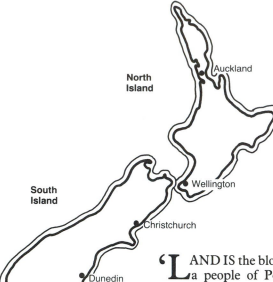

The Maori Wars in New Zealand all had the same cause: land. The European settlers wanted it the Maoris were unwilling to give it up, even for payment.

The Fire in the Fern

The 'discovery' of New Zealand by Captain Cook in 1769 turned out to be a disaster for the indigenous Maori people, for the Europeans brought with them not only drink and disease, but also firearms which they traded for the natural produce of that fertile country.
Sporadic inter-tribal warfare had always been part of the fierce Maori tradition, but the arrival of modern weapons caused havoc and resulted in an estimated 65,000 casualties up to 1840. By the time the tribal leaders realized that the threat to their way of life came not from their neighbours, but from the white men from across the seas, it was too late. Their homeland had already become a European settlement in the South Pacific Ocean, and so it remains to this day.

'LAND IS the blood of man' said the Maoris, a people of Polynesian origin who, for about a thousand years, had occupied the land we now call New Zealand. So, with the arrival of increasing numbers of settlers from Europe in the early years of Victoria's reign, came quarrels over land claims. These were followed by 'atrocities' and 'massacres' of the *pahekas* (white men), and intermittent fighting between them and the original inhabitants for nearly thirty years.

It was not until January 1840 that the first British colonists landed in New Zealand. The following month the British Governor, Captain William Hobson RN, signed the Treaty of Waitangi with some 500 Maori chiefs by the terms of which they surrendered all their sovereign rights to the Queen of England. In return they were guaranteed possession of their lands and forests, and it was agreed that the Crown would have the sole right to purchase any land they wished to sell. Hobson then proclaimed British sovereignty over the whole country, making Auckland the seat of government.

In the same year a British force of about 150 men of the 80th Foot (the Staffordshire Volunteers, now the South Staffordshire Regiment) arrived. Their tasks were to maintain public order, build defences and prevent fighting between the Maoris and the colonists and between the Maoris themselves. This force was soon strengthened by companies from the 96th Regiment (later the Manchester, now the King's Regiment) and the 99th (later the 2nd Battalion the Wiltshire Regiment, now embodied in the Duke of Edinburgh's Royal Regiment). Ships of the Royal Navy were in New Zealand waters at the time, and in the coming fighting they supported the land forces with guns, marines and seamen. The protection of these forces was soon needed. For settlers poured into the new British colony, all demanding land at the lowest prices. Inevitably there were disputes with the Maoris, who soon felt duped and disillusioned with the *pakehas*, and these soon turned into violent clashes and then into open warfare.

Though ferocious and inclined to cannibalism, the Maoris were a staunchly independent and gifted people, with an innate skill in the tactics of war. In addition to primitive clubs, axes and spears, they armed themselves with muskets and light artillery sold to them by European traders. Strong, agile and cunning, they proved first-class fighting men and earned the healthy respect of the Victorian soldier – who offended their code of war (for a fair fight at a fixed time and place, when the bravest men should win), but never shook their proud courage or degraded their proud honour.

A peculiar feature of Maori warfare was the *pah*, a rapidly-built earthwork 'fort' with interconnecting trenches and rifle-pits, protected by palisades of timber stuffed and lined with flax to form an elastic armour. The trenches were roofed with branches supported by timbers and covered with a thatch of ferns. When attacked the Maori defenders were invisible, being hidden in the trenches and firing at their attackers through loopholes at earth-level. If too hard pressed the Maoris would quietly evacuate a *pah* and retire to another where they would continue their stubborn defence. When a strong British force attacked a well-defended Maori *pah* in 1864, they could see nothing except the red-and-white Maori flag flying above the palisades but they were met with an intense fire from the invisible defenders. When they at last forced their way inside, the *pah* appeared to be unoccupied, and they laid down their arms and set about looting. 'Suddenly from under their very feet from chambers dug in the earth and skilfully camouflaged . . . arose a large number of Maoris. The fierce volleys they poured into the astonished white troops caused them to panic and flee from the *pah*.'

In the formal attack on a strongly-held *pah* in 1845, the 58th Foot (later the 2nd Battalion The Northamptonshire Regiment) was joined by sailors and marines, and a third of the assaulting force was lost. Corporal William Free of the 58th was with the 'forlorn hope' (the storming party):

We formed up in close order, elbows touching when we crooked them; four ranks, only the regulation 23 inches between each rank. There we waited in a little hollow before the *pa*, sheltered by the fall in the ground and some tree cover. We got the order 'Prepare to charge'; then 'Charge'. Up the rise we went at a steady double, the first two ranks at the charge with a bayonet . . . we were within 100 yards of the *pa* when the advance began; when we were within about 50 paces of the stockade front we cheered and went at it with a rush . . . The whole front of the *pa* flashed fire and in a moment we were in a one-sided fight – gun flashes from the foot of the stockade and from loopholes higher up, smoke hiding the *pa* from us, yells and cheers and men falling all around. A man was shot in front of me and another was hit behind me. Not a single Maori could we see. They were all safely hidden in their trenches and pits, poking the muzzles of their guns under the foot of the outer palisade. What could we do? We tore at the fence, firing through it, thrusting our bayonets in, or trying to pull part of it down, but it was a hopeless business.

This verdict was confirmed by Major Cyprian Bridge, also of the 58th:

When I got up close to the fence and saw the strength of it and the way it resisted the united efforts of our brave fellows . . . my heart sank within me lest we should be defeated . . . a bugle in the rear sounded the retreat . . . and then all that were left prepared to obey its summons carrying off the wounded with us. We had suffered very severely and many were killed or wounded whilst retiring as the enemy increased their fire upon us as they saw us in retreat. It was a heartrending sight to see the number of gallant fellows left dead upon the field and to hear the groans and cries of the wounded for us not to leave them behind . . .

Sporadic fighting, known as 'the fire in the fern', flared up again in the 1860s. By this time more and more European settlers were arriving and the 56,000 remaining Maoris realised they were being out numbered. A separatist movement was formed under a leader called Wiremu Kingi, and for nearly ten years guerilla warfare followed. Not until the settlers had all the land they wanted and the Maoris had been decimated did the fighting come to an end. Three hundred Maori warriors made a last stand in a *pah* near Orakau. 'We have been beaten because the *pakeha* outnumber us in men,' declared a Maori later; 'not one *pakeha* can name the day when we sued for peace.'

Two of the VC's awarded in the course of the Maori Wars went to men of the Royal Navy. The first to be won in New Zealand went to

William Odgers of HMS *Niger*. According to the citation, on 28 March 1860 he 'displayed conspicuous gallantry at the storming of Pa Lum Pah. He was the first to enter it under heavy fire and assisted in hauling down the enemy colours'.

The second VC went to Samuel Mitchell, who was Captain of the Foretop of HMS *Harrier*. He took part in an unsuccessful assault on a *pah* at Tauranga, which was built on a headland. After a heavy, eight-hour bombardment a frontal assault was mounted by a mixed party of British soldiers and men of the Naval Brigade. No fire was returned, so it was assumed that the defenders had either been killed by the shelling, or had withdrawn.

In fact, they had sheltered underground and waited until their attackers were almost upon them before opening up. The results were devastating, and in the disorderly retreat that followed many wounded men were left behind. Mitchell saw that Commander Hay was among those who had fallen and, with a total disregard for his own safety and despite protests from the wounded man himself, returned to carry him away from the heavy fire. No further attempt was made to capture the position that day, and when the attack was resumed the following morning it was discovered that the Maoris had slipped away during the night.

Maori tribesmen, trained in the art of war from early boyhood, had their faces tattooed to make themselves look more fierce, and performed war dances with blood-curdling shouts, yells and gestures to frighten their enemies. An instinctive use of ground cover and other tactical skills made them formidable opponents, while their bravery in battle and a strict code of honour won the respect of all those who fought against them. When the wars finally came to an end in the 1870s, ordinary British soldiers subscribed to a memorial tablet which read, quite simply, 'I say unto you, love your enemies'.

Taking the Queen's Shilling

Rudyard Kipling described men who took the Queen's shilling as 'the sons of those who for generations had done over-much work for over-scanty pay, had sweated in drying rooms, stooped over looms, coughed among the whitelead, shivered on the lime barges . . .

THE BRITISH Army has always been an army of volunteers, except in the two World Wars of this century. At the beginning of Victoria's reign recruits were required to enlist for life, but in 1847 the term was reduced to twenty-three years, and in 1870 'short service' was introduced. This meant enlistment for twelve years – up to seven of them to be served with the colours, and the rest with the reserve.

Who joined the Army?

The War Office and nearly everybody else assumed that unemployment drove men to enlist, but even if this was true, there were always many thousands of unemployed men who could have joined the Army but chose not to – evidently finding a pauper's life more attractive than that of a soldier or sailor. Poverty was not the only motive for joining the Army, and as the first Royal Commission on Recruiting noted in 1861 'few enlist from any real inclination for military life.' For many the Army was a refuge, a means of escape from debt, from a nagging wife, from a pregnant girlfriend (and her father) or simply from a dull and unrewarding existence.

Colour-sergeant John Mitchell of the 58th Foot who joined the Army in 1841, fought in the first Maori War, and later settled in New Zealand, is a good example. 'At the age of twenty,' he wrote in his diary, 'I held a responsible position [in a brewery in Stamford] at a weekly salary of 11/- without any prospect of increase.' So he decided to leave the job in which he was 'so wretchedly paid & take service under the Queen, taking care to let no one know of my design, not even my dearly beloved Father & Sister Mary.' Chance led him to enlist in the 58th. 'I met a soldier of the 58th Regt on the recruiting service whom I knew who came from a village near Stamford. I told him I would enlist, with that he gave me the Queen's shilling & took me to a magistrate who swore me in, from thence to a Doctor who examined me & passed me, the soldier then took me to his billet. The next day I was marched off to Leicester with seven other recruits . . .'

'It was on a bright May morning in 1833,' recalled RSM Loy Smith, 'that a cavalry regiment marched into a pretty country town and formed up in the market place directly opposite my master's shop [a chemist and druggist] . . . This was the first time I had seen a regiment of cavalry with their mounted band and I became enchanted with them, particularly when I thought of what a glorious life theirs must be to mine, they marching from town to town and seeing the world, and appearing so light-hearted, and I, condemned to stand behind a counter from Monday morning to Saturday night . . . On 10 June 1833, less than one month later [when he was just over sixteen], I took the oath of allegiance to serve the King, his heirs and successors, in the 11th Light Dragoons.' RSM Loy Smith later served with his regiment, renamed the 11th Prince Albert's Own Hussars (later The Royal Hussars, Prince of Wales Own) in India, Ireland and the Crimean War, and took part in the Charge of the Light Brigade, which was doubtless a good deal more exciting than life behind a shop counter.

No matter what their motive, over half of the recruits were casual labourers, the least skilled members of the working class, and more and more of them were being recruited from the growing towns rather than from the country – to the dismay of those officers who considered,

'The guard falling in at the head of the column'. Officers and men of the 8th (King's) Regiment in Guernsey, 1840. In the foreground (*l to r*) stand a Captain, Lieutenant, Sergeant and Drummer.

with some reason, that agricultural labourers were stronger, fitter and made better soldiers.

Recruiting had always been a problem in peacetime, which the War Office tried to solve from time to time by improving terms and conditions of service and by lowering physical standards for recruits. But the regular means of persuasion were recruiting parties and posters. Colonels of regiments would send out parties to areas where likely men might be found – often to pubs and fairgrounds. It was 'only in the haunts of dissipation and inebriation, and among the lowest dregs of society,' recounted one possibly censorious former recruiting sergeant, 'that I met with anything like success. I could seldom prevail on even the uneducated to enlist when they were sober-living and industriously inclined.'

Recruiting sergeants' sales talk was generally unscrupulous and misleading. Potential recruits would be flattered, plied with drinks, promised an easy and adventurous life, with rapid promotion, in the gallant regiment they were being invited to join, offered an immediate cash bounty (without mentioning that this was merely an allowance to pay for necessary articles of kit). 'Tell your man,' advised one sergeant, 'how many recruits had been made sergeants, how many were now officers . . . that where your gallant and honourable regiment is now lying everything may be had for almost nothing, that the pigs and fowls are lying in the streets ready roasted . . . keeping him drinking – don't let him go to the door without one of your party with him, until he is past the doctor and attested.'

Recruiting posters offered similar blandishments, 'men will not be allowed to hunt during the next season more than once a week' and 'gallant and spirited young men of good character are certain to be promoted as there are at present upward of forty sergeants and corporals wanting to complete the corps.' After 1870, however, these abuses were stopped. Recruiting parties were not allowed to operate in public houses, enlistment bounties were prohibited, advertising had to be factual and honest.

Private Ryder remembers . . .

In this contemporary account, a young soldier recalls how he came to join the British Army in 1844:

I am a native of Twyford, in the county of Leicester, and from my childhood have had a strong inclination for the army; although my father (who is an old soldier, and was at Waterloo) always tried to set me against it, by telling me that for the least offence the

cat-o'-nine tails would be made use of. He would also describe to me the horrors of the battle of Waterloo, thinking in that way to turn my mind from a soldier's life; but instead of turning me, this only made me the more anxious to become a soldier; and I never was so happy as when I was listening to him talking about it; till at last he would say, 'Boy, don't ask me any more foolish questions, for you will not understand me if I talk for a month, until you have been to see.'

At the beginning of 1844, I made myself known to sergeant Dyer, of the 32nd regt, who was then recruiting at Nottingham. He was a very fine-looking man, and dressed very smartly. He was trimmed all over with silver lace, and wore an officer's cap; he did not lose an inch of his height, for he was very proud. One night he took me to his home (for he was a married man) to measure me, as I would not go to a public-house with him. The sergeant measured me and said, 'Barely 5ft 6in my lad; but you're young, and I shall try to get you passed.' I had not quite made up my mind, so I did not enlist that night; but a few nights after I was going down the Long Row on some business for my master, when I met the sergeant, and I said to him, 'Well, I want a place.' 'That's right, my lad; thrust your body into the army, and make a man of yourself,' said the sergeant. At the same time he held out a shilling, but I told him I should not take it there; so we went to his house, and thus I enlisted in the 32nd regiment, being then in my twentieth year.

In a room in the 'Hampshire Hog' in Charles Street, Westminster, sergeants of the Light Cavalry enlist new recruits for service in the Crimea.

Doctor Brydon's Ride

These extracts are taken from an account by the only survivor of the retreat from Kabul, written shortly after his arrival at Jellalabad . . .

'Jan. 6th. The retreat commenced this day about 9am, a temporary bridge having been thrown across the Cabool river for . . . the infantry; the guns, baggage, etc fording the river . . . We moved so slowly that it was near midnight before we reached our encamping ground across the Loghur river, a distance of only about five miles. But even this short march, with the darkness and deep snow, was too much for the poor native women and children. Many lay down and perished . . .

Jan. 7th . . . This day our march was to Boothak, a distance again of about five miles; and the whole road from Cabool was at this time a dense mass of people. In this march, as in the former, the loss of property was immense, and towards the end of it there was some sharp fighting . . . Few had anything to eat, except those who, like myself, followed the Afghan custom of carrying a bag of parched grain and raisins at their saddle-bow . . .

Jan. 8th. This morning we moved through the Khoord Cabool Pass with great loss of life and property; the heights were in possession of the enemy, who poured down an incessant fire on our column. Great numbers were killed . . . All the stragglers in the rear were cut up . . .

Jan. 10th. Resumed our march about 10am and were immediately attacked, and numbers fell in a small rocky gorge . . . just outside the camp . . . This was a terrible march . . . the fire of the enemy incessant, and numbers of officers and men, not knowing where they were going from snow-blindness, were cut up . . . So terrible were the effects of the cold and exposure on the native troops that they were unable to resist the attacks of the enemy . . . and a mere handful remained of the native regiments which had left Cabool . . .

Jan. 11th. We marched all night, the cavalry and the advanced guard, and arrived at Kutta Sung this morning, having sustained more loss from the enemy firing on us from the heights all the way . . .

The confusion now was terrible; all discipline was at an end.

We had not gone far in the dark [on the 12th] before I found myself surrounded . . . I was pulled off my horse and knocked down by a blow on the head by an Afghan knife, which must

have killed me had I not had a portion of a *Blackwood's Magazine* in my forage cap. As it was a piece of bone the size of a wafer was cut from my skull, and I was nearly stunned . . . those who had been with me I never saw again.

I regained our troops . . . The men were running up the hill on the sides of the road and on in front, throwing away their arms to lighten themselves, and could not be kept together or controlled; so Captain Bellew [the QMG] assembled all he could find mounted, and formed us into an advanced guard (about forty). We moved steadily on, fired at from the hills . . . During this night we all suffered from most intense thirst . . .

We shortly came in sight of the village of Futtehabad on the plain, about fifteen miles from Jellalabad; all here seemed quiet [in which they were deceived and] the villagers fired on us and the cavalry charged among us . . . and it became a case of utter rout, out of which all that got clear were Captains Hopkins and Collyer, Dr Harper, Lt Steer and myself. The three former being well-mounted left Lt Steer and me behind, telling us that they would soon send us help; after riding a short distance, Lt Steer said he could go no further, as both he and his horse were done (the latter was bleeding from mouth and nostrils) – he would hide in one of the many caves . . . in the hills . . . so I proceeded alone, for a short distance unmolested, then I saw a party of about twenty men drawn up in my road . . .'

Somehow he managed to get clear of them and two more parties of horsemen, but by then 'I was quite unarmed, and on a poor animal I feared could not carry me to Jellalabad, though it was now in sight. Suddenly all energy seemed to forsake me, I became nervous and frightened at shadows, and I really think I would have fallen from my saddle, but for the peak of it and some of the people from the fort coming to my assistance . . . Immediately on my telling how things were, General Sale dispatched a party to scour the plain in the hopes of picking up any stragglers, but they only found the bodies of Captains Hopkins and Collyer and Dr Harper. [The poor pony 'lay down and never rose again'.]

First Afghan War

BY THE beginning of Victoria's reign British power in India, exercised through the Honourable East India Company, was paramount and expanding. As the British extended their domination in India, so did the Russians in Asia. A real or imagined Russian threat to invade India through the ancient invasion routes in the North-West was the preoccupation of British Governors-General and Viceroys throughout the century, giving rise to the diplomatic and military moves known as 'The Great Game'. Hence the three Afghan Wars.

In 1838, the Persians, with Russian 'advisers', were planning to capture Herat in western Afghanistan, and Lord Auckland, the British Governor-General of India, decided to 'attempt to save Afghanistan' by invading the country with an army of British, Indian and Sikh troops. The Afghan ruler, Dost Mahomed, had been ill-advised enough to intrigue with the Russians and to write Lord Auckland a letter ending 'consider me and my country as yours' – which seems to have been the equivalent of 'yours faithfully' in English. So a huge army of British,

'The Remnants of an Army'
the painting which brought home to the Victorian public the stark horror of the retreat from Kabul

Dr William Brydon (1811-1873) was a Surgeon in the Bengal Army of the East India Company Army – whose service he entered in 1835. In 1839 he was medical officer of a native infantry regiment in Afghanistan. On the disastrous retreat from Kabul he escaped with five other officers and reached Fattehabad, where the others were killed. Wounded, Brydon made his away alone to Jellalabad – providing the theme for the famous painting illustrating a defeat which, like Dunkirk, became a legend for the British to cherish.

Surgeon Brydon returned to Kabul with General Pollock's army of retribution, and fifteen years later he was involved in another British-Indian legendary disaster – the siege of Lucknow in 1857. He left India in 1859 and lived quietly in his native Scotland until his death at Westfield, Ross, in 1873.

Hardly one of the Queen's 64 years on the throne passed without her Army fighting a war in some distant part of her growing Empire, to protect her peoples from envious invaders – or from themselves. Mostly the British public were thrilled to read of victories, but sometimes, as in the First Afghan War, they would be shocked by news of a terrible disaster . . .

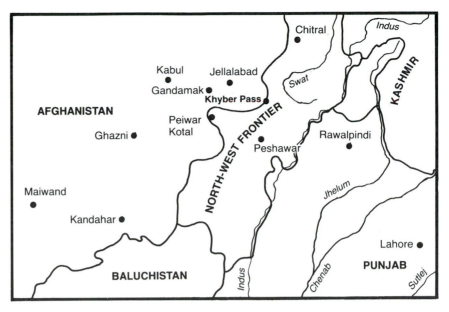

Indian and Sikhs, hated enemies of the Afghans, was assembled to invade Afghanistan and replace Dost Mahomed with a British protégé named Shah Suja.

The 'Army of the Indus' with 38,000 camp followers and 30,000 camels wound its way through the Bolan Pass to Kandahar and on to the great Afghan fort at Ghazni in July 1839. Here, having left its heavy artillery behind, it devised the technique of breaching the gate with gunpowder so that a storming party could charge through. Colour Sergeant John Clarke of the 17th Foot, which later became the Royal Leicester Regiment, gives this vivid eye-witness account of the assault on Ghazni:

That night the whole army had to parade at eight o'clock and were served out with sixty rounds of ammunition, and flints each, with orders to fall in at twelve o'clock on the same ground. There was not a word to be spoken above a whisper, and we were to turn our belts inside out and also the scales of our caps, in order to make everything as dark as possible. The artillery had their horses' hoofs muffled and also the wheels of the guns and chains.

We all had to lie flat on the ground till the gate had blown open, which was done with two 'Mussacks' of gunpowder, screwed to the gate. At the end of the drawbridge was a mortar to fire red-hot shot. Now the whole army got the silent word to march, and not a word could be heard from the men. Our regiment, the 17th, were first after the storming party. The 13th Light Infantry (later the Somerset Light Infantry) went to the opposite side of the city to fire blank cartridge to take the attention of the enemy.

The whole army had to lie down, until crossing the drawbridge, the artillery firing from the heights and also firing from the Citadel, with rockets shooting, bullets and cannon-balls flying about our heads like a swarm of bees.

Now the work began, the bugle sounded the advance, up we got, charged the drawbridge and took it, and got into the fort the best way we could. The first man we saw was General Sale (*General Sir Robert 'Fighting Bob' Sale, 57 at the time*), wounded with a sabre cut across his cheek. He led the storming party.

We were the first company into the fort . . . The Company faced about and fired a volley, and when the smoke cleared away not a man could be seen standing. All were either killed or wounded . . . After we had taken the Citadel the remainder of the city had to be taken and that took the remainder of the day. We had not much time to look about . . . Next day to Cabul, a very long march. We had not much fighting there. Some big guns were fired from the forts, but they soon ceased. It took the whole army all day to march around it. It was a beautifully rich city.

'A SIGNAL CATASTROPHE'

But the British were even more unwelcome in Kabul than were the Russians nearly 140 years later. 'British officers were insulted by shopkeepers, sentries were killed in the night, lone soldiers had their throats cut . . .' By 1841 the Afghans were in open revolt, and the British forces found themselves under siege in Kabul, Kandahar and Ghazni. After days of indecision they decided to retreat to India, and on 2 January 1842, 4,500 troops (700 of them British from the Queen's 44th Regiment) the remainder Indian cavalry and sepoys of the East India Company army, left Kabul for Jellalabad (British-held fort on the Afghan border) accompanied by officers' wives and children and some 10,000 camp followers. Waiting for them in the snow-covered passes were Ghilzais tribesmen – 'the best marksmen in the world' – with their *jezails*, long-barrelled rifles with a greater range and accuracy than the British smooth-bore muskets. A week later, officers of the 13th Regiment on the walls of Jellalabad spotted a lone horseman riding in from the direction of Kabul. It was Surgeon William Brydon – the only survivor of the Kabul army.

'Fighting Bob' Sale was in command of Jellalabad, with about 2,000 troops including 700 men of the 13th Light Infantry. Repeated Afghan attacks were beaten, and Sale joined the ranks of Victoria's heroes as the 'defender of Jellalabad'. Meanwhile an avenging army commanded by Major-General George Pollock marched into Afghanistan – the first army in history to force the Khyber Pass – recaptured Kabul, released the British prisoners, burned down the city's Great Bazaar, and marched out again. Dost Mahomed was released and re-established on his throne. Despite bombastic proclamations from the British, subsequent events in Afghanistan showed how futile was the sacrifice of lives and the waste of money.

One party of unmounted 20 officers and 45 men (most of them from the 44th) succeeded in reaching the village of Gandamak, some 30 miles from Jellalabad, where they were confronted by a large force Afghans. Outnumbered and having only 20 muskets between them, they formed a square and fought with bayonet and sword until, except four who were taken prisoner, not one man of the party was left alive.

Sir George Pollock

General George Pollock, the now forgotten Victorian hero who saved the Army's reputation after the disaster of Kabul by forcing the Khyber Pass (the first general in history to do so) and visiting retribution on the Afghans. The son of a saddler, he was commissioned at the Royal Military Academy Woolwich as a Lieutenant 'Fireworker' in 1803. He fought in the Maratha War under General Lake and at the capture of Rangoon in the First Burma War (1824). Thereafter, although promoted to Major-General, he saw no action until the First Afghan War. Ill-health forced him to leave India in 1843, but he lived on in faded glory, becoming a Field Marshal and Constable of the Tower, until his death in 1872.

'Fighting Bob' Sale

General Sir Robert Henry Sale was the second son of an East India Company colonel and on fame as 'the defender of Jellalabad'. At 13 he was given an ensign's commission in the 36th Foot (later the 2nd Bn The Worcestershire Regiment) beginning the career which won him his reputation as 'Fighting Bob'. He served under Sir Arthur Wellesley (later Duke of Wellington) at the siege of Seringapatam in 1798, and later campaigned in Travancore and Mauritius. He commanded a column in the Burma War of 1824, and killed the Burmese C.-in-C. in single combat. At the storming of Ghazni he was nearly 60, stout and double-chinned, but he could still 'cleave the skull' of one of the Afghan defenders of the fort.

1845

FEROZESHAH:
First Sikh War
  3rd Hussars
  Royal Norfolk
  Worcestershire
  East Surrey
  South Staffordshire
  Royal West Kent
  Wiltshire
  Royal Munster Fusiliers
  (then 1st Bengal
  European L.I.)
MOODKEE: First Sikh War
  3rd Hussars
  Royal Norfolk
  East Surrey
  South Staffordshire
  Royal West Kent

1846

ALIWAL: First Sikh War
  16th Lancers
  East Surrey
  Royal West Kent
  King's Shropshire L.I.
  2nd Gurkha Rifles
SOBRAON: First Sikh War
  3rd Hussars
  9th Lancers
  16th Lancers
  Royal Norfolk
  Royal Lincolnshire
  Worcestershire
  East Surrey
  South Staffordshire
  Royal West Kent
  King's Shropshire L.I.
  Wiltshire
  Royal Munster Fusiliers
  2nd Gurkha Rifles

1846-1847

NEW ZEALAND: Maori Wars
  Northamptonshire
  Wiltshire
  Manchester
SOUTH AFRICA
  7th Dragoon Guards
  Royal Warwickshire
  Cameronians
  Royal Inniskilling Fusiliers
  Black Watch
  Sherwood Foresters
  Argyll and Sutherland
   Highlanders
  Rifle Brigade

General Sir Charles Napier

ONE OF THE MOST extraordinary personalities of his age – swashbuckling and eccentric, hard-swearing but religious, sentimental but quarrelsome, witty but extremely ambitious – General Sir Charles Napier loved war. But after the battle of Miani, where he 'saw no safety in misery', he wrote 'God knows I was very miserable when I rode over the fields and saw the slain.'

Over 60 when he conquered Sind, he was short of stature and wore steel-rimmed spectacles. His general appearance was scruffy; he had a long white beard and straggling grey hair, and he rarely wore uniform.

A great-great-grandson of Charles II and grandson of the fifth Lord Napier, Charles James Napier was the eldest son of Colonel George Napier, a veteran of the American War. He was bought a commission in the 33rd Foot at the age of twelve; served in the Peninsular War with his two brothers, William and George; was seriously wounded six times and spent over a year as a prisoner of war.

Later he served in Bermuda, France and Greece, where he was a close friend of the poet Byron, quarrelled with his superiors, and fell in love with a Greek girl named Anastasia, by whom he had two daughters. He spent ten years on half-pay, and then was given Northern Command in operations against the Chartists, with whom he was in some sympathy.

'To try my hand with an army is a longing not to be described,' he wrote when he was sent to Sind in 1841. But he also told a friend: 'I am too old for glory now . . . If a man cannot catch glory when his knees are supple he had better not try when they grow stiff . . .' When he took command in Sind he wrote in his journal, 'Charles Napier! Take heed of your ambition for military glory . . . I have worked myself to this great command, and am thankful at having it, yet despise myself . . . the weakness of the man and the pride of war are too powerful for me.'

In his dispatches after Miani he mentioned individual NCOs and men, and even Indian soldiers, something never done before. He also collected £70,000 in prize money, and seized a truckle bed on which was lying the pregnant wife of one of the Mirs because it concealed a store of gold.

Napier – *which* Napier?

Queen Victoria's heroes included so many *Napiers* that it must have been confusing even for the Queen (who never seemed to forget a name or face), especially as Admiral Sir Charles Napier (1796-1861) and his three cousins, General Sir Charles James Napier (1782-1853), the conqueror of Sind, General Sir George Napier (1784-1855), Governor of Cape Colony, and General Sir William Napier (1785-1861), the historian of the Peninsular War, were all prominent in the first decades of her reign. The more distinguished bearers of the Napier name in her day included two Admirals, seven Generals, a Field Marshal, a Governor of Madras, and a successful marine engineer.

The Admirals and all but one of the Generals were descended from a long line of Lairds of Merchiston in Scotland, and among their ancestors was John Napier, the inventor of logarithms. This remarkable family also produced Admiral Henry Napier, General Mark Napier, General Thomas Napier, General Elers Napier (who was only a Napier because he took the name of his stepfather, Admiral Sir Charles Napier), Lord Francis Napier, Governor of Madras, and a plain Mr Robert Napier, a distinguished marine engineer who built one of the first ironclad warships. The famous Napier who was totally unrelated to all the others was Field Marshal Lord Napier of Magdala (1810-1890).

The famous Latin pun – *Peccavi*: I have sinned – which he is said to have uttered after his successful conquest of Sind, is completely in character with the man, but must in fact be credited to a *Punch* cartoonist celebrating the event. If anyone had sinned it was the British, who ignored their earlier treaties with the Amirs and showed no compunction in annexing the territory to their growing Indian empire.

A radical in politics but an autocrat in government, Napier had no doubts about the superior benefits of British rule. Like most of his contemporaries, he assumed that the 'natives' would naturally prefer British notions of law and order to their own. Noting that the poor in Sind 'live in a larder and yet starve', he set up a complete civil government, social, financial and judicial. Contrary to the practice of the East India Company, he did not hesitate to attack religious practices which he considered inhuman. So he abolished 'suttee', the age-old Hindu custom by which a widow threw herself on her husband's funeral pyre. When Brahmins defended the custom, he replied: 'My nation also has a custom. When men burn women alive we hang them . . . My carpenters shall therefore erect gibbets on which to hang all concerned when the widow is consumed. Let us all act according to national custom.'

As Commander-in-Chief in India after the Second Sikh War, Napier – then nearly seventy and in poor health – attempted to make drastic reforms in the army, whose discipline even the Governor-General, Lord Dalhousie, described as 'scandalous', but he soon found himself at loggerheads with the Military Board in India, the East India Company Directors in London, and with Dalhousie himself. He offended the Directors by ordering roomier, healthier, and therefore more costly barracks for the soldiers: 'Make the rooms high and narrow, for that not only gives pure air, but debars overcrowding.' He offended the Board when he criticised the cost of officers' messes: 'The damning sin of the magnificent armies in India . . . is an outrageous and vulgar luxury . . . This I hold to be my duty to the parents of hundreds of these boys . . . to reduce the expense and drinking of messes.' He was reprimanded by Dalhousie and even censured by his much-revered Wellington when he exceeded his powers and suspended an order on cutting pay. He resigned at once: 'Government, Court, Duke and Governor-General may all go to the devil!'

At the funeral of the Duke of Wellington in 1852, Napier was a pall-bearer – though ill and in great pain from internal ulcers. 'I cannot get rid of his face,' he wrote, 'as I saw it young in battle, and old in peace.' Barely a year later, on 29 August 1853, he died.

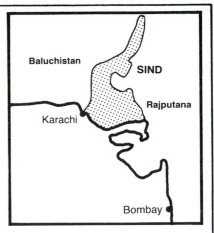

The Seizure of Sind

'We have no right to seize Sind, yet we shall do so, and a very advantageous, useful, humane piece of rascality it will be.'

So wrote the British conqueror of Sind, Sir Charles Napier in his diary. 'The great recipe for quieting a country,' he added, expressing a general Victorian view of 'the natives' (and of their own children), 'is a good thrashing first and a great kindness afterwards: the wildest chaps are thus tamed.'

In 1843 the wildest chaps for the British in India were the Baluchi Mirs (or 'Ameers' or 'Amirs') of Sind (or 'Scinde'), who 'governed Scinde by the sword alone' . . . and 'were at full liberty to mutilate or kill any Scindian or Hindu at their pleasure or caprice. They disliked the presence of all foreigners.' Moreover, Sind (now a province of Pakistan), lying in the valley between India and Afghanistan, stood in the path of British imperial expansion. During the First Afghan war they had, not surprisingly, been less than friendly towards the British forces marching through their land. So General Napier was sent to Hyderabad, Sind, with a treaty making stringent demands on the Mirs. Assuming they would refuse to sign, he seized a number of forts and got ready to conquer the country. Hearing that a Baluchi army of some 25,000 had assembled at Miani (or Meanee) a few miles north of Hyderabad, he attacked them on 17 February 1843 with a force of under 3,000 men, all Indian troops except for 500 men of HM 22nd Regiment (now The Cheshire Regiment, then mostly Irish).

Napier's small army advanced in columns under heavy artillery fire to within 200 yards of the Baluchis, deployed in line and charged. 'The Beloochees,' wrote Sir William Napier (colonel of the 22nd and brother of Sir Charles), 'having their muskets laid ready in rest along the summit, waited until our troops were within fifty yards ere they poured in their fire. The rapid pace of the British, with the steepness of the slope, deceived them in aiming, yet the loss was great . . . looking down at the closely-packed mass of weapon-waving tribesmen waiting to receive them, the men halted and staggered back in utter amazement at the flashing forest of sword-blades that glittered in their front.' The Baluchis 'dashed forward with demoniac strength and ferocity full against the front of the 22nd. But with shouts as loud, and shrieks as wild . . . and hearts as big and arms as strong [as theirs], the Irish soldiers met them with that queen of arms, the bayonet, and sent their foremost masses rolling back in blood.'

'No fire of small arms, no thrust of bayonets, no sweeping discharge of grape from the guns . . . could drive these gallant soldiers back. They gave their breasts to be shot; they leaped upon the guns by twenties at a time; their dead rolled down the steep slope by hundreds; but the gaps in their masses were continually filled up from the rear . . . For three hours that living tide of valiant Beloochees held their ground against that still more valiant little band, when they began to give way . . .' Sir Charles had sent his cavalry to charge the Baluchi rear. The British losses were some 20 officers and 260 other ranks; the Baluchi losses were estimated to be 6000 dead.

A month later, Napier clinched his conquest of Sind in another ferocious battle at Dubba, also near Hyderabad. With 5,000 men (including the indomitable 22nd, 1000 cavalry and 19 guns, he attacked an army of 26,000 Baluchis. Napier (then 60 years of age) led the final charge himself. This final victory cost him 270 officers and men (147 of the 22nd); the Baluchis lost 5,000 men – and Sind, which became a British Province, with Sir Charles Napier as its first Governor.

PUNJAUB: Second Sikh War
3rd Hussars
9th Lancers
14th Hussars
Royal Lincolnshire
South Wales Borderers
Gloucestershire
Worcestershire
Duke of Cornwall's L.I.
King's Shropshire L.I.
King's Royal Rifle Corps
North Staffordshire
Royal Munster Fusiliers
(then 1st Bengal Europeans)
Royal Dublin Fusiliers
(then 1st Bombay
Europeans)

*In the first three decades of the
Queen's reign the British in India
pursued a forward policy: securing
the frontiers, annexing states
with 'unsatisfactory' rulers and
conquering others – such as
Maharajah Ranjit Singh
in the Punjab . . .*

Heroes of the Punjab

THE SIKHS were, and still are, a monotheistic Hindu sect living in that part of northern India known as the Punjab – the land of the five rivers. Founded in the 16th century, they created a powerful military state ruled, when Queen Victoria came to the throne, by their greatest leader, the one-eyed Maharajah Ranjit Singh (1780-1839). The Sikhs made fine soldiers and they maintained a large army, trained and led by mercenary European officers, mostly French. Their artillery was at the time probably more powerful than anything the British could put in the field. The Sikhs were an obvious menace to British security in India, but as long as Ranjit Singh lived an uneasy peace was kept. After his death, the Sikh army, led by a supreme military body called the Khalsa, became the greatest power in the state and they were determined to make war with the British.

In 1844 the new British Governor-General of India, Sir Henry Hardinge, was confident that the Sikh army would not cross the Sutlej, the river forming the boundary between British and Sikh territory. But on 12 December 1845, they did just that, and over 12,000 Sikh troops,

infantry, cavalry and artillery, marched on Ferozepore.

THE FIRST SIKH WAR (1845-46)
The first Sikh-British clash was at Mudki at night on 18 December 1845 – nicknamed 'Midnight Moodkhee' by the British soldiers, who still wore the scarlet coats, white cross belts and shakos of Napoleonic wars. Sir Hugh Gough, the Commander-in-Chief and Hardinge, both in their mid-sixties, had marched a 10,000-strong army 120 miles from Ambala to confront 22,000 Sikhs. The 3rd Light Dragoons (later the 3rd Hussars) made a spectacular charge to turn the Sikh left flank, and a brave infantry charge forced the Sikhs back with heavy losses, but the battle ended inconclusively. 'I might have killed several Sikhs at Mudki,' wrote one officer of Dragoons, 'but I was foolishly merciful.'

Two days later, at Ferozeshah, came the bloodiest battle of all – again partly at night – of which the following account was written by a lieutenant of the 50th Foot, which later became the Royal West Kent Regiment:

No one can imagine the sickening uncertainty. A burning camp on one side of the village, mines and ammunition exploding in every direction, the loud orders to extinguish the fires as the Sepoys lighted them, the volleys given should the Sikhs venture too near, the booming of the monster gun, the incessant firing of the smaller one, the continual whistling noise of the shell, grape and round shot, the bugles sounding, the drums beating and the yelling of the enemy, together with the thirst, fatigue and cold, not knowing whether the Army were conquerors or the conquered – all contributed to make this night awful in the extreme.

In his own official despatch Sir Henry Hardinge wrote: 'When morning broke we drove the enemy, without a halt, from one extremity of the camp to the other, capturing thirty or forty guns . . .' But the British casualties were sickening – more than 2,400 of an army of less than 18,000 men all told.

A week later, on 28 January 1846, the Peninsular veteran, Sir Harry Smith won what he

At the time of his death in 1839 – brought on by drink and debauchery, or so the British claimed – the dominions of Maharajah Ranjit Singh embraced the whole of the Punjab, from the Indus to the Sutlej

called 'a stand-up gentleman-like battle' at Aliwal. Private, later Sergeant, John Pearman, aged 27, of the 3rd Light Dragoons described the action in his Memoirs:

Our army came into line as steady as a field day. I sat on my horse and looked at the two armies. It was a lovely sight . . . At about 700 yards from the enemy, the Colonel shouted: 'Action! Front! Unlimber and prepare for action!' . . . We all dismounted and held the horses, when 'bang' went our guns. About the third shot I saw was making holes in the ranks in front of us . . . At this time the firing was terrific, and looking back, the plain was covered with wounded and dead men, and horses and pieces of broken guns . . . We were in a cross fire from the enemy's guns and we had seven horses down at once in my guns (no. 5) out of the eight horses.

We limbered up again and I and Jack Reeves rode on ammunition boxes, when a shot came and struck the wheel close to me, smashed it, and the spoke struck Reeves in the thigh, but did not hurt him much. It all missed me . . . We now galloped close to the enemy, about three hundred yards, and 'Bang! Bang!' went our guns to a good tune and they had something to think about.

At this time I looked to the left and saw the 16th Lancers (later The 16th The Queen's Lancers) coming on at a trot, then a gallop. I took off my cap and hollered out: 'The first charge of the British Lancers!' The enemy formed square, but the 16th Lancers went right on and broke it. Such cutting and stabbing I never saw before or since.'

This First Sikh War ended disastrously for the Sikhs at Sobraon on 10 February 1846. Private Pearman watched the British infantry charge:

Oh, what a brave sight to sit on your horse and look at those brave fellows as they tried several times to get into the enemy's camp; and at last they did but oh, what a loss of human life. God only knows who will have to answer for it.

A Sikh gunner saw it rather differently:

Nearer and nearer they came, as steadily as if they were on their own parade ground, in perfect silence . . . At last the order came, 'Fire', and our whole battery as if from one gun fired into the advancing mass. The smoke was so great . . . I . . . fully expected that we had destroyed the demons, so what was my astonishment . . . to see them still advancing in perfect silence, but their numbers reduced to about one half. I fired again and again into them, making a gap or lane in their ranks each time; but on they came, in that awful silence, till they were within a short distance of our guns, when their colonel ordered them to halt to take breath, which they did under a heavy fire. Then, with a shout . . which is still ringing in my ears, they made a rush for our guns . . . In ten minutes it was all over.

The British took the Sikh capital at Lahore, and everybody thought the Sikhs' power was finally broken – everybody except Sir Charles Napier who said 'this tragedy will be re-enacted a year or two hence'.

Sir Harry Smith (1787-1860)

Lieutenant-General Sir Harry Smith, Bart., was one of several colourful characters who first acquired renown in the Peninsular War. The son of a surgeon, he was commissioned at 18 in the 95th Foot (later the Rifle Brigade). He fought at Corunna and at Badajoz – where he rescued two beautiful teenage Spanish girls from the troops, and later married one of them, Juana Maria Dolores de Leon. Theirs was a lifelong love match, and she went with him on all his campaigns and travels. Smith fought at Waterloo as assistant quartermaster-general. He was commandant of the forces in Cape Colony during the Kaffir War (1834), and achieved fame for riding from Capetown to Grahamstown – 700 miles – in six days.

In 1840 he was appointed adjutant-general to the Queen's Army in India and took part in the Gwalior War in 1843. In the First Sikh War he commanded a division and was made a baronet for his victory at Aliwal.

Returning to South Africa, Smith was Governor of the Cape of Good Hope from 1847 to 1852. He defeated the Boers at Boomplatz in 1848. Ladysmith in Natal was named after his wife.

Hugh Gough
1st Viscount Gough
1779-1869

Like many another Victorian hero, Hugh Gough was a veteran of the Peninsular War. He commanded the 2nd Battalion of the 87th Prince of Wales' Irish Regiment (later the Royal Irish Fusiliers) and was severely wounded at the Battle of Talavera in 1809.

Born in Limerick, he was commissioned at the age of 14 and promoted lieutenant in the 78th Highlanders when he was 16, at which age he first came under fire at the taking of Capetown in 1796. In 1837, the year Victoria became Queen, he was appointed to command the Mysore Division of the Madras Army. He held the chief command in the Opium War in China (1841-42), and returned to India as Commander-in-Chief. His first Indian triumph was in the Gwalior War (1843) when he finally destroyed the Mahratta power.

In the Sikh Wars of 1845-46 and 1848-49 Gough won a series of indecisive victories against well-armed, highly-trained and more numerous armies, and he was on the point of being replaced by Sir Charles Napier when at last he broke the Sikh power at Gujerat (1849).

Gough fought in more campaigns than almost any soldier of his day, except Wellington and was much loved by his troops for his personal bravery: in battle he always wore a white coat so that he could be easily recognised. After his last battle, he returned in triumph to England, received the Freedom of the City of London and was given the then handsome pension of £2,000 a year, and was promoted to full General. Later he became a Privy Councillor and a Field Marshal. He died greatly honoured at the age of 90.

CHILLIANWALLAH:
Second Sikh War
3rd Hussars
9th Lancers
14th Hussars
South Wales Borderers
Gloucestershire
Worcestershire
Royal Munster Fusiliers
(then 2nd Bengal
Europeans)

GOOJERAT:
Second Sikh War
3rd Hussars
9th Lancers
14th Hussars
Royal Lincolnshire
South Wales Borderers
Gloucestershire
Worcestershire
Duke of Cornwall's L.I.
King's Shropshire L.I.
King's Royal Rifle Corps
Royal Munster Fusiliers
(then 2nd Bengal
Europeans)
Royal Dublin Fusiliers
(then 1st Bombay European
Fusiliers)

MOOLTAN: Second Sikh War
Royal Lincolnshire
Duke of Cornwall's L.I.
King's Royal Rifle Corps
Royal Dublin Fusiliers
(then 1st Bombay European
Fusiliers)

THE SECOND SIKH WAR (1848-49)

Napier was right: late in 1848 the Sikhs again took the field against the British. On 13 January Gough attacked their army when it was strongly entrenched in dense jungle near Chillianwala, outnumbering his troops and guns by four to one. During the battle the 24th Foot (later The South Wales Borderers) were ordered to charge the Sikh guns, unsupported and using the bayonet only, when they were still too far away. They 'actually broke the enemy's line and took large numbers of guns,' reported General Sir Colin Campbell 'without a shot being fired by the Regiment . . .' But nearly half the regiment was lost, of whom 238 were killed. Gough called it 'an act of madness' – like the Charge of the Light Brigade, but not celebrated in verse. Sergeant Pearman was there:

The battle lasted until dark at night, when both armies stayed on the ground, and the killed and wounded lay where they fell. Our small army lost about two thousand and the enemy it was said lost near five thousand, so what with men and horses, the place was covered with dead and dying . . . In the night it came on to rain, which did not improve our very nice condition, but we had to put up with it, and I am proud to say the men did not grumble about it. Sometimes they would wish they had some grog.

But Gough's 'butcher's bills' in indecisive battles appalled the British government: 'the news from India is very distressing,' wrote Queen Victoria, and . . . Sir Charles Napier is instantly to be sent out to supersede Lord Gough.' But by the time Napier arrived in India Gough had attacked the main Sikh army at Gujrat on 21 Februay 1849, and won a brilliant victory, which was achieved, as he emphasised, 'with comparatively little loss on our side' – 96 killed and 700 wounded in a force of some 24,000 men. Again, Sergeant Pearman was in the thick of the battle and saw how it ended:

The battle was now at its highest, and the air had become filled with shot, shell and smoke. Trumpets were sounding, drums beating, bugles sounding, colonels and other officers hollering, when all of a sudden came the order for the 3rd Light Dragoons to charge. I could see the 9th Lancers and the black cavalry doing the same. But we did not get much at them this time, as they made a quick movement back into their line . . . (*Later*) I could now see that the whole of the cavalry was to the front, as far as I could see right and left. It now seemed that the battle was drawing to a close, as we could see the enemy in full retreat. Lord Gough came down the front with his staff. His leg was bleeding at the knee. A piece of shell had struck him I afterwards heard. The old man said: 'Thank you, 3rd Light, a glorious victory, men!' As soon as he had been down the cavalry front, we got the order to advance in pursuing order. The whole of the regiments . . . covered eight or ten miles of front . . . We pursued the poor flying devils to the banks of the Indus river.

After Gujrat the Sikhs surrendered unconditionally and the British annexed the Punjab.

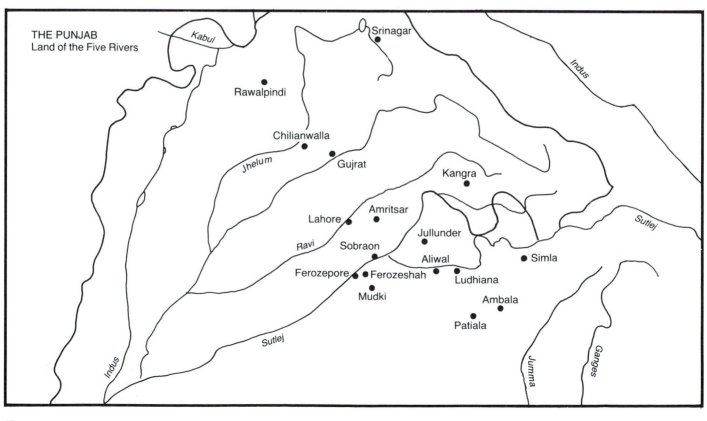

THE PUNJAB
Land of the Five Rivers

The 'thin red line' was not kept straight and steady by men who asked questions

A Soldier's Life

The 41st Regiment encamped on Dover Heights

FIVE OFT-QUOTED words neatly expressed what it meant to be soldiers of the Queen: 'Theirs not to reason why'. In an army in which mutiny was punishable by shooting, hanging or, for Indian sepoys, blowing from guns; in which breaches of discipline could earn a brutal flogging or (after 1881) 'Field Punishment No. 1', which meant lashing a defaulter to a gun wheel for several hours a day; and in which even such an offence as appearing on parade with dirty buttons could earn days of confinement to barracks, a wise soldier knew better than to ask 'why?' He obeyed orders and kept his mouth shut. And even then he could be put on a charge for 'dumb' insolence.'

From the day a recruit accepted the Queen's shilling, he found himself in a world of blind obedience and ramrod rigidity on parade. Drill was the beginning and end of every soldier's training. A perfect march-past demonstrated a unit's fitness for war. All army training and exercises, even rifle and artillery practice, were performed with drill-book precision according to strict rules to be followed regardless of time, place, or potential enemy. The army's bayonet exercises, remarked Sir Evelyn Wood unkindly, were 'more suitable for a Music Hall than for training men to fight.' Drill movements first introduced in 1780 were still in use on the parade-grounds and battlefields of 1900 – with humiliating consequences. For during the Boer War British-trained troops faced many defeats at the hands of a numerically inferior enemy, who never drilled or saluted his officers properly.

In the first half of the Queen's reign most soldiers were accommodated in cramped, poorly ventilated barracks, where they had to live, eat, drink and sleep in less than 300cu.ft. of space compared with the 1,000cu.ft. allotted to convicts. There were no chairs, and a soldier had to perch on his bed to eat his meals from a trestle table, using his own utensils and 'eating irons'. Coal-stoves and dim oil (later gas) lamps provided fitful heat and light. Men slept on folding iron beds with straw mattresses (changed quarterly), two sheets (washed monthly) and four blankets (washed only when filthy). Often the communal washing tub served as a night urinal, and the latrine was outside in the open. Small wonder that deaths from tuberculosis were 18 per 1,000 among civilians of the same age. A soldier's daily food ration, from which until 1870 sixpence a day was deducted from his pay, was a pound of bread and twelve ounces of meat, including bone, offal and fat. For his breakfast he had biscuits, known as 'hard tack', dipped in coffee; for dinner a stew and sometimes a roast with potatoes, and supper usually consisted of nothing more than a piece of bread and a bowl of tea.

Only six out of every hundred men were allowed to have wives 'on the strength', and they too lived in the barrack room, with only a curtain to give some privacy. After the Crimean war, married soldiers were allowed separate quarters, and all barracks were renovated and repaired to provide adequate if not luxurious accommodation with proper ventilation, drainage, heating, washing and cooking facilities.

In India, where most regular soldiers were likely to spend a significant portion of their service, barracks were more spacious. Of necessity, they were also better ventilated, even although they remained unbearably stuffy in the

41

hot weather. However, for the ordinary Tommy, there was the unheard luxury of having beings of a lower order than himself to fetch and carry and clean – and, of course, to browbeat and curse. He could even have himself shaved in bed. Otherwise, service in India could be boring in the extreme, with little to do but spend long hot hours stretched on one's charpoy (bed), getting drunk in the canteen – or visiting the local brothel. Later in the reign, thanks to the efforts of Lord Roberts, regimental libraries were established to help relieve the tedium of camp life.

The British soldier's uniform changed very little before the last two decades of the reign. In burning deserts, humid jungles or snow-swept mountain passes, he continued to wear the scarlet tunic, the leather stock, tight trousers and the shako of Wellington's day. Kilted Highlanders marched to the relief of Lucknow in their feather bonnets and white spats, and over forty years later under the South African sun their descendants suffered agonies from blistered legs. But when sun-helmets and lightweight khaki uniforms began to replace shako and scarlet, many ordinary soldiers disliked the change, preferring the smart to the practical.

For Indian other ranks ('sepoys' in the infantry, 'sowars' in the cavalry), life was rather easier than for their British fellow-soldiers. They were not liable to be flogged, they were permitted to wear their own clothes when not on parade, and each man could prepare his own food in accordance with the conventions of his caste or community. Above all, the sepoy had the consolation of serving in his own country, among his own kind, and, apart from the loss of esteem suffered by the Bengal army in the years before and after the Great Mutiny, his profession earned him respect whenever he returned to his village and family.

In the first ten years of the Queen's reign a soldier's life tended to mean just that: the recruit enlisted for unlimited service. From 1847 he could enlist for an initial ten years, or twelve in the cavalry, artillery and engineers, but he was not entitled to a pension unless he served a further eleven years with the Colours (or twelve with the other branches). In 1870 short service was introduced: a soldier enlisted for six years with the Colours followed by six in the Reserve.

A soldier's pay – 1s a day for infantrymen, 1s 3d for cavalrymen (plus 1d a day for beer) – did not compare too well with the average wages of unskilled labourers, but it was regular, and many a soldier could earn more by using his civvy-street skills (tailoring, shoe-repairing etc) or by working as a mess servant, officers' batman or groom, or as a bandsman. Extra pay could be earned for special duties, and from 1836 good conduct pay was paid at 1d a day for every five years of 'unblemished' service.

However, many a recruit failed to notice that the shilling a day promised by the recruiting sergeant was subject to deductions. Not only did the rations have to be paid for but also such items as kit, laundry, haircutting and barrack-room damages. Even though charges for food were abolished in 1873 and other stoppages were later reduced, very few men actually saw the promised shilling a day as actual cash in hand. Those who demanded better pay on his behalf were usually told that the ordinary soldier enlisted not for the money but for the excitement of the military life.

Other rewards there certainly were. During the Queen's reign more medals and honours were bestowed than ever before or since, many of them on her personal initiative. Following the

It was General Sir Charles Napier who insisted that all new barracks built for British troops in India should be light, airy and well-ventilated

success of the first campaign medals to be issued, for those who fought at Waterloo, medals were awarded for most of the many campaigns undertaken during Victoria's reign, and they were greatly prized by all ranks. Individual awards began in 1833 with the Long Service and Good Conduct Medal for soldiers who had served for eighteen years without blotting their copybook. The Meritorious Service Medal was awarded from 1845 to senior NCOs for excellent service other than in action. The first medal for gallantry available to Other Ranks was the Distinguished Conduct Medal awarded to those who had served in the Crimea. Apart from medals awarded for individual bravery – of which the most prized was, of course, the Victoria Cross – 'mentions in dispatches' were a time-honoured way of recognising outstanding conduct in battle. In his dispatches from Sind, Sir Charles Napier included Other Ranks among those mentioned, which became standard practice from that time on.

Promotion came slowly, if at all. NCOs needed to be able to read and write, which meant that they had to be found among the fewer than 10% of all British soldiers who were literate – at least until the last quarter of the century. Scotsmen, being rather better educated than the English or the Irish, tended to form the majority of corporals and sergeants. The highest non-commissioned rank, Warrant Officer, was instituted, but promotion to commissioned officer rank was very rare – perhaps some 3% of all officers – and was discouraged. The soldiers of Victoria's army wanted to be led by 'real gentlemen' whom they could respect for their natural bravery. And as Field Marshal Sir William Robertson and others found, life in the officers mess was not always very comfortable for the commissioned ranker.

Pensions were paid to old soldiers after twenty-one years in the army, but a veteran's pension might well amount to litte more than his first pay as a recruit. The neglect of time-expired soldiers was callous and notorious. The lucky few might find places as Yeomen of the Guard, as Yeomen Warders at the Tower (the 'Beefeaters'), or in the Royal Hospital, Chelsea. Those whose only skills had been learned on the parade-ground or battle-field were lucky to find ill-paid menial jobs as porters, watchmen and the like. Skilled men fared rather better. There were several voluntary societies who helped old soldiers to find employment, notably the Army and Navy Pensioners or Time-Expired Men's Employment Society founded in 1855 and the Corps of Commissionaires founded in 1859. But, despite their efforts, all too often men who had worn 'the Widow's uniform' were sooner or later driven to charity, drink or petty crime, or begging in the streets.

Field Marshal Sir William Robertson

From Footman to Field-Marshal

Unique among the heroes for Victoria was William Robertson (1860-1913), who joined the army as a private and rose to the rank of Field-Marshal. One of seven children of a country tailor, he was educated at the village school and then went into service as a footman in the household of none other than Lord Cardigan.

Discontented, he decided to enlist in the army. 'I would rather bury you than see you in a red coat,' declared his mother, reflecting the common attitude of the day towards anything to do with 'Tommy Atkins'. Nevertheless, as soon as he reached the age of 17, Robertson joined the 16th Lancers [later the 16th/5th The Queen's Royal Lancers], and rapidly rose to be troop sergeant major. Encouraged by his officers, he accepted a commission when offered, and went to India with the 3rd Dragoon Guards, who were later amalgamated with The Carabiniers and The Royal Scots Greys to form The Royal Scots Dragoon Guards.

As one of the mere 3% of all officers commissioned from the ranks, Robertson had a hard struggle against poverty and unspoken social prejudice. His father made his 'gentleman's clothes', he drank only water in the Mess, and he earned extra pay by learning six languages in three years. In a letter to his father, he wrote:

It is so miserable out here . . . So far as I know, not *once* has anyone in my present sphere taken offence at being in my company, but there is such a difference between this and sincere mutual interest; this naturally cannot be between a born gentleman and one who is only now beginning to *try* to become one . . . Here, among all the gaiety and apparent friendship, I feel that if I were not an officer tomorrow, there would perhaps be none to recognize me . . .

These sentiments echoed Wellington's view, expressed a generation earlier, that rankers 'do not make good officers; it does not answer. They are brought into a society to the manners of which they are not accustomed . . . they are men of different manners altogether.'

All the same, Robertson became a captain after only two years, and was awarded the D.S.O. He was the first ex-ranker to be admitted to Staff College, and he married the daughter of an Indian Army general. By the time he died in 1933, he had become Field-Marshal Sir William Robertson, Baronet, (Knight) Grand Cross of Bath, (Knight) Grand Cross of St Michael and St George, Knight Commander of the (Royal) Victorian Order and Chief of the Imperial General Staff. It was in this capacity during the First World War that he had supreme command of all British armies, and tried hard to deny civilian ministers any say on strategy. The Prime Minister Lloyd George wanted supreme power in his own hands and succeeded in getting Robertson dismissed.

'The Best Officers in the World'

THE OFFICERS of Queen Victoria's army were, with very rare exceptions, all gentlemen born and bred. The sons of titled families, country squires, army officers, clergymen, civil servants, and lawyers had little difficulty in obtaining a commission – if their families could afford the purchase price and

could provide the private income all officers needed to live a decent life in the Army and pay their mess bills. As Kipling wrote: '. . . God has arranged that a clean-run youth of the British middle classes should in matter of backbone, brains, and bowels, surpass all other youths. For this reason a child of eighteen will stand up . . . with a tin sword in his hand . . . until he is dropped. If he dies, he dies like a gentleman.'

No other qualifications or professional training were necessary. As a gentleman an officer had received the kind of upbringing and education that made him a natural leader, and always provided he showed courage in battle, nothing else really mattered. Not even physical defects or age. Several of Victoria's generals had only one arm, including Lord Raglan, Lord Hardinge, and Sam Browne (the designer of the Sam Browne belt), and two of the most successful – Roberts and Wolseley – had only one eye apiece, while one of the winners of the VC at Rorke's Drift was almost completely deaf. Almost all of the generals in the Crimean War were over 60, and one, Sir John Burgoyne, was 72. Viscount Gough and Lord Roberts were 70 when they fought their last campaigns. Sir Charles Napier was 67 when he conquered Sind, and when Sir Colin Campbell led an army to relieve Lucknow he was a mere 65. Over half the colonels in the 1846 Army List had joined the army in the previous century, and in 1850 no general in Britain was under 61.

The purchase system tended to block the promotion of able officers with no money and over-promote the rich but incompetent – who could purchase senior ranks over the heads of more deserving but less wealthy officers. Captain James Algeo of the 77th Foot (later the 2nd Middlesex Regiment) was still only a captain after thirty-nine years in the army. One of the heroes of the Indian Mutiny, Henry Havelock, remarked that he had been purchased over by 'two fools and three sots' before becoming a captain, but he at last became a major-general. But the ambitious, able and well-heeled officer could enjoy very rapid promotion and become a lieutenant-colonel in a very few years.

Not all army officers had to purchase their commissions. Officers in the Royal Artillery and the Royal Engineers were commissioned after completing a course of training at the Royal Military Academy, Woolwich, and after 1842 cadets from the Royal Military College at Sandhurst could be awarded commissions without purchase. Officers were also sometimes promoted from the ranks – but all too rarely. In 1849, for example, out of the 461 commissions awarded, 24 went to NCOs, 25 to Sandhurst cadets, and only 74 of the remainder were obtained without purchase.

Officers, being gentlemen, were assumed to have the means to serve the Queen without depending on the niggardly salaries she paid them. Throughout her reign little or nothing was done to pay army officers a living wage. Pay varied according to regiment and service, but at the time of the Crimean War a subaltern was paid about £96 a year and a lieutenant-colonel about £328. Cavalry, artillery and engineer officers all received rather more. A major-general was paid just over £1,000 a year and a full general nearly £4,000.

To live on these salaries was practically impossible for officers without private means. Not only was an officer required to buy his uniform, equipment and weapons, but he also had to pay his mess bill – which might well be higher than his pay – as well keep a batman and pay subscriptions for almost anything from the regimental band to its wine cellar or pack of hounds. All officers were expected to live up to the standard of their rank and to participate in the social life and activities of the mess. Only the sons of the rich could afford to live in such regiments as the Household Cavalry, the Foot Guards and the Scots Greys. Even in an ordinary infantry regiment a subaltern needed a private income of £100 a year; in the cavalry he would need four times as much. When serving overseas, as in India, officers were paid rather more; an infantry subaltern received about £160 a year. As the cost of living was cheaper, Indian army officers enjoyed a higher standard of living than they could afford on returning to England.

Promotion by Purchase: 'A Sordid and Degrading Traffic'

In 1830 Lord Brudenell – later Earl of Cardigan and leader of the charge of the Light Brigade at Balaclava – purchased the lieutenant-colonelcy of the 15th Hussars [later amalgamated with the 19th Hussars to form the 15th/19th The King's Royal Hussars] for the formidable sum of £40,000. He had bought his first commission, as cornet, in 1824, when he was 27 years of age, and so his great wealth enabled him to achieve very rapid promotion. From early in the 18th century it had been the custom to purchase commissions for young boys – some from the day of their birth.

The going rates established by Royal Warrant in 1821 varied according to regiment and rank. The regulation price of a first commission – that of an ensign or cornet – was £450 in a Line Regiment of Foot, and £1200 in such socially prestigious regiments as the Foot Guards, Life Guards and Royal Horse Guards.

Promotion to higher ranks cost much more: a lieutenant-colonel in an infantry regiment had to find £4500, and in a cavalry regiment £6175. But many had to pay 'over-regulation' rates. In the cavalry, for example, officers had to pay almost double the regulation rate: it can be seen that Brudenell paid nearly six times the proper price for the privilege of buying himself into the Hussars.

This system of promotion by purchase, so curious as it now seems to us, had its detractors as well as its defenders. One distinguished colonel, reporting to the Purchase Commission in 1856, described it as a 'sordid and degrading traffic in commissions in the higher grade.' But the Duke of Wellington, whose word no doubt weighed more heavily, maintained that the system brought into the Army 'men of fortune and education who have some connexion with the interests and fortunes of the Country, besides the Commissions they hold . . .' For this reason, the Army was not a mercenary army, but 'a safe and beneficial force.'

Not surprisingly, once the Purchase Commission had heard all the available evidence, it proceeded to take no further action. The system was far too beneficial to the Government, who not only made money from the sales but who were also spared the expense of recruiting, training, paying and pensioning officers in Her Majesty's armed forces.

Most Victorian army officers came from a rural background and brought with them a great enthusiasm for hunting and shooting – recreations which their regiments naturally encouraged. So it was not surprising that the young Garnet Wolseley should write home from the Crimea that 'Man shooting is the finest sport of all . . . the more you kill the more you wish to kill.' Many officers, however, felt that the actual fighting was not for gentlemen; their principal duty was to lead their men into battle, sometimes armed only with a stick, like General Adrian Carton de Wiart who fought unarmed in four wars, explaining:

I never carried a revolver, being afraid that if I lost my temper I might use it against my own people, so my only weapon was a walking stick.

The actual fighting and killing – that was for the men. Above all else, an officer had to be brave and gallant, never flinching under fire. Garnet Wolseley, then a subaltern still in his teens, saw his first action in Burma in 1853: 'Like all young soldiers, I longed to hear the whistle of a bullet fired in earnest', he said, and when he was badly wounded in that battle: 'What a supremely delightful moment that was!' Later, in the Crimean War he lost an eye, but like many another of Victoria's heroes his physical disability did not prevent him from serving his sovereign in war.

SOUTH AFRICA
12th Lancers
Queen's
Royal Warwickshire
Suffolk
Black Watch
Oxford and Bucks L.I.
King's Royal Rifle Corps
Highland L.I.
Argyll and Sutherland
    Highlanders
Rifle Brigade

1852

PEGU:
Second Burmese War
Royal Irish
South Staffordshire
King's Own Yorkshire L.I.
Royal Munster Fusiliers
(then 2nd Bengal
Europeans Fusiliers)

facing page
Launched in 1867 the
Crocodile, like her sister
ships, was built to carry
a full battalion of infantry,
with their married families
and auxiliaries

Troopships and Transports

WHEN VICTORIA's soldiers went to war they also went to sea, usually for weeks at a time. All the numerous wars and military expeditions of the Queen's reign required her troops to endure long voyages to distant lands. Early in her reign the 2000-ton steamship *Hindostan*, one first of the great P & O vessels and the largest ship of its time, took 91 days for the voyage to Calcutta, having run out of coal on the way! Even in the 1890s ships were still taking several weeks to reach India.

But voyages Out and voyages Home were not all: troopships conveyed armies from Bombay to Suez on their way to the Crimea, from Calcutta to China for the second China War and back to Calcutta for the Indian Mutiny, from Bombay to Zula on the Red Sea coast for the Abyssinian campaign, and so on year after year. Ordinary soldiers and their officers, the generals and their staffs, sailed to and fro, fighting wars and pacifying the natives in the Queen's enormous empire.

Trooping was in the hands of the Admiralty, and the transport of troops was either undertaken by navy transport vessels or by ships bought or hired for the purpose. Such ships were not always well chosen, as Private Wickens of the 90th Foot discovered in April 1857 when he embarked on HMS *Transit* at Portsmouth bound for China.

Transit was in trouble from the start:

. . . Our first mishap took place at the mouth of the Needles. On the morning of the 7th [of April, the day after embarkation] . . . we found, a little to the surprise of all on board, that there were four feet and a half of water in the forehold. The captain therefore immediately on the discovery weighed anchor and put back into Portsmouth . . . The *Transit* was immediately taken into dock for the purpose of being botched up. Soon it was evident that she was not properly repaired and in fact was never seaworthy from the time she was launched. This done . . . we again started on our road, but ill-luck was all we were to meet with, for in passing through the Bay of Biscay, we met strong head winds. Our jibboom was carried away and the jib-sails flew into ribbons. The ship was leaking in several places and the troops never had a dry place to sleep in . . .

The 'ill-luck' of the *Transit* continued: 'she was continually leaking and the pumps were going night and day night and day.' After surviving a severe storm lasting five days the ship 'appeared a complete wreck' with her main yard snapped in two, her jib boom and jib sheets lost, and leaks in the hull and head 'so large that the men stuffed their blankets in to keep the water out.' No sooner had the main yard been spliced

The Loss of the *Birkenhead*

On 25 February 1852 the steam troopship *Birkenhead* sailed from Simonstown, the British naval base at the Cape, carrying reinforcements to Port Elizabeth for the Kaffir War in Natal. She had 648 persons on board including detachments from ten different regiments – the 2nd, 6th, 12th, 43rd, 45th, 60th, 73rd, 74th, and 91st regiments of Foot and the 12th Lancers, as well as a number of women and children. At two o'clock the following morning the ship struck a rock near the ominously named Danger Point, just over a mile from the shore, and it became immediately obvious that she was doomed. There were only three boats, and these were got clear of the sinking ship, carrying all the women and children, just before she broke in two.

Meanwhile all the troops were standing quietly in line as if on morning parade, and most of them went down with the *Birkenhead*. First-hand accounts of the disaster came from two men and an officer. Corporal John O'Neill of the 91st Argyll and Sutherlanders recalled the Captain of the ship and 'the last words he uttered':

'Lower your boats, men,' said he, 'we are all lost!' I never saw him again. Major Wright (also of the 91st) gave the order, 'All hands fall in on deck,' and we fell in, every man. He told off so many soldiers, and so many sailors to each boat, to get them out and save the women and children . . . No man was allowed to leave the ranks till the boats were pushed off. (The horses, those unsung 'heroes for Victoria', were blindfolded and driven overboard.) Major Wright threatened to shoot any man who stepped towards the boats, but no one thought of doing it . . . The ship went down twenty minutes after striking. It was a terrible time, but we stood on. We all expected to die . . . The water rose as the ship was sinking. Before we left her we were up to our necks in water on the top deck . . .

Private John Smith of the 2nd Regiment, Queen's Royals, who had been asleep below when he was woken by 'a tremendous crash', told a somewhat different story:

I stood at the gangway and assisted to hand the women and children into the boat. The men all stood back until they got safely away; but there was no 'falling in' on deck. When we went down I was in the long boat. There were about a hundred of us in it altogether, but when the ship broke in two the falling funnel caught our boat, and smashed it, throwing us all into the water . . .

Whether the troops left on board the *Birkenhead* as she went down stood in parade order or not, Major Wright undoubtedly echoed the sentiments of the Queen and all her subjects:

. . . the men's conduct was all the more to be wondered at, seeing that most of the soldiers had been but a short time in the service . . . Everyone did as he was directed; and there was not a murmur or cry among them until the vessel made her final plunge.

Of all those on board the *Birkenhead* when she struck, only 193, including all the women and children, were saved.

than on 10 July the ship hit a sunken reef in the Straits of Bangka, between the islands of Borneo and Sumatra. In ten minutes it was sinking, but the troops got away in boats and landed safely on a rock three miles from Bangka Island. They had lost all they possessed. However, they were soon rescued by naval vessels and conveyed by way of Singapore to Calcutta to join the troops fighting the mutineers.

Not all troopships were as unseaworthy as the *Transit*, but troop accommodation was inevitably cramped and unsavoury. The conditions for some 600 men below decks on a 2,000-ton paddle steamer making the voyage around the Cape to India can be imagined, but on sailing ships they could be much worse: troops were often taken as deck passengers – frozen in winter, burned in the tropics, and in rough weather crammed into already packed troop decks.

However, conditions were rather better in the troopships built by the Navy for the Indian Government, five rigged screwships named *Crocodile*, *Euphrates*, *Jumna*, *Malabar*, and *Serapis*, each able to accommodate a battalion of infantry with their families – about 1,200 bodies. Though a vast improvement on the old sailing troopships, accommodation was depressingly inferior to passenger ships of the day. The junior officers' quarters, below the water line, were described as 'unattractive', so presumably standards for the Other Ranks were even lower. However, the troops had the consolation of a free daily issue of a dram of rum, which officers had to pay for, and the quantities of bullocks, cows, sheep and fowl carried suggested that all ranks ate reasonably well. For thirty years these famous five troopships conveyed thousands of Victoria's heroes to and from India.

After the Crimean War the Royal Navy found that it had neither the men nor the ships to meet the demand for overseas movement of troops, and the Admiralty turned to the commercial shipping companies. Several famous lines competed to meet the Army's trooping requirements: P & O (Peninsular & Oriental Steam Navigation Co.), the Bibby Line, B.I. (British India Steam Navigation Co.), and Union-Castle. Bibby and B.I. were troopship lines, and with P & O they virtually monopolised regular trooping to and from India. Ships of the Union and Castle Lines (Union-Castle from 1900) were used for trooping Africa during the Zulu and Boer Wars. Such lines had the fleets needed to convey armies and large expeditionary forces when called upon. Nine B.I. and six P & O vessels transported Napier's force to Abyssinia. Twenty-five B.I. ships carried troops to Suakin during the Egyptian campaign, and thirty-seven were engaged during the Boer War. In the same conflict P & O used nine of its liners to move some 150,000 troops.

The Triumph of Steam

IN THE FIRST half of Victoria's reign three contests were being fought out among naval and merchant seamen: Sail vs Steam, Paddle vs Screw, and Wood vs Iron. In the first year of her reign it became possible to travel all (or almost all) the way to India by steamship, for in September 1837 the Peninsular Steam Navigation Company (later the P & O) proudly announced a new service:

'Steam conveyance from Lisbon and Falmouth to Vigo, Oporto, Lisbon, Cadiz, Gibraltar, Malta, Greece, the Ionian Isles, Egypt and India.'

Passengers for India left London on the 1st and 29th of the month. They sailed with the Peninsular Company's steamships ('the largest and most powerful that have yet been put afloat') to Gibraltar, then by Admiralty steam packet to Alexandria via Malta; they crossed Egypt via Cairo to Suez in two-wheeled horse-drawn vehicles (the Overland Route); and sailed from Suez to Bombay in one of the East India Company's new steamships. Until the opening of the Suez Canal in 1869 this was the route favoured by many Indian army officers, but regular troopships sailed via the Cape to India and the Far East.

Steam had come to stay, but sail put up a fight. The Admiralty feared that a successful steam warship would make the whole of the British fleet obsolete, but as the French planned to build steam warships, there was no choice but to do the same. Against steam was the high cost of building steamships compared with sailing ships. The weight and bulk of coal carried by steamships severely reduced their payload, and on long voyages they needed coaling stations. Mechanical failure could completely immobilise a ship without sails, and so for many years ocean-going steamships were rigged with sails.

The early steamships were propelled by paddles, which had the disadvantage for naval vessels of being vulnerable to gunfire and taking up space needed for guns. When screw propulsion was introduced, the Admiralty organised a contest to determine the merits of the two systems. A tug-of-war was arranged between two steam sloops of similar size and power. The *Alecto* with paddles and the *Rattler* driven by the new screw were connected stern to stern by a tow rope. Once the tug-of-war got under way, the *Rattler* towed the *Alecto* behind with her paddles turning uselessly in the water. The *Rattler* also easily won a series of races with the *Alecto*.

But the capital ships of the Royal Navy, though invariably steam-powered from the Fifties, continued to be built of wood; the ships of the line with their huge decks, masts and square-rigged sails still looked much as they had done in Nelson's day. The last wooden three-decker, HMS *Victoria*, was launched in 1859, and by the Seventies the 'wooden walls' were protected by thick iron armour-plating. Once again, the French had threatened to make the British fleet obsolete by building ironclads. Well before the end of the reign, masts, rigging, sails, and wood had disappeared completely from the British battle fleet, replaced by steel armour, huge gun turrets housing 12-inch guns, and great funnels belching smoke.

*In March 1854, 'shouting,
cheering, singing,
the nation swept into war.'*
CECIL WOODHAM-SMITH

War in the Crimea

'THE FINEST army that has ever left these shores' was *The Times* description of the expeditionary force of approximately 27,000 men that left England for Gallipoli in the spring of 1854. Twenty-five battalions of infantry, sixteen squadrons of cavalry and three battalions of Guards sailed with the force, and in support were troops and batteries of the Royal Artillery, and detachments of the Corps of Royal Sappers and Miners, soon to be renamed the Corps of Royal Engineers.

There were five divisions of infantry, each of two brigades of three regiments apiece. Only six of the infantry battalions had seen active service

in the past thirty years, and indeed very few of all its officers and men had ever heard a shot fired in anger. Waved goodbye by the Queen, the Prince Consort and their children, cheered by war-fevered crowds, they went on their way, bands playing and flags flying, confident of an early victory over the Tsar and his hordes.

With them went the Commissariat, the civilian body 'that was to take charge of their supplies and transport needs'. A department of the Treasury, it was headed by Mr James Fidler aged sixty-six, specially recalled from retirement, and it was noticeably ill-equipped for the task ahead', although *The Times* judged it fit 'to act

At the Alma the 42nd Royal Highland Regiment – the Black Watch – advances on the enemy with fixed bayonets.

48

with a vigour heretofore unknown' – a verdict it was soon forced to reverse.

Commander-in-Chief of this army was Lord Raglan, then aged sixty-six, whose experience of war had ended at the Battle of Waterloo. Only two of his divisional commanders – the Duke of Cambridge and the Earl of Lucan – were under sixty, and only two had previously held a command above battalion level. Lord Raglan and his staff were at the time and since subjected to fierce criticism on their conduct of the war. 'We have no Wellington here', remarked one officer, himself revealing the backward-looking attitude which was at the root of the tragedies in the Crimea. If Raglan lived in the shadow of Wellington, so did most of the Queen's Army, her government and her subjects.

Lord Raglan's force was joined in the Crimea by a somewhat larger French army commanded by Marshal Armand St Arnaud, and the two commanders were joint commaders-in-chief of the entire allied expeditionary force, which was transported to Turkey by a fleet of some 150 warships and transport vessels. Before it left no one had prepared any estimate of the forces required or made a reconnaissance of the proposed invasion areas. But then the Russians seem to have had no plans to oppose an Allied landing.

□ □ □

Probably very few of the soldiers and sailors bound for the Crimea could have said why they were going to fight a war there, but as the poet of the war's most memorable action was to say: 'Theirs not to reason why.'

The origins of the Crimean War grew from the suspicions of Russia long held by Western European Powers particularly by Britain. The relentless expansion of the Tsarist empire in Asia was seen as a menace to Britain's power in India. Tsar Nicolas I's ill-concealed ambition to carve up the decaying Ottoman Empire of the Turks, and so secure Constantinople and the Dardanelles as a Russian naval base, was a threat to Britain's naval supremacy in the Mediterranean and to her route to India. In addition, the autocratic tyrannies of Tsarist Russia were offensive to the more liberal-minded British.

The immediate occasion for the war arose from a dispute between Turkey, France and Russia over 'The Holy Places' in Jerusalem – a city revered by Roman Catholic and Greek Orthodox pilgrims, and then part of the Ottoman empire. Napoleon III of France, anxious to win Catholic votes and military glory, quoted an old treaty giving the French rights custody over The Holy Places, which in practice the Turks were looking after. The Turks were willing to recognise French claims, but not the Russians

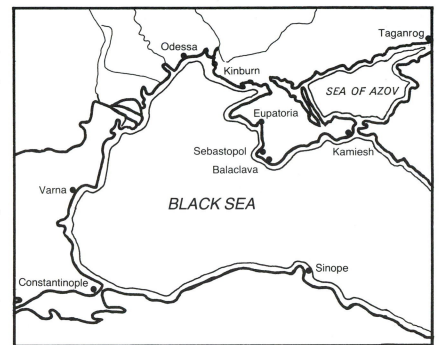

who, in their turn, claimed the right to protect the millions of Orthodox Christians in the Turkish empire. Turkey rejected their demand.

Russia thereupon occupied the Turkish-controlled provinces of the lower Danube (now part of Rumania). Britain and France supported Turkey, and the British fleet was ordered to Constantinople. On 30 November 1853 the Russian fleet attacked and destroyed a Turkish squadron off Sinope in the Black Sea. The news of 'the massacre at Sinope' stirred up war fever in London and Paris, destroying any chance of peace. British and French fleets entered the Black Sea to protect the Turkish coasts and shipping, and in March 1854 both governments declared war on Russia. They were joined later by Piedmont-Sardinia, led by the astute Count Cavour, bent on securing an Italian voice at the peace conference after the war.

'The English go and come by sea; but there is little chance of them reaching Sebastopol; they would be afraid to,' said a Russian officer '. . . let them try and fight us on land and we would soon see them off. The French we know can fight, but the English, pshaw! They are only used to fighting savages in a far-off country . . .' His scornful comments pointed to the reasons why the Allies chose to attack Russia in the Crimea and the Baltic. Russia was still the strongest military power in Europe, and Napoleon's experience did not encourage the idea of an invasion by land. But the loss of a major naval base such as Sebastopol would force her to come to terms: it would also frustrate her hopes of controlling the Dardanelles and gaining access to the year-round warm waters of the Mediterranean.

The London military outfitter Edmiston advertised a complete kit of clothing and equipment for 'officers proceeding to the seat of war' at an inclusive price of 18 guineas.

49

Lord Raglan

'Lord Raglan has arrived – a kind-looking old gent,' remarked an officer of the 8th Hussars at Varna in May 1854. The Commander-in-Chief of the British Forces in the Crimea was in fact 67 years of age at the time. Born in 1789 Lord Fitzroy Somerset (he did not become Lord Raglan until 1852) was the youngest of the Duke of Beaufort's eleven children. When he was fifteen, and still a schoolboy at Westminster, a commission was bought for him as a cornet in the 4th Light Dragoons (later the Queen's Royal Irish Hussars).

He showed remarkable promise and enthusiasm as an officer, calm and steady in moments of great danger and confusion, and always very cool under the heaviest fire. In 1810 Sir Arthur Wellesley, hero of the Peninsular War, made him his Military Secretary, but this post did not keep him far from the firing line. In 1812, for example, he scaled the hotly-defended bastion of San Vicente at Badajoz and helped to bring about its surrender.

At the age of 23 he was a Lieutenant-Colonel in the 1st Foot Guards and principal ADC to Wellington. At Waterloo in 1815, he was at Wellington's side when a ball from a sniper's musket smashed his right elbow. He walked back to a cottage used as a forward hospital, and a surgeon amputated the arm and tossed it away. 'Hey, bring my arm back,' shouted the still unruffled Colonel Lord Fitzroy Somerset, 'There's a ring my wife gave me on the finger.'

After Waterloo his military career continued to flourish, and he remained Military Secretary to Wellington until the old Duke died. Wellington always thought highly of his abilities, and in turn Lord Fitzroy revered the Duke, not without reason, as the greatest commander of the age. By the age of 39 he was promoted Major-General and appointed ADC to King George IV, and was also elected MP for Truro. He served on a number of important diplomatic and military missions, and was a Knight of the Order of the Bath, the Order of Maria Theresa of Austria, of St George of Russia, of the Tower and Sword of Portugal, amongst others. He enjoyed a happy family life, he was well-to-do, had many friends, and was popular and well-liked by the whole army.

When the old Duke died in 1852, he was succeeded as Commander-in-Chief by Lord Hardinge. This came as a disappointment to Lord Fitzroy, who was Hardinge's senior and who considered himself to be Wellington's natural heir in the post. Instead he was appointed Master-General of the Ordnance and given a peerage as Lord Raglan.

Two years later he was chosen to command the Army on its way to the Dardanelles to fight the Russians. Since Waterloo he had seen no action, and in fact he had never before had a senior command in the field. He was deeply conservative in all army matters, and rarely saw the need for the smallest change. All he knew of the art of war he had learned from Wellington – which for him and most of his fellow-officers was more than enough.

In the Crimea he caused embarrassment by frequently referring to the Russians as 'the French', and he often appeared indecisive and unclear in his orders. Although loved and respected by his troops, he failed to take advantage of this to project himself as their leader, and would even try to avoid being seen. Whether or not he can fairly be blamed for the sufferings and defeats experienced in the Crimea, it is to be remembered that the Army he led so modestly emerged victorious.

The Queen showed her trust in her Commander when she wrote after the battle of Alma; 'Lord Raglan's behaviour was worthy of the old Duke's – such coolness in the midst of the hottest fire.' Later, however, she became critical and wrote of her 'astonishment at the meagre and unsatisfactory reports from Lord Raglan which contain next to nothing.'

Undoubtedly the burdens of a commander-in-chief proved too heavy for Lord Raglan, and in June 1855, ten days after the disaster at the Redan when so many lives were needlessly lost, he died, possibly of cholera, certainly of exhaustion and depression. 'It was impossible not to love him,' said Florence Nightingale when she heard the news at Scutari. 'He was not a *very great* general, but he was a *very good man.*'

In British accounts of the war, pre-eminence is naturally given to the exploits and sufferings of the British forces, overlooking the fact that France provided over half the total troops taking part. The French appear to have been much better armed, equipped and organised than their allies, who drifted into war as ill-prepared at sea as they were on land. Towards the end of the war this imbalance of the Allied forces was even more obvious when 10,000 well-equipped Sardinian troops played a significant role in the victory at Tchernaya in 1855. The Turks, on whose behalf the war was ostensibly being waged, took part in all the battles, but after their flight at Balaclava they were rarely used again in the front line.

The Army of the East, as the British Expeditionary Force was called, and their French Allies, made first for Varna on the Bulgarian coast, intending to march to the relief of Silistria where the Turks were holding out against a 120,000-strong Russian army. The regiments fresh from Britain were beautifully turned out: column after column of bearskins and bayonets, shakos and lances, the infantry in scarlet jackets with white cross belts, riflemen in green, hussars and other light cavalry in blue and gold, and heavy dragoons in scarlet with gleaming brass helmets. Inexperienced, ill-trained and ill-equipped, apparently more fit for the parade ground than the battlefield, these were the troops that fought the Russian army to a standstill at the Alma, Balaclava and Inkerman, and despite great sufferings and losses survived a Crimean winter.

The armies enjoyed their first weeks in Bulgaria: the weather was fine, rations were good, forage was plentiful, the troops got on well with their allies, and the enemy was retreating. But then another enemy appeared: cholera, first in the French army, then in the English, and by late August RSM Loy Smith of the 11th Hussars wrote in his diary: 'The English Army from cholera alone had lost up to this time over 600 men.' Depression set in: 'Such is the state of apathy we are reduced to,' wrote a Coldstream Guards officer, 'that no one seems to care whether we go to Sebastopol or South America,' and Sergeant William McMillan of the same regiment noted in his diary:

The men are all impatient to be off, they say that if we are to take Sebastopol let us go and do it at once, not keep us here until there is not a man who is able to go. They want something to excite them, something to turn their minds from brooding over this awful disease . . .

As a foretaste of the sufferings and privations to come a huge fire at Varna destroyed thousands of pounds worth of stores, including 150 tons of biscuit and 16,000 pairs of boots. At the time hardly anyone seems to have been concerned about the inadequacies of the services for providing food, clothing, shelter, medical treatment, and transport (only twenty-one wagons for the entire army).

Having received his government's instructions to invade the Crimea and attack Sebastopol, Lord Raglan reconnoitred the coast with the French second-in-command, General Canrobert, and at once decided that the troops should land on a long sandy beach at the unfortunately-named Calamita Bay near Eupatoria, thirty-five miles north of Sebastopol. RSM Loy Smith described the sea-voyage and the landings:

About 10am [on Thursday, 7th September 1854] the whole fleet moved off, a sight never to be forgotten – the day was beautifully fine. At night, each ship showed at the masthead the number of lights that corresponded with the line it belonged, so that the sea was illuminated as far as the eye could reach. No berths or hammocks were provided (every available part of the ship being taken up for the horses) so that the men had to shift for themselves. The cholera still followed us. During that voyage we, the cavalry, lost over 20; the infantry more than twice that number; and between 300 and 400 had to be left on board sick . . .

Thursday 14th September
In the morning we all eagerly crowded the head of the vessel to witness the landing of the French and English infantry. For nearly a mile, flat-bottomed boats filled

The Duke of Cambridge

Lord Raglan's Divisions and their Commanders

The 1st Division included battalions of the Grenadier, Scots Fusilier, and Coldstream Foot Guards, together with the 42nd (Black Watch), 93rd (Argyll & Sutherland Highlanders) and the 79th (Cameron Highlanders) Regiments of Foot under General Sir Colin Campbell.

In command was Major-General **HRH The Duke of Cambridge** (1819-1904), who was a cousin of the Queen. Colonel of a Hanoverian regiment when he was nine and a major-general at twenty-six, the Royal Duke had never before seen active service. Amiable, well-intentioned, hard-working, he was deeply conservative. His role in the campaign was minimal and, much to the indignation of the Queen, 'nervous prostration' caused him to leave the Crimea before the end of the war. He lived on to become Commander-in-Chief of the Army from 1856 to 1895, dedicating a long career to opposing any kind of change in the Army.

Lt Gen Sir George de Lacy Evans

The 2nd Division included the 30th (East Lancs), 41st (The Welch Regt), 47th (Loyal North Lancs), 49th (Royal Berkshires), 55th (Border Regt), and the 59th (Sherwood Foresters) Regiments of Foot.

Lieutenant-General **Sir George de Lacy Evans**, the most battle-stained and most radical of Raglan's staff was in command. Born in Ireland in 1787, he fought in India, the Peninsula, where he was wounded, and in America, where he commanded the British force that seized the Congress House in Washington. Elected a Radical MP for Westminster, he later commanded the British Legion in Spain during the Carlist War. At the Alma he was severely wounded while leading his division. On his return to England he was formally thanked by Parliament. He died in 1870.

Lord Raglan's Divisions and their Commanders

The 3rd Division included the Royal Scots, the 28th (Gloucesters), 38th (South Staffs), 44th (Essex Regt), 50th (West Kents), and 68th (Durham Light Infantry) Regiments of Foot.

In command was Major-General **Sir Richard England**. Born in Canada in 1793, son of an Irish general, he had fought at Walcheren, in the Kaffir War and with the Scinde Field Force, when his retreat in face of the enemy was thought timid. Promoted major-general in 1851, he was nominally second-in-command to Lord Raglan, but the likelihood of his succeeding Raglan was considered to be a 'public danger'. He insisted on sharing the sufferings of his troops, and the army doctors invalided him home in 1855. He died in 1883.

□ □ □

The 4th Division included the 4th (King's Own), 20th (Lancashire Fusiliers), 21st (Royal Scots Fusiliers), 46th (Duke of Cornwall's Light Infantry) and the 63rd (Manchester) Regiments of Foot.

In command was Major-General the Hon **Sir George Cathcart** who was sixty. A cornet's commission in the Life Guards was purchased for him at the age of fifteen, and he became lieutenant-colonel of the 7th Hussars at twenty-six. He fought at Waterloo, but had not distinguished himself since. However, he was given a 'dormant commission' by the government to command the army if Lord Raglan were to be killed. He kept it in a waterproof bag in his breast-pocket and told his ADC he was relieved when it was cancelled and he could return it to Lord Raglan – with whom he was at loggerheads anyway, complaining that he was never consulted.

In the event, Sir George died before the man he was chosen to succeed. Attempting to charge uphill at Inkermann in the face of the advancing Russians, he called out 'I fear we are in a mess', and fell from his horse, shot through the heart.

□ □ □

The Light Division included the 7th (Royal Fusiliers), 19th (Green Howards), 23rd (Royal Welch Fusiliers), 33rd (Duke of Wellington's), 77th (Middlesex) and 88th (Connaught Rangers) Regiments of Foot.

In command was General **Sir George Brown** (1790-1865), the most senior of the divisional generals, a ferocious martinent whose policy was 'pipe-claying, close-shaving and tight-stocking'. 'An old imbecile bully', according to his subalterns, and yet his kindness to his men when cholera raged at Varna endeared him to them. At the Alma his

Gen Sir George Brown

horse was shot under him and he himself was severely wounded in the chest, but he refused to be invalided home. After the war he was appointed Commander-in-Chief in Ireland.

□ □ □

The Cavalry Division was composed of a Heavy Brigade and a Light Brigade. In the Heavy Brigade were the 4th and 5th Dragoon Guards, the 1st Royal Dragoons (Royals), the 2nd Dragoons (Royal Scots Greys), and the 6th Dragoons (Inniskillings). The Light Brigade included the 8th and 11th Hussars, the 4th and 13th Light Dragoons, and the 17th Lancers.

In command was Major-General **Lord Lucan**: (*see panel overleaf*).

□ □ □

The Heavy Brigade was commanded by Major-General the Hon **James Scarlett** (1799-1871). Gazetted a cornet in the 18th Hussars (later the 13th/18th Royal Hussars), by 1840 he was Colonel of the 5th Dragoon Guards (later the 5th Royal Inniskilling Dragoon Guards) and had spent five years as Tory MP for Guildford. Like most of his fellow commanders, he lacked campaign experience, but unlike them he was kindly and unassuming, and full of good sense. Also unlike them, he welcomed experienced 'Indian' officers on his staff. 'They are all fond of him and will follow him anywhere,' said one of them. And at Balaclava follow him they did when the Heavy Brigade performed 'one of the greatest feats of cavalry in the history of Europe.'

The Light Brigade was commanded by **Lord Cardigan** (*see panel overleaf*).

with armed men – our Light Division being first – were being towed by sailors rowing in other boats. We saw them leap cheerily on to the beach. Grave thoughts now passed through my mind: how many of these fine fellows will never again leave that shore!

Friday 16th September
Early next morning three days' rations and three days' forage was issued to each man; the former consisted of 3lbs of salt-pork, 3lbs biscuit, and a small quantity of tea and sugar. The pork became so rancid the second day that we could not eat it. A ration of rum . . . was likewise handed over to the quartermaster for issue on our landing but, by some mishap or mismanagement, this was lost.

By this time Sergeant McMillan was already ashore and inland:

It was dark when we halted last night [14th September] and the rain came down in torrents. We got a few dead weeds to lay on and we lay all night exposed to the pelting storm . . . We kept our belts on all the time and our firelocks piled near us. When I got up this morning I was that stiff I scarce could stand, the men got together some of the weed we had to lay on and made fires. I managed to boil about half a pint of water . . . and made some tea. Went to a small village about 2 miles off to get some water. They had plenty of corn in small stacks and put in long rows along the walls . . . There was a lot of Frenchmen there and they were taking everything they could lay their hands on, fowls of every description, calves, sheep, lambs, water . . . They even took the bell out of the church . . .

The French seem to have been generally better organised, having been first ashore and supplied with tents and other essentials, and they were permitted to 'live off the land', that is, plunder, to a degree officially forbidden to the British troops. RSM Loy Smith takes up the story:

About 9am [Tuesday 19th September], the Allied armies commenced their march towards Sebastopol. The French and Turks consisted of 37,000 men with 68 guns, the English 27,000 including 1,000 cavalry and 60 guns. The French and Turks marched next to the sea, then came the British infantry in columns of divisions, the artillery between the divisions. We the 11th, the 13th and the 'I' Troop RHA formed the advanced guard, the 13th skirmishers in front . . .

The 8th Hussars, the 17th Lancers and 'C' Troop RHA protected the flank, five miles from the sea, and the 4th Light Dragoons brought up the rear. The allied armies advanced steadily on a front of nearly five miles across beautiful undulating country and in brilliant, hot sunshine. Before long many of the troops were suffering badly from exhaustion and thirst after their meagre breakfast of dry biscuit and salt pork, and the growing line of stragglers included many dying of cholera. 'After nine or ten miles we came in sight of the enemy,' wrote Sergeant McMillan:

and at half past three the first cannon was fired by England in the defence of Turkey. There was three or four thousand of the Cossacks and Russians but we soon put them to flight and then bivouacked for the night.

20th September

Advanced again at 6.00am. Had not got far when we came in sight of the enemy. They expected us and retired as we advanced, without firing a shot . . . we could see the Russians marching in columns in the Alma Heights about 5 or 6 miles off.

The whole expedition were marching by divisions. We halted on a beautiful plain before reaching the Alma River and we loaded our rifles and deployed into line, then advanced. The Light Division extended in skirmishing order. We had not gone far before the Russians opened fire on us with the big guns. Their shots came rolling along so we opened ranks and let the shot go through.

With the 11th Hussars in the advance guard, RSM Loy Smith also saw the start of the battle:

As I stood up in my stirrups and gazed around, I thought to have the privilege of seeing such a sight as was worth a man's life to view. We were now in full view of the Russian Army that crowned the opposite heights of Alma, their lance points, swords and bayonets glistening in the sun – it was a lovely day. Between us ran the River Alma . . . From our elevated position we could see over a forest of bayonets on our right and far away over the Black Sea, which was covered with the combined fleets, all steaming and sailing in the same direction. The colours of our infantry regiments were unfurled. Glorious sight! At one glance could be seen the armies of four of the mightiest nations of Europe in battle array, and the fleets of three of them . . .

The Russian Army confronting the advancing Allies consisted of over 33,000 infantry, 5,000 cavalry and 96 guns, commanded by Prince Menschikov. The Russian infantry wore ankle-length greatcoats and were armed with old smooth-bore muskets (compared with the new Brititsh Minié rifles), and they fought stolidly in massed battalions.

Prince Menschikoff planned to halt the Allied armies at the heights above the River Alma, a natural barrier strengthened by earthworks ('redoubts') containing batteries of guns, and protected on the flanks by field artillery, squadrons of cavalry, and massed infantry. It was called Kourgane Hill, and the Prince had good reason to be confident that no troops in the world would dare storm it. So confident was he that he invited a party from Sebastopol to a picnic lunch on a nearby hill where they could watch the destruction of the invaders. However, Kourgane Hill was soon to be 'the scene of a great feat of British arms'.

'Up the hill we went,' recalled a sergeant of the Royal Fusiliers, 'step by step, but with fearful carnage. The smoke was so great that we could hardly see what we were doing, and our fellows were falling all round; it was a dirty, rugged hill . . .' As the massed Russian columns moved slowly down the hill towards the long thin line of red-jacketed British infantry advancing towards them.

Sergeant McMillan, who was in the thick of it with the 1st Division, continues the story:

We had to take these heights before we could proceed any further. So we set to work and at 1.30pm the first gun was fired by our Artillery which was taken up by the French on our right. There began the bloody fight, our Artillery advancing as opportunity afforded. The Light Division advanced and cleared the enemy out

The Allied fleet of transports and warships at Varna, where cholera killed about 800 men as they waited to embark

Lord Lucan

George Charles Bingham, later 3rd Earl of Lucan, was born in 1800. When he was sixteen a commission was purchased for him in the 6th Foot Regiment. The Bingham family wealth was founded in the reign of Elizabeth I by three soldiers of fortune who amassed vast estates in Ireland, and Lord Lucan drew a huge income from his Irish rents.

By means of exchanges and high payments for promotion, he became Lieutenant-Colonel of the renowned 17th Lancers when he was only twenty-six. Filled with military ambition, he had great courage but little common-sense, and above all, like his brother-in-law Lord Cardigan, he was a martinet, a stern, harsh and ruthless commanding officer who was determined to enforce Army regulations and procedures to the letter. He spent vast sums on uniforms and horses for his Lancers, and made their turn-out so smart that they became known as 'Bingham's Dandies', but the price he demanded was fault-less performance.

The officers and men of the 17th Lancers were subjected to endless parades, inspections and drills, after which came severe reprimands for the officers, merciless floggings for the men. Not surprisingly, the regiment hated him, but as one officer remarked – 'He's brave, damn him!' In 1828 he had fought for the Russians in their war with Turkey, and had proved he could endure the dangers and hardships of campaigning.

Lord Lucan and his brother-in-law Lord Cardigan detested each other and quarrelled openly on every possible occasion. So when in 1854, Lord Lucan was appointed to command the cavalry division in the Expeditionary Army for the forthcoming war with Russia, with Lord Cardigan subordinate to him as commander of the Light Division, the stage was set for the tragedy that happened at Balaclava.

After the charge Lord Raglan was, not surprisingly, bitterly angry. His first words to Lord Lucan were: 'You have lost the Light Brigade!' Lord Lucan furiously retorted that all he had done was carry out orders. 'You were a Lieutenant-General' he was told, 'and you should therefore have exercised your discretion, and, not approving of the charge, should not have caused it to be made.'

Lord Lucan had misinterpreted the order, according to Lord Raglan and had taken no steps to find out the dispositions of the Russian army, had not asked for the assistance of the French cavalry (which the order told him were on his left), and had not called up his Heavy Brigade or the Horse Artillery.

Determined not to accept any blame, Lord Lucan wrote to the Secretary for War, and was dismayed to find himself recalled from his command. Back in England, he demanded a court-martial, which was refused, and the row dragged on, with speeches in Parliament, court cases, pamphlets and counter-pamphlets and letters to *The Times*.

Unlike Lord Cardigan, who was welcomed as a hero, Lord Lucan was unpopular with the public and was mocked as 'Lord Look-on'. However, like many another affronted hero for Victoria, he was consoled by military honours: he was in turn appointed a full General, Gold Stick in Waiting, Colonel of the 1st Life Guards, Knight Grand Cross of the Order of the Bath, and finally Field-Marshal in 1887. He died in 1888 – 'a marvellous survival,' said *The Times* correspondent, William Howard Russell.

of the foot of the hill . . . Our artillery was too much for them, they soon silenced the enemy's batteries. We then advanced and supported the 2nd Division in going through a vineyard [where many of the troops picked bunches of grapes which they held clenched in their teeth as they advanced]. In crossing the vine-yards the bullets fell like hell and ever so many of our men were wounded. We got to the foot of the hill where we got out of the fire for a few minutes and got formed . . . and we advanced halfway up the heights. The hill right up to the top was covered with the enemy who showered their cannon balls down towards us but they fell short. We then advanced some distance without firing. When we were within good range we commenced firing. About this time there was an order given by some of the commanders to retire . . . And the enemy seeing us retire came out of the rifle pits after us thinking they had beat us, and I do believe without any word of command the whole line faced about again and advanced, and about this time there was a tremendous shout commenced on the right by the French and it was taken up by each division all along the line, it was just like a clap of thunder. This frightened the Russians and they retired and we advanced after them and shot them down by hundreds with the Minié rifle. They retreated up the valley in such confusion as no person ever saw.

RSM Loy Smith wrote of the end of the battle:

At this time, the crest of the heights of the Alma were crowned with the bright scarlet uniforms of the British infantry . . . Lord Raglan with his staff now rode in front of us, then went up a cheer as I doubt the like was ever heard on earth before.

After burying the dead and removing the wounded and sick, the Allied armies prepared to move on towards Sebastopol. Allied casualties, mostly British, had been heavy, over 2,000 of them from the Light, 1st and 2nd Divisions. Other infantry divisions and the Cavalry, to their fury, had scarcely been engaged. The Russian losses were much heavier, probably some 6,000 men. An opportunity to assault Sebastopol at once may have been missed, but at the time the French and British commanders felt their armies were too exhausted to do more.

This delay allowed time for the Russians' chief engineer, the famous Colonel Franz Todleben, to strengthen the defences of Sebastopol. Already, a line of ships had been sunk across the harbour mouth, making it impossible for Allied warships to get in or for the Russian Black Sea Fleet to get out, which brought tears of frustrated rage to Admiral Korniloff's eyes. Now Todleben established a four-mile long chain of bastions and gun emplacements encircling the port. Every night he rode along his line of emplacements, siting guns, extending fields of fire, and linking batteries so that they supported one another. The Allied bombardment of Sebastopol killed many of its defenders but did little real damage to its defences, whereas the

Russian counter-fire caused heavy losses among the besiegers.

After his defeat on the Alma Prince Menschikov retreated into the city of Sebastopol, but when the Allied armies made a flank march around the fortress to establish siege bases at the ports of Balaclava and Kamiesch to the south, he moved his forces out again to threaten their flank and rear. In fact, the two armies marched closed by one another, each unaware of the other's presence. On Tuesday 26th September Allied forces reached the North Balaclava Valley: RSM Loy Smith later observed in his diary:

. . . How little did many a fine fellow of our brigade think that, that day, the following month, he would be lying dead, unburied on that very ground . . .

Wednesday 27th September 1854

As we approached Sebastopol, we passed several farmhouses, vineyards and orchards. At last we came in full view of the town. What a glorious sight to look down on the beautiful town and harbour, and the Russian fleet riding at anchor. As we sat gazing at them with admiration, a cannon ball came whizzing along towards us, as much as to say 'Halt'.

The battle of Balaclava began on 25 October when a Russian force of some 25,000 men was seen advancing on the Allied positions in the

Lord Cardigan

James Brudenell, seventh Earl of Cardigan (1792-1868), Commander of the Light Brigade at the battle of Balaclava, was perhaps the most colourful and controversial of all Victoria's heroes in the Crimean War. Fearless, arrogant, disdainful of all criticism, a regimental disciplinarian of quite exceptional severity, he was the commander his brother officers loved to hate. And yet, in spite of the merciless floggings he ordered so freely, his men seemed to have admired him as 'the ideal cavalry leader.' After the disastrous Charge, some of them told him: 'We are ready to do it again, my Lord.'

Fifty-seven years old when he rode 'into the valley of death' at Balaclava, Cardigan had pursued a personal and military career filled with extraordinary incidents and scandals. He had twice been an MP; had eloped with another man's wife, with whom he later had a disastrous marriage; had been sued for adultery by an angry fellow peer; had purchased the command of the 15th Hussars (later the 15th/19th King's Royal Hussars) reputedly for £40,000 and, after a series of trivial-sounding but notorious and demoralising disputes with his officers, he had been removed from his command by Court-Martial and reprimanded for spying on officers of whom he disapproved – a practice, declared the court, 'revolting to every proper and honourable feeling of a gentleman'.

Next he purchased the command of the 11th Hussars (later the Royal Hussars), but his re-instatement in the Army had to be approved by Parliament. Once again he was in constant dispute with his officers, and he even fought a duel with one of them. Tried by his peers for attempted murder, he was acquitted by them – to the intense indignation of *The Times*, and indeed of the public at large. Completely unperturbed by public disapproval and even by a severe reprimand from the Duke of Wellington, Lord Cardigan set about turning the 11th Hussars into

the smartest regiment in the entire British Army using penalties and punishments which were harsh even by the Draconian standards of the day. Always he demanded more glitter, more polish, pipeclay, smarter drill, greater perfection in turnout. In the year before the Crimean War he loved to be seen around Town and to be saluted smartly by his 'cherry-pickers', the nickname given to the 11th Hussars from the colour and tightness of their pants.

Lord Cardigan had never seen active service and like almost all British cavalry officers, other than those who had fought in India and were therefore discounted, he knew little of the business of war. Nevertheless, when war with Russia loomed, he was given command of the Light Brigade with the rank of major-general. Unfortunately, his brother-in-law, Lord Lucan, whom he hated, was put in command of the Cavalry Division which made him Lord Cardigan's superior officer. The two of them quarrelled so violently that Lord Raglan arranged for them to operate separately like 'two spoilt children', said one of their fellow officers.

Lord Cardigan was given special permission to dine and sleep aboard his yacht *Dryad* every night. A superb horseman and utterly unmoved by the heaviest cannon and musket fire, he led his brigade wherever ordered, with the greatest dash and élan. If not ordered nothing would move him. 'Theirs not to reason why' expressed perfectly his own idea of a cavalryman's duty. After the loss of the Light Brigade he was, and always remained, sure that he had done his duty. 'My Lord,' he said to Lord Raglan, 'I hope you will not blame me, for I received the order to attack from my superior officer in front of the troops.'

On his return to England, Lord Cardigan was greeted as a hero. Wherever he went, crowds cheered, women wept, bands played 'See the conquering hero', mayors made speeches, cities gave banquets in his honour, and the Queen invited him to stay at Windsor. The woollen jacket he had worn at Balaclava was copied, given the name Cardigan and sold by the thousand. He was appointed Inspector-General of Cavalry (in which role every officer dreaded his coming, for the smallest fault never escaped his eye), and he realized his dearest ambition when he was made Colonel of the 11th Hussars. Appropriately, he ended his life in the saddle: he fell from his horse after suffering a stroke, and died from his injuries.

heights above the port. The Turkish garrisons of four of the six redoubts along the Causeway Heights (see plan) resisted stubbornly but were quickly overwhelmed by superior numbers, and soon a strong Russian cavalry force with artillery support was advancing steadily towards Balaclava. All that stood between them and the British base was Sir Colin Campbell and his 550 Argyll and Sutherland Highlanders, the 'thin red line' whose deadly volleys caused the Russians to waver, steady their ranks, waver again, then wheel and withdraw.

Lord Raglan then ordered the Heavy Brigade to go to the support of the Turks and the Highlanders – two squadrons each of the 4th and 5th Dragoon Guards and the Scots Greys and Inniskillings, fewer than 600 troopers, led by General Scarlett. Their route took them straight across the front of the massed Russian cavalry, some 3,000-4,000 strong, only a few hundred yards away. The Heavies wheeled to face the enemy, dressed their ranks with parade-ground precision, and waited for the trumpeters to sound the charge. One of General Scarlett's officers appeared wearing a forage cap instead of the regulation cocked-hat. The general sent him back to change it. 'My staff shall be properly dressed', he said. When all was in order, he drew his sword and called to his trumpeter: 'Sound the charge!'

Scarlett immediately galloped off with his staff. Halfway down the hill the Russian cavalry had halted and sat motionless in their saddles, a dense grey mass in their long, thick greatcoats, while two flanking wings moved out to crush the British line. To the watchers with Lord Raglan

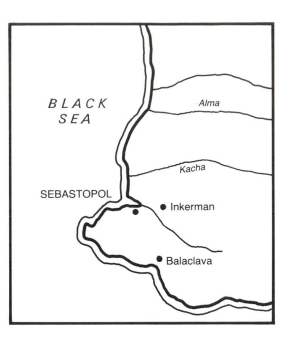

and his Staff on the cliffs above the valley, the vastly out-numbered British squadrons appeared as specks of scarlet against the sea of British grey. Fifty yards ahead of his front line, Scarlett galloped straight into the Russians and disappeared, quickly followed by squadrons of Scots Greys and Inniskillings who charged headlong into the Russian mass and seemed to be swallowed up.

'How can such a handful resist, much less make a headway through such a legion?' remarked one observer. 'Their huge flanks lap round that handful, and almost hide them from our view. They are surrounded and must be

'The Thin Red Line'; Robert Gibbs' famous painting of the 93rd Sutherland Highlanders facing Russian cavalry at the battle of Balaclava in 1854.

annihilated!' But Scarlett and his men were alive and could be seen fighting like madmen, hacking and chopping furiously with their swords, whose points were turned by the thick Russian great-coats. After a few minutes the Russian ranks began to waver, and when the other Heavy Brigade squadrons crashed into the mass, they backed away, broke and fled.

Sergeant McMillan noted in his diary that day:

We were just on the brow of the hill where the cavalry charge was and we saw it all. Our Cavalry were on their [the Russians] right and they charged them in fine style and indeed they did cut them up. They sent horses and men flying all ways, such running and shouting there was after the charge to catch the Russian horses whose riders were killed or wounded as never was, after the Scots Greys had charged.

A simple message from Lord Raglan was handed to General Scarlett: 'Well done, Scarlett.' But Lord Cardigan of the Light Brigade, who had not attempted to move to the support of the Heavies because, he said, he had been 'ordered into a position by . . . my superior officer [Lord Lucan], with orders on no account to leave it . . .', declared 'Those damned Heavies have the laugh of us this day.' RSM Loy Smith recalled what happened:

Our Heavy Cavalry now advanced and charged into them; we then expected to be ordered to sweep down on their right flank. Had we done so at the proper moment, I feel that few of them would have escaped . . . But, much to our chagrin, we were held as spectators of this unequal combat for more than ten minutes . . . being only a few hundred yards off. But, to our joy and relief, we saw this mass of Russian cavalry retreat over the Causeway Heights the same way they came. Had we received the order, in all probability the charge down the North Valley would not have taken place.

In this way the Russian advance on Balaclava was blocked, although they still held part of the Causeway Heights. Accordingly, Lord Raglan ordered the Cavalry to 'advance and take advantage of any opportunity to recover the heights'. But for reasons which are by no means clear Lord Lucan failed to respond.

When the Commander-in-Chief saw the Russians trying to move the captured British guns he followed up his earlier order by sending one of his aides, Captain Nolan, with a hastily scribbled note urging Lucan 'to advance rapidly to the front, follow the enemy and try to prevent the enemy carrying away the guns. Troop horse artillery may accompany. French cavalry is on your left. Immediate.'

What followed – the reason why – is a matter for conjecture even today, so persistent is the cloud of uncertainty and confusion that hangs over this most celebrated of all military follies.

Sir Colin Campbell

'This distinguished, gallant and loyal general', as Queen Victoria described Sir Colin Campbell, was 61 years of age when he took command of the Highland Brigade in the Crimea. Oddly, his real name was Colin McIver, the eldest son of a Glasgow carpenter and his wife Agnes Campbell, a family that had 'come down in the world.' When he was presented to the Duke of York, the Commander-in-Chief of the Army, by his uncle Colonel John Campbell, he was given a commission. 'What! Another of the clan!' exclaimed the Duke, entering his name as 'Colin Campbell' – and that name he thereupon adopted as respectable enough for a Scottish officer.

In his later career he fought under Wellington and Sir John Moore in the Peninsular War, and was wounded four times. He served and fought all over the world, including Spain, America, China, and India, and spent thirty years in garrison duties in such places as Gibraltar, Barbados and Demerara. In the year Queen Victoria came to the throne he took over command of the 98th Foot (later the North Staffordshires). In the 2nd Sikh War he commanded an infantry division as a local brigadier-general, and served with such distinction that he was appointed a Knight Commander of the Order of the Bath. By then he felt he was growing old and fit only for retirement, but instead he spent three years in the North-West Frontier leading operations against the unruly tribesmen. Then he quarrelled with his superiors and retired on half-pay.

But when the Crimean war broke out, Sir Colin returned to the army and was promoted major-general in command of the Highland Brigade, which consisted of the 42nd (The Black Watch), 93rd (later the Argyll and Sutherland Highlanders) and 79th (later the Queen's Own Highlanders (Seaforth and Camerons) Regiments of Foot. He was the most respected of all the brigade commanders in the Crimea, and with him at their head his Highlanders would rather die than retreat.

At the Alma he gave them orders to advance in a steady unbroken line on the massed Russian columns, firing as they advanced. Their enemies were unnerved at the sight of the tall figures in 'skirts' and strange plumed headgear, marching quietly towards them through the smoke, the silence broken only by the crack and whine of their rifle bullets. The Russian columns broke and fled. The triumphant cheers of the Highlanders, permitted at last to break their silence, could be heard miles away.

At the battle of Balaclava Sir Colin's Highlanders stopped a determined charge by 400 Russian cavalry, and saved the day. As the Russians advanced on the 93rd, Sir Colin ordered the regiment to reform on the forward crest of a hill, saying, 'There is no retreat from here, men! You must die where you stand!'

The men of the 93rd showed themselves eager to rush forward, 'Ninety-third!' shouted Sir Colin, 'Ninety-third! damn all that eagerness!' And the mere sound of his voice steadied the line. When the Russians came within range of the Minie rifles, the Highlanders fired volley after volley, and soon the squadrons started to retreat. The battle was won.

It was from their unflinching steadiness in the Crimea that the 93rd – the only infantry regiment awarded the battle honour 'Balaclava' – came to be known as 'The Thin Red Line'.

During the Indian Mutiny Sir Colin Campbell led the relieving force that retook Cawnpore and Lucknow. Although his extreme caution and his lack of dash earned him the nickname 'Sir Crawling Camel' in India, in the eyes of his men, the general public and the Queen, he was a very great hero. When he died in 1863, the man who was once Colin McIver had become Field-Marshal Lord Clyde.

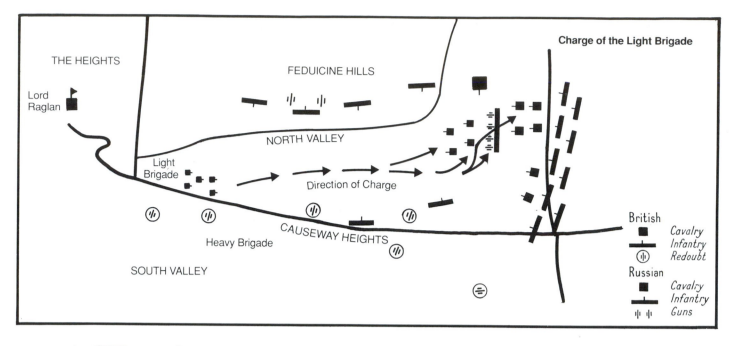

THE HEIGHTS

Lord Raglan

FEDUICINE HILLS

NORTH VALLEY

Light Brigade

Direction of Charge

Heavy Brigade

CAUSEWAY HEIGHTS

SOUTH VALLEY

British
Cavalry
Infantry
Redoubt

Russian
Cavalry
Infantry
Guns

One explanation, more plausible than many others, is that from his position down in the valley Lord Lucan simply could not see the captured guns beyond the ridge of the Causeway Heights. From his standpoint the only enemy guns in view were those at the far end of the North Valley, where the Russian cavalry had regrouped after their defeat.

In a slow, deliberate manner that was the despair of his staff, Lucan read the message and then, according to his own, later account, urged the 'uselessness of such an attack and the dangers attending it.' By this time the impetuous Nolan had lost all patience and, with great insolence, declared that 'Lord Raglan's orders are that the cavalry are to attack immediately.'

'Attack, sir?' Lucan demanded angrily. 'Attack what? What guns, sir?'

'There, my lord, is your enemy', replied Captain Nolan, with a dramatic wave of the arm in the direction of the valley. 'There are your guns.'

Without further comment or question Lucan passed the order to Lord Cardigan, who received it with icy courtesy. Not even the heat of imminent battle could thaw the hostility that existed between the two men: had they been on more cordial terms it is just possible that by discussing the situation and examining its implications the impending disaster might still have been averted.

It is true that strict military etiquette, then as now, required that orders were not to be questioned. Cardigan understood this more than most, but even he – lowering his sword in salute to a superior officer – allowed himself to observe that 'the Russians have a battery in the valley on our front, and batteries and riflemen on both sides.'

'I know it,' replied Lucan, 'But Lord Raglan will have it. We have no choice but to obey.' Lord Cardigan saluted once more, received a further brief instruction from his brother-in-law, and then swung round in the saddle. 'Well,' he said aloud to himself, 'here goes the last of the Brudenells', and galloped away to rejoin his Light Brigade, drawing up about two horse lengths in front of his staff officers and five lengths ahead of his front line. RSM Loy Smith recalled the moment:

We took up a position facing directly down the North Valley. We could distinctly see the Russian position. The 11th was on the left of the first line, the 13th Light Dragoons on the right and the 17th Lancers in the centre; the 4th Light Dragoons and the 8th Hussars formed the second line. We had not been in this position long when Lord Cardigan received the order from Lord Lucan to attack the batery of guns which was placed across the valley immediately in our front about a mile off. There was likewise a battery on the Fedioukine Hills on our left and the enemy had possession of the Redoubts Nos 2 and 3 on our right. This Army in position numbered about 24,000 and we (the Light Brigade) not quite 700.

He noted that although twelve Horse Artillery guns were close at hand, they were not used before the charge, adding mildly: 'this was a most unfortunate omission for us . . . for it was the enemy's guns and infantry posted there [on the Causeway Heights] that caused us the greatest losses – both going down the valley and returning.'

'I remember as if it were but yesterday', wrote Private Wightman of the 17th Lancers years later:

Cardigan's figure and attitude, as he faced the brigade and in his strong hoarse voice gave the mementous

Captain Nolan – did he try to avert the disaster?

1854

ALMA: Crimean War
4th Hussars
11th Hussars
13th Hussars
17th Lancers
Grenadier Guards

command, 'The brigade will advance! First squadron of the 17th Lancers direct!' Calm as on parade – calmer indeed by far than his wont on parade – stately, square and erect . . . He was in the full uniform [cherry colour and royal blue] of his old corps, the 11th Hussars, and he wore the pelisse [fur-trimmed jacket], not slung, but put on like a patrol jacket, its front one blaze of gold lace. His drawn sword was in his hand at the slope, and never saw I a man fitter to wield the weapon . . . turning his head towards his trumpeter, Britten of the Lancers, he quietly said 'Sound the Advance!' and wheeled his horse, facing the dark mass at the farther end of the valley . . . The trumpeter sounded the 'Walk'; after a few horse-lengths came the 'Trot'. I did not hear the 'Gallop' but it was sounded . . . Britten was a dead man in a few strides after he had sounded the 'Gallop'.

It was at this point that there occurred one of the most extraordinary incidents during that most extraordinary day. Captain Nolan, who taken a place in the front line, suddenly broke ranks and raced at full speed ahead of the formation. He then cut diagonally in front of Lord Cardigan and across the line of advance, turning in his saddle as if to give an order or to address the Brigade. Had it suddenly dawned on him that the advance was heading in the wrong direction, and that his impetuous wave of the arm had been misinterpreted?

The answer to that question will never be known for as Nolan turned to speak he was struck by a Russian shell. No words came from his open mouth, only an appalling shriek. His terrified horse turned and bolted back through the ranks of advancing cavalrymen, with its rider's body still upright in the saddle.

Lord Cardigan seethed with fury. Never in his long experience as a commander had there been so gross a breach of discipline by a junior officer, or so flagrant a display of military bad manners. What was the impudent young puppy trying to do? Take command of the Brigade, and lead the charge himself? These and similar thoughts, as he later admitted, filled his mind as he carried on riding towards the Russian guns.

Other matters were uppermost in the minds of the men who followed him, as RSM Loy Smith describes:

As we moved off, the Russians opened fire from all their batteries. The round shot passed us and the shells burst over and amongst us, causing great havoc. The first man of my troop that was struck was Private Young, a cannon ball taking off his right arm. I, being close on his right rear, fancied I felt the wind from it as it passed me. I afterwards found I was bespattered with his flesh.

We now came under a terrific fire, for the infantry in and about the Redoubts kept up a continual fusi-lage [meaning 'fusillade'?] as we came opposite them, but the men hung well together, keeping their line and closing in as their comrades fell back wounded or killed. Many riderless horses were now galloping with

Coldstream Guards
Scots Guards
Royal Scots
King's Own
Royal Fusiliers
Green Howards
Lancashire
Royal Scots Fusiliers
Royal Welch Fusiliers
Gloucestershire
East Lancashire
Duke of Wellington's
Border
South Staffordshire
Welch
Black Watch
Essex
Sherwood Foresters
Loyal North Lancashire
Royal Berkshire
Royal West Kent
Middlesex
Manchester
Durham L.I.
Cameron Highlanders
Connaught Rangers
Argyll and Sutherland
  Highlanders
Rifle Brigade

Despite its inconclusive outcome, Balaclava remains a glorious episode in British military history

us, forcing their way into the ranks and keeping their places as well as though their masters had been on their backs.

Meanwhile, Private Wightman was riding almost directly behind Lord Cardigan:

Later, when we were in the midst of our torture and, mad to be out of it . . . were forcing the pace, I heard again, high above the turmoil and din, Cardigan's sonorous command, 'Steady, steady, the 17th Lancers!' and saw him check with outstretched sword Captain White, my squadron leader, as he shot forward . . .' As they got near the guns and broke into the charge, Wightman 'got a musket-bullet through my right knee and another in the shin, and my horse had three bullet wounds in the neck . . . It was about this time that Sergeant Talbot had his head clean carried off by a round shot, yet for about thirty yards further the headless body kept the saddle, the lance at the charge firmly gripped under the right arm.' As cool as his commander, Wightman was unshaken and rode on: 'so I pressed my spurs well home and faced it out with my comrades' [later regretting that his narrative seemed 'barren of incidents'!] until they were 'close on those cursed guns'. Cardigan was still straight in front of me, steady as a church, but now his sword was in the air; he turned in his saddle for an instant, and shouted his final command, 'Steady! steady! Close in!' Immediately afterwards there crashed into us a regular volley from the Russian cannon. I saw . . . Cardigan disappear into the smoke. A moment more and I was within it myself . . . the smoke was so thick I could not see my arm's length around me . . . I was through and beyond the Russian battery before I knew for certain that I reached it.

I then found that none of my comrades were close to me. There was no longer any semblance of a line . . . Lord Cardigan was nowhere to be seen, nor did I ever again set eyes on the chief who had led us down the valley so grandly.

Like the rest of the Brigade, including Cardigan, Wightman was now on his own to find his way back. Soon he was joined by two other survivors: '. . . we were all three wearied and weakened by loss of blood; our horses wounded in many places; there were enemies all about us, and we thought it was about time to be getting back . . .' From his reading in the regimental library he recalled the saying 'We have done enough for honour'; that was our humble opinion too, and we turned our horses' heads.'

Only 195 of nearly 700 light cavalry returned, and 500 horses were killed. The 17th Lancers were reduced to 37 troopers, and two officers and eight men were the only survivors of the 13th Light Dragoons. Small wonder that the French General Bosquet, who was watching, was moved to utter the famous comment: *C'est magnifique, mais ce n'est pas la guerre.* Indeed, without the intervention of the French Chasseurs d'Afrique, who charged the Russian artillery and infantry on the Feioukine Hills, the disaster could have been even worse. However, the Allies

held Balaclava, and from then on the Russians retained a healthy respect for British cavalry regiments.

Ten days later came the Battle of Inkerman. Once again, the diary of Sergeant McMillan provides a vivid, eye-witness account of events:

Sunday 5th November
This has been a Sunday as man never saw before. As soon as daylight broke our outlying piquets on the right of our position [on Inkerman Ridge] found the enemy close upon them in massive columns. They had crept up in the night which was very foggy. Well our piquet was forced to retire and the enemy advanced. The alarm was soon given and we were under arms in no time, so was the Second Division. We advanced to meet the Russians . . .

What happened at Inkerman was a determined Russian attempt to break out of Sebastopol and overwhelm the Allies by sheer weight of numbers. Prince Menschikov's forces were by this time half as great again as the combined Allied armies. The main attack that cold foggy morning fell on the British infantry positions, some 8,000 against 40,000 Russians (though accounts, as always, vary) supported by heavy artillery fire. Taken by surprise in the gloom, the British had little time to organise their defence. As one officer replied when asked where the enemy were: 'They are all around us, but the thickest there,' pointing to the right of the British position.

Sergeant McMillan's account of his own experience illustrates the desperate and confused nature of the fighting that morning and shows why Inkerman came to be called 'the soldiers' battle':

There was not above half of the Guards there as the others were coming on and off duty. I don't think in all there was a thousand of us. We tackled the Russians who were in columns and columns advancing up the hills amongst the brushwood, and such a fight commenced as was never known before. We were firing about four and a half hours, sometimes gaining and sometimes losing ground but we stuck to them, our men fell so fast, so did the Russians. There was a re-doubt on the hill and we were hard pushed, so our men soon filled it, the Russians came up close to the re-doubt . . . we kept firing away as fast as we could, kneeling on the ground to keep out of the line of fire, some of our men had spent all their ammunition. We fought hard, though so did the Russians and nearly overpowered us. But just at that moment another regiment of ours came, so we advanced out of the re-doubt and charged them with our bayonets . . . we drove them back and followed them down the hill some distance. Never shall I forget the sight I saw. Hundreds of them lay killed . . . We thought we had done them all away. But there was a valley to our left and fresh columns of them poured up there and completely surrounded us.

. . . There was only about 30 of us. Well, we faced about and drove them down the valley. I gave myself up for lost, I thought I should be either shot down or taken prisoner and cruelly murdered . . . when we got a short distance further we met about 100 of the enemy again right in front of us. Our ammunition was all expended . . . so we came down to the charge and charged this lot in front, it was our only chance . . . but before we got up to them, a French column advanced and drove them back, so we effected our escape. I cannot express the joy I felt, many a man burst into tears as soon as the danger was over. What few of us that was left we formed up behind the French. The Duke of Cambridge [his Divisional Commander] came up and said 'Where is my men, where are all my men.' When told that we were all that was left he seemed sadly hurt, he then said, 'Come, my lads, come my lads, let's retire and get some ammunition.' We did so, had half an hour's rest and then advanced again . . .

The French drove them all back, so we retired about 5.00pm, called the Roll and the Duke of Cambridge was there, there was very few of us left . . . about this time the enemy had ceased firing.

At Inkerman the Russians lost some 12,000 men and failed to relieve Sebastopol. The Allies lost about 2,300, mostly British.

The objective of the Allied Expeditionary Force was to cripple Russian sea power in the Black Sea by capturing and destroying the naval base at Sebastapol. To drive the Russians out of this powerfully defended fortress city took them almost exactly a year from the landing at Calamita Bay in September 1854.

After the Allied victory at the Alma Lord Raglan wanted to attack Sebastopol without delay. His French joint C-in-C, General Canrobert (Marshal St Arnaud being on the point of dying from cholera) wanted to wait for the siege trains to be landed. Lord Raglan's adviser from the Royal Engineers, 72-year-old General John Burgoyne, agreed with the French: an assault without a siege train was an 'unjustifiable risk'. Having surveyed the fortress, he had concluded that bombardment of the Malakov tower was the key to the capture of Sebastopol. A year later events proved him right.

'Land the siege trains!' exclaimed General Cathcart of the 4th Division, confident that the Allies could easily march straight into Sebastopol. 'But my dear Lord Raglan, what the devil is there to knock down?' At the time he had a good point, for Colonel Todleben had not yet begun to strengthen the port's defences.

Bombardment of Sebastopol began on 17 October, and continued without decisive effect through that terrible Crimean winter. Through what Sergeant McMillan called 'dreadful firing every night' and day, the British troops experienced great hardships. Rather than continue his 'daily description of this winter' in his diary he summarised it all on slip of paper:

. . . the men were continually going to hospital through wet and cold which was followed by diarrhoea, dysentery and death. There was scarce a man in

camp that was actually fit for duty, our clothes were in rags, our boots nearly off our feet, there were all sorts of contrivances to keep out the cold, and a bit of old cloth or blanket was most acceptable when it could be got, to wrap round our legs and tied up with pieces of twine to keep the wet and snow off. The trenches were in a most miserable condition by so many men being continually in them. They were up to their knees nearly in mud and slush, the cold north winds came whistling over the bleak heights piercing through the thin rags that covered us . . . The fuel became very scarce now, indeed we had to forage for it the whole time in the Crimea . . . I have gone days without, as well as my comrades, one single thing warm or cooked inside of my lips. Raw pork, biscuit and a drink of cold water has been all we have had. We still get green coffee served out to us, but as we could not roast it, it was of very little use.

In 1855 the Allies were strengthened by the arrival of 10,000 well-trained Sardinian troops, and the much better organised French army was increased to 78,000 men with a new, vigorous and ruthless commander, General Pélissier. Bombardment of Sebastopol at Easter destroyed most of its defences, and the Allies' capture of Kerch cut Russian communications with the mainland.

Allied assaults on the strongpoints at the Malakoff and the Redan resulted in huge casualties on both sides. The British attack on the Redan, without prior bombardment, was caught in crossfire from 100 guns, and many lives were needlessly lost. Lord Raglan, already a sick man, blamed himself and ten days later he died from exhaustion and depression. He was succeeded by General Sir James Simpson, who was 'appalled by the responsibility' thrust upon him.

Sebastopol was taken on 8 September 1855 as a result of a well-planned bombardment and assault led by the French General Bosquet. The Allies occupied the city, having lost a total of some 250,000 men in the war to capture it.

The Russian attempt at Inkerman to break the siege of Sebastopol was a costly failure, but nearly a year was to pass before the port finally fell to the Allies

West Yorkshire
Royal Leicestershire
Royal Irish
Green Howards
Lancashire Fusiliers
Royal Scots Fusiliers
Royal Welch Fusiliers
Cameronians
Gloucestershire
East Lancashire
East Surrey
Duke of Cornwall's L.I.
Duke of Wellington's
Border
South Staffordshire
Dorset
South Lancashire
Welch
Black Watch
Essex
Sherwood Foresters
Loyal North Lancashire
Northamptonshire
Royal Berkshire
Royal West Kent
Middlesex
Wiltshire
Manchester
Durham L.I.
Highland L.I.
Seaforth Highlanders
Cameron Highlanders
Royal Irish Fusiliers
Connaught Rangers
Argyll and Sutherland
  Highlanders
Rifle Brigade

'Why have women passion, intellect, moral activity – these three – and a place in society where no one of these three can be exercised?'

FLORENCE NIGHTINGALE

Calamity in the Crimea

When cholera broke out among British troops at Varna, not long after their arrival, the victims were sent in ever-increasing numbers to the Turkish Barrack Hospital at Scutari. Because it was classified as a 'General Hospital' the authorities assumed that it would be adequate. In fact, it was a vast, dilapidated, filthy set of barracks. Beneath its four miles of corridors and rooms were great overflowing sewers which fouled the air of the whole building. It was damp and bare of any furniture – no beds, chairs, tables, buckets, or hospital equipment – and there was only one kitchen. No staff was available to clean the place, and there were not enough doctors, drugs, bedding, and sanitary equipment to cope with the hundred of cholera cases and battle casualties arriving daily. The men were laid in rows on the dirty floors, often left unattended for days, without even a drink of water.

'Such scenes of horror were nothing new,' as Cecil Woodham Smith points out, 'similar miseries had been endured by the British Army many times before.' What was new in 1854 was the presence of the world's first war correspondent – William Howard Russell of *The Times* whose despatches 'burst on the nation like a thunderclap'. Russell's revelations, not least his comparison with the French, started a national uproar, and accusing fingers were pointed at Sidney Herbert, the Secretary at War. As the minister charged with the financial administration of the army, he was naturally blamed for the 'criminally inadequate arrangements,' and yet no man was in fact more concerned for the welfare of the troops.

However, he was in the hands of the military authorities, who assured him that Russell's reports were grossly exaggerated. Unconvinced, Herbert turned for help to an old friend, Florence Nightingale, the Superintendent of the Institution for Sick Gentlewomen, knowing her to be not merely a highly dedicated and experienced nurse, but an organising genius. He wrote asking for her help on the day she wrote to him offering her services. Within days the Cabinet had unanimously approved her appointment as 'Superintendent of the Female Nursing Establishment of the English General Hospitals in Turkey,' and four days later, on 21 October she left London for Scutari, with a party of thirty-eight nurses.

On hearing of their coming, the Army Medical Department and the doctors at Scutari were indignant and aggrieved. Overworked and under-staffed, they could hardly be expected to welcome the arrival of a Society lady with a party of nurses who knew nothing of army methods and procedures. In their eyes common soliders were little more than 'animals'; 'you will spoil the brutes,' they told Florence Nightingale.

However, they were well aware that she had the support of the Secetary at War and the Cabinet, so they could not openly oppose her, but they could and did ignore her. For herself and her thirty-eight nurses she was allotted only five damp and dirty small rooms and a kitchen, containing only two beds and a few chairs. That night there was no food, only some tea without milk. Nobody seemed to want their help. But Miss Nightingale made no complaint. All she could do was wait until the doctors asked for the skills and services of her nurses – and the ample supplies of drugs and medical stores she had brought with her.

So for days she kept them sorting linen, checking stores, making shirts and slings, and she would not permit any of them to enter a ward unless invited by a doctor. Although this meant that they had to see wounded men suffer without lifting a finger to help them – which made some of her nurses think their Superintendent was unfeeling – she was determined to demonstrate that they were there to work with and not against the doctors,

continued on far right

Florence Nightingale

'IT WAS AS IF I HAD WANTED to be a kitchenmaid,' said Florence Nightingale (1820-1910) of her family's horrified opposition to her plans to train as a nurse. How could she, they protested, she who was the beautiful, cultured younger daughter of a wealthy country gentleman, she who had been presented at Court and could expect to make a good marriage, how *could* she want to spend her days with nurses whom everyone knew were a coarse, ignorant, disreputable class of female, all too often drunk or worse. How could any lady of good breeding dream of being a nurse – it would shame her family. But Florence Nightingale, like Joan of Arc, had heard voices, and she knew that she must devote her life to nursing.

Indifferent to the charms of Society and turning her back on marriage proposals, she spent her days studying official reports on health, sanitation and hospital conditions. In her first London Season, she took to inspecting military hospitals, and by the time she was thirty she had visited and worked in hospitals all over Europe. Her training included periods at the renowned hospitals at the Kaiserwerth Institution in Germany and the Maison de la Providence in Paris.

But she was more than a gentle, caring nurse; she was a woman who knew exactly what she wanted to do and was determined to do it. She had a fine brain, and she made herself an expert in public administration and statistics – an unusual field of study for a woman at that time. She became a recognised authority on everything to do with hospitals and health care, and in 1853 she was appointed superintendent of the Institution for the Care of Sick Gentlewomen in Harley Street. Her position in society undoutedly helped her, and it was her friendship with Sidney Herbert, Secretary at War at the start of the Crimean War, that led to her being asked to go to Scutari.

The popular image of Florence Nightingale has always been 'The Lady with the Lamp', moving from bed to bed to comfort the sick and dying at Scutari. And such was the troops'

Miss Nightingale and
Mr Bracebridge survey
Sebastopol from Cathcart's
Heights, May 1855.

memory of her, but probably her achievements as an administrator were of greater long-term value. Her great aim was to reform medical organisation not only at Scutari but within the whole of the British army, and above all to secure recognition of the value of women as nurses. In all these aims she succeeded brilliantly. At Scutari, as soon as she and her nurses were asked to help, she used initially the large sums of money available to her from *The Times* fund for the sick and wounded, from friends and from her own resources to pay for whatever was needed 'from a milk pudding to a water-bed'.

What came to be known as 'Nightingale Power' had the wards repaired, cleaned and equipped. Until her arrival only seven shirts had been washed in the whole hospital, and bedding had to be washed in cold water. 'Nightingale Power' rented a house, installed boilers and paid soldiers' wives to do the washing. The kitchen in her quarters was fitted out and stocked to provide invalid food to all patients needing it. By the end of December, the hospital had been supplied with many of its urgent needs, and she was able to report to Sidney Herbert:

Orderlies were wanting, utensils were wanting, even water was wanting. I supplied all the utensils, including knives and forks, spoons, cans, towels etc . . . and

and that their services were really needed.

She had not long to wait. A few days after the battle of Inkerman on 5 November the casualties began pouring into the Barrack Hospital, reinforced by victims of the Crimean winter. When a blizzard blew down the troops' tents and wrecked ships bringing fresh supplies of clothing, food and forage, the men were forced to spend the winter in the open, without fuel or adequate food – even the coffee sent out by the commissariat was in the form of unroasted berries. When the hospital wards and corridors were crammed with men suffering from dysentery, cholera, rheumatic fever and malaria, in addition to the wounded, the doctors turned to Miss Nightingale for help.

By the end of December the Barracks had been transformed into a hospital, but meanwhile conditions before Sebastopol were getting worse. The troops had to sleep on the ground, in muddy water, with only a blanket to cover them. There was no bread, tea, or fuel, and food had to be eaten raw. Turns of duty were often thirty-six hours, because so many men were sick. Early in January, there were only 11,000 in camp before Sebastopol, compared with 12,000 in hospital. Most of them were suffering from scurvy or diarrohoea, or both.

It was, said Miss Nightingale, a 'calamity unparalleled in the history of calamity.' To her indignant fury, she discovered that large stocks of preserved foods, lime juice, tea, blankets, clothing, medical supplies, and other necessaries had been sent to the Army and should have been available – except that they had either disappeared into the Turkish Customs House (which she dubbed 'a bottomless pit') or they were being held in the Purveyor's store because they had yet to be officially examined.

To compound this 'calamity unparalleled,' an epidemic broke out in the hospital itself. Similar to cholera but variously described as 'famine fever', Asiactic cholera, and goal fever, it killed so many in the wards that officers and nurses began to be afraid to go on their rounds. Thanks to the timely arrival of an official Sanitary Commission, the cause was traced to the sewers beneath the hospital, which were in fact overloaded cesspools from which poisonous gases blew into the wards. When the sewers and privies were flushed and cleaned, and the walls limewashed, the death-rate dropped dramtically. And as the Crimean winter drew to a close, and the sun shone again, men found it hard to believe they had lived through such hardships. At home the people's fury was such that the government fell.

An early representation of Florence Nightingale on her nightly rounds in the wards of the hospital at Scutari.

Illustrations such as this captured the heart and mind of the Victorian public, and fostered the image of 'The Lady with the Lamp'. It was an image not without foundation, but below her gentleness and compassion lay an iron will, unflagging energy and a relentless determination to get things done in the face of official complacency, indifference, corruption and inefficiency.

was able to send instant arrowroot in huge milk pails (two bottles of port wine in each) for 50 men . . .

I am a kind of General Dealer in socks, shirts, knives and forks, wooden spoons, tin baths, tables and forms, cabbages and carrots, operating tables, towels and soap, small tooth combs, precipitates for destroying lice, bedpans and stump pillows.

Small wonder that men arriving at Scutari to find clean beds, warm food and cheerful nurses said they 'felt they were in heaven.'

She nursed the worst cases herself. Sometimes she was on duty for twenty-four hours at a stretch, and still she found time to write long and detailed reports and attend to all the administrative work of the hospital. During that terrible Crimean Winter she calculated that she saw 2,000 men die, and she never let any man under her care die alone. There are many moving recollections of her night rounds:

I believe there was never a severe case of any kind that escaped her notice [wrote a doctor who worked with her] and sometimes it was wonderful to see her at the bedside of a patient who had been admitted perhaps an hour before, and of whose arrival one would hardly have supposed she could already be cognisant.

It seemed an endless walk [recalled one of her nurses] and one not easily forgotten. As we slowly passed along, the silence was profound; very seldom did a moan or cry from those deeply suffering fall on our

ears. A dim light burned here and there. Miss Nightingale carried her lantern which she set down before she bent over any of the patients. I much admired her manner to the men – it was so tender and kind.

What a comfort it was to see her pass even [said a soldier]. She would speak to one, and nod and smile to as many more; but she could not do it all you know. We lay there by hundreds; but we could kiss her shadow as it fell and lay our heads on the pillow again content.

She was wonderful at cheering up anyone who was a bit low [said another soldier]. She was full of life and fun when she talked to us.

By this time she was already a popular heroine in England, and inevitably the Queen sent a message:

. . . I wish Miss Nightingale and the ladies would tell these poor noble wounded and sick men that *no one* takes a warmer interest or feels *more* for their sufferings or admires their courage *more* than their Queen . . .

And in a personal message to Florence Nightingale, expressing her admiration for her work, the Queen invited her to suggest something that she could do to show how much she appreciated the courage of her sick soldiers. Her Majesty received a prompt reply requesting that sick mens' pay should be improved – which it was.

Florence Nightingale's concern for the troops was not confined to care for the sick and wounded; she also found time to look after the interests of those who were well. She found and furnished reading rooms for them, arranged classes and lectures, and devised and personally supervised a scheme to help them save their pay – which their more cynical officers firmly believed they spent only on drink, so that in six months they sent home over £70,000.

In a few weeks she had transformed the old Barracks at Scutari from a den of death, disease and misery into something like a hospital, and so she determined to 'arrange things,' as she called it, at the military hospital at Balaclava in the Crimea. But all the many tasks she had undertaken and the burden of responsibilities she had shouldered proved too much, even for her, and she collapsed with Crimean fever. For days she lay near death. It was said that on hearing that she might die, men in the hospital at Scutari turned their faces to the wall and wept.

That she survived the crisis was due as much to her iron will as to her robust constitution. As she lay on her bed recovering from the fever, nursed by her best nurse, a horseman rode up to her hut, and asked to see her. 'Who are you?' asked the nurse, barring his way. 'Only a soldier, but I must see her . . . My name is Raglan, she knows me very well.'

Her position as a national heroine, even the gift from the Queen of a brooch designed by the Prince Consort 'as a mark of the high approbation of your Sovereign' gave her little pleasure: 'praise, popularity, prints, jewels left her unmoved.' The country longed to welcome her home with flags flying and bands playing. The government offered to send a warship to bring her home in state, but she would have none of all that. She slipped, unnoticed, back to London, took a train north, and walked home to her family. She never once appeared in public or made any public speech or statement.

For the rest of her long life Florence Nightingale devoted her immense energies to the reorganisation of the army medical service, the reform of hospitals and the establishment of nursing as a professional service. Aware that the 73% mortality from disease in the Crimea could have been prevented and was due almost entirely to the Army system – which was still in existence – she set out single-handed to change it. She won over the Queen and the Prince Consort, she wrote ceaselessly to the politicians and administrators, and she bullied her friends, such as Sidney Herbert and the poet Arthur Hugh Clough, to work for her until they too collapsed, exhausted. But she achieved her aim. By 1861 the death-rate in army barracks was halved.

By then she had founded the Nightingale School for Nurses at St Thomas's Hospital in London. Her health wrecked by her efforts in the Crimea, she became a semi-invalid. From her couch in her London home, which she rarely left, she inspired and directed hospital and nursing reform all over England and in a number of other countries, including India.

Florence Nightingale died in 1910, three years after being rather belatedly awarded the Order of Merit in recognition of her heroic achievements.

In the closing years of her long life, when her sight and her memory began to fail, honours were heaped on Florence Nightingale from all corners of the globe. Her wish not to be buried in Westminster Abbey was respected. Six sergeants carried her coffin to the family grave at East Wellow, and on the tombstone was inscribed a single line: 'F.N. Born 1820. Died 1910.'

It was largely due to the influence of Florence Nightingale that medical examinations were introduced in the Army and Navy

65

Newspaper correspondents – 'those newly-invented curses who eat the rations of fighting men, and do no work at all.
SIR GARNET WOLSELEY

The World's First War Correspondent

IT WAS DURING the Crimean War that newspaper readers at home were first given day-by-day reports on the conduct and progress of a great international conflict – thanks to the enterprise of a great editor, Thomas Delane of *The Times*, and to the first professional war correspondent, William Howard Russell. Russell's despatches from the scene of action revealed, as never before, the government's feeble direction of the war and in particular the gross incompetence of the War Office. For perhaps the first time a 'bad press' was a major factor in the fall of a government.

Like so many of the British troops and their officers whose courage and sufferings he reported so vividly, William Howard Russell was an Irishman. Born in County Dublin in 1820, he was a man of humble birth whose parents managed to give him a good education. Though he had no experience of writing for newspapers, he set about earning an income as a freelance journalist while reading for the Bar in London.

He joined *The Times* as a parliamentary correspondent, and got his first experience of war reporting in the Schleswig-Holstein war in Denmark in 1850. Four years later he was sent to cover the war in the Crimea by Thomas Delane, who had earned for *The Times* its formidable reputation as 'The Thunderer', for when he spoke people listened. Even he was reluctant to accept the accuracy of Russell's first reports from the Crimea, but with the revelations about the needless hardships being endured by British troops at Varna and Gallipoli there was a national outcry.

Roger Fenton (1819-1869) was the official British photographer in the Crimea. Photography was then in its infancy, and involved cumbrous processes for developing and printing, so Fenton took his own 'Photographic Van' with him. However, the 350 or so photographs he later exhibited in London tended to show the war in a favourable light, with few of the horrors and hardships as reported by William Russell

66

In the Crimea itself, Russell's despatches caused bitter resentment. Lord Raglan took them as an unjust criticism of his conduct of the campaign – which they were not. Russell was shunned by Staff Officers, denied the facilities he needed as a reporter, and even refused rations. 'Lord Raglan never spoke to me in his life', wrote Russell on one ocasion: 'I was regarded as a mere camp follower . . .' But he was not discouraged by such attitudes, and his brilliantly-written reports continued to appear in *The Times*.

For the next quarter of a century, Russell was 'The Thunderer's' special correspondent in many of the world's major conflicts, including the Indian Mutiny, the American Civil War, the Prusso-Austrian Seven Weeks' War in 1866, and the Franco-Prussian War of 1870, the Zulu War in 1879, and the Egyptian campaign of 1882. He was knighted for services to journalism in 1895, and died in 1907.

Though heartily disliked by such Victorian generals as Lords Wolseley and Roberts – who each became adept at providing misleading information without actually lying – war correspondents had come to stay, and the same two generals and many others quickly learned how to use publicity to benefit their careers. In the steps of William Howard Russell followed such prominent writers as Windwoode Reade, who reported the Ashanti War for *The Times*, G. A. Henty of *The Standard*, and Conan Doyle, who coined the phrase 'Black Week' during the Boer War. The explorer H. M. Stanley represented the *New York Herald* in the campaigns in Abyssinia and Ashantiland.

The Crimean War on Victorian breakfast tables

Russell's graphic reports from the Crimea – with no detail spared in deference to Victorian susceptibilities – shook the complacency of Britain's establishment and brought home to ordinary men and women, for the first time, the true horrors of war. Nothing like Russell's despatches had ever been seen before. Their impact on public opinion can be compared only with that of television news coverage of the Vietnam War on the American nation. Two brief examples from his considerable output – one from the Alma and the other from Balaclava – are typical of Russell's treatment and style:

Can it be said that the battle of the Alma has been an event to take the world by surprise? Yet . . . there is no preparation for the commonest surgical operations! Not only are the men kept waiting, in some cases for a week, without the hand of a medical man coming near their wounds, not only are they left to expire in agony, unheeded and shaken off . . . it is found that the commonest appliances of a workhouse sick ward are wanting, and that the men must die through the medical staff of the British Army having forgotten that old rags are necessary for the dressing of wounds . . . The worn out pensioners who were brought as an ambulance corps are totally useless . . . there are no dressers or nurses to carry out the surgeon's directions, and to attend on the sick during the intervals between his visits. Here the French are greatly our superiors. Their medical arrangements are extremely good . . .

□ □ □

A large number of sick and, I feared, dying men, were sent into Balaclava on the 23rd on French mule litters . . . They formed one of the most ghastly processions that ever poet imagined. Many of these men were all but dead. With closed eyes, open mouths, and ghastly attenuated faces, they were borne along two and two, the thin stream of breath in the frosty air alone showing they were still alive. One figure was a horror – a corpse, stone dead, strapped upright in its seat, its legs hanging stiffly down, the eyes staring wide open and teeth set on the protruding tongue, the head and body nodding with frightful mockery of life at each stride of the mule over the broken road. No doubt the man died on his way down to the harbour. Another man I saw with raw flesh and skin hanging from his fingers, the naked bones of which protruded into the cold air, undressed and uncovered . . .'

War in the Gulf

With British attention diverted by the Crimean War and its aftermath, Persia – despite repeated warnings – decided in 1856 to seize its chance of occupying the disputed Afghanistan province of Herat. Britain replied by sending an expeditionary force of 7,000 men from Bombay to the Persian Gulf, where the town of Bushire was captured. Six weeks later a second expedition, of similar strength, was despatched, commanded by General Outram with General Havelock as his second-in-command.

In March 1857 an attack was launched up the River Tigris against the fort of Mohammerah and the nearby main camp of the Persian army. In a series of actions the Persians were defeated with heavy loss, forcing the Shah to pull out of Herat and sue for peace.

Sailors on Land and Sea

1856

BUSHIRE (Persia)
North Staffordshire
Durham L.I.

1856-1857
PERSIA
14th Hussars
North Staffordshire
Durham L.I.
Seaforth Highlanders

1857
CANTON: 2nd Chinese War
East Lancashire
KOOSH-AB (Persia)
North Staffordshire
Durham L.I.
Seaforth Highlanders

WHEN THE Crimean War broke out the Royal Navy was very undermanned, so generous bounties were offered to merchant seamen, to tempt them to transfer. The ploy worked only too well, for when the authorities had to face the task of moving an expeditionary force to the Crimea, they found that they had plenty of ships but not enough trained crews to man them.

Many of the vessels belonged to P & O and other pioneering steamship companies, who had been subsidised by the Government on the understanding that in times of war their ships would be made available for troop-carrying duty at low cost.

There were also some large sailing ships built to carry emigrants out to New South Wales during the gold rush. Scratch crews were got together, and the formidable task began of transporting many thousands of British soldiers, with guns, ammunition and other military supplies, to the fields of battle. It was the first large-scale movement of troops to be undertaken in the age of steam.

Conditions in the camps were so bad that cholera soon broke out, reducing the force to an

Sailors were very popular in Victorian times. These two examples of Staffordshire pottery of the 1850s depict a sailor helping his wounded soldier comrade, and two sailors manning a gun

68

army of invalids. Meanwhile, the Turks had managed to raise the siege of Silistria on their own account, without any assistance from their allies. Tsar Nicholas I ordered his invading army to retire, enabling the British and French to turn their minds to the real purpose of the campaign, the destruction of Sebastopol.

This involved moving the army from Varna to Calamita Bay on the northern shore of the Black Sea. The men were crammed as tightly as possible into all available vessels, leaving behind stores and medical supplies which – it was hoped – might follow later. 'My God!' cried one senior army surgeon, 'they have landed this army without any kind of hospital transport, litters or carts or anything.'

In all these sea transport operations, from home waters across the Bay of Biscay, into the Mediterranean, through the Dardanelles and up into the Black Sea, ordinary British seamen performed prodigious tasks. They did all that was asked of them, often under difficult and dangerous conditions. But their duties, onerous as they were, did not call for acts of individual bravery. It was not courage that was required, so much as resourcefulness, endurance, cheerfulness and determination – qualities which many people regard as representing the heart of Britain's seafaring tradition, even today.

Before war was formally declared, a Franco-British fleet sailed through the Bosphorous and into the Black Sea to patrol the northern coast of Turkey. One of the first engagements of the war was the bombardment by the Royal Navy of shore batteries near the Russian port of Odessa. Now that hostilities were under way plenty of opportunities for heroic behaviour arose, and few seized their chances more avidly than the Naval Brigades, consisting of men who sailed on board naval vessels but whose duties were mostly on land, in support of their army comrades.

Mrs Duberly, wife of Captain Henry Duberly of the 8th Hussars, noted in her Crimea diary:

These seamen appear to work with the greatest energy and goodwill. One meets a gang of them harnessed to a gun, and drawing with all their might and main; or digging at entrenchments singing, and laughing, and working heartily and cheerily . . . There was certainly no camp in which more kind consideration for others, more real active help, has been afforded to all than in that of the sailors; and their willingness and cheerfulness to abour encouraged and comforted all through the difficulties and sufferings of last winter.

One young rifleman serving with the Green Jackets at the siege of Sebastopol observed that the 'Jack Tars are curious animals in camp'. But

British sailors embarking at Portsmouth Harbour for the Baltic fleet

that the Naval Brigades were much admired is shown by this typical extract:

The signal [for the attack] was given by fireworks from batteries one hour before daylight, and the riflemen, with about two dozen *volunteer* Jack Tars, made a dash, and in spite of the sweeping volleys of grape and canister etc., some of them mananged to reach the Russian works, but where was the support? . . . These were detained in the advanced trenches, and out of 160 of my comrades, 70 were killed and wounded, and, I am sorry to state, a number of the sailors were killed.

God bless them! They are England's bravest men. I saw one sailor, a very little man, struggling through a crowd of soldiers with his chum, who was twice his size and mortally wounded, on his back. The soldiers expostulated with the impropriety of carrying him home, but Jack was determined to effect his object, or die in the attempt. A sailor will run a mile to give a wounded rifleman his grog.

Many other stories about the heroism of the Naval Brigades started to circulate within the British ranks, bringing much needed cheer to the hard-pressed men. One army officer described their behaviour in the front line:

There is a recklessness about the seamen's courage . . . whenever a particularly effective shot issued from one of their embrasures, the tars would leap *en masse* upon the parapet, wave the Union Jack, and cheer like devils. A defiance that had the effect of bringing upon the brave, but thoughtless fellows, an augmented dose of iron.

The main tasks of the Allied fleet in the Black Sea, once the troop transports had been safely convoyed from Varna to Eupatoria, were to blockade the Sea of Azov to make it difficult for the Russians to reinforce the Crimean peninsula, and to bombard shore batteries. However, in May 1855 came action of a more spectacular kind when a combined Allied expedition landed at Kamiesh, a Russian base on the eastern shore of the Crimea commanding the entrance to the Sea of Azov. Large quantities of food, stores and ammunition were destroyed, and enemy guns spiked. In the engagements that followed, the Russians lost no fewer than 250 ships of various kinds.

In this way the Sea of Azov came under Allied control, and their flotilla pressed home its advantage by raiding and destroying more enemy depots, penetrating as far as Taganrog on the north-eastern shore. This port was a vital link in the supply route between the granaries of central Russia and her armies in the Crimea. However, the shallow sea approaches made it difficult for the Allies to bring into action their larger ships with their heavier guns.

On board the *Stromboli* an ingenious solution was found. A wooden raft 45ft long and 15ft wide was built on 29 casks, on which a 32-pounder gun weighing well over two tons was firmly secured. Drawing only 20 inches of water, this

The '*Lady Nancy*' bombards Taganrog

remarkable gunboat – promptly dubbed the *Lady Nancy* – was brought inshore with 100 rounds and a crew of 18 on board. It then proceeded to bombard Taganrog 'with a precision that elicited hearty cheers from our allies', according to one contemporary account. The names of the crew are not recorded, but it must have taken a special kind of heroism to sail so flimsy a craft, let alone fire a heavy gun from it.

Shallow depths also presented problems in the Baltic Sea, where elderly and lumbering three-deckers, under Royal Navy commanders of even greater age, were sent in the early spring of 1854 as part of an expedition to enforce a blockade, destroy enemy shipping and attack fortifications, ports and shore supply depots.

Vice-Admiral Sir Charles Napier, then aged 68, was appointed Commander-in-Chief, whereupon he urged the men under his new command 'to sharpen your cutlasses, and the day is your own.' So quaint an expression from a bygone age did not go down at all well with his masters in London, but in most other respects he seems to have had few illusions about the nature of his task. 'I am going out', he wrote to one of his captains, 'with a raw squadron to attack an efficient fleet in their own waters.' Events were to prove him right, for apart from blockading the Baltic, the only success that year was the capture, after much delay and difficulty, of a group of islands commanding the Gulf of Bothnia.

'We have to deal with shallow waters and granite walls,' said a gloomy, perceptive leading article in *The Times*, 'and find ourselves too gigantic for the petty warfare, and giants though we are, we are so far baffled.' Sir Charles Napier echoed these thoughts in a letter to the First Lord of the Admiralty, written in July 1854, about a possible assault on a naval arsenal at Sveaborg, near Helsingfors (now Helsinki):

The only successful manner of attacking . . . that I can see . . . is by fitting out a great number of gunboats carrying one gun with a long range . . .

The end of the wooden line-of-battle ship, and deep draught ships of all kinds, was now in sight, hastened by the destruction of the Turkish fleet at Sinope and the operational difficulties encountered in Russian waters. The day of the modern gunboat had dawned.

By midsummer 1854 six vessels of an entirely new design were ordered by the Admiralty, and a few weeks later this number was increased by a further 20. In 1855 a new Anglo-French fleet sailed for the Baltic in two divisions, the first of which left Spithead watched by Queen Victoria and the First Sea Lord.

Under the command of Admiral Dundas, who was not related in any way to the former C-in-C in the Mediterranean of similar name, the new

expedition – consisting of more than 50 ships, including 18 gunboats – was more effective than its predecessor. It inflicted a loss of more than 80,000 tons of shipping upon the Russians, as well as the destruction or dislocation of many of their shore installations.

In an action near Viborg (now Viipuri) in the Gulf of Finland, the gunboat *Ruby*, towing cutters from the *Magicienne* and *Arrogant*, came under heavy fire from a concealed shore battery at a range of not more than 350 yards. Riflemen also opened fire, creating a confusion in the two boats which was much increased when a rocket accidentally exploded. Two crew members of *Magicienne* – a lieutenant and an A.B. – acted with a great courage and presence of mind, and were later each awarded the Victoria Cross. Covering fire from *Ruby* saved the day and, with the loss of only one midshipman, the British seamen and marines escaped from the trap which had been carefully laid for them.

The major action of the year, in which the Royal Navy had to sweep mines for the first time, took place in August, when the long-awaited

attack on Sveaborg was launched. During the bombardment, which lasted two days and one night, over 2,000 Russians were killed, 23 ships destroyed and a huge amount of ammunition detonated. Allied losses were one man killed and 15 wounded, mostly by bursting rockets.

This foretaste of modern warfare had a profound effect upon the Russians, who feared that similar onslaughts might be made upon Kronstedt and St Petersburg if the war were allowed to continue. It helped to bring about their acceptance of peace terms put forward by Austria, which brought the Crimean War to an end early in 1856. By this time, the British had 64 gunboats in their fleet, and had ordered 120 more.

In many ways the most poignant naval story concerns not a hero of the Crimean War but a Victorian anti-hero – a man whose death provides a backcloth against which all the many deeds of daring, of valour and of gallantry might well be set by way of contrast. It is a story that comes not from the Baltic Sea or the Black Sea, but from the Pacific Ocean, where a British squadron was ordered to attack shipping at the port of Petropavlovsk. In command was Rear-Admiral David Price, who had served with great distinction in the Napoleonic War, reaching the rank of Captain in 1815.

But after all the glory there followed 39 barren years of inactivity, broken only by a brief appointment as a commander of a 50-gun ship and, later, by a spell as the commissioner of a naval dockyard. He made his way slowly up the list, from one pair of dead man's shoes to another, increasingly losing touch with all his earlier training and hard-won battle experience, and becoming more and more unfit to command men in action.

When, at long last, the challenges of leadership confronted him once more he found he could not accept them. After ordering his ships to go into action Rear-Admiral David Price left the bridge, went to his cabin, took out a gun and shot himself.

The gunboat *Ruby* provides covering fire during the attack on Viborg

The Victoria Cross

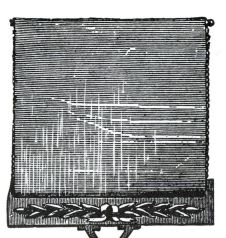

THROUGHOUT her reign Queen Victoria took a deep interest and pride in her sailors and soldiers, as many of her letters and her actions show. The Victoria Cross – which of all military decorations carries the highest prestige – was instituted by her personal inspiration and initiative. At a time when the only medals awarded to British soldiers and sailors were for good conduct and long service, the Queen saw the need for public recognition of individual acts of exceptional bravery.

The Queen wanted awards that would be 'highly prized and eagerly sought after by the officers and men of Our naval and military services'. The Victoria Cross was announced in the *London Gazette* in February 1856, and the first awards were to include acts of bravery performed in the recently-concluded Crimean War.

The new award was democratic in character. The Royal Warrant instituting the Victoria Cross for 'Officers or Men who have served Us in the presence of the Enemy and shall then have performed some single act of valour or devotion to their Country', laid down that 'neither rank nor long service nor wounds nor any other circumstance or condition whatsoever save the merit of conspicuous bravery or devotion shall be held to establish a sufficient claim to honour'. In this way, all were eligible to receive for the decoration, and this equality of the brave was demonstrated when the Queen presented the first Victoria Crosses: all 62 recipients stood shoulder to shoulder regardless of rank.

The Queen supervised every detail of the award and its design. When it was proposed that the motto should be 'For the Brave' she commented that this suggested that only those who have received the Victoria Cross are considered brave, and she insisted that the medal should be awarded 'For Valour'. She wanted the initials BVC (Bearer of the Victoria Cross) to follow the names of holders of the award, saying that 'VC would not do' because no one could be a Victoria Cross. But popular usage defeated her on this: everybody always knew what VC stood for.

From the beginning the Victoria Cross has always been manufactured by the same firm of goldsmiths and silversmiths, Messrs Hancock of Bruton Street in London, founded in 1848. The Queen took a close interest in its manufacture, and even tried the pins which she found 'will answer very well'.

The Victoria Cross is made in bronze from Russian guns captured at Sebastopol. The name of the recipient and the date of his act of bravery are engraved on the reverse. The medal, suspended by a 1½" ribbon, is worn on the left breast, and takes precedence of all other awards and orders

Queen Victoria presented the first VCs in Hyde Park on 26 June 1857. Without distinction of rank, 62 heroes of the Crimean War stood shoulder to shoulder as she pinned the new medal on each of them.

At Rorke's Drift no fewer than eleven VCs were won

The first man to win the VC was Charles Lucas on board HMS *Hecla*.

selecting one or more of their number for the VC. During the Indian Mutiny several awards were made on this basis, but thereafter the practice died out. The VC is in its essence a recognition of individual acts of exceptional courage.

A pension of £10 a year (increased to £100 in 1959) was granted to all non-commissioned winners of the VC, and a sum of £50 was paid into the estate of a posthumous recipient. Presumably it was thought that officers would not expect a monetary reward. The original Warrant stated that a recipient's VC could be forfeited and his pension stopped if he were convicted of 'any infamous Crime' including treason and felony.

Only seven of the 500 or more VCs awarded during the Queen's reign were forfeited – including that of Gunner Collis of the Royal Horse Artillery, who won his VC in the Second Afghan War and fifteen years later was imprisoned for bigamy, but that did not stop him from re-enlisting in 1914. Forfeitures for misconduct were stopped by her grandson George V. 'Even were a VC to be sentenced to be hanged for murder,' he wrote, 'he should be allowed to wear the VC on the scaffold.'

The first-ever award of the Victoria Cross was to Charles Lucas, a mate on HMS *Hecla*, during the Fleet's bombardment of Bomarsund in the Crimean War. Lucas almost certainly saved his ship and the lives of all on board when he snatched up a live shell that had fallen on the deck

Later warrants extended eligibility to Indian and other colonial services and to 'Non-Military Persons Bearing Arms a Volunteers', and cases of 'Conspicuous Courage and Bravery under Circumstances of Danger but not before the Enemy' were also included. In line with its stress on equality, the Victoria Cross could also be awarded in cases of conspicuous bravery by a body of sailors or soldiers, and in such cases officers and other ranks had the privilege of

and hurled it into the sea – where it exploded with a tremendous roar. Lucas was promoted Lieutenant on the spot, and was one of the first 62 VCs decorated by the Queen in 1857. He later rose to be a Rear-Admiral and died aged 80 in Tunbridge Wells.

A number of the early winners of the VC later achieved high rank. Of these perhaps the most remarkable were Field-Marshal Earl ('Little Bobs') Roberts and Field-Marshal Sir Evelyn Wood, both of whom won the VC for deeds of spectacular bravery in action during the Indian Mutiny – and both of whom might well have been awarded it on several other occasions.

Most winners of the VC were in their early twenties – junior officers and other ranks in the thick of the action – and it has never been awarded to a woman. The two youngest winners of the VC were Hospital Apprentice Andrew Fitzgibbon, aged 15, who displayed conspicuous coolness and courage while attending the wounded under fire during the assault on the Taku Forts in 1860, and Drummer Thomas Flinn of the 64th Foot who was also only 15 when he was recommended for the VC for his bravery in hand-to-hand fighting against sepoy gunners during the Indian Mutiny. The oldest VC was undoubtedly Lieut (later Capt) William Raynor of the Bengal Veteran Establishment who was 62 in 1857 when he was one of the nine men defending the Delhi Magazine against overwhelming odds.

Very few men have ever been recommended for the VC on more than one occasion, entitling them to add a bar to their original Cross, and no such bars were awarded during Victoria's reign. Six VCs were awarded for conspicuous bravery *not* in the presence of an enemy, and four civilians received the award – three during the Indian Mutiny and one in the Second Afghan War. Awards seem to have been made rather more freely at first, 111 being given during the Crimean War and 182 (as many as in the Second World War) during the Indian Mutiny, but it needs to be remembered that at that time there were no other medals for bravery. The greatest number of VCs received in any one action was the eleven awarded to the defenders at Rorke's Drift in 1879 – seven to the 24th Regiment (later The South Wales Borderers), the greatest number awarded to any one regiment.

Five of the eleven VCs won at Rorke's Drift went to privates and two to NCOs, and throughout the Queen's reign well over half of all winners of the VC were Other Ranks. While this may not be proportionate to their numbers, it showed that ordinary Privates, Troopers, Gunners, Sappers, Drummers, Seamen, Stokers and NCOs could be and were recognised as Heroes for Victoria.

Lieutenant Roberts (later Field-Marshal Lord Roberts) won his VC by recapturing the regimental Colours from sepoys during the Indian Mutiny.

Lieutenant F.H.S. Roberts (only son of Lord Roberts) won the VC when he was killed while trying to save the guns at the battle of Colenso on 15 December 1899 – just before his father took over as Commander-in-Chief of the British forces in South Africa.

Among the more lasting benefits conferred upon the maritime world by the Queen's Navy were British Admiralty charts, still in wide use today

Charting Uncertain Seas

In charge of the huge task of charting many of the world's coastlines for the British Admiralty was Hydrographer of the Navy, Admiral Sir Francis Beaufort. In 1805 he devised a system of measuring the wind speeds, later adapted to include sea conditions, used by mariners for more than 150 years. He also has the rare distinction of having a sea named after him – part of the Arctic Ocean off the coast of northern Canada.

THE SYSTEMATIC and scientific charting of most the world's coastal waters by the Royal Navy during the 19th century was rarely heroic in a literal sense, but was certainly undertaken on a heroic scale. Although largely a self-imposed task it made good strategic and commercial sense, at a time when Britannia really did rule the waves, to produce up-to-date, reliable charts to improve navigation and reduce the number of shipwrecks, saving lives and valuable cargo.

Before 1840 the East India Company held a monopoly of ocean survey work in Far Eastern waters, but after the First Chinese War, so-called, the task was transferred to the Royal Navy. The preparation of accurate charts for merchant shipping was not the only benefit to accrue from the work of naval hydrographers: it was through their efforts that deposits of coal were found off the shores of the Chinese mainland as well as the islands of Formosa, Japan and the Pescadores. Although only very lightly armed, survey ships were expected to play their part in naval engagements. The small gunboat *Dove* saw action in the Yangtse and at Taku, and was also later

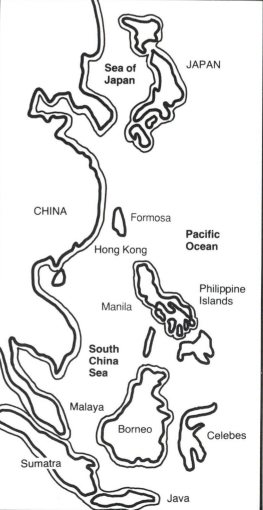

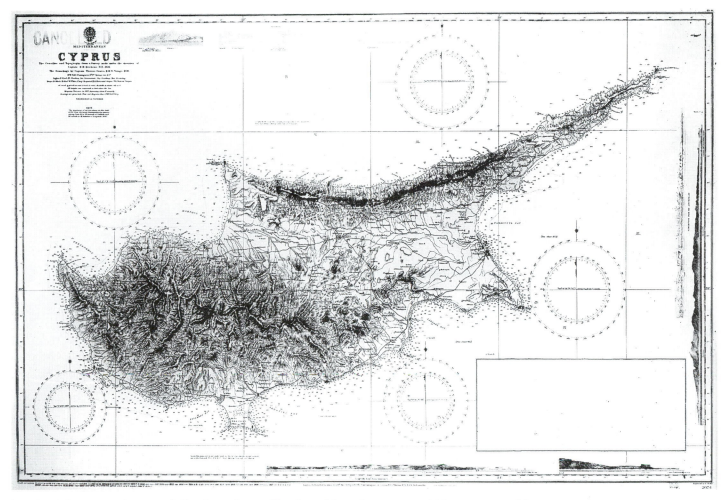

MEDITERRANEAN
CYPRUS

involved in an exchange of fire in a bay off Formosa, which appeared in due course identified as Attack Bay in the appropriate chart.

So accurately were they prepared that many of these charts, issued by the British Admiralty, are still used today by countries all over the world, often amended and updated – but not always so. There is perhaps a gentle irony in the fact that one of the most permanent and useful benefits to be bestowed upon the maritime world by the most powerful Navy in the world, should be the result of years of painstaking and humdrum work, usually well away from the sound of gunfire and the drama of battle.

The senior officer in charge of these operations, the Hydrographer of the Navy, was Admiral Sir Francis Beaufort. Among other things, he gave his name to the Beaufort Wind Scale, a system of classifying wind speeds which has only recently been replaced. By the time he retired in 1855 no fewer than 2,000 separate charts, covering all parts of the world, had been prepared. In that year alone, 140,000 copies were printed for the use of the Royal Navy, or for sale to other seafarers.

Surveying was not at all popular with naval ratings, who found the work tedious and repeti-

tive. Often the men would have to spend hours of duty in open boats, exposed to the heat of the tropical sun or to temperatures well below zero, taking soundings to establish the depth of the water at fixed and regular intervals in accordance with a pre-determined plan. One inaccurate measurement, or one move slightly out of position, could ruin the work of a whole day. For their officers back on board ship, working from the comparative comfort of the bridge, fixing positons with sextant and compass and steadily building data on their charts, it was probably a far more interesting exercise. And the task was not entirely without its dangers, for landings had often to be made on hazardous, rocky shores to plot the configurations of bays, inlets, estuaries, headlands and other coastal features.

One of the Royal Navy's survey vessels in the early 1840s was HMS *Samarang*, under the command of Captain Sir Edward Belcher CB. Irascible and capricious in manner, he was a remarkably fine surveyor, well regarded by his superior officers, including Beaufort. After the treaty between England and China at the end of the Opium War in 1842, Captain Belcher was ordered to chart the Eastern Archipelago from Korea to Singapore.

Part of an heroic legacy – an Admiralty chart of the coastline and topography of Cyprus, amended in 1917 to show the latest magnetic variations, exemplifies the accuracy and draughtsmanship of Victorian surveyors and hydrographers.

HMS *Plover* at anchor at
the mouth of a creek
near Hong Kong

Once, off the coast of Gillolo, he was fired on by a group of hostile natives and forced to take shelter in his barge for a short time. In the manner of Sir Francis Drake, he then returned to complete and check his calculations before leading a punitive raid in which he put his attacker to flight, collecting a bullet wound in the thigh for his pains. Belcher managed to convince the authorities that the natives were, in fact, pirates – despite the fact that they fought under the Dutch flag – and secured for his officers and men a bounty of £10,000.

Despite this windfall, the crew of HMS *Samarang* were not happy under Belcher's command, and when the commission came to a premature end – after a row in Hong Kong with the Commander-in-Chief – there was great rejoicing among the officers and men, who deeply resented his arbitrary manner and lack of concern. On one occasion, for example, when the ship had made a safe and comfortable anchorage in Manila Harbour in time to celebrate Christmas, Belcher suddenly gave orders on the morning of Christmas Day to weigh anchor and sail to a remote and inhospitable bay in order to undertake further routine survey work.

Although his task remained unfinished, Belcher's achievement was nevertheless very considerable. He covered much of the vast sea area allotted to him, together with the coast of Borneo, parts of the Korean coast and the islands of Majico Sima. In addition, during his extensive voyaging he had from time to time signed treaties of friendship with a number of local rulers on behalf of Her Majesty's Government. For all his oddities and quirks of character, Captain Sir Edward Belcher CB was a loyal servant of the Queen, and one of her most devoted heroes.

The Admiralty's systematic charting of bays, creeks, inlets and estuaries in many parts of the world drew its impetus partly from a spirit of exploration and adventure, partly from the commercial benefits thus derived, and partly from humanitarian motives – a desire to reduce the loss of life at sea and a determination to stamp out slave trading and piracy throughout the

A cyclone strikes
HMS *Samarang* in the
South China Sea

world. It was as an intelligence-gathering operation that the charting of the east and west coasts of Africa, of Latin America and of the China Seas proved of special value. Knowing where the traders embarked their human cargo and the routes they took to reach their markets, opened up the possibility of patrolling the seas in an attempt to stem the traffic.

Most slave trading was carried out along the west coast of Africa to provide cheap labour for South America, the Caribbean and the United States. The Navy's principal task force was the West African squadron – 'the most disagreeable, arduous, and unhealthy service that falls to the lot of British officers and seamen . . .' as the Medical Director General of the Admiralty observed. Malaria, yellow fever, blackwater fever and other scourges carried off hundreds of British sailors each year, and often it was only the rare prospect of a visit to St Helena or Ascension Island, to enjoy fresh food and fresh water in a cooler climate, that sustained morale.

By the 1840s a number of countries favoured abolition, in theory at least, and agreed that their ships could be searched at sea. The West African squadron was accordingly strengthened,

from seven to 30 or more cruisers and from 700 to 3,000 men. The advent of steam made it possible, for a time, to run down the traders, although the more successful of them soon learned the lesson and acquired steam vessels of their own. The trade continued to flourish until 1861, when the inauguration of President Lincoln destroyed the market virtually overnight. He was a confirmed believer in abolition and hanged a convicted American slave trader during his first year of office to prove the point.

The situation on the east coast of Africa, however, remained more or less unchanged. Slavery was not prohibited under Muslim law, so the trade out of Zanzibar to Arabia, and south to Madagascar, carried on throughout Victoria's reign and well into the present century. It was only contained by interception on the high seas by the Royal Navy, whose officers and seamen knew exactly where they stood in respect of their arduous and often dangerous task. They had no doubt about the morality of their position. With Victorian certainty they knew that trafficking in slaves was an abomination: their Christian as well as their patriotic duty was to suppress it and punish the traders, so far as it lay in their power.

Captain Sir
Edward Belcher CB

On a slaveship
off Zanzibar

The Queen's Other Army

In India two separate armies served the Queen and her expanding empire; the East India Company's army of Indian troops ('sepoys') under British officers, and the Queen's Army of British troops paid for by the Company.

The Company's own army (the Queen's 'other army') numbered some 300,000 men and was divided into three Presidency areas, of which the largest was Bengal; the other two were Bombay and Madras.

The Queen's army, often referred to as the 'British Army in India', consisted of four regiments of cavalry and 22 of infantry stationed in India in 1857.

The number of British officers and other ranks of both armies was about 40,000. The two armies, through their commanders, came finally under the authority of the Governor General, who was appointed by the Crown. On the eve of the Great Mutiny this crucial post was held by Lord Canning.

In the Company's Bengal Army three out of four sepoys were high-caste Hindus, Brahmins or Rajputs, and the majority were enlisted in Oudh, the northern kingdom now known as Uttar Pradesh, with its capital at Lucknow.

Though paid only a third of a British soldier's pay and never promoted to a higher rank than the most junior British subaltern, the average sepoy was content in the army. Although he had to wait years for promotion, his living conditions and income were good by local standards, his position was secure, and his profession earned him prestige in his village.

He could respect, even like, his British officers, and until some years after the Queen's accession he could feel that they respected him and that they 'knew how to treat the sepoys in their own way'. 'The sepoy, said an English officer of the Bengal artillery, was 'perfectly happy with his lot, a cheerful, good-natured fellow, simple and trust-worthy.' It was, indeed, almost an article of faith with many British officers of Indian regiments that their men were totally loyal and dependable.

So why did the sepoys turn on their officers and mutiny in 1857?

The immediate trigger of the Sepoy Mutiny in 1857 was the replacement of the familiar Brown Bess musket with the new Enfield rifle. In loading the Enfield the sepoy had to bite off the end of a greased cartridge, and a rumour was put about that the grease was cow or pig fat. The cow being sacred to Hindus and the pig an abomination to Muslims, the change was seen as contempt for the religion of both, and perhaps an attempt to force sepoys to become Christians.

But the root causes of the Mutiny lay much deeper. From their earliest days in India the British stance was one of strict neutrality in religious matters, and they took great care not to offend the Hindus, Muslims or any other community. Trade, not conversion, was the sole concern of the East India Company, and any attempt to interfere with local customs and beliefs – other than on unassailable commercial grounds – was frowned upon by the Court of Directors.

However, as British power grew so did pressure from Westminster and elsewhere to improve the lot of the Queen's 'subject peoples'. Various reforms were introduced, with entirely predictable results. The abolition of suttee, the legalisation of re-marriage by widows, the introduction of English-style education, English-style courts, English-style land laws, the railways, the new roads, the canals, the electric telegraph, and, perhaps most disturbing of all, the Christian missionaries who now roamed the land – all these changes were seen as attacks on the religious feelings of the Indian people.

Already unsettled by such changes, Sepoys also found that some of their officers were holding bible and prayer meetings to convert them from their 'idolatrous' religion. Unlike the old officers of 'John Company', many of the new officers did not trouble to understand the sepoys or to speak their language. Some even called them 'niggers' and 'pigs'. And now there was a new army regulation compelling sepoys to serve overseas, even though it was well known that a Hindu lost his castle when he crossed 'the black water' and would be spurned by his friends on his return.

Only a few British officials saw where such breaches of religious neutrality could lead. As one of them said, 'a blow will be struck at our power in India, which in the course of time may prove fatal'. That blow was struck on 10 May 1857 in Meerut.

The Great Mutiny

'OUT OF THE question' was the average British officer's reaction when warned that there was going to be a revolt in which the sepoy army would take the lead. There had been mutinies before, and they had all been put down. But this time there were fewer British troops (only one battalion between Lucknow and Calcutta) and many of them were in the recently-annexed Punjab. Quite suddenly in the first half of 1857 the seething unrest became an explosion.

The first shot in the Great Indian Mutiny was fired at Barrackpore, near Calcutta, when a sepoy named Mangal Pande of the disturbed 34th Native Infantry ran amok and attacked his officers. The regiment was disbanded and Mangal Pande was hanged, but from then on mutineers were known as 'Pandies'.

But the first real revolt was at Meerut, about 40 miles north of Delhi, on Sunday 10 May 1857. Eighty-five cavalry sepoys had refused to use the new cartridges. They were thereupon court-martialled, given long prison sentences, and paraded in their fetters in front of the whole

Before embarking for the Crimea the 42nd Highlanders were inspected at Chobham, Surrey, by Queen Victoria and the Prince Consort attended by the King of Hanover and Lord Cardigan.

(facing page)

Soldiers of the 73rd Perthshire Regiment stand fast during the sinking of the troopship *Birkenhead* in 1852. Other Scottish drafts on board were from the 74th and 91st Highlanders. Oil painting by Thomas Henry.

A contemporary aquatint showing the Scots Fusilier Guards cheering the Queen at a parade before their departure for the Crimea in 1854.

The Bombardment of Sebastopol, 1854. The Crimean War was the last major conflict in which traditional wooden men-of-war, built to designs little changed over the centuries, saw active service. The first appearance of iron-clad warships was on 16 October 1856, when a French flotilla attacked the Russian port of Kinburn at the mouth of the Bug River.

The 42nd Royal Highlanders at the Battle of the Alma, 1854.

The 93rd Highlanders at
Balaclava. In the foreground
is their commanding officer
Colonel Ainslie.
Watercolour by Orlando
Norie.

The Battle of Inkerman. On
5 November 1854 the
Russian commander
Menshikov made a second
attempt to drive a wedge
between the Allied forces
besieging Sebastopol and
their field support. The
main assault fell upon British
units, whose dogged
resistance wore down the
Russians, who withdrew
when Bosquet's French
division finally arrived on
the field of battle.

One of a series of 12 reliefs
issued at the time of the
Queen's Diamond Jubilee,
featuring 'Heroes of the
Victoria Cross'. This scene
depicts Sergeant Hartigan,
unarmed, attacking four
mutineers, who had entered
the 9th Lancers camp
disguised as musicians and
had murdered a fellow-
sergeant.

Colonel John Ewart leads
the 93rd Sutherland
Highlanders as they storm
the Secundrabagh at
Lucknow in November
1857. Watercolour by
Orlando Norie.

The 90th Perthshire Light Infantry, formerly the Scottish Rifles, repel a Zulu attack during the battle of Ulundi in 1879. Painting by H. Oakes-Jones

Since the Victoria Cross came into being after the Crimea War 23 men of the South Wales Borderers have won this much-coveted award, ten of them during the Zulu campaign of 1879. Many of the medals are proudly displayed in this 'VC Case' in the regimental museum.

The battle of Tel-el-Kebir in 1882 crushed Arabi Pasha's revolt in the Sudan and set the seal on General Wolseley's brilliant career.

The King's Own Scottish Borderers were one of the many regiments engaged in the long series of campaigns and expeditions on the North-West Frontier of India. Here they are seen capturing the heights of Maidan during the Tirah campaign of 1897.

The uniforms of 29 Colonial Regiments are shown in this chromolith supplement entitled 'Types of Our Empires Defenders' – one of a series issued by *The Boy's Own Paper* from 1880 onwards.

British horse artillery comes under sniper attack as General Redvers Buller makes the final crossing of the River Tugela during the Boer War.

garrison. While the British officers and men were in church that Sunday, the native regiments released the 85 from gaol, set fire to European bungalows and officers, and attacked and killed many officers and their families. Before British troops could be summoned, the mutineers had set off on the road to the south.

The mutineers reached Delhi the following day, and were promptly joined by the sepoy garrison and the city mob. Most of the resident British army officers and civilians, with their families, were hunted down and murdered that day. A small group of army officers and men, led by Lieutenant George Willoughby, blew up the city ammunition store, killing several of themselves and hundreds of attacking sepoys. Of the survivors four officers were awarded the Victoria Cross.

That afternoon two young Eurasian telegraph signallers tapped out a message to Ambala saying 'the sepoys have come in from Meerut' and ending 'we must shut up.' In the palace the eighty-year-old King of Delhi, Bahadur Shah II, reluctantly allowed himself to be proclaimed Emperor of Hindustan. For a few weeks the sepoys and their supporters considered themselves to be victorious, for there was no sign of the British.

The news of the fall of Delhi spread like a prairie fire across northern India, and soon the entire Bengal army and countryside from Delhi to Calcutta had taken up arms against the British.

At Ambala, a British force was assembled consisting of the 9th (Queen's Royal) Lancers, the 75th Foot (the Gordon Highlanders), the Royal Horse Artillery, and several Native Regiments – of which one mutinied and went to Delhi, and one had to be disarmed.

The Commander-in-Chief, 69-year-old General Sir George Anson, a veteran of Waterloo who had seen no action since, was noted for his prejudice against the Company Army. He never saw an Indian soldier, he said, 'without turning away in disgust at his unsoldierlike appearance.' He had heard for himself from sepoys their strong objections to the use of greased cartridges, but he refused to believe that they were about to mutiny.

As soon as news of the Delhi uprising reached him, he organised a counter-blow as quickly as possible, personally leading to a column of troops out of Ambala on the road to the capital.

He had not gone far before he was struck down by cholera, an enemy more lethal to the British troops than the mutineers' muskets. His successor, 57-year-old General Sir Henry Barnard, also died of cholera a few weeks later, and was succeeded by General Thomas Reed. He, too, fell ill and was in turn succeeded by General Archdale Wilson.

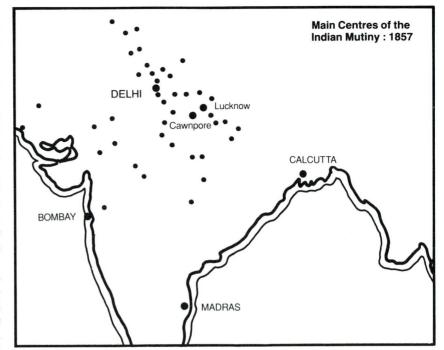

Main Centres of the Indian Mutiny : 1857

DELHI
Lucknow
Cawnpore
CALCUTTA
BOMBAY
MADRAS

Before he succumbed General Barnard had defeated a strong force of some 30,000 mutineers with 30 guns at Badli-ki-Serai a few miles from Delhi. The triumphant British force then occupied a strong tactical position on the Ridge overlooking the north walls of the city, clearly expecting to recapture it in a matter of days. Lieutenant Roberts arrived there on 28 June: 'scarcely able to believe my good fortune. I was actually in Delhi and the city was still in the possession of the mutineers.' Two weeks later he received his first wound – then an essential item in an officer's CV.

THE SIEGE OF DELHI

But weeks went by while the Force waited for reinforcements and endured a dreadful camp. 'We are altogether in a false position here,' wrote General Archdale Wilson, in a letter to his wife. 'We want 25,000 to 30,000 men to take such a strong position as Delhi.' Not all his officers agreed. 'It is as clear as noonday,' wrote the Chief Engineer of the Force, 'that our sole chance of taking Delhi is by an assault which grows more difficult with every day's delay.'

Keeping the rebels at bay cost many lives. Particularly heavy losses were suffered by the Gurkhas who were given the task of defending a mansion known as Hindu Rao's house, on the right of the British lines, which was repeatedly attacked. Their commander, Major Charles Reid, entered in his diary:

The Pandies, as they are called, made their *twenty-first* attack on my position yesterday. They turned out of the city at half-past seven in the morning and kept us at it until dark. Not a thing had we to eat, and we all

Only Bengal of the East India Company's three 'Presidencies' was involved in the Great Mutiny (or 'Sepoy Revolt') and of the Bengal Army's 150,000 sepoys only about 25% took part in the fighting.

facing page
Indian sepoys at rifle practice

Sir John Lawrence

Chief Commissioner of the recently annexed Punjab when news of the mutiny came from Delhi, was that hero much admired by Victorian writers and their readers, the resolute and ruthless Sir John Lawrence, one of whose deputies was Lieutenant-Colonel John Nicholson.

Within days they had occupied every commanding position, secured every arsenal and treasury, disarmed every suspect regiment, rounded up and dealt with deserting sepoys, and had leaders of mutiny shot or blown from guns.

To strike promptly at mutinous units wherever they happened to be and to prevent them from joining forces, Nicholson proposed a Movable Column (a lightly-equipped but well-armed and highly trained cavalry corps) and a strong levy of Multani horsemen to be commanded by himself. Lawrence agreed, and eventually Nicholson was commander of both these forces.

So successful was Lawrence in preventing an uprising in the Punjab that by August he was able to send a strong force with the Movable Column and John Nicholson (now a Brigadier-General) to the support of the Force besieging Delhi. His resolute actions so impressed the people of the area that men poured in to enlist with the British, and eventually 34,000 new troops were raised.

As a result, he was able to send to Delhi three regiments of Punjabi cavalry, seven battalions of Punjabi infantry, a siege train and a Punjabi corps of sappers and miners. Convinced of the paramount importance of retaking Delhi, he even denuded the province of European troops, sending to Delhi a cavalry regiment, six battalions of infantry and a large artillery force.

Not all British officers appreciated John Lawrence's ruthlessness. Some Colonels of Indian regiments, firmly believing in the total loyalty of their sepoys, felt themselves dishonoured when the order came to disarm, and many of them threw their swords on the piles of arms. At least one burst into tears, and another committed suicide rather than see his beloved regiment disgraced.

Born in 1811, John Lawrence was educated at Haileybury, then the college for cadets in the East India Company services. He was posted to the Bengal civil service, and rose slowly to be a commissioner in the North Western province at the time of the Sikh Wars. A masterful and, indeed, autocratic ruler of his province (and later of India as Viceroy from 1864 to 1869), John Lawrence had some endearing characteristics, one of which was a lack of interest in things of value, that almost amounted to carelessness.

Typical was the way he nearly lost the famous Koh-i-noor diamond which now graces the imperial crown of England. At the end of the second Sikh War the crown jewels of the late Maharajah Ranjit Singh were handed over to the East India Company. These included the great Koh-i-noor diamond, which was wrapped in cloth inside a little box and handed over to John Lawrence for safe keeping.

Weeks later the Governor General wrote to Henry Lawrence, his brother and then Resident at Lahore, saying that Queen Victoria wanted it at once. Henry mentioned this to his brother:

'Well, send for it at once,' said John.

'But *you* have it,' said Henry.

'Ah yes,' said John, 'I'd forgotten.'

Later he sent for his personal servant and asked him if he'd found a small box which he'd put in his waistcoat pocket some weeks ago. When his servant said he'd found the box and put it in one of his master's trunks, Lawrence ordered him to bring it and let him see what was inside. The servant opened the little box and unfolded the cloth.

'There's nothing here, sahib,' he said, 'but a bit of glass.'

After the capture of Delhi, the victors exacted a terrible retribution from its defenders and citizens. Officers and men, British and native, went from house to house collecting vast quantities of plunder, and hundreds of sepoys and suspects were shot or hanged. 'Lots of the blackguards are hanged every morning', wrote one winner of the VC, 'the more the merrier.'

Sir John Lawrence was one of the few who condemned this wholesale vengeance. He wrote to the Commander in Delhi: 'I believe we shall be lastingly, and, indeed, justly abused for the way in which we have despoiled all classes without distinction.' Unfortunately his voice went unheard.

came home dead beat. I never felt so completely done up before. The sun was something fearful . . .

Over a hundred of his Gurkhas were lost in a fortnight, and Major Reid began to wonder whether there would be 'any of them left for the attack.'

'Come and join us, Gurkhas!' the attacking mutineers would shout, 'We won't fire on *you*!' 'We are coming,' the Gurkhas would reply, getting out their kukris. The Gurkhas were the only native troops, apart from the Sikhs, who were popular with the British troops. Their bravery and their cheerfulness was greatly admired, as Major Reid notes:

They called one another 'brothers'. They shared their grog with each other and smoked their pipes together. Often were the [60th] Rifles seen carrying a wounded Gurkha off the field and vice versa. My men used to speak of them as 'Our Riffles', and the men of the 60th, when mentioning the Gurkhas, said. 'Them Gurkhees of ours.'

The Sikhs were also liked and admired by British troops, as Richard Barter noted:

They were always together, and seemingly in close and amusing conversation which must have been curious as both were almost totally ignorant of each other's lingo . . . 'Liquor' seemed to go a long way.

Conditions in the camp on the Ridge were appalling. 'I heard several men say,' wrote Captain Barter, 'that we should never take the city and that it was only a question of time before we should all perish.' As many men were being killed by cholera, dysentery, heatstroke and sheer exhaustion as by the 'Pandies'. The chaplain who visited the fourteen hospitals noted that they were crowded to the doors and was saddened to see:

. . . nearly every man . . . languishing from that terrible disease cholera. It required strong nerves to withstand the sickening sights of these infirmaries. The patients constantly retching . . . The flies, almost as innumerable as the sand on the seashore, alighted on your face and head, and crawled down your back, through the openings of the shirt collar and occasionally flew even into your throat.

Below the camp the dead bodies of mutineers lay rotting in the heat. On one of his piquets an officer noted 'about fifteen dead Pandies within ten yards in a state of decay and the stench was quite overpowering, inhaling it as we did for 38 hours.' Small wonder that some soliders grew desperate and dashed at the enemy, getting killed on purpose to be rid of such an existence as soon as possible. Somehow the besiegers kept up a constant fire on the mutineers, which did little or no real damage, while the enemy had plenty of guns which easily out-matched the British artillery in accuracy and rapidity of fire. 'The siege is on their part, not on ours,' said Major Reid, and if the British were not going to be starved or worn out, they had to decide quickly to attack and take the city.

'Nikalseyn': Hero of Delhi

WHEN BRIGADIER-GENERAL John Nicholson arrived at Delhi on August 7, his mere presence raised the spirits of the British force encamped on the Ridge, as they waited for their commanders to decide when and how to attack the city. Close behind Nicholson came an army of some 4,000 troops, including his 'Movable Column', the lightly-equipped, fast-moving force which he had employed with such success in the North-West to disarm mutinous sepoy regiments and restore British control and prestige. 'Nicholson has come on ahead and is a host in himself,' said Major William Hodson of Hodson's Horse. The camp is all alive at the notion of something decisive taking place soon.'

John Nicholson was thirty-four years old, the eldest of five sons of an Irish doctor. At the age of fifteen he was given a cadetship in the Bengal Infantry by an uncle who was a Director of the East India Company. He arrived in India in 1839, just in time to serve as an infantry officer in the First Afghan War. In the Second Sikh War he fought under Sir Hugh Gough, and later held a number of civil posts in the Punjab, with the task of pacifying the province. His treatment of criminals was severe to a degree; their severed heads would be displayed on his office desk.

His forceful character, his pale, unsmiling, black-bearded face and his reserved and silent manner so impressed the Pathans, Afghans, Multanis and the people of Punjab, that they regarded him as a god, and worshipped him. The corps of Multani horsemen he raised were ready to follow wherever he led, and to the Sikhs he was their revered 'Nikalseyn'. But he was unmoved by such adulation, for he disliked India

The siege train advances on Delhi

83

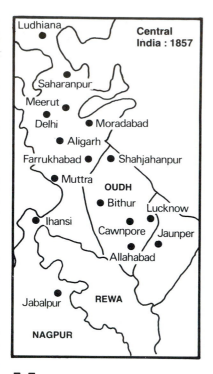

Central India : 1857

Ludhiana
Saharanpur
Meerut
Delhi
Moradabad
Aligarh
Farrukhabad
Shahjahanpur
Muttra
OUDH
Bithur
Lucknow
Ihansi
Cawnpore
Jaunper
Allahabad
Jabalpur
REWA
NAGPUR

Massacre at Cawnpore

'All is well at Cawnpore,' reported the Divisional Commander, Major-General Sir Hugh Wheeler, a few days after the fall of Delhi. Cawnpore, a prosperous city of some 60,000 people, was the headquarters of the military command of Oudh, the most disaffected province in British India. Wheeler, who had spent half a century in India, which he loved, and had married an Indian woman, trusted his sepoys absolutely. He spoke their language as well as they did, and he simply could not believe that they would mutiny. So he was not worried that they outnumbered the British troops by ten to one, and he echoed the opinion of the English lady who said that Cawnpore was 'quiet and the regiments staunch'.

On 6 June Wheeler was informed that his garrison was about to be attacked. All he had for the defence of Cawnpore was about 300 British officers and men, many of them sick, and a few loyal Indian troops. This tiny force was encumbered with about 500 non-combatants, most of them women and children. Thinking it safer than the city or the barracks, he moved them all into a small entrenchment outside the city and about a mile from the river Ganges. This consisted of a few half-finished barrack huts surrounded by a low earth rampart,

also unfinished. It was inadequately provisioned, and although there were about ten loaded muskets for every man who could use one, there were only a few light guns, all of them in dangerous positions.

The siege lasted three weeks. Surrounded and constantly under fire from 3,000 well-trained and well-armed sepoys, the defenders endured agonies from the heat – the sun was at its hottest – and from hunger and thirst. Their only diet was a daily ration of a few ounces of flour and lentils. Many were killed or suffered horrifying wounds from shot and shell, and by the end of the siege 250 were dead.

When the ammunition and food and water were nearly exhausted, General Wheeler was forced to agree with the leader of the rebels, Dondhu Pant (known as the Nana Sahib) to surrender on the promise of a safe passage of all the survivors down the Ganges to Allahabad. As they were embarking, they were raked by musket and gunfire, and 'cavalry waded into the river with drawn swords and cut down those who were still alive, while infantry boarded the boats to loot'. All the remaining men were cut down or shot, including General Wheeler.

The few surviving women and children were kept captive, but when the Nana Sahib was told that General Havelock was on his way to Cawnpore with a strong army, they were all murdered and their bodies thrown down a well. The news of this massacre horrified the world, and the Queen expressed what her people felt when she wrote: 'The horrors committed on the . . . women and children are unknown in these ages, and make one's blood run cold. Altogether, the whole is so much more distressing than the Crimea – where there was glory and honourable warfare . . .'

The Queen and her husband, however, did not share the widespread demand for indiscriminate and wholesale vengeance: 'The details of the atrocious crimes committed by the sepoys in India,' wrote the Prince Consort, 'are most harrowing . . . the difficulty will be to bring the punishment home to the real offenders and it is to be expected that many an innocent person will suffer . . .'

Heroes for Victoria were not only her successful soldiers and sailors, and their commanders, but all those who suffered in the course of doing their duty, or who were caught up in the aftermath of powerful events over which they had little or no control.

and Indians, and above all he hated sepoys 'with a hatred no words could describe'. His response to the news of the Mutiny was ferocious and implacable.

'Let us propose a Bill,' he wrote to the Civil Commissioner at Peshawar, 'for the flaying alive, impalement, or burning of the murderers of the women and children at Delhi. The idea of simply hanging . . . is maddening.' And he issued an order that no Indian should pass a white man riding, without dismounting and salaaming.

Happy as were the troops encamped on the Ridge to see Nicholson arrive, his seniors – though they had called for him – were less content. He was so clearly in command that already the troops called him 'The General'. The self-assurance, the overbearing manner, the air of silent disapproval, perhaps – above all – the youth of this obviously able East India Company Army officer, did not endear him to the elderly generals of the Queen's Army. While they were not sure what to do next, Nicholson made it painfully clear that he knew exactly what needed to be done and how to do it.

'Soon he was visiting all our piquets,' an officer wrote in his diary, 'examining everything, and making the most searching enquiries about their strength . . .' Everywhere he went the troops gave him the salute due to a Commanding Officer, for to them he was 'The General.' In fact, he had no official status, but, as the same officer noted, 'He was a man cast in a giant mould . . . There was something of immense strength, talent and resolution . . . and a power of ruling men on high occasions which no one could escape noticing.'

Not long after the arrival of the Movable Column, Nicholson marched it out to attack a strong force of mutineers threatening to capture the British siege-train on its way to Delhi. At Najafgarh, some fifteen miles from the city, he gave the time-honoured order 'Line advance!' and led his men into a fierce hand-to-hand battle with the rebels, which ended with the killing of hundreds of sepoys and putting the rest to flight. This was a small victory but it saved the siege-train and put new heart into the tired troops waiting to mount the assault on Delhi itself.

Early in September the siege-train arrived: huge guns drawn by elephants were followed by long lines of carts containing 'enough ammunition to grind Delhi to powder.' Even so, the Commander of the Field Force, the elderly and cautious General Archdale Wilson, hesitated to attack at once. 'Delhi must be taken,' declared Nicholson to Lieutenant (later Field-Marshal Lord) Roberts, '. . . and if Wilson hesitates longer I intend to propose at today's meeting [to decide whether to assault at once or not] that he should be superseded.' Roberts was 'greatly startled, and ventured to remark' that if that course of action were followed Nicholson would become the senior officer with the Force. 'I have not overlooked that fact,' replied Nicholson.

However, an immediate assault was agreed, and by 12 September heavy guns were pounding the northern walls and bastions of the city. After three days of bombardment Nicholson led the column which entered through a breach in the Kashmir Gate bastion. Just before the assault, Captain Charles Ewart of the 2nd Bengal Fusiliers wrote a letter to his mother which gives a vivid picture of what was expected of a Victorian army officer:

I believe we are to escalade. You know what that will be – rush up a ladder with men trying to push you down, bayonet and shoot you from above. But you must wave your sword and think it capital fun, bring your men up as fast as you can and jump down on top of men ready with fixed bayonets to receive you. All this is not very pleasant to think coolly of, but when the moment comes excitement and the knowledge that your men are looking to you to lead them on and bring them up with a cheer makes you feel as happy as possible . . . It will be fearfully exciting work. I hope it won't make me swear . . .

Captain (later Lt Gen) Richard Barter of the 75th Highlanders recalled the night before the assault:

There was not much sleep that night in our camp . . . Each of us looked carefully to the loading of our pistols, the filling of our flasks and getting as good protection as possible for our heads which would be exposed so much in going up the ladders. I wound two turbans round my old forage cap with my last letter from the hills in the top . . .

Last orders read to all ranks a little after midnight included: any officer or man who might be wounded was to be left where he fell, as there were no men to spare to help him; no plundering – all prizes taken to be put into a common stock for fair division; no prisoners to be taken; and care taken not to injure any women or children.

Officers swore on their honour and their swords to abide by these orders, and the men all promised to follow their example.

At 3am on 14 September the guns ceased firing and the signal for the attack was given, as Captain Barter recorded:

We had been watching anxiously for it, and now in columns of fours we rushed at the double through a high archway into a garden of roses and through this to the foot of the glacis. The dark forms of the 60th Rifles [The King's Royal Rifle Corps] seemed to spring out of the earth as they lined the bank at the side of the garden, keeping up a galling fire on the walls and breach . . . Day had broken and the sun was showing like a large red ball in the east as, passing through the line of the 60th who cheered us loudly, we emerged on the glacis and there, straight before us, was the breach. It was a huge gap in the wall, full of men whose heads showed just over the edges of it. Along the walls they swarmed as thick as bees, the sun shining full on the white turbans and the black faces, sparkling brightly on their swords and bayonets. Our men cheered madly as they rushed on. The enemy, whose fire had slackened when ours ceased, at first seemed perfectly taken aback by our sudden appearance, but recovering from their surprise they now began firing again in earnest. Round shot came screaming from the guns far on our right, while grape and shell whistled from those nearer, and the walls seemed one line of fire all along our front. Bullets whipped through the air and tore up the ground about our feet and men fell fast . . . Three times the ladder parties were swept away, and three times the ladders were snatched from the shoulders of the dead and wounded.

Meanwhile the massive Kashmir Gate was blown in by a party of Royal Engineers, most of whom were shot dead while attempting to place the charge. Colonel (later Field Marshal Sir Colin) Campbell led a column of the 52nd Foot through the shattered gate. Inside the city Nicholson was leading an attack down a narrow lane towards the Lahore Gate, through which he planned to let in another British column. Many of his officers were already killed or wounded, but heedless of the guns and sharpshooters all around, he charged on, calling his men to follow him. A sepoy on a roof nearby took careful aim . . . Nicholson fell, shot in the back.

Delhi was taken, but 'Nikalseyn' was dead. Without him, said John Lawrence, in tears, the city might not have fallen, and the back of the Mutiny might not have been broken. The price seemed too high. At Nicholson's funeral, the men of his Multani Horse, for whom tears were unmanly, 'sobbed and wept as if their very hearts were breaking . . . For him they had left their Frontier homes, for him they had left their beloved hills to come down to the detested plains.'

Once the Kashmir Gate had been captured, Delhi fell to the British – a turning-point in the Mutiny

Sir Henry Havelock

IN COMMAND of the column advancing from Allahabad, to deal with Nana Sahib and his mutineers at Cawnpore, was Brigadier-General Sir Henry Havelock. Perhaps the ablest commander then in India, his name became a symbol of heroism and sacrifice for countless Victorian children. His official instructions were to 'take prompt measures for dispersing and utterly destroying all mutineers and insurgents' at Allahabad, Lucknow and Cawnpore. But by the time he arrived at Allahabad, Colonel (later Brigadier-General) James Neill had already bombarded and retaken the town, disarmed the mutineers and restored order with great speed and severity.

Havelock therefore prepared to move on to Cawnpore. Sometimes unkindly described in Indian society as 'fussy and tiresome,' and 'an old fossil dug up', he was sixty-two years old when he arrived in India after a successful campaign in Persia with General Sir James Outram. The son of a Sunderland shipbuilder, whose business had failed, Havelock obtained a commission in the army and elected to serve in India, where life was easier for impecunious officers.

Ambitious and hard-working, he was what is now called a 'born-again Christian' (like Henry Lawrence, Outram, Neill and many other officers of his day), and he believed it was 'his solemn Christian duty' to hold prayer meetings and Bible classes for his troops – a practice which must have confirmed the suspicions of sepoys who believed the Raj was planning to force them to become Christian. As a soldier he had shown great coolness and reliability, but he had frequently been passed over by 'sots and fools'. Now his moment had come.

Havelock's force was unimpressive, consisting of about a thousand men of the 64th Foot, the 84th Foot, the 78th Highlanders, the Madras Fusiliers, a detachment of Sikhs, about 20 cavalry, and six guns. Their progress was slow, for many of the men were untrained and, not having received hot-weather uniforms, were wearing their heavy woollen tunics. After exhausting marches by day and night the column came upon a large force of mutineers near Fatehpur. Havelock's despatch after the battle told the story:

[The enemy] 'insolently pushed forward two guns, and a force of infantry and cavalry cannonaded our front, and threatened our flank . . . I estimate his number at 3,500, with twelve brass and iron guns . . . I might say that in ten minutes the action was decided, for in that short space of time the spirit of the enemy was entirely subdued. The rifle fire, reaching them at an unexpected distance, filled them with dismay; and when Captain Maude was enabled to push his guns through flanking swamps, to point blank range, his surprisingly accurate fire destroyed their little remaining confidence.

There were few casualties. Havelock told his wife that his lifelong prayer had been answered:

I have lived to command in a successful action . . . I captured in four hours eleven guns and scattered the enemy's whole force to the winds . . . but away with vain glory! Thanks to Almighty God who gave me the victory . . . I now march to retake Cawnpore.

Hodson of Hodson's Horse

Head of Intelligence of the British force outside Delhi was Major William Hodson, of Hodson's Horse. A superb linguist and master of all the idioms, phrases and accents of the districts where he had campaigned, Hudson maintained a network of spies in the city who kept him fully informed of every move the mutineers made. What he learned led him to press for an immediate assault. The rebels, he claimed, were 'perfectly ignorant of any intention of so bold a stroke . . . The surprise would have done everything.' But he was told it was 'a mad idea'.

'As a cavalry officer he was perfection,' was Hugh Gough's opinion of William Hodson, founder and leader of the irregular regiment of cavalry bearing his name. The son of an archdeacon, Hodson was born in 1821 and educated at Rugby under Thomas Arnold and at Trinity College, Cambridge. He became an officer in the Militia, but transferred to the army of the East India Company in time to fight at the battle of Mudki in the first Sikh War ('I enjoyed it all', he said).

He was appointed Adjutant and then Commander of the Corps of Guides, another irregular fighting force raised on the North-West Frontier, but lost his command when he was convicted, but later cleared, of misappropriating regimental funds and of cruelty to natives. When the Mutiny started he was asked to form a new corps of irregular cavalry, and Hodson's Horse rapidly won fame as a brilliant fighting unit. His troopers wore scarlet turbans, scarlet sashes and dust-coloured tunics. His brother officers had vivid recollections of Hodson: 'It was beautiful to see him [wrote one of them] riding a little in front and in the centre of his troopers, and to see how quietly he controlled their eagerness to press on by motioning them back, first on the right, then on the left, by a mere wave of the hand . . . I fancy I see him now [recalled another] laughing, parrying most fearful blows, as calmly as if he were brushing off flies, all the time calling out "Why, try again!" . . . "Do you call yourself a swordsman?" etc.'

After the capture of Delhi, Hodson secured General Wilson's approval to find, capture or kill the old King of Delhi, Bahadur Shah, who had given his name and support to the mutineers. Taking fifty of his horsemen he rode out to Humayun's tomb, about six miles from the city, where the emperor had taken refuge with his family and court. On the promise that his life should be spared, Bahadur Shah surrendered and was led back to captivity in his palace of the Red Fort in Delhi.

Next day, Hodson returned to Humayun's tomb with one hundred troopers, and demanded the surrender of the king's three sons, who were surrounded by several thousand armed retainers. They gave themselves up without resistance and Hodson sent them off towards the city, under armed guard. Having stayed to ensure that the retainers gave up all their arms, Hodson galloped after his prisoners, and found them surrounded by a resentful mob.

Supported by his troopers, Hodson ordered the three princes to dismount and strip. He then seized a carbine and himself shot each of them. Their bodies were then displayed in a Delhi bazaar, for all to see 'the fate of those who murdered British women and children'. His action was much criticised at the time, and according to Lord Roberts 'cast a blot on his reputation'.

Some six months later, at Lucknow, Hodson accompanied Colonel (later Field Marshal Lord) Robert Napier in the storming of one of the city palaces occupied by mutineers. As he charged into a room, sword in hand, shouting 'Come on!', he was shot in the chest and killed.

The little army tramped grimly on under the burning sun, hoping to rescue the women and children they had heard were held captive by the Nana Sahib. A few miles from the city he waited for them with 5,000 men and eight guns posted in a strong position. Havelock and his men were soon under fire from well-protected guns. He vividly desribed the course of the battle, and its outcome, in his official dispatch:

My artillery cattle, wearied by the length of the march, could not bring up the guns to my assistance, and [his troops], formed in line, were exposed to heavy fire from the 24-pounder on the road.

I was resolved that this state of things could not last; so calling upon my men, who were lying down in line, to leap on their feet, I directed another steady advance. ['The longer you look at it, men,' he said, 'the less you will like it. Rise up! The brigade will advance!'] It was irresistible. The enemy sent round shot into our ranks until we were within three hundred yards, and then poured in grape with such precision as I have seldom witnessed. But the 64th, led by Major Sterling and my aide-de-camp [his son Henry Marsham Havelock], who had placed himself in their front were not to be denied. Their rear showed the ground strewed with wounded; but on they steadily and silently came, then with a cheer charged and captured the unwieldy trophy of their valour. The enemy lost all heart, and after a hurried fire of musketry gave way in total rout. Four of my guns came up, and completed their discomfiture by a heavy cannonade . . . and it was evident that Cawnpore was once more in our possession.

It was the first real battle of the mutiny and the first real British victory over the mutineers. But sadly it came just one day too late to save the captive women and children in Cawnpore.

The campaign medal struck
for the Indian Mutiny

The Siege of Lucknow

THE SIEGE of the Residency at Lucknow lasted in all four and a half months, from 30 June 1857 until 17 November. On 25 September, Sir Henry Havelock and Sir James Outram fought their way in and reinforced the garrison, but the siege was then resumed until Sir Colin Campbell arrived with a stronger force six weeks later. The garrison and surviving civilians were evacuated at that time and the Residency and the city were abandoned to the mutineers. Not until March 1958 was Lucknow finally recaptured by Campbell in the course of his reconquest of Oudh.

Statue of Sir James Outram
on the Thames Embankment

Sir Henry Lawrence

A week before the mutiny at Meerut the sepoys of the 7th Oudh Irregulars at Lucknow had refused to bite their greased cartridges and threatened to murder their officers. They were promptly disarmed. The Chief Commissioner of Oudh, Brigadier General Sir Henry Lawrence, elder brother of Sir John, realised that the sepoy mutiny that he had long foretold was about to start, and he began to prepare for the siege he knew would come.

There was only one British regiment in Lucknow, the 32nd Foot, and part of these he brought into the area of the Residency and part were stationed north of the city to keep watch on the sepoy lines. The Residency itself was fortified, walls were strengthened, windows blocked up, gun emplacements built, and provisions and ammunition brought in. Sir Henry made it clear that he did not expect any immediate trouble, but was merely taking sensible precautions.

Born in Ceylon in 1806, Henry Lawrence had spent nearly all his life in India. After being educated at Addiscombe College, the school for cadets of the East India Company, he was commissioned in the Bengal Artillery. Serious and hard-working, he set himself to learn Indian languages and study administration. His efforts were rewarded when he was appointed Resident in Lahore after the annexation of the Punjab, and was knighted.

A few months before the Mutiny he was appointed to Oudh by the new Governor General, Lord Canning.

Like Havelock, Nicholson and others, he was a convinced Christian, but unlike some of his fellow commanders his religious beliefs seem to have led him to be better disposed towards the people he administered, although he certainly had no sympathy with the mutineers.

When Lawrence arrived in Oudh the province was seething with discontent. Its annexation by the British and the deposition of the king, corrupt and tyrannical as he had been, were bitterly resented – particularly as the corruption continued and the new British officials were overbearing and tactless to a degree. Oudh had been 'the great nursery of sepoys' and in the days of the kingdom they had been a privileged class. Annexation put an end to all that, and the affair of the greased cartridges lowered the prestige of the sepoy. 'I used to be a great man when I went home,' complained an Oudh sepoy, 'The rest of the village rose when I approached. Now the lowest puff their pipes in my face.'

So Sir Henry Lawrence was not surprised when one of his staff warned him on 30 May about a report that the firing of the nine o'clock gun that night was to be the signal for a general mutiny. Not surprised, but unconvinced, for when a long silence followed the gun that evening Sir Henry leaned across the dinner table and said to his colleagues with a smile, 'Your friends are late'. Almost at once shouting and musket shots could be heard in the nearby sepoy lines. The great mutiny had come to Lucknow.

There followed serious rioting, killing and looting in the city, and uprisings all over Oudh. On 12 June Lawrence reported:

'Every outpost I fear has fallen, and we daily expect to be besieged by the confederated mutineers and their allies.'

At the end of the month he led out a small force to meet the approaching mutineers at Chinhat, and was heavily defeated. Lawrence wrote to General Havelock:

'The enemy has followed us up, and . . . unless we are relieved quickly, say in fifteen or twenty days, we shall hardly be able to maintain our position.'

The remaining troops, women and children were then withdrawn into the Residency. The siege of Lucknow had begun.

Two days later a shell burst into Sir Henry Lawrence's room in the Residency, mortally wounding him; forty-eight hours later he was dead.

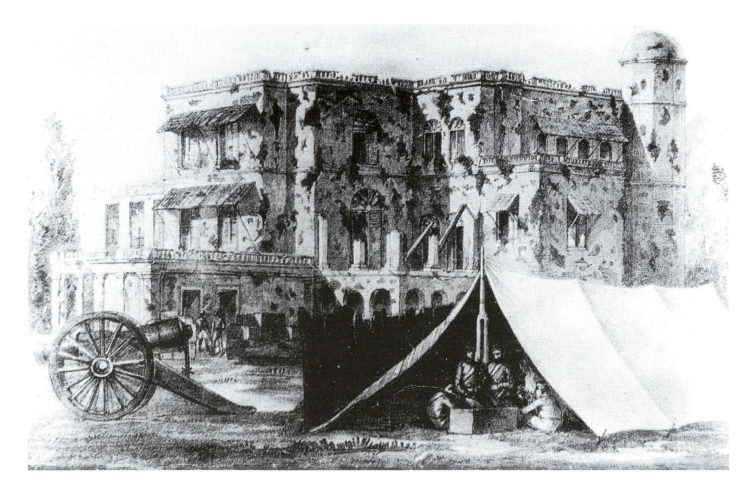

The Residency at Lucknow – scene of one of the most bitterly contested sieges in the whole of the Indian Mutiny

In a sense all, or almost all, of the besieged at Lucknow could be called Heroes for Victoria. From the first day they were subjected to an intermittent but terrifying bombardment of cannon fire and musketry, and constant sniping made it death to linger in any exposed position. Some days there would be concerted attacks when the defenders were faced with 'a sea of heads and glittering weapons,' showers of grapeshot and musket balls, while trumpeting elephants hauled big guns into position. All these assaults were driven off at great cost, but the men in the outposts lived in fear of being over-run. A captain of the 25th Native Infantry, who had fortified his house in advance wrote of this dread;

We well knew what we had to expect if we were defeated, and therefore each individual fought for his very life. Each loophole displayed a steady flash of musketry, as defeat would have been certain death to every soul in the garrison . . . During this time even the poor wounded men ran out of the hospital, and those who had wounds in their legs threw away their crutches and deliberately knelt down and fired as fast as they could; others, who could do little else, loaded the muskets.

Though some of the European women in Lucknow felt 'utterly unable to cope without their husbands and servants', most rose to the situation, carrying out unaccustomed nursing duties in the Banqueting-Hall-turned-hospital, improvising uniforms for soldiers who had lost theirs (one officer 'wore a shirt made out of a floor cloth'), keeping records of rations and casualties, collecting scarce firewood, organising ever-welcome cups of tea (or brandy!) for men on duty, and loading their muskets.

Disease killed or weakened almost as many as the enemy's guns. Cholera, dysentery and small-pox took their daily toll, and many suffered from boils, rashes, scurvy, and the effects of heat, poor diet and nervous strain. In the make-shift hospital the wounded and sick lay in rows on beds, sofas, mattresses, or cloaks, or just on the floor, and every day new casualties were brought in to lie 'covered with blood and often with vermin . . . Everywhere cries of agony were heard, piteous exclamations for water or assistance.' One of the wounded was Dr Brydon, the only survivor of the retreat from Kabul in 1842.

When General Havelock's relieving column was forced to halt on the road to Lucknow, he sent a message to Colonel John Inglis, who had taken over command on the death of Sir Henry Lawrence: 'When further defence becomes impossible, do not negotiate or capitulate. Cut your way out to Cawnpore.' To this Inglis replied with an outline of the desperate situation at Lucknow:

We have only a small force . . . it is quite impossible, with my weak and shattered force, that I can leave my defences . . . I have upwards of 120 sick and wounded, and at least 220 women and 230 children, and no carriage of any description.

If you hope to save this force, no time must be lost in pushing forward. We are daily being attacked by the enemy, who are within a few yards of our defences . . .

My strength now in Europeans is 350, and about 300 natives, and the men are dreadfully harassed; and, owing to part of the Residency having been brought down by round shot, many are without shelter. Our native force . . . are naturally losing confidence, and if they leave us I do not see how the defences are to be manned.

THE RELIEF OF LUCKNOW

General Havelock pushed on to relieve Lucknow, having retaken Cawnpore, but his small force was so weakened by cholera and casualties that he had to retreat and wait for reinforcements. At that moment he learned that he had been superseded in his command by Major-General Sir James Outram (1803-1863), who was senior to him. Outram, however, announced that he would 'cheerfully waive his rank' in favour of Havelock, so that 'to him should accrue the honour' of relieving Lucknow.

Not surprisingly, this arrangement did not work very well. Reinforcements arriving with Outram increased the relieving force to some 3,000 men, 2,000 of them British infantry. These included the 6th Fusiliers and the 90th Light Infantry.

In the final attack the two generals placed themselves at the head of the column that fought its way, yard by yard, into the besieged Residency. As they advanced through the narrow streets, they met volley after volley from the loop-holed houses, and General Neill was killed by a shot in the head. Havelock recalled the scene:

At length we found ourselves at the gates of the Residency, and entered in the dark in triumph. Then came three cheers for the leaders, and the joy of the half-famished garrison, who, however, contrived to regale us, not only with beef cutlets, but with mock-turtle soup and champagne.

But Outram, one officer noted, 'did not seem to be very pleased . . . and said that losses had been very severe; he feared 800 killed.' In fact, 500 seems to have been nearer the mark, apart from all the earlier losses. So he may not have been amused when a lady asked him: 'Is Queen Victoria still alive?'

The besiegers now became the beseiged, for the force that fought its way in under Havelock and Outram was much too weakened by death and disease to fight its way out again. The siege of Lucknow continued for another six weeks.

Its second relief was achieved in November by Sir Colin Campbell, recently appointed Commander-in-Chief, who brought fresh troops with him, including his famous Highlanders (the 93rd) and a Naval Brigade with naval guns. When Sir Colin rode down the lines to inspect his army before the attack most of the men he saw were weary, and wore patched and torn uniforms. There were, however, some exceptions. The 9th Lancers were resplendent in their blue uniforms and white turbans, as were the Sikh cavalry with their shining sabre and silver-mounted pistols. Also on parade were Sir Colin Campbell's beloved 93rd in full Highland costume, with feather bonnets, waving plumes and many a Crimean medal proudly worn. Sir Colin addressed his men in a strong Scots accent:

When we make an attack you must come to close quarters as quickly as possible. Keep well together and use the bayonet . . . You are my lads. I rely on you to do the work!

The Naval Brigade consisted of 250 sailors and marines from HMS *Shannon*, under the command of Captain William Peel. They sat astride their ships' guns and sported a strange assortment of naval uniforms. It was the task of Peel's guns to breach or batter down buildings as, once again, the attackers had to fight their way from street to street. 'Captain Peel,' reported Campbell, 'behaved very much as if he had been laying the *Shannon* alongside an enemy's frigate.' The losses on both sides were enormous: the bodies 'were literally in heaps,' wrote Lieutenant Roberts, 'some dead, but most wounded and unable to get up from the crush.' When Sir Colin and his force had secured a safe escape for the women and children, the sick and wounded, he abandoned the city for the time being.

His priority now was to quell the uprisings and restore the Queen's Peace throughout Northern and Central India. The forces at his disposal were daily increasing, thanks to the arrival of reinforcements from Britain and the recall of troops from Burma, Ceylon, Persia, and from the force on its way to China. It needs to be remembered, too, that throughout the Mutiny the British had the Sikhs and the Gurkhas fighting on their side, as well as the sepoys of the Company's army who remained loyal. Without this 'native' support, they might have been overwhelmed before reinforcements could reach India.

Once fresh troops began to arrive, the end was inevitable. Cawnpore was recaptured in

Listening for miners in a cellar of the Residency

How Thomas Kavanagh won his VC

Much of the fighting at Lucknow took place underground. The mutineers dug mines under the Residency, and in turn the defenders would tunnel through into enemy mines to kill or capture the miners.

Thomas Kavanagh, a debt-laden Irish government clerk, aged 36, with fourteen children, seeing the siege as his great opportunity for life, took on the dangerous, unpleasant and much-disliked duty of counter-mining. He would sit for hours in the tunnels, pistol in hand, listening for the sound of picks and spades. As soon as there was an earth collapse and a hole appeared he would dash through, firing at the enemy miners.

Hearing that Sir Colin Campbell, the new Commander-in-Chief, was leading a force to relieve Lucknow, Kavanagh saw a chance for greater glory. He offered to make his way through enemy lines, disguised as a native, carrying a message to Sir Colin. He could then show him a better route to the Residency than the one followed by Havelock and Outram.

So late on 9 November he and a native spy slipped silently through the lines and the city into the countryside. He was wearing suitable clothes, his fair hair tucked into a turban, his skin darkened with oil and lampblack. After losing their way more than once, crossing a swamp and bluffing a suspicious sepoy patrol, they arrived at an outpost of the relieving force. The message was delivered, and as a result of what Campbell called 'one of the most daring feats ever attempted' he was able to lead his successful flanking attack on Lucknow.

A few days later, during that attack, Kavanagh dashed with eight officers dodging the bullets, across the half-mile space separating Campbell from Havelock and Outram. Five of them were killed. General Havelock, then too ill to run, walked slowly across the space to welcome Campbell. A few days later he died.

Thomas Kavanagh was duly recommended for the Victoria Cross. Being a civilian, he was at first declared ineligible, and instead he was given £2,000 and a civil service post. However, on appeal, he was awarded the VC – and kept the £2,000.

December 1857 and Lucknow in March 1858. In Central India, General Sir Hugh Rose (later Field Marshal Lord Strathnairn, 1801-1895) defeated the only two outstanding leaders produced by the mutineers: Tantia Topi, who had brilliantly defeated the British at Cawnpore, and the Rani of Jhansi.

The Rani raised and led a number of armies against those of Sir Hugh Rose. She rode into battle dressed as a man, 'using her sword with both hands and holding the reins of her horse in her mouth.' She was defeated, first at Kalpi in May and again at Kotah-ki-Serai, near Gwalior, in June, where she was killed. According to one British cavalryman whose squadron was sent in pursuit of the Rani, she was 'a wonderful woman, very brave and determined. It is fortunate for us that her men are not all like her.'

His words expressed the basic reason why the British were able to defeat the Mutiny. The mutineers were well-trained, well-armed, acclimatised, strongly motivated, at fighting against foreign rulers. The one advantage they lacked was effective leadership. In the end they were defeated by the kind of leaders Wellington had called 'the best officers in the world.'

The news of the Indian Mutiny – or Sepoy Revolt, as some called it – caused such horror and outrage to the British people, from the Queen down, that they were compelled to reconsider the way their Indian Empire was governed. By Royal Proclamation, which was read aloud in Allahabad and other major cities of India on 1 November 1858, 'the government of the territories of India, heretofore administered in trust for us by the Honourable East India Company' was transferred to the Crown, and the Company was abolished by Act of Parliament.

By the same Proclamation the Queen appointed Viscount Canning, then the Governor-General, 'our first Viceroy and Governor.' 'The Crown,' wrote Vincent Smith, 'in the person of Queen Victoria, took an interest in Indian affairs more personal than that of most [East India Company] Directors, and she contrived to convey that interest, in some almost magic way, both to her military and civil servants and to the People of India at large.'

A new Cabinet Minister, the Secretary of State for India, became responsible for all the policies of the Government of India, and the officers and men of John Company's army were embodied in the Queen's army. By the time the reorganisation was complete the new Indian Army consisted to 140,000 Indian and 65,000 European troops. During the remainder of the reign, the Indian army fought alongside British regiments in numerous campaigns throughout the Empire, and produced many Indian heroes for Victoria.

The Royal Marines

THE MARINES first won 'immortal honour' at the capture of Gibraltar in 1704, some forty years after the Duke of York (later James II), the Lord High Admiral, first raised a regiment of foot soldiers to accompany the 'Navy Royall and Admiralty'. Britain's maritime strategy in her wars with France and Spain in the 18th century called for a force trained to serve as ships' gunners and sharpshooters as well to fight on shore. By the end of the Seven Years War in 1759, Parliament had approved a permanent establishment of some 20,000 Marines in 135 companies. In the decades to come Marine battalions took part in the conquest of French Canada, the capture of Manila in the Philippines, Pondicherry in India, Havana in Cuba, and Belle Isle off the coast of Brittany. Marines sailed with Captain Cook on each of his voyages of discovery. Marines landed in Sidney Cove with Captain Arthur Phillip RN at the founding of Australia. Marines fought 'with uncommon gallantry' at the battles of Bunkers Hill, Concord and Yorktown in the American War of Independence, and played a decisive role in such great naval victories as 'the Glorious First of June' in 1794 and Cape St Vincent in 1797. Some 5,000 Marines served with Nelson at the battle of Trafalgar. Such was the Marines' reputation for courage and loyal service that in 1802 King George III directed that the Corps should 'in future be styled the Royal Marines'.

Soldiers who could fight on sea and land proved a powerful weapon in the hands of Victoria's foreign secretaries and empire-builders. When Mehemet Ali, Viceroy of Egypt, attempted to seize Syria from the Turks in 1840, Britain, Austria, Russia and Prussia formed an alliance to stop him. In September 1840 a force of 1,500 Royal Marines under the command of Commodore Sir Charles Napier, cousin of the general of the same name, promptly turned the Egyptian invaders out of Beirut and Sidon.

Two months later the British fleet bombarded and destroyed the great fort of Acre, which was defended by 5,000 Egyptian troops. War and piracy in the Far East provided plenty of action

for the Marines. In the 'Opium Wars' with China in the Forties and Fifties Marines landed and stormed fortifications on the Canton and Yangtse Kiang Rivers, including the heavily fortified Bogue Forts. In the years 1857-60, Royal Marines landing parties played a leading role in obtaining the surrender of the great Chinese city of Canton and of the Taku Forts.

For decades the Royal Marines filled the role of international policemen, destroying pirate strongholds and keeping sea lanes clear for international trade. Typical was the force of over 300 marines and seamen commanded by Captain Talbot RN which sailed in 27 boats up the Songibesar River in Borneo and destroyed a notorious nest of pirates. In the same year, 1845, the Argentinian dictator Manuel de Rosas closed the Parana River to all foreign vessels, and an Anglo-French fleet was sent to force the floating barrier and chain boom. Commanded by Captain Hotham RN, a party of some 320 marines and sailors stormed the Argentinian barricades and fortifications, and cleared the river.

HMS *Powerful* was among the Allied warships that took part in the bombardment of Acre in November 1840.

The Crimean War was very largely a war of sieges. In the Baltic the Royal Marines played a leading part in the reduction of the Russian fortresses on Bomarsund in the Aland Islands in August 1854, and the Royal Marine Artillery got what they called 'most excellent practice' at the prolonged siege of Sebastopol. Several of the first VCs awarded in 1856 went to marines for their supreme valour during the war.

The Indian Mutiny of 1857-59 found the Royal Marines in action thousands of miles from their ships. Captain William Peel's Naval Brigade sailed up the Ganges to Allahabad, bringing with them big guns from HMS *Pearl* and *Shannon*. Their heavy fire, and the Marines' invincible fighting spirit was decisive in breaking the mutineers' resistance at Lucknow and Cawnpore.

The policeman's role of the Royal Marines often meant a life of inaction and even boredom for the men. In the little-known 'Pig-War' (which never became a fighting war) of 1860-72, involving the island of San Juan off the coast of British Columbia, Britain and the United States both claimed the island, and so both countries stationed troops there. When the Americans installed their garrison the British sent a detachment of Royal Marines, and the two 'enemy' garrisons remained there together quite amicably for the next twelve years.

Japan was another venue for Royal Marines' 'policing' duty. The highly conservative Samurai warrior class of Japan deeply resented the presence of foreign traders and diplomatic officials in their country, and encouraged attacks on the British Legation in Yedo and Yokohama. In 1862 a British trader and several legation guards were killed, and even when the forts at Kagoshima were bombarded by an Anglo-Dutch fleet, the attacks continued. So in 1863 a battalion of the RMLI was sent from Plymouth to 'show the flag', and they joined a fleet of British, American, French and Dutch warships to break a Japanese blockade of their Inland Sea. A storming party of marines attacked and rapidly cleared Japanese forts at Shimonoseki, an action that broke the back of the anti-foreign movement. Thereafter the duties of the Royal Marine battalions in Japan became purely ceremonial. The Japanese were much impressed by the marines, from whom they learned some useful military lessons.

Corporal John Prettyjohn (RMLI) winning the VC at the battle of Inkerman, 23 February 1855. When his party ran out of ammunition, he picked up the nearest Russian soldier and threw him at the others. He then checked the assault with a fusillade of stones. Prettyjohn was awarded the VC by ballot in his battalion.

Detachments and battalions of Royal Marines fought with distinction and panache with most of the numerous British expeditions in Africa in the latter half of the Queen's reign. A force of a little more than a hundred marines and seamen met and crushed some 2,000 ferocious Ashanti warriors not far from Elmina on the fever-ridden Gold Coast in 1873. A year later fifty Royal Marines of Sir Garnet Wolseley's expeditionary force held out for two days when attacked by 10,000 Ashanti warriors. In the Ninth Kaffir War of 1877-78 Marines from HMS *Active* of the Africa station landed close to East London in South Africa and marched with the column that overcame the massed tribesmen at the Battle of Quintana Mountain in February 1878. A year later HMS *Active* put them ashore again to join Lord Chelmsford's forces in the war with the dreaded Zulu *impis*. On the day of the disaster at Isandhlwana, a small force of marines defeated 5,000 Zulus in a desperate struggle.

In General Wolseley's brilliant Egyptian campaign of 1882, a detachment of 700 marines armed with Gatling guns occupied Alexandria after the bombardment in order to restore order. At Port Said, an officer and six marines landed from an open boat, took the Egyptian sentries by surprise and so enabled two companies of marines with Gatling guns to surround and occupy the town without having to fire a shot. At Tel-el-Kebir eight companies of Royal Marines took a prominent part in routing the Egyptian army. Four of them were extended to form a firing line, followed by four as supports, and in the words of an officer who was there:

We advanced by rushes, lying down to fire. The enemy's bullets were falling thickly . . . when the bugles – to the relief, I think, of everyone – sounded the 'Charge'. The whole line, every man burning to get at the Egyptians, rushed forward at the double with a continuous shout or roar rather than a cheer.

At the battle of El Teb against the followers of the Mahdi, in March 1884, the Royal Marines' battalion formed the left face of the 'square'. When the advancing Dervishes got about 200 yards from the square 'they charged down in their thousands, shouting, yelling and brandishing their formidable spears and swords. The stream of Martini bullets that rushed to meet them brought them down in their scores, but the survivors hurled themselves upon the bayonets . . .' In three hours it was all over, and 3,000 of the Mahdi's followers were dead or wounded. Of the Royal Marines there were four dead and twenty wounded.

A few days later, at Tamaii the Mahdists were again routed – but not before they had become the first enemy force to break a British square. This happened when the order to charge was given and the companies forming the square

A Private of the Royal Marines Light Infantry c. 1865. Throughout most of Victoria's reign the Corps of Royal Marines consisted of two Divisions: the Royal Marine Artillery (RMA 1804-1923) and the Royal Marines Light Infantry (RMLI 1855-1923).

failed to charge at the same time, thus opening a space for the enemy to rush into. The Marines, who were on the right face of the square, were forced back and the naval guns captured. It was a bad moment, but the square rapidly re-formed, recovered its lost ground, and recaptured the guns.

Royal Marines repulsing an attack while manning a 'zareba' during the defence of Tofrek in March 1885.

Britannia Waives the Rules

IN THE YEARS following the Napoleonic Wars the Royal Navy, emasculated though it was by cuts in expenditure, found itself increasingly acting as world policeman in support of Britain's growing interests abroad. Freedom of passage, that vital component of free trade, had first to be obtained and then guaranteed. The suppression of piracy and the hunting down of slave traders also came to be regarded as proper policy objectives for a major maritime power. If force had to be used in order to uphold liberal principles, that was the price that Victorian England had to pay for the assumption of international moral leadership.

Whatever doubts senior officers may have entertained, British sailors carried out their tasks with characteristic cheerfulness and ingenuity. But with an ageing fleet of cumbersome sailing ships at the mercy of wind and weather, their successes were more often than not due to good luck, courage and brilliant seamanship.

The advent of wooden, steam-powered gunboats changed this situation profoundly. Almost by chance, or so it seems, the need to develop a small vessel of shallow draft, which was easy to maneouvre and able to bring considerable firepower to bear upon shore positions, produced an ideal weapon of war for Western European powers – especially Great Britain – to further imperialist ambitions during the second half of the 19th century.

Conventional defence systems that relied on coastal forts, shore batteries and shallow waters were made obsolete almost overnight. Harbours, shorelines and rivers, even those barely navigable, were now all vulnerable to attack. With the end of the Crimean War, as the Chinese soon discovered, gunboats could turn rivers into 'daggers pointing at the very heart of a country', as one contemporary writer rather colourfully put it.

That gunboats were cheap to build and easy to maintain were other points strongly in their favour. Provided the major European powers managed to keep peace with each other and with the USA, there would no longer be a need to build large and expensive battleships, except for reasons of research and development. Gunboats were more than a match for pirate junks, slave-trading dhows and warrior canoes.

Politicians of all persuasions thought it in no way contradictory to place more responsibilities upon the Royal Navy, and to cut naval estimates each year. Both the Radicals and the Liberals in Britain were wedded to the principles of *laisser faire* and determined to reduce public spending, so where defence expenditure was concerned it made little difference which party was in power.

The gunboat offered a way of discharging what were perceived as Britain's responsibilities at comparatively low cost, and satisfied one other cherished principle of mid-Victorian Britain – namely, that power should be used to exert influence, and not to gain territory. What

Civis Romanus Sum!*

Even before the heyday of the gunboat, naval power was being applied more and more to secure concesions or to uphold national honour, as in the notorious Don Pacifico affair.

After an anti-Semitic mob had set fire to his house in Athens in 1847, the Greek government declined to compensate Don Pacifico, a naturalised Portuguese subject who acted as consul in the city. He had taken out a British passport, but otherwise had little claim on British citizenship.

After lengthy negotiations with the local authorities failed in 1850, he appealed for help to the British Foreign Secretary, Lord Palmerston, who immediately responded by sending a British fleet to blockade Piraeus harbour and to seize Greek shipping.

In defence of this action, he delivered a 4½ hour speech in the House of Commons which called upon MPs to decided 'whether, as the Roman, in days of old, held himself free from indignity when he could say *Civis Romanus Sum*; so a British subject, in whatever land he may be shall feel confident that the watchful eye and the strong arm of England will protect him against injustice and wrong.'

So resounding a peroration could hardly fail to win the support of the House, who cheered the Foreign Secretary to the echo. His triumph was completed when the Greek government caved in and awarded Don Pacifico the compensation he demanded.

Palmerston himself thus became a national hero – but not a hero for Victoria, who considered him to be 'unprincipled' and 'very reckless'. Writing to her uncle King Leopold, after the Palmerston's death, she said that he had 'many valuable qualities, though many bad ones, and we had, God knows! terrible trouble with him about Foreign affairs.'

*I am a Roman citizen

96

useful purpose was served by taking on all the burdens of government of a foreign land if British interests there could be promoted just as well by other, indirect, means? This gives the lie to the maxim, 'Trade follows the flag', for until the unbridled grab for land in Africa during the latter part of the 19th century, the reverse was more often true. The British flag followed British trade – sometimes with great reluctance, as many an Admiralty memorandum on the subject shows.

THE FIRST OPIUM WAR

The three wars fought with China during Queen Victoria's reign offer a fascinating case study, which clearly illuminates the point. They were not really wars at all – at least, not in the sense that we understand them in the West – but a series of naval and military engagements, sometimes quite bloody, to uphold the principles of free trade and to protect the commercial interests and prestige of European traders. At another level, they were a tangible sign of the fundamental clash between European and Chinese civilisations – both of which held themselves to be superior to all others. Most Chinese were convinced that all foreigners were barbarians:

most Europeans took exactly the same view of them.

It is an irony, to say the least, that Britain first took action against China during 1839-42 to protect the lucrative drug trade carried out by the East India Company, at that time the world's largest producer of opium. China was their main market, and after years of turning a blind – and doubtless bribed eye, the Chinese authorities decided that the time had come to stamp out drug addiction and to suppress the opium trade completely. They also insisted that foreign merchants should respect their customs and conventions, even if these offended European notions of justice and dignity.

British officials were considered ill-mannered when they refused to kow-tow before Chinese mandarins of equal or superior rank. The British, in turn, felt humiliated when they were not allowed to meet provincial governors. When the British Chief Superintendent of Trade – another Lord Napier (William, 8th Baron Napier) – was not permitted to reside in China, he wrote home asking for 'three or four frigates and brigs, with a few steady British troops, not Sepoys . . .', no doubt to teach the Chinese manners and respect for the British way of life.

HMS *Condor* – one of the Navy's most famous gunboats

Stinkpots and Tridents

One action typical of many during the First Opium War, took place at Fatshan Creek on 1 June 1841, where a fleet of junks was attacked by a British force of 250 men, led by 12 officers and 22 NCOs.

The junks, heavily armed, were supported by a hill fort on one side of the creek and by a six-gun shore battery on the other, and were positioned to sweep the channel as the enemy flotilla came into view.

British gunboats opened fire on the junks as Marines landed to attack the fort. The hill was steep and the Chinese gunners were unable to depress their guns sufficiently to fire into the attacking force. Even volleys of grape shot passed harmlessly overhead, so the Chinese started to roll 32-pound shot down the hill and to throw showers of stinkpots and three-pronged spears.

The British officer in charge of naval operations, Commodore Elliot, together with Captain Boyle, commander of the Marines, and a midshipman, ran neck-and-neck up the hill. On reaching the fort Captain Boyle saw one of the defenders aiming a matchlock at him. So he took out his revolver and, still panting from the climb, fired a shot which went wide of its mark. The Chinese soldier replied by rolling two huge shot at him and, for good measure, by hurling a trident at the midshipman. But these were his last acts of defiance, for he was then struck down by a bullet from Commodore Elliot.

The Chinese stuck to their guns until the main body of Marines was within 50 paces of the embrasures. Then suddenly, to a man, they deserted their posts and ran helter-skelter down the hill to seek sanctuary.

With the fort safely in their hands, the British expedition pressed home its advantage and destroyed the enemy ships.

In 1839 an Imperical edict declared that the opium trade must cease and all stocks surrendered. Foreigners who disobeyed were simply to be shut up in their own factories. War began when two British frigates defeated a fleet of 29 Chinese war junks, and in 1840 a British Expeditionary Force arrived with orders to occupy Chusan, blockade Canton and force the Chinese government to sign a treaty. Commanded by Major-General Sir Hugh Gough, the troops included the Royal Irish, the Cameronians, the 55th Foot, and the Hertfordshire Regiments.

The Chinese ridiculed these barbarians. They were convinced that in their quaint, tight uniforms they would fall over and not be able to get up again. Even if this turned out not to be the case, they would certainly run away 'on display of the celestial terror'. Gough and his men regarded their opponents as 'contemptible', although as a military nation they 'were not wanting in courage or strength . . .'

The Chinese were certainly superior in numbers and often fought to the last man, but they were always outclassed by the better-armed, better-led and better-disciplined British infantry, marines and naval brigades. Most Chinese soldiers were armed either with out-of-date matchlocks or more primitive weapons such as pikes, swords and, in many cases, bows and arrows. According to one British colonel:

. . . their arms are bad and they fire ill, and having stood well for a while, give way to our rush, and are then shot like hares in all directions . . . The Chinese are robust, muscular fellows and no cowards, the Tartars desperate; but neither are well commanded or acquainted with European warfare.

The British had little difficulty in capturing all the major seaports, including Shanghai, Ningpo, Foochow, Canton and Amoy. At the heavily-defended city of Chusan, with its 30ft high walls and great stone towers every 300 yards, the small British force encountered much more determined opposition. The walled town of Ching-Kiang-Fuo also put up fierce opposition: its hidden Tartar garrison inflicted heavy losses on Gough's men.

However, in August 1842 the Chinese were forced to sign the Treaty of Nanking, which gave Britian favourable trading rights in these ports as well as special privileges and legal immunity for British residents in China. Hong Kong became a Crown Colony, which particularly pleased the Queen, 'Albert is so amused at my having Hong Kong,' she wrote to her uncle, venturing the thought that the Princess Royal might also be called Princess of Hong Kong. In more serious vein she also wrote to her Prime Minister, Sir Robert Peel:

The Queen wishes Sir Robert to consider, and at an *early* period . . . how to recompense and how to mark her high approbation of the admirable conduct of all those meritorious persons who have by their strenuous endeavours brought about the recent brilliant successes in China and Afghanistan.

Sir John Bowring, commander of the Far East station in 1856, later became Governor of Hong Kong

The Second China War

THE CHINESE are a pragmatic people and, having been obliged to sign the Treaty of Nanking, they saw no good reason why thereafter they should comply with its more stringent terms. There were other matters to attend to, of which the most pressing was internal unrest in the country. Not that internal unrest was in any way unusual in China, but on this occasion it had broken customary and tolerable bounds by developing into open revolt against the Emperor himself.

The Son of Heaven was an enthroned godhead, into whose presence only the most privileged of his own people were admitted. That he should fall under the gaze of an Outer Barbarian was unthinkable. Consequently, no diplomats were allowed to approach the Imperial Court or even to enter the forbidden city of Peking, which was a source of considerable irritation to the British.

The main focus of tension between the Chinese and the foreign devils was to be found in the large and prosperous port of Canton, where the inhabitants had banned European traders in direct contravention of the terms of the treaty. The Imperial Government did nothing; either it was too supine or too caught up with its own problems to deal with the affair. A number of clashes took place between Cantonese citizens and British merchants, and a local proclamation threatened death to any member 'of the vile race' of English attempting to enter the city.

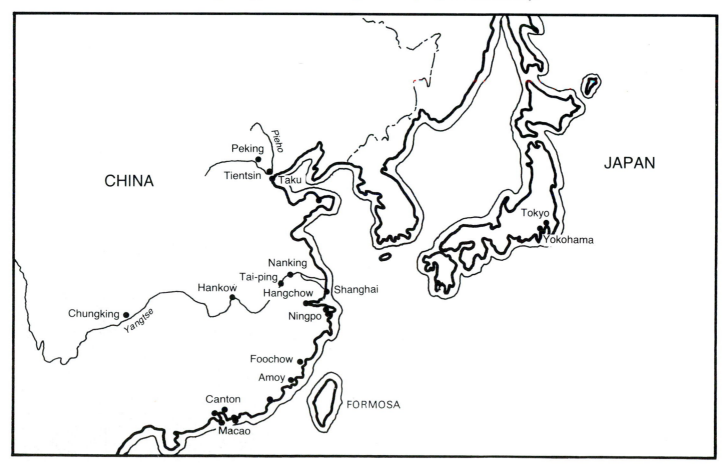

Matters came to a head in 1856 when a British schooner out of Hong Kong was boarded by the Chinese authorities, who claimed that certain members of her crew were pirates. A demand for their immediate release from Sir John Bowring, commander of the Far East station, was rejected out of hand by local Imperial Commissioner Yeh. Ships of the Royal Navy were then sent to bombard the Barrier forts guarding the approach to Canton, before sailing on up-river to the city itself. On October 29 an assault party of 200 marines, commanded by Captain Penrose of the Royal Marine Light Infantry, breached the city walls but were then repulsed. Further attacks followed, with supporting fire from the naval units; a fleet of war junks was destroyed, and forts with about 200 guns were captured. Infuriated by these assaults, Commissioner Yeh ordered that British factories should be burned down; the British retaliated by setting fire to other parts of the city. One member of the punitive expedition reported later that the Chinese

. . . maddened by the loss of property and life, manned the house tops to hurl bricks and stones down on our heads, and the Chinese soldiers who were very thick, tried hard to cut us off; but as they had only spears we knocked them down like ninepins.

Although the British suffered few casualties it was clear that their force was not large enough to occupy Canton. So the Governor General of

India was asked to send 5,000 troop reinforcements and the Admiralty was asked for a flotilla of gunboats. These requests came from Rear-Admiral Sir Michael Seymour KCB, Commander-in-Chief East Indies and China Station, a senior officer who had served with some distinction in the Baltic in 1855 and had lost an eye while examining a Russian mine.

The Indian Mutiny intervened, so some months passed before these new forces could be brought into play. Meanwhile, Lord Elgin was appointed as the new Plenipotentiary and instructed to obtain compensation for loss of life and damage to property in Canton, to insist on the strict observance of the Treaty of Nanking, and to press for diplomatic representation at the Imperial Court in Peking. By this time France had become involved in the dispute, ostensibly because the Chinese had been unwise enough to murder a French missionary. It is much more likely that France was determined to muscle in on the negotiations to prevent the British gaining any unfair trading, naval or military advantages.

Once again the Chinese rejected all demands and at dawn on 28 December 1857 the British opened fire on the city of Canton, 'demonstrating the benefits of Western civilisation by dropping shells on Yeh's house', as the authors of *Send A Gunboat!* observe.

Landing parties followed three days later. A number of important officials were taken prisoner, including Yeh himself, and a puppet administration in the city was set up. With

The heroism of Lieutenant Pim

Junior officers were keen to serve on gunboats because they offered the only chance of command of an armoured ship at the rank of Lieutenant, and rare opportunities of distinguishing themselves in action – especially against pirates – and so coming to the attention of their superiors. But there was a price to pay, for these eager young officers had to spend by far the greater part of their time on routine patrol duties which often became extremely tedious. To vary the monotony they would venture ashore from time to time, despite the obvious dangers involved in leaving ship.

In December 1857 Lieutenant Pim, the commanding officer of the gunboat *Bantam*, decided that a creek near Sai-Lau needed to be explored. So he took a boat and 14 men, found a suitable landing place some way up the creek and, after leaving two men behind to

guard the boat, led his party ashore. When they returned some time later they were horrified to see a large, yelling crowd round the boat, pelting their comrades with stones and other missiles. Although considerably outnumbered, they charged the crowd with drawn cutlasses, managed to scramble aboard and push their boat off the mud. But by this time some of the crowd had got hold of weapons and started to fire at the British sailors, five of whom were killed in the first fusillade and most of the others wounded.

With great coolness Lieutenant Pim stood in the bows and, armed only with his revolver, returned the sustained fire coming from the bank. He was hit no fewer than six times, but by presenting himself as the main target he drew the enemy's fire and gave his men a chance to get their boat out of range and make good their escape.

Canton secured, Elgin felt able to press ahead with the next stage of the plan. Having persuaded the American and the Russian trade ministers to back the Anglo-French initiative, he warned Peking that representatives of the four Western powers now wished to meet senior Chinese officials in the capital.

He lost no time in setting out, by way of Shanghai, for the Gulf of Pechili and the mouth of Peiho River guarding the approach to Peking. He was to have met a force of gunboats there but, to his fury, reached the rendezvous point before they did. He wrote to the Foreign Secretary, Lord Clarendon:

At the moment I am writing this despatch, the French flag is represented by two gunboats within the bar of Peiho, the English by two despatch-boats aground on top of it.

The Chinese were not impressed, but took advantage of the delay by strengthening forts commanding the estuary. More than 80 guns and many thousands of Tartar cavalrymen could be seen among the earthworks, and along every stretch of river bank, as far as the eye could see, pointed stakes had been planted to discourage landings.

However, the defenders had reckoned without the gunboats, for when they did arrive on the scene the mud-built fortifications collapsed under their sustained bombardment, and the invading fleet was able to proceed further up-river to deal with remaining outposts. At Taku, some Chinese warships were moored in the shelter of a barrier of junks, but once this line was broken the Allied flotilla, led by the gun-vessel *Cormorant*, continued to sail slowly up the narrow waterway as far as Tientsin. This was a centre of great strategic importance since it controlled the northern end of the Grand Canal,

British gunboats supported the artillery attack on the Taku forts

Mr Midshipman Kennedy has a busy day

In February 1858 Midshipman Kennedy of HMS *Calcutta* was ordered to take two boats and place himself under the command of Lieutenant Forbes of the 80 hp gunboat *Algerine*, on a pirate-hunt in the China Seas. At Grass Island a junk was sighted, but it turned out to be a decoy sent by the pirates to divert attention from one of their larger contraband vessels, known as a *lorcha*. This they sailed round the south side of the island but, after a brief exchange of fire when they saw Kennedy waiting for them, they turned and headed for the shore in a rising gale. With daring seamanship the pirates dropped anchor at the very last moment to swing the stern of their vessel almost on to the rocks, over which they escaped inland.

Kennedy realised that the ship could not be left to fall back into the hands of the pirates, so he drew his cutter alongside and jumped aboard with three of his crew. They found the *lorcha* deserted except for one Chinese seaman, who became his prisoner, and an old man in manacles who had been tortured and was in a very weak condition. After releasing him, Kennedy decided that the only option was to set fire to the pirate ship and then return to his own boat. However, as the cutter approached it was nearly swamped by the rising sea. Two Chinese fishing boats came to the rescue, but they were smashed against the bows of the *lorcha* and their crews drowned.

By now, the fire had taken a firm hold and, fanned by the wind, was creeping towards the powder magazine. In desperation, Kennedy ordered two of his men to jump overboard and swim for the cutter as it made a further attempt to draw alongside. He threw the old man into the boat and, with his prisoner and the remaining member of his crew, jumped into the sea. All three were hauled aboard the cutter, which then pulled away just in time to escape the full force of a huge explosion which blew the *lorcha* out of the sea.

None the worse for his exploit, Kennedy immediately pressed on to rejoin the *Algerine*, now heavily engaged in action against two Chinese

junks. A well-placed shell from the gunboat hit the magazine of one of them, which blew up, and a short time later the second junk was hit in the bows. By this time the pirates had had enough. They jumped overboard and swam for the shore hotly pursued by a party of British sailors, who followed them inland and set fire to their village.

To Lieutenant Forbes and his officers the cash value of the day's activities was nil, because they had not captured any of the pirate vessels. No bounties were paid for vessels destroyed, and it was little consolation when, many months later, a grateful Parliament awarded a sum of £180 to be divided equally between the crews of *Algerine* and *Calcutta*. Fate was rather kinder to our hero, however, for in due course he recorded his many adventures in a lively autobiography entitled *Hurrah for the Life of a Sailor! Fifty Years in the Royal Navy*. By that time he had become Sir William Kennedy, Admiral of the Fleet.

Peking's main channel of trade and communication with central and southern China.

Here Sir Michael Seymour and his force met no resistance; on the contrary, people swarmed to the river bank in their thousands to stare at the strange foreigners and their even stranger vessels. Local traders came out to supply provisions, including fresh meat: only the officials remained aloof, doubtless awaiting instructions from the Imperial Court.

Word was sent to Lord Elgin, and within eight days the Treaty of Tientsin was signed, in which the Chinese conceded all demands. On the face of things it seemed that Anglo-French combined action had carried the day but, as before, the Chinese delayed putting the Treaty into effect, especially the provisions that within one year it was to be ratified at Peking.

To make matters worse, the Chinese resumed their harassment of the British in the Canton area. During a retaliatory raid letters were found, or so it was claimed, indicating that the Emperor had no intention of honouring the Treaty of Tientsin. Furthermore, the British were to be prevented from re-entering the Peiho River and no British trading on the River Yang-tse would be tolerated. Confirmation followed that in an attempt to safeguard the river approach to their Imperial capital, Peking, the Chinese had closed the Peiho River once more and were busy strengthening the Taku forts.

Another show of naval strength was clearly necessary. Rear Admiral Sir James Hope, anxious to restore a reputation somewhat tarnished during the Crimean War, took over as Commander-in-Chief in April 1859. With a flotilla of eleven gunboats and gunvessels he sailed north to the Peiho River, confident that he could force the entrance without difficulty and so repeat Seymour's success of the previous year.

But the Chinese were not to be caught napping twice. The British mistimed their action by going into the attack on a falling tide, and succeeded in dismantling only the first of the three barriers erected across the river mouth. Moored below the middle barrier, the ships were easy targets for the shore batteries, especially as some of them had grounded on the mud. Casualties were heavy. On board Hope's flagship *Plover* 26 men had been killed or wounded, while only three members of *Kestrel's* crew escaped uninjured. After heavy fire both ships sunk at their moorings, and Admiral Hope had to move his flag to the gunvessel *Cormorant*.

Undaunted by these reverses he then ordered the landing parties ashore, with disastrous results. The sailors and the marines, weighed down by their rifles and equipment, found themselves wallowing in thick, foul mud. Faced with heavy enemy fire from the shore, including fireballs that caused the most dreadful injuries, the British attack faltered and then broke. Many of the survivors threw away their weapons in desperate attempts to regain the comparative safety of the gunboats. 89 men were killed in the fighting and 345 wounded, including 118 of the gunboat crews.

Although Hope displayed a characteristic lack of judgement throughout the engagement, his personal courage was of the highest order. He stuck to his command throughout the action despite having part of his thigh torn away by a shell splinter. At the height of the battle a neutral vessel, the USS *Toeywhan*, commanded by Flag Officer Josiah Tattnall, drew alongside and offered to take Sir James on board, together with other wounded officers and men. Legend has it that during his conversation with the British admiral, Tattnall looked round and saw some of his own crew helping to fire the *Plover's* forward gun. He reprimanded them severely, but with a smile turned to Hope and uttered the now-famous phrase, 'Blood must be thicker than water'.

The day following the battle attempts were made to refloat some of the British vessels, but three proved to be total losses, presenting the Royal Navy with its worst defeat in more than a hundred years of minor engagements. Nothing remained for the flotilla except a humiliating return to the shelter of Hong Kong. British public opinion was outraged and demanded retribution: there had to be a third attack on the Peiho River and the Taku forts.

In planning a fresh assault many hard-learned lessons were applied. It was acknowledged that the Chinese could not be brought to heel by naval action alone and that, as in the Crimea, the Army would have to carry the main attack to the enemy, with the Royal Navy in a supporting role. New commanders were appointed, including General Sir Robert Cornelis Napier who later distinguished himself in Abyssinia. Rear Admiral Sir James Hope, having recovered from his wound, was re-appointed naval C-in-C, to the delight of his friends and astonishment of his critics.

On 8 March 1860 an ultimatum was sent to the Imperial Government demanding an apology, full compensation for the Peiho River action and ratification of the Tientsin Treaty. Not surprisingly, this was rejected by the Chinese. By this time, an Expeditionary Force of some 14,000 men, including a number of infantry and cavalry regiments of the Indian Army, had been assembled in Hong Kong under the command of Lieutenant-General Sir James Hope Grant. This force was later joined by a contingent of 6,700 French soldiers, mostly colonial, commanded by General de Montauban. Some of the senior British officers regarded the presence of their allies as more of a hindrance than a help: according to one commentator the French were at pains to avoid the fighting, but were always ready to claim as much of the glory as possible.

After establishing a depot at Odin Bay the allied armies, supported by the Royal Navy and a French squadron, overcame Chinese resistance at Sin-Ho and reached the mouth of the Peiho River. The main assault on the Taku forts opened on 21 August 1860 with a heavy bombardment from land-based artillery supported by allied

gunboats moored in the river. The Chinese defenders returned fire with equal vigour, but after two arsenals were destroyed their guns started to falter and the way was clear for the infantry to attack the northern fort, the crucial strategic point. The storming parties met very stiff resistance at the outset, but one by one white surrender flags started to appear, and by night-fall the way to Tientsin was open.

With the Taku forts now safely in their hands, the allies were able to remove the river barriers. Gunboats and land forces moved up-river to Tientsin, where a familiar sequence of events unfolded. Their welcome by the local people was as cordial as before, but Chinese officials span out negotiations as long as possible, and set a series of traps, ambushes, and other stratagems to delay the allied advance.

But in the end all these proved abortive and, leaving the gunboats behind to keep their lines of communication secure at Tientsin, the two armies took the road to Peking, where British and French soldiers plundered the Emperor's Summer Palace. The Chinese tried to bargain with the lives of European envoys they had earlier captured, but swift action by Sir Hope Grant secured the surrender of the city. At this point it was discovered that the hostages had been tortured and that many of them had died.

Having fled his capital, the Emperor empowered Prince Kung as one of the envoys to make peace with the Anglo-French force. On 24 October 1860 a treaty was signed, but Grant ordered that the Yuen-Ming-Yuen, or Round Bright Garden, an exquisite group of palaces and gardens dating back to 1709, should be burned to the ground. One of the sappers who had to carry out this act of revenge was Captain Charles Gordon R.E., soon to win renown as 'Chinese Gordon', before moving on to even more illustrious fame. Although one of his closest friends had been tortured to death by the Chinese, he showed little enthusiasm for his task. 'You would scarcely conceive the beauty and magnificence of the palaces we burnt,' he wrote. 'It made one's heart sore . . .'

The British attack on the Peiho river forts on the evening of 25 June 1859 in which marines and seamen, trapped in thick river mud, became easy targets for Chinese shore batteries

The North-West Frontier

THE CONQUEST of Sind and the annexation of the Sikh state made British India the immediate neighbour of the turbulent kingdom of Afghanistan, with its disputed mountainous frontier stretching from Bokhara to Baluchistan. These wild border lands with their rocky hillsides and narrow winding passes were, for the British, 'the North-West Frontier'. Here, year after year, stolid British infantrymen, Scottish Highlanders, Bengal Lancers, Sikhs, Gurkhas, gunners, sappers and miners, engaged in intermittent conflict with the fiercely independent and warlike Pathan tribes.

For the British these lawless tribes were a constant threat to the peace and security of the most sensitive border of their Indian empire. Across that border were the restless Afghans, kinsmen of the Pathan tribesmen, whose kingdom all too often seemed on the point of falling under Russian domination. British army officers and government officials viewed the tribesmen with mixed feelings, sometimes as mere savages, sometimes as gallant foes, sometimes as murdering thieves, sometimes as small players in 'The Great Game' which was the power struggle in Central Asia:

. . . men of predatory habits, careless and impatient of control . . . fierce and bloodthirsty . . . utterly faithless to public engagements . . . perpetually at war with each other . . . Reckless of the lives of others, they are not sparing of their own. They possess gallantry and courage themselves and admire such qualities in others . . .

Their ordinary occupation consisted of incursions into the plains . . . and in robbing and murdering peaceful traders in our territories . . .

They are poor but brave, and although turbulent and difficult to deal with, still have a great love of their country and cherish their independence . . .

For centuries the tribes had led a free and active existence in their remote mountain lands, subject to no ruler. British notions of law and order meant nothing to them. All they knew was that whenever the British moved in to 'protect' a territory, they took it over. Savage but skilful fighters, armed with matchlocks, usually stolen, they would creep up on an unwary British picket or column, pick off stragglers, launch a sudden attack, slash and kill, gather up dropped rifles and swords, and disappear. Similarly they would suddenly swoop down into the plains, attack forts, steal cattle and guns, kidnap rich merchants or unguarded British officers or civilians, and even their families.

Such outrages invariably called for a British punitive expedition. A force would be sent to locate the offending tribe, kill as many of them as possible, rescue the kidnapped, recover the stolen arms, and burn a few of their villages. Between 1849 and the end of the Queen's reign, well over forty such expeditions were mounted, but the tribes remained unsubdued.

THE AMBELA CAMPAIGN

Most of the British punitive expeditions in the North-West Frontier Province were minor affairs, involving field forces of no more than about a thousand troops, but from time to time tribal raids would become so frequent and widespread that the authorities would be forced to intervene on a major scale. Such was the trouble with the Hindustani Fanatics which resulted in the Ambela (also spelt Ambala, Ambeyla, Umballa, Umbela, and Umbeylah) Campaign. The Hindustani Fanatics were a religious sect who preached a *jihad* (holy war) against all infidels, but particularly against the British. By 1860 they had organised an extensive network of conspirators throughout northern India, with headquarters in Patna. During the Mutiny of 1857 they supplied rebellious sepoys with arms and bolt-holes.

In and around the remote village of Satana, deep in the wild mountainous region about 75 miles northwest of Peshawar, the Fanatics created a stronghold with stocks of arms and ammunition. From there they despatched raiding parties to loot and plunder trade caravans, and despite the expeditions sent to punish them — notably by Sir Sydney Cotton who in 1858 led a 5,000-man force, which burnt down their villages, blew up their forts and drove them from their base – their numbers continued to increase.

As long as the border could remain a 'No-man's land' – as it were 'a great gulf fixed' – all was well; but if any power was to be supreme, that power must be neither Russia nor Afghanistan.

WINSTON CHURCHILL

By the 1860s their raids had become so destructive and demoralising that the Government decided that all the Fanatics' strongholds had to be destroyed and they themselves slaughtered or driven out.

To block their usual escape route into the mountains, Sitana was to be attacked from the north. This called for a march through the mountainous territory of the Bunervals, a large and powerful tribe mistakenly thought to be unfriendly to the Fanatics and well-disposed to the Government.

Sir Neville Chamberlain agreed, reluctantly, to lead the expedition but, as so often happened, he was given troops and supplies that were inadequate for the task. His initial force of 6,000 men included the 71st Highlanders, the 4th and 5th Gurkhas, the Corps of Guides, the 11th Bengal Cavalry (Probyn's Horse), the 101st Royal Bengal Fusiliers, several battalions of native infantry and batteries of mountain guns.

He chose the Chamla valley as his base of operations, but to reach it the only practicable pass was the Ambela – in the territory of the Bunerwals. When the expeditionary force arrived at the entrance to the pass on 23 October 1863, they issued a proclamation stating that they only wished to march through the tribe's territory and intended no harm. But as their political officer observed:

Was it likely that a brave race of ignorant men would pause to consider the purport of a paper they could not read when the arms of a supposed invader were glistening at their door?

'The (Bunerval) people having taken a hostile part against us,' reported Chamberlain, '. . . has altered our whole position.'

Soon everything went wrong. There was no road, and as his force advanced, Chamberlain noted that 'the hills on either side grew higher and closer together, and masses of rock had to be worked round or scrambled over.' The guns had not arrived, and he decided to camp at the head of the pass before descending into the Chamla valley on the way to the Fanatics' stronghold.

Sir Neville Chamberlain

As unlike his namesake, the 20th century prime minister, as perhaps any man could be, General Sir Neville Chamberlain was one of the bravest and most battle-scarred of the many now-forgotten Heroes for Victoria. He fought in so many actions and was seriously wounded so many times that he was forced to retire from active service at the then early age of forty-three. Despite his aching scars and recurrent malaria, however, he lived to a great age and died a Field-Marshal. If he is remembered at all today it is probably as the inventor of snooker, the game based on billiards and pool which he devised in 1875 – some say it was in Ootacamund, some in Jubbulpore – to help relieve the boredom of under-employed army officers. At that time 'snooker' seems also to have been the name given to artillery officer recruits at Woolwich.

Neville Bowles Chamberlain was born in 1820 in Rio de Janeiro, the second of five sons of the British consul-general at Rio. Like his three brothers, he was commissioned when he was seventeen into the East India Company's army. He soon made a name for himself as a skilful swordsman and dashing cavalry leader. In his first campaign, the Afghan War of 1839-42, he was wounded six times. The slaughter and destruction he saw in that disastrous conflict led him to write that he was 'disgusted with myself, the world, and above all with my cruel profession,' but this seems to have been a passing feeling, for his subsequent career showed that his real love was the excitement and glory of military action. He fought with great distinction at the battle of Maharajpore in the Gwalior Campaign (1843) and in both Sikh Wars. Like John Nicholson, he came to be revered as some kind of a demigod among the tribes of the North-West Frontier, where he spent many years in command of irregular forces. Year after year he led punitive expeditions against such tribes as the Orakzais, Afridis, Mahsuds, and Waziris. When he was sent on long sick leave in 1852, he 'rested' by spending eighteen months lion-hunting in South Africa. When the Mutiny came he was instrumental with John Nicholson in forming the famous Movable Column. At the siege of Delhi he was adjutant-general of the army, and was wounded by a musket ball in his shoulder. This did not stop him from directing part of the assault – even though he could hardly move and had to be propped up near the city wall.

After the Mutiny he continued to take part in almost yearly punitive expeditions against the troublesome Pathan tribes. By 1863, when he was asked to lead an expeditionary force against the Hindustani Fanatics and destroy their power for ever, he had lost his zest for the glory of leading men into battle: 'I have no wish for active service,' he told his brother. 'I want to turn my sword into a shepherd's crook.' But his sense of duty prevailed. In the ensuing Ambela campaign he was wounded yet again and was forced to hand over his command. He had fought his last battle. Famous in his day as 'the bravest of the brave', he was rather belatedly given some of the honours he had earned, being appointed KCSI in 1866, GCB in 1875, and Field-Marshal in 1900. He was Commander-in-Chief of the Madras army from 1876 to 1881, when he retired and lived quietly in Southampton until his death in 1902.

'Storming the Heights of Laloo' – a sketch drawn by an unknown officer in the Ambela campaign

But the Bunervals had been persuaded by the Fanatics that the British were about to occupy their lands, and they mounted a night attack on Chamberlain's force, which was described by one of his officers:

(After a wild shout of 'Allah! Allah!') the matchlocks flash and crack from the shadows of the trees; there is a glitter of whirling swordblades, and a mob of dusky figures rush across the open space and charge almost up to the bayonets. Then comes a flash and a roar, the grape and canister dash up the stones and gravel, and patter among the leaves at close range. The whole line lights up with fitful flashes of sharp file-fire, and, as the smoke clears off, the assailants are nowhere to be seen; feeble groans from the front and cries for water in some Pathan patois alone tell us that the fire has been effectual . . . High up on a little knoll we see the tall form of the General . . . looking intently into the darkness before him . . .

The attack had failed, but Chamberlain and his men were surrounded and pinned down on the summit of the pass. During the next few weeks their numbers were reduced, and by late November the sick and wounded numbered over 450. While leading a counter-attack Chamberlain suffered his ninth wound, and became so seriously ill that he had to hand over command to the inexperienced General John Garvock, who was instructed not to move until

the Commander-in-Chief, General Sir Hugh Rose, arrived to take charge. But, reinforced by the 7th Royal Fusiliers, the 93rd Highlanders and the 24th Punjabis, Garvock disobeyed orders and broke out of the trap, as reported by the same officer:

5,000 men rose up from their cover, and, with loud cheers and volleys of musketry, rushed to the assault – the regiments of Pathans, Sikhs, and Gurkhas all vying with the English soldiers as to who should first reach the enemy. From behind every rock and shrub at the foot of the conical peak small parties of mountaineers jumped up and fled as the advancing columns approached them. It took but a few minutes to cross the open ground, and then the steep ascent began, our men having to climb from rock to rock . . . and though many of the enemy stood their ground bravely and fell at their posts, their gallantry was of no avail; and ere many minutes had elapsed the peak from foot to summit was in the possession of British soldiers.

The campaign was over. The Bunervals, chastened, agreed to burn the Fanatics' village themselves, in the presence of British officers, one of whom was Major Frederick Roberts VC. The British troops marched back the way they came, and in spite of ignoring his C in C's orders, General Garvock was appointed KCB.

The people love their Navy
and believe in it
THE DAILY TELEGRAPH: 1887

The Queen's Navy

LIKE HER uncle, 'the Sailor King' William IV, Queen Victoria was extremely proud of the Royal Navy. She regularly visited ships, and took the salute at Fleet Reviews; on her State visits abroad there was always a naval escort for the royal yacht; she insisted on a naval career for her gifted second son, Prince Alfred, who on his own merits rose to become an Admiral of the Fleet. The British public shared her enthusiasm, and there were many songs celebrating the gallant deeds of jolly Jack Tars and of their life at sea.

As conservative as the monarchy itself, the Royal Navy nevertheless underwent many changes during the reign. Square-rigged wooden ships armed with muzzle-loading cannon gave way to iron-clad steamships with gun turrets. In the face of competition from abroad the Navy was obliged to introduce armour-plating, breech-loaders, torpedoes, mines, submarines and many other innovations.

An Act of 1889 laid down that the Royal Navy must be as large as the next two most powerful navies combined. So Britain's supremacy at sea was never in doubt. Naval Brigades, in which many of the Navy's 40 VCs were won, played a vital part in many military expeditions, often marching far inland, as in the Indian Mutiny, the Abyssinian campaign and the 2nd Boer War. Warrant Officer Thomas Holman fought with a Naval Brigade at Tofrik in the Sudan in 1884, when it was attacked by Arabs before they were able to position their guns and barricades:

There we lay, an isolated party of Britons, infuriated and as callous to danger as the Mohammedan fanatics around us . . . A mass of white, black and brown wounded humanity, mad with pain and excitement, slashing, hacking and heaving at everything around us . . . Panting, howling, bleeding, cursing, raving, praying, kicking, biting the dust; it was sad, grand, bewildering, awful to view . . .

But increasingly, as the years passed, the Royal Navy also acted as an international policeman, protecting British citizens and their inter-ests, fighting piracy and slavery, surveying the world's oceans and exploring unknown regions. During a voyage lasting three years and covering 68,890 miles the corvette *Challenger*, for example, in the course of her oceanographic work, set up no fewer than 362 observation stations all over the world.

After the Crimean War the sailors' life on board was still tough and rough, but easier than it had been for their fathers. There were fewer brutal floggings (after 1879 the practice was suspended); shore leave became a right no longer to be withheld at a captain's whim; with the introduction of preserved food, diet improved and rations were more generous; many ships had libraries. Most important, from 1853 sailors could sign on for continuous service, with the prospect of a modest pension, and were no longer laid off at the end of each voyage. A new rank, leading seaman, came into being; promotion prospects and pay steadily improved throughout the reign.

Uniforms were standardised and smarter; blue cloth jacket and trousers, with a blue serge frock tucked in with three rows of white tape sewn on, a black silk scarf, a wide straw hat and a working hat of blue canvas with a ribbon on which the name of the ship was embroidered in gold. White duck trousers and white drill frock were worn in the tropics. Such was the prestige of the Navy that generations of small boys and girls were proud to wear a 'sailor suit', as many family photograph albums show.

Despite the triumph of steam, all Victorian sailors had to 'know the ropes' and be able to go aloft to furl and loose a ship's sails, however rough the weather . . .

Rescue in Abyssinia

1867-1868

ABYSSINIA

3rd Dragoon Guards
King's Own
Cameronians
Duke of Wellington's
Sherwood Foresters

27th Bombay Native
Infantry (1st Baluchis)
Commanding Officer:
Major H. Beville

KING THEODORE III of Abyssinia, King of Kings, Emperor and Chosen of God, the successful bandit who had seized the crown at the age of 37, proved a tyrannical and cruel ruler who slaughtered all possible rivals and pillaged their lands.

He was undoubtedly mentally disturbed. In 1863 he sent a letter to Queen Victoria proposing an offensive alliance against his Muslim neighbours. Unluckily, the letter went astray. When he received no reply, the King felt himself slighted, and incarcerated the British envoy, several British officials and their wives, as well as a number of European missionaries, lay preachers, and others, keeping them in chains. From time to time he had some of them tortured and flogged, and they lived under constant threat of being killed.

After years of patient negotiation failed to secure their release, the British Government decided in 1867 to send an expeditionary force to rescue all the prisoners. The man they chose to lead it was General Sir Robert Napier, the commander-in-chief of the Bombay army, for most of the force was to be drawn from India.

'What is desired,' the Duke of Cambridge, the C-in-C, told Napier, 'is that a flying column or succession of flying columns should be pushed forward and operate to the front, so as to make a dash if possible and finish the business before the rains set in.'

Basically, this was the strategy that Napier adopted – except that 'flying column' was no way to describe the large, fully-equipped force he assembled to march 400 miles into the unknown tropical and mountainous terrain of

Abyssinia. Aware that he might be blamed for exceeding his budget, but never forgiven for failure, and determined not to let his troops or his future fall victim to demands for economy, he left his C-in-C and the government in no doubt as to the scale and cost of the operation: 'The expedition will consist of a force that may be stated in round numbers: 4,000 British, 8,000 native troops; with at least an equal number of camp followers, and 25,000 head of cattle of various kinds . . .' adding that as many as 150 transports would be needed at any one time, as well as a good harbour and landing-point, ample water and stores.

Eventually it took some 300 steam and sailing ships to convey about 62,000 men and 36,000 animals (including 1,800 camels and 44 elephants) from India and land them at Annesley Bay on the Red Sea Coast. The expedition disembarked over a period of two months (December 1867/January 1868). Napier then divided his army into a striking force for the assault on Magdala, and a support force to cover his line of communications. By early April the striking force had marched nearly 400 miles and had reached a point only a few miles away from Magdala itself.

Napier's 4,000 strong fighting force consisted of five British regiments: the 4th King's Own, 26th Cameronians, the 33rd (Duke of Wellington's), the 45th Sherwood Foresters, and the 3rd Dragoon Guards, together with fourteen Indian regiments – four cavalry and ten infantry. Attached to the force was a Naval Brigade with rockets, together with a Royal Artillery detachment armed with new breech-loading, long-range mountain guns. Napier did everything possible by the standards of the day to safeguard the health and fitness of his men; camps were established ahead of the marching column, with fresh water pumped from the coast, as well as all necessary food and other supplies

In the 1860s the Queen's Armies were in a state of transition. Some of Napier's troops wore the traditional scarlet uniforms with white cross-belts, while others wore the new khaki disliked by many older officers. Some (especially the

Lord Napier of Magdala

Robert Cornelis Napier (who was not related to any of the other distinguished Napiers of Victoria's reign) was born in Ceylon in 1810 – the year in which his father, an artillery major, was killed in action at Fort Cornelis in Java. He was educated at Addiscombe College, Croydon, and at 18 he sailed to India as a lieutenant in the Bengal Engineers.

He had a very active fighting career. In the Sikh Wars he fought at the battles of Mudki, Ferozeshah, Sobraon, and Gujarat. Twice he had his horse shot under him, and at Ferozeshah he was severely wounded when he charged on foot with the 31st Regiment. On the North-West Frontier he commanded a column in the First Black Mountain Hazara Expedition in 1852, and the next year he was fighting the Jowaki Afridis in the Peshawar district.

He served with Havelock and Outram at the relief of Lucknow, and was active in the mopping-up campaigns in Oudh and Gwalior as the Mutiny came to an end. He was a divisional commander in the war with China in 1860, and when selected to lead the Abyssinian expedition, he was commander-in-chief of the Bombay Army.

The remarkable success of the Magdala expedition at so small a cost in lives brought Napier a rich harvest in rewards and honours, recommended by the Prime Minister, Benjamin Disraeli, who said to the Queen:

'So well planned, so quietly and thoroughly executed, the political part so judiciously managed, the troops so admirably handled during the long, trying march, the strength of the Anglo-Indian organization so strikingly demonstrated, wiping out all the stories of Crimean blundering – the Abyssinian expedition stands apart, and merits, Mr Disraeli thinks, perhaps an exceptional award.'

So Robert Cornelis Napier became Lord Napier of Magdala, and was voted a pension (and their thanks) by Parliament. He was appointed Knight Grand Cross of the Order of the Bath, Knight Grand Commander of the Star of India, and honorary Colonel of the 3rd London Rifles. He was made a Freeman of the City of London, an honorary citizen of Edinburgh, and a Fellow of the Royal Society. He was appointed Commander-in-Chief of the Army in India, and held the rank of Field Marshal when he died in 1890.

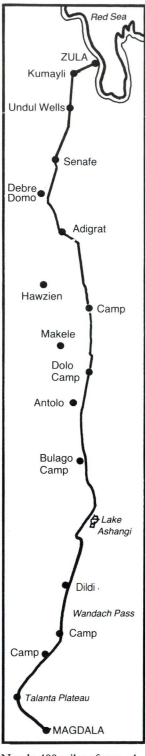

Indians) were armed with out-of-date muzzle-loading muskets, others had the new breech-loading Enfield-Snider rifles which had a firing rate of eight or nine rounds a minute and could kill at 800 yards.

Magdala, Theodore's capital, where his prisoners were held, was an almost inaccessible mountain fortress, 300 feet above a plateau, itself 7,000 feet above sea level. As Napier's assault force approached from the coast, Theodore was collecting an army of 7,000 warriors, camp-followers, and artillery, as well as prisoners, and leading them on a terrible march towards Magdala, burning, pillaging and slaughtering on the way. Once in the fortress he had his guns trained on the advancing British and Indian columns, while he himself watched them through a telescope as they scrambled up the steep slopes.

When he saw a long line of baggage mules emerge from a defile into the plain directly beneath his guns, Theodore sent his troops into the attack under cover of a heavy bombardment. Much to his annoyance, and to the relief of Napier's infantry racing to protect the baggage train, the shots passed noisily but harmlessly overhead. Theodore's gunners were unable to aim accurately from a great height.

However, 6,000 of his troops swarmed down the precipitous hillside, halted at the bottom, formed a seven-deep front, three quarters of a mile long, and then advanced at a trot. Led by the king's favourite general, they saw the baggage-train as an easy plunder. But they found themselves faced with three hundred well-placed

British infantry and Punjab Pioneers directing rapid fire into their ranks from 250 yards, supported by a stream of rockets from the Naval Brigade firing from a small crest nearby. Halted for a moment, the Abyssinians still came on, but continuous volleys from the Snider-Enfield rifles stopped them and forced them back. By the end of the day seven hundred of Theodore's troops lay dead and a further 1,200 were wounded. 'The British have destroyed my army with just their advance guard', lamented the king, 'what will they do with their main force?'

Nearly 400 miles of rugged terrain separated the coastal town of Zula and Theodore's fastness at Magdala, more than 9,000 ft above sea level

This huge mortar was one of nine in the formidable artillery encountered by Napier during his advance

He sent a delegation, including two of the prisoners, to Napier to discuss terms. The reply was brief: '. . . submit to the Queen of England and bring all the Europeans in Your Majesty's hands and deliver them safely this day in the British camp.' Hearing this, the king fell into a rage and threatened to kill all the prisoners, but in a calmer mood he decided to conciliate Napier and let all the prisoners go. Unmoved, Napier prepared to storm Magdala, while Theodore relieved his frustration by having some hundreds of his Abyssinian prisoners thrown, in chains, over a 100-foot precipice. 'The sight of wholesale slaughter,' observed one of Napier's staff, 'caused a deep feeling of hatred to Theodore among the British soldiery.'

The Royal Engineers and the 33rd Foot led the assault up the steep, narrow path to the fortress. The Sappers' task was to blow in the gate and set up scaling ladders, so that the men of the 33rd could charge through and scale the walls, but at the critical moment the gunpowder and scaling ladders were not to be found! The 33rd (who had been in disgrace with Napier for their rowdy behaviour on the march) saved the day and their good name by fighting their way over the wall. One of them, Private Bergin, heaved a drummer boy, Drummer Magner, with the aid of a rifle butt, to the top of the twelve-foot wall. While Bergin opened fire on the defenders, the boy hauled more of the 33rd's men, sweating and cursing, to join the attack.

Soon Ensigns Mellis and Wynter of the 33rd were waving the Queen's and the regimental colours from the top of the wall. 'I shall never forget the exhilaration of that moment,' said Ensign Wynter, 'the men firing and shouting like madmen.'

Seeing his men flee, Theodore shot himself – with a pistol presented to him by Queen Victoria years before. The campaign was over. Magdala was put to the torch, and by the middle of June not one soldier, sailor, ship or animal from Napier's force was left in the country.

The financial cost had been high, but the casualties, at under 400, were gratifyingly small. The Queen was delighted with her soldiers' success in this extraordinary campaign, from which she and her growing empire gained not an inch of new territory but a great deal of prestige.

After the capture of Magdala, the fort and the village were set on fire by the British, and all Theodore's guns destroyed

facing page (top)
The ever-capricious Theodore released some of his prisoners and then changed his mind. But he was too late: they had already made good their escape and reached the safety of British lines

Cardwell's Army Reforms

IT SEEMS DOUBTFUL whether Edward Cardwell should be classified as a hero for Victoria since, like her cousin, the Duke of Cambridge, Commander-in-Chief of the Army, the Queen did not look kindly on changes in the way *her* army was organised. However, as a good constitutional monarch, she accepted her ministers' advice, and there is no doubt that Cardwell's reforms amounted to an heroic achievement. The changes he initiated helped, in David Ascoli's words, 'to create, within the limits of political parsimony, an army fit to fight a war rather than play at peace.'

Cardwell's reforms changed the army from top to bottom. He moved the Commander-in-Chief from the Horse Guards to Pall Mall and made him responsible to the Secretary of State for War (who thereby became in effect the army's head), at the same time giving him command of all the land forces of the Crown, regular and auxiliary, at home and overseas. The Surveyor-General of the Ordnance and the Financial Secretary were made responsible to the Secretary of State, not to the Commander-in-Chief. But Cardwell was unable to persuade the conservative Duke to set up a General Staff for giving central direction to the army in time of war – the kind of direction that might have avoided the blunders of the Boer War.

To open the door to promotion by merit and to a more professional army, Cardwell abolished the purchase of commissions and promotion. The mere proposal started a political storm. All but a small minority of officers – who included Colonel Garnet Wolseley and Captain Evelyn Baring (the future Lord Cromer) – were implacably opposed to abolition. Echoing Wellington, the diehards said a professional army would be a mercenary army and a potential threat to the state. Officers had to be gentlemen born and bred to lead and to serve the Crown, and most gentlemen were also born to money; for them purchase was an investment, their pension fund. Cardwell's reponse to political and army opposition was to abolish purchase by Royal Warrant and to pay officers compensation at the current market value for their commissions.

Owing to the ever-increasing demands of Empire, the army was stretched far beyond its means, with only about 3,500 reserves available for overseas service. Cardwell effectively increased its strength by withdrawing troops from self-governing colonies such as Canada and New Zealand, unless they paid for them. At the same time he reorganised the regimental system in order to stimulate recruitment and create a reserve of trained soldiers.

The old regiments of the line, the traditional focus of the infantryman's loyalty, were normally known by their numbers, and had no association with the militia or the volunteers, which were territorially based. Most regiments had a special title in addition to their number; county or regional titles were adopted towards the end of the eighteenth century. The title of a regiment did not necessarily reflect its character or composition. Not all Highland regiments were manned by Highlanders, or Welsh regiments by

Edward Cardwell 1813-1864

After taking a double first at Oxford, Edward Cardwell became an MP at the age of 29 and a loyal supporter of Conservative Sir Robert Peel. He had held a number of senior government offices, including President of the Board of Trade, Chief Secretary for Ireland, Chancellor of the Duchy of Lancaster, and Colonial Secretary before in 1868 Gladstone appointed him Secretary of State for War in his first ministry.

A man who had never served in the army and who hated violence, Cardwell then wore himself out in the immense task of modernising the army, and became, in the words of an eminent historian of Victorian England, 'the greatest British army reformer during the nineteenth century. In him economy and efficiency met.' After Gladstone's government fell in 1874, he was created a Viscount and retired into private life.

Welshmen, and a county regiment was as likely to contain Irishmen as men of the county.

Until 1881 all infantry regiments, except the Sovereign's three regiments of Foot Guards, were numbered 1 to 109 in order of historical precedence. The Foot Guards and Horse Guards, the 30-odd cavalry regiments, the Royal Engineers, the Royal Artillery, and the Rifle Brigade were not included in Cardwell's reorganisation.

Under his localisation scheme each infantry regiment was assigned to a county or city as its 'home', with which it was identified and where it expected to find its recruits. The country was divided into sixty-six regimental districts defined by county boundaries, each containing the depot of the associated regiment. Thus, the 5th Foot became the Northumberland Fusiliers, the 9th Foot the Norfolk Regiment, the 11th Foot the Devonshire Regiment and so on. By the end of the century more than twenty-five percent of all infantrymen were serving in regiments of their native county or city.

Cardwell realised that two-battalion regiments made more effective and economic units for training, for service at home and overseas and for creating a reserve of trained soldiers. Under his 'linked battalion' system, which came into being in 1881, all but a few single-battalion regiments with numbers higher than 25 were linked in pairs; for example, the 50th and 97th Foot became The Royal West Kent Regiment. Linked regiments had to conduct themselves as if they were two battalions of one regiment. However, they carried their histories, their traditions, their battle honours, their nicknames, and even their old numbers with them to their new regimental homes; so the old 3rd Foot became The East Kent Regiment but were still called 'The Buffs' and kept 'Blenheim' in their colours, and the 57th joined the 77th in The Middlesex Regiment, but remained 'The Die-hards' with 'Albuhera' proudly shown on their colours. Even as late as 1977 an old soldier could refer to his regiment, the Gloucesters, as 'the 28th Foot'.

Of the two regular battalions of the linked regiments, one was kept at home to recruit and train, while the other served overseas. The 44th

(East Essex) and the 56th (West Essex) Regiments, for example, were merged to form the 1st and 2nd battalions of the Essex Regiment; in 1884 the 1st battalion was at Colchester and the 2nd in Egypt. The Essex Rifles and the West Essex Militia formed the 3rd and 4th battalions. The regimental depot was at Warley.

Not all old soldiers (or their officers) welcomed these changes. When the 75th Foot (Stirlingshire) was amalgamated with the 92nd to become the 1st battalion of the Gordon Highlanders, one sergeant wrote their epitaph:

But under God's protection
   They'll rise again in kilt and hose
A glorious resurrection!
   For by the transformation power
Of Parliamentary laws,
   We go to bed the Seventy-Fifth
And arise the Ninety-Twas

As a further encouragement to recruitment, the ordinary soldier's period of engagement was reduced from twelve to six years with the colours and six in the reserve, although he could serve longer if he wished and was accepted. A private's pay was raised to a shilling a day, and meat and bread were provided free. Flogging in peacetime was abolished except on active service, where the punishment was still inflicted until 1880. Such reforms did not merely make a soldier's career less like penal servitude for life, they also helped to build the needed reserve of trained men in the prime of life. Senior officers and old sweats alike shook their heads sadly, but in the event army service became more popular and attracted a higher grade of recruit.

Alongside these reforms, Cardwell strengthened and rearmed the army. He provided the infantry with a vastly improved firearm – the breech-loading Martini-Henry rifle, which was effective up to 1,000 yards. He was unable, however, to prevent the conservative artillery from *returning* to muzzle-loading cannon, even though breech-loaders had proved their worth in China and Abyssinia, but he increased artillery strength by 5,000 men and 156 field guns. The cavalry, too, he increased by some 1,600 men, but the social and political influence of the cavalry was too strong for him to attempt any other changes.

Edward Cardwell 'left the army estimates lower than he found them', wrote Sir Robert Ensor, 'and yet he had increased the strength of the army in the United Kingdom by 25 battalions, 156 field guns and abundant stores, while the reserve available for overseas service had been raised from 3,545 to 35,905 men . . . he exhausted his prime on this single specialised task; rendering his country a unique service, for which he has not always been too generously remembered.'

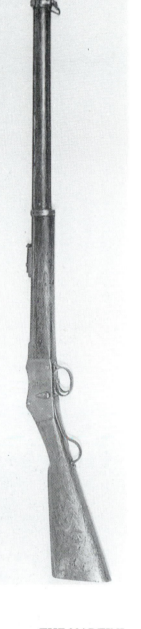

THE MARTINI-
HENRY RIFLE

The Enfield rifle was converted to a breech-loader by means of a Snider breechblock in 1866, but five years later a purpose-built breech-loader, the Martini-Henry, was approved and remained standard for nearly twenty years. It was sighted for a range of 1,000 yards and fired a heavy bullet with great power.

The Ashanti War

In June 1873 a large Ashanti army, reported to be 12,000 men, invaded the British colony on the Gold Coast (now Ghana). The Royal Navy landed marines and sailors and, with native troops, beat off the attack, but the British government saw that if they wished to keep the Gold Coast they had to send a more powerful force to subdue the Ashantis. As commander, they chose Major-General Sir Garnet Wolseley, who had made a name for himself for his successful and bloodless Red River campaign in Canada.

Wolseley's force numbered about 4,000 men: the 23rd Regiment (The Royal Welch Fusiliers),

Sir Garnet Wolseley receives news from the front during the Ashanti War

the 42nd Regiment (The Black Watch), a battalion of the Rifle Brigade, a 250-strong Naval Brigade, two battalions of West Indian troops, some local troops, a battery of mountain-guns with Hausa gunners, and a party of Royal Engineers. In January 1874 he led his men into the fever-ridden jungles of the Gold Coast to show the Ashanti army, with its vastly superior numbers of trained warriors, what it meant to challenge the might of the British Empire.

Apart from the Ashantis themselves, Wolseley and his men had to face two other formidable enemies: the unhealthy climate of the region (known as 'the white man's grave') and the dense, river-crossed jungle where thousands of fierce Ashantis lay concealed waiting to pour volleys of bullets and slugs into the advancing British column.

Wolseley and his brilliant staff (known as the 'Wolseley Gang', almost all of whom became generals) had a plan of campaign which had been worked out very carefully. The basic strategy was to invade Ashantiland in the healthier dry months of December-February, making a swift dash inland to smash the Ashanti army with overwhelming firepower, destroy the Ashanti capital at Kumasi, and return as quickly as possible to the coast.

So that his troops should spend as little time as possible in the disease-ridden climate Wolseley planned to get them in and out of the country in a few weeks. Hutted camps were built at intervals on the route, with hospitals, stores, bakeries, abattoirs, and water purifiers. The men were given a daily dose of quinine and were issued with veils, cholera belts and respirators. For every three men there was a native porter to carry their equipment. In place of their heavy scarlet or green uniforms they wore grey homespun 'tropical' suits. These and other precautions paid remarkable dividends because during the whole campaign – which did, in fact, last only a

114

Wolseley's expedition made a hazardous landing on the West African coast before marching inland to attack the Ashantis

few weeks – no more than 55 of the total force of 4,000 men died of disease.

'Fighting in the bush,' Sir Garnet told his men, 'is very much like fighting by twilight with no one able to see further than a few files to right or left.' Giving them a detailed description of the jungle terrain and of Ashanti fighting tactics, he laid down that all fighting was to be undertaken in skirmishing order by small tactical units, and urged them, in terms typical of Victorian imperialism, not to feel discouraged by the superior numbers encircling them:

Each soldier must remember that, with his breech-loader, he is equal to at least twenty Ashantis, wretchedly armed as they are with old flint muskets firing slugs or pieces of stone . . . It must never be forgotten that Providence has implanted in the heart of every native of Africa a superstitious dread and awe of the white man, that prevents the negro from daring to meet us face to face in combat. A steady advance or charge made with determination always means the retreat of the enemy.

The Ashanti army waited for Wolseley's force at Amoaful, about thirty miles from Kumasi, drawn up in their traditional extended horse-shoe formation but completely invisible amidst the tall trees and thick undergrowth. The battle that followed was confusing, but decisive. All sounds were amplified amid the tall trees: the roar of the Ashanti muskets, the hiss of bullets, the swish of the naval rockets, and the yells and beating of drums was such that no unit was certain of the position of the others. An eye-witness noted that the fight . . .

. . . consisted simply of five hours of lying down, of creeping through the bush, of gaining ground foot by foot, and of pouring ceaseless fire into every bush which might contain an invisible foe. Nothing could have been better than Sir Garnet Wolseley's plan of battle, or more admirably adapted for the foe with whom we had to deal. Wherever he attacked us, he found himself opposed by a continuous front of men, who kept his flanks at bay, while the 42nd pressed steadily and irresistibly forward. To that regiment belong, of course, the chief honours of the day, but all did excellently well.

The victory cost Wolseley's force 250 men, and it was estimated that the Ashantis lost around 2,000. But the defeated Ashantis continued to harass the British column as it pushed on to Kumasi. Late on 4 February the Black Watch led Wolseley's men into the deserted city, horrified to find piles of human skulls, evidence of long-practised human sacrifice. They thereupon burned the city to the ground and returned to the coast.

The defeat had no lasting effect on the Ashanti people. Though they signed a treaty renouncing their claims on the coast and undertaking to give up slavery and human sacrifice. Twenty years later another British force had to be sent to quell Ashanti resistance. Finally, in 1897, their country was declared a British protectorate.

Meanwhile, the Black Watch, the Royal Welch Fusiliers and the Rifle Brigade added 'Ashantee' to their Battle Honours, and Sir Garnet Wolseley was appointed Knight Grand Cross of the Order of St Michael and St George, Knight Commander of the Bath, presented with a Sword of Honour by the City of London, thanked by Parliament and awarded £25,000 by a grateful nation.

1873-1874
ASHANTI: (West Africa)
Royal Welch Fusiliers
Black Watch
Rifle Brigade

115

THE ZULU WAR

The Washing of the Spears

At Isandhlwana on 22 January 1879, the Zulus inflicted what was probably the most crushing defeat a European army had ever suffered at the hands of 'native' troops. 'How this could happen we cannot yet imagine,' Queen Victoria asked in her journal when news of the disaster reached London. So how did it happen?

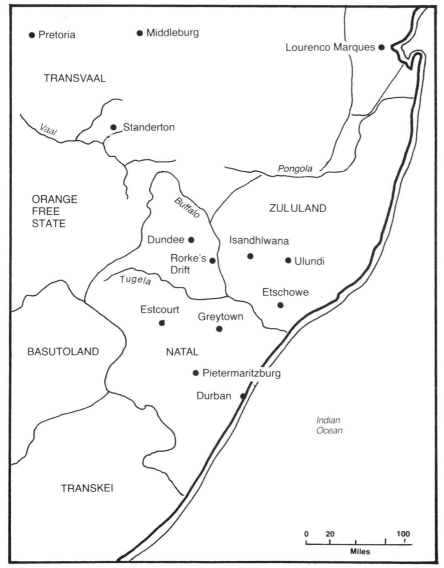

The Zulus were a highly militarised nation with a standing army of some 50,000 well-trained, fearless warriors, all eager for battle, waiting on the will of their king, Cetewayo. Their existence constituted a threat to their neighbours, particularly to Boer settlers in the Transvaal, the British in Natal, and the Swazis.

By tradition a new Zulu king had to go to war so that his warriors could 'wash their spears'. But Cetewayo, who had allowed himself to be crowned in the name of Queen Victoria by the British Administrator of the Transvaal, had undertaken not to go to war – not even 'one little swoop.' But the king could not hope to keep his 'impis' (field armies) in idleness indefinitely, nor could he disband them. Besides, the Zulus naturally resented European colonisation of their land, and they wanted to lead all African peoples in a war to drive out the white men.

For their part, the British under the High Commisioner for South Africa, Sir Bartle Frere, realised that there could be no security for the white communities until the Zulu military machine had been destroyed. Peace in South Africa, he declared, no longer depended on the colonial governments, but on 'the caprice of an ignorant and bloodthirsty despot' with a powerful standing army at his command and clamouring for war. Using a series of incidents on the Zulu border, Frere had an ultimatum sent to Cetewayo with a list of unacceptable demands, including the disbandment of the Zulu army – demands with which the king could not have complied even if had wanted.

The ultimatum expired, and the British mobilised an army to invade Zululand. Its objectives were to destroy Cetewayo's impis in battle, and capture the king and his capital at Ulundi. In command was Frederick Augustus Thesiger, Lord Chelmsford (1827-1905). A conservative and rather indecisive officer, who had served in the Crimea, in India during the Mutiny, and on Napier's staff in Abyssinia, he was one of those who believed that the British thin red line was still the best defence against any attacking force.

Chelmsford's invading army consisted of about 5,000 European troops supported by 8,000 armed Natal Kaffirs. His British infantry battalions were drawn from the 3rd (The Buffs), the 4th (King's Own), the 13th (Somerset Light Infantry), the 24th (South Wales Borderers), the 80th (South Staffordshire), the 90th (Cameronians), and the 99th (Lanarkshire) Regiments. For cavalry support he had a number of irregular mounted corps of white colonists, boasting such names as the Frontier Light Horse, the Isipongo

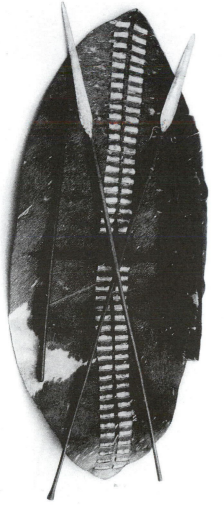

Rorke's Drift

That same afternoon a Zulu impi of 4,500 warriors, fresh from their triumph at Isandhlwana, swept down on the little post at Rorke's Drift, a few miles away. The post was a mission station used as a small field hospital and supply centre. The men there numbered about 400, including a detachment of about 100 men of the 24th, a company of the Natal Kaffirs, 36 hospital patients, a surgeon and a chaplain. The senior officer was Lt Chard of the Royal Engineers, and Lt Bromhead commanded the 24th.

When the war-cry and tramping feet of the approaching impi were heard, the native troops, with their colonial officers and NCOs, all fled, leaving the two lieutenants with only 140 men, all told, to defend the posts, and just a few hours to build some makeshift barricades with the aid of mealie bags and biscuit boxes. About 4.00pm, a look-out on a hill behind the station, yelled: 'Here they come, black as hell and thick as grass!'

For the next twelve hours the defenders, including the patients, held off attack after attack. Shooting with deadly accuracy at close range, the soldiers accounted for hundreds of their attackers. All around the perimeter and even in the hospital, the fight went on until about four o'clock in the morning, when the Zulus withdrew. By then Chard and his men had fired 20,000 rounds of ammunition and had killed or wounded at least 500

Zulu warriors, for the loss of seventeen of their number. Almost all the defenders were wounded, but they still had the strength to clear up the cookhouse and make a cup of tea.

Eleven Victoria Crosses were awarded to the defenders of Rorke's Drift, including Lieutenants Chard and Bromhead, who were also invited to Balmoral by the Queen.

All but one of the officers of the 24th Regiment stayed in the camp at Isandhlwana and were killed with their men. The odd one out was Lieutenant Melvill who had been ordered to save the Queen's Colour. He escaped as far as the Buffalo River, joined on the way by Lieutenant Coghill. While trying to cross the river, they were caught by the Zulus and killed. Both officers were posthumously awarded the VC. The Colours were lost but later recovered and restored to the 24th. The following year the Queen decorated them with a wreath of immortelles, and to this day the Queen's colour staff of the successor regiment carries a silver wreath of immortelles.

Mounted Rifles and the Royal Natal Carbineers. To support his Royal Artillery batteries, he looked to the Royal Navy, HMS *Active* of the Africa Station landed a Naval Brigade of 170 sailors and marines, armed with two 12-pounder Armstrong guns, a Gatling, and two rocket tubes. The chief means of transport in South Africa at the time was the ox wagon, and to convey Chelmsford's columns with their equipment and supplies called for over 5,000 oxen and 750 wagons and carts.

Chelmsford divided his forces into five columns, three of which were to invade from different points on the Zulu border while two were held in reserve against Zulu (or Boer) attacks. The three invading columns crossed the Zulu border early in January 1879, with orders to converge on Ulundi. This division of the British forces seems to have been a major cause of the disaster that soon followed. The central column, with Chelmsford in personal command, crossed the Buffalo river at Rorke's Drift and moved on to camp near a hill called Isandhlwana, a site which he himself had chosen on an earlier scouting mission.

Chelmsford and his men seemed to have had

little idea that they were now facing the largest and best trained army in Africa. Ignoring the advice of experienced Zulu-fighters, who told him 'the Zulus are more dangerous than you think,' he neglected to laager and entrench his camp, and he again divided his forces. He took about half of them to support a scouting party reported to be in contact with the enemy, leaving in camp six companies of the 24th Regiment with some colonial volunteers and Kaffir troops. In his absence the main Zulu impi emerged from hiding to attack his camp. The future General Sir Horace Smith-Dorrien (then a Lieutenant with the 95th Regiment, who was delivering a message) described the attack in a letter to his father:

At about 10.30 the Zulus were seen coming over the hills in thousands. They were in perfect order, and seemed to be in about 20 rows of skirmishers one behind the other. They were in a semi-circle round our two flanks and in front of us and must have covered several miles of ground. Nobody knows how many there were of them, but the general idea is at least 20,000 . . . Before we knew where we were they came right into the camp assegaiing everybody right and left. Everybody then who had a horse turned to fly. The enemy were going at a kind of very fast half-

At the battle of Ulundi a Zulu attack is repulsed by the 90th Perthshire Light Infantry. Painting by H. Oakes-Jones

Lord Chelmsford

walk and half-run. On looking round we saw that we were completely surrounded and the road to Rorke's Drift was cut off.

Contemptuous of the 24th's deadly volleys, the barefoot Zulu warriors hacked and stabbed their way through the defences until all who stood their ground had been cut down. All the officers of the 24th and all but two of the men were killed, and of the 1,800 men at Isandhlwana, 800 Europeans and 500 Natal Kaffirs only about 300 survived. The Zulus admired the bravery of the 'red soldiers': 'how few they were, and how they fought!' A Zulu observer told a British newspaper correspondent:

They threw down their guns when their ammunition was gone, and then commenced with their pistols, which they fired as long as their ammunition lasted; and then they formed a line, shoulder to shoulder, back to back, and fought with their knives.

When Lord Chelmsford saw what had happened, he was horror-struck, 'I can't understand it,' he said, 'I left a thousand men here.'

The English had allowed Cetewayo to wash his spears.

The Battle for Ulundi

'We have certainly been underestimating the power of the Zulu army,' was Lord Chelmsford's verdict on his crushing defeat, and he always maintained that his camp could have been defended, if only his orders had been followed. However, the heavy Zulu losses in attacks on his forces at Etshowe, Ginginhlovo, Kambula, and Inhoblane, where the British losses were minimal, supported his contention that even the fearsome Zulu impis could be crushed and destroyed by the discipline and firepower of a modern army.

At the battle of Ulundi six months later he proved his point and won a satisfying victory. His 5000-strong force was formed into one enormous square. The infantry, four deep, manned the sides, with the field guns and Gatlings at the corners and centres. Inside the square were the cavalry, native troops, irregulars, engineers, wagons and carts with ammunition, and Chelmsford and his staff. When all was ready, the square moved slowly towards Cetewayo's capital, flags flying and bands playing. There was at first no sign of the Zulus. Private Tuck of the 58th Foot, who was in the front rank, described the scene:

'After advancing about three miles (during which time our mounted men were out in front and on our flanks burning some of the large Zulu military kraals), the enemy could be seen approaching from all sides in immense numbers. I should estimate their number at 20,000.'

The British troops faced out and closed ranks. The two front ranks knelt, and the two rear ranks stood, waiting for the Zulu advance. Private Tuck was watching:

'. . . a hot engagement ensued for one hour and a half, inflicting severe loss on the enemy's side but few on the British. Our cavalry was surrounded by them, we standing perfectly steady until the enemy coming too close, when the cavalry retired into the square, and then the infantry artillery opened such a fire that no living being could possibly come within a hundred yards of us as shells and volleys went into their midst. Still, on they came with great determination but they could not stand against our fire and advance, so they turned and ran. No sooner had they turned to flee than out of our square popped the 17th Lancers, Mounted Volunteers and all mounted men cutting the enemy down like grass before the scythe . . .'

On that day, 4 July 1879, the Zulu military power was finally broken, Ulundi was captured, and Cetewayo fled. 'An assegai has been thrust into the belly of the nation,' he said. 'There are not enough tears to mourn for the dead.'

The Queen received the news 'with the greatest satisfaction and gratitude,' especially pleased 'that this great success should have been achieved by Lord Chelmsford after so much anxiety.' He, however, had been replaced by Sir Garnet Wolseley – who arrived too late to influence the conduct of the war. It was left to Wolseley to capture Cetewayo and his chief, and to pacify the Zulus.

1878

ALI MASJID (Afghanistan)
10th Hussars
Royal Leicestershire
Loyal North Lancashire
King's Own Yorkshire L.I.
Rifle Brigade

1878-1879

AFGHANISTAN:
Second Afghan War
10th Hussars
Royal Leicestershire
East Surrey
Loyal North Lancashire
Rifle Brigade

A combined British and
Indian force, commanded
by Maj Gen Roberts, in
the Kurram Valley

The Second Afghan War

RUSSIAN ADVANCES into central Asia in the decades after the Crimean War were seen in London and Calcutta as a threat to the Indian empire. By absorbing Tashkent, Samarkand and Khiva the Tsar's armies had come dangerously close to Afghanistan and the traditional route for invaders of India. So when in 1877 Amir Sher Ali of Afghanistan welcomed a Russian mission to Kabul, the Viceroy of India, Lord Lytton, prepared to send a British mission to the Amir, with a demand that he should dismiss the Russians. The Amir replied by turning back the British mission's advance party as it crossed the Afghan border in September 1878.

Lytton then sent an ultimatum to Sher Ali, calling for an apology for this rebuff and the immediate acceptance of a British mission. No reply was received and three British columns invaded Afghanistan at dawn on 21 November 1878.

Mindful of the disasters of the First Afghan War, the Indian government assembled a large and well-equipped invasion force. The cavalry component of the three columns included squadrons of the 9th Queen's Royal Lancers, the 10th Royal Hussars, and the 15th King's Hussars, as well as the famous Bengal Lancers, the Corps of Guides, and other Indian cavalry

The Afghans 'were no more friends of the Russians than of the British; they were friends of Afghan independence.'

VINCENT A. SMITH

units. The British infantry units included the Rifle Brigade and the 60th King's Royal Rifle Corps, together with battalions from nine regiments: the 5th (Northumberland Fusiliers), the 8th (The King's), the 17th (Leicestershire), the 25th (King's Own Borderers), the 51st (King's Own Light Infantry), the 59th (2nd Nottinghamshire), the 70th (Surrey Regiment), the 72nd (Duke of Albany's Own Highlanders), and the 81st (Loyal Lincoln Volunteers). The Native infantry included battalions of the Corps of Guides and five Gurkha regiments, as well as Sikh, Punjabi and other Indian infantry regiments. The Artillery provided a siege train and over twenty batteries of field and mountain guns. There were nine companies of Bengal Sappers and Miners.

The largest of the invading columns was the Peshawar Valley Field Force of some 16,000 men in two divisions. Commanded by Lieutenant-General Sir Samuel Browne (the one-armed designer of the 'Sam Browne' belt), this force entered the Khyber Pass and surrounding hills during the night of 20 November, and after a long artillery duel captured the fort at Ali Masjid. Jellalabad was occupied four weeks later.

The second largest column, the Kandahar Field Force of about 13,000 men in two divisions under Lieutenant-General Sir Donald Stewart, marched up through the Bolan Pass to Quetta. On 8 January 1879 they reached Kandahar, already evacuated by the Afghan garrison.

The smallest column was the Kurram Valley Force of 6,300 men commanded by Major-General Sir Frederick Roberts. After marching into the valley and taking the Kurram fort, it found its progress valley blocked by a line of Afghan defences based on Peiwar Kotal, a ridge between the hills. The road to the Kotal was covered by Afghan artillery and sharpshooters and could be raked from end to end by gun and musket fire. When Roberts realised that thousands of Afghan regular soldiers and hordes of tribesmen were waiting to annihilate his small force, he experienced, he said, 'a feeling very nearly akin to despair.'

1878-1880

AFGHANISTAN:
Second Afghan War
9th Lancers
15th Hussars
Royal Northumberland
   Fusiliers
King's
Suffolk
King's Own Scottish
   Borderers
East Lancashire
Royal Hampshire
King's Own Yorkshire L.I.
King's Royal Rifle Corps
Seaforth Highlanders
Gordon Highlanders
2nd Ghurka Rifles

1879

CHARASIAH:
Second Afghan War
9th Lancers
Royal Hampshire
Seaforth Highlanders
Gordon Highlanders
KABUL: Second Afghan War
9th Lancers
Royal Norfolk
Royal Hampshire
Seaforth Highlanders
Gordon Highlanders
2nd Gurkha Rifles

1879-1880

AFGHANISTAN:
Second Afghan War
6th Dragoon Guards
9th Hussars
Royal Fusiliers
Royal Norfolk
Devonshire
West Yorkshire
East Yorkshire
Royal Irish
King's Own Shropshire L.I.
Manchester
Royal Berkshire
Seaforth Highlanders

1880

AHMAD KHEL:
Second Afghan War
East Lancashire
King's Royal Rifle Corps
KANDAHAR:
Second Afghan War
9th Lancers
Royal Fusiliers
Royal Berkshire
King's Royal Rifle Corps
Seaforth Highlanders
Gordon Highlanders
2nd Gurkha Rifles

Major Sir Louis Cavagnari, KCSI

The treaty signed at Gandamak on 26 May 1879, which was supposed to have brought the Second Afghan War to an end, allowed Britain a free hand in the management of Afghan affairs and placed the strategic Khyber Pass under the complete control of British forces. Another crucial provision concerned the appointment of a permanent British Resident in Kabul.

The man chosen for this important post was Major Sir P. L. N. Cavagnari, KCSI, an officer much experienced in negotiating with border tribesmen. He set out for the Afghan capital with an impressive escort commanded by Lt. W. R. P. Hamilton, VC. The party arrived on 24 July 1879, but within a fortnight local hostility towards the Mission and its members had become very apparent.

Nevertheless Sir Louis sent a telegram to the Viceroy assuring him that all was well. On the morning of the following day, 3 September, Afghan troops rioted when the authorities failed to meet their pay arrears. A party of rebels attacked the stables set aside for the Mission, and in a very short time the whole of the British Residency at the Bala Hissar, the citadel of Kabul, was under siege.

A message to the Amir brought his son and the Afghan Commander-in-Chief to the scene but their presence had no effect on the rebels, who continued to attack the building. Shortly before noon a force of not more than 25 men, led by three British officers, charged the Afghans in a vain attempt to subdue them. This was followed by two further charges, which also failed. Finally, with all the British officers killed, a gallant Sikh Jemadar rallied the remaining defenders and led a fourth attempt to break the siege.

By this time the gates of the courtyard had been forced, and the rioters had set fire to the building in which the members of the Mission were now making a desperate final stand. The structure itself started to collapse, allowing the mob to rush in at a number of points. Soon the British Resident, all his staff and the survivors of his military escort, were slaughtered.

When news of the massacre reached India it was immediately decided to resume the war by marching on Kabul in order to re-impose British rule and punish the rebel ringleaders. As troops moved into their forward positions it was recognised that the most serious problem to be overcome was the long line of communication over extremely difficult terrain, along which huge amounts of ammunition and supplies would have to be moved to sustain the expedition. It was recommended that the Government should 'use every endeavour to collect, purchase or otherwise, some 20,000 camels' to keep the crucial supply line going.

The Second Afghan War was, by far, the most important single campaign in which the Indian Army took a major part during the second half of the 19th century. Many famous Indian cavalry, artillery, engineer and infantry regiments went into action, whose bravery won the admiration of their British comrades-in-arms.

The imagination of the British public at home was also fired, and many people considered it unjust that Indian other ranks were not, at that time, entitled to receive the Victoria Cross. However, in 1837 a military division of the much-coveted Indian Order of Merit had been created, and at the end of the war more than 200 of these awards went to 'all ranks for conspicuous gallantry in the field.'

Two special medals were also struck to commemorate the campaign: these were the Second Afghan War Medal and the Kabul to Kandahar Star.

Camped just outside the range of the Afghan guns, he made a careful reconnaissance, and decided on the risky plan of dividing his force. Leading the bulk of his troops on a flanking march by night and climbing the left side of the hill on which the Afghans were posted, he ordered the force remaining in his base camp to make it obvious that a frontal attack was planned. At dawn his Gurkhas, Sikhs, and Highlanders took the Afghans completely by surprise, stormed their defences and put them to flight. At about the same time the base camp force opened a frontal attack. Soon the Afghan camp and guns were in British hands. For the loss of twenty killed and seventy-five wounded, the little general had won Peiwar Kotal and opened the way into Afghanistan. On hearing the news, the Queen sent a message to the Viceroy which he passed to General Roberts:

I have received the news of the decisive victory of General Roberts, and the splendid behaviour of my brave soldiers, with pride and satisfaction, though I must ever deplore the unavoidable loss of life . Pray inquire after the wounded in my name. May we continue to receive good news.

The 5th Gurkhas still celebrate 'Peiwar Kotal Day' every year. Roberts was appointed Knight Commander of the Bath and was formally thanked by Parliament.

The Amir Sher Ali fled to Turkestan and died a few months later. His son, Yakub Khan, signed a treaty with the British at Gandamak under which the Amir agreed to welcome a British envoy at his court, and to allow Britain to control his foreign policy in return for a subsidy and protection.

The Second Afghan War seemed to be over; in fact, it was only half over. As forty years earlier and a century later, the Afghans did not appreciate the advantages of foreign protection. Barely two months passed before the British envoy and all his officers were murdered in Kabul.

General Sir Frederick Roberts headed the force sent to 'assist the Amir in putting down the disturbances.' His 6,500-strong force, which included battalions of the 72nd and 92nd Highlanders together with Gurkhas and Sikhs, routed a much larger Afghan army at Charasiah, a few miles from Kabul. It was in this action the British army used Gatling guns for the first time; they tended to jam, and did not impress Roberts. A triumphal entry was made into Kabul and the Amir abdicated. 'Now I am really King of Kabul,' Roberts told his wife. 'It is not a kingdom I covet, and I shall be right glad to get out of it.' The Afghans, too, were eager to see him get out, especially after his 'rough and ready' trial and execution of those accused of murdering the British envoy and his escort.

Learning that several large and hostile Afghan forces were advancing on Kabul, he reluctantly decided to withdraw his forces to Sherpur, a fortified area north of the city. The Afghan army returned to Kabul, while at Maiwand in southern Afghanistan the British suffered a major disaster on 27 July 1880. A field force of about 2,000 men under General Burrows was surprised by an Afghan army of about five times their number. In the ensuing action, the British lost over 1,300 men, including 308 out of 488 men of the 66th (Berkshire) Regiment. The survivors retreated into Kandahar, which the Afghans then beseiged.

A strong column was at once assembled in Kabul for the relief of Kandahar. As before, Roberts was in command. His force consisted of the 72nd Highlanders, the 92nd Highlanders, the 60th Rifles, the 9th Lancers, the 2nd, 4th, and 5th Gurkha Regiments, a number of Sikh and Punjabi infantry and cavalry units, and three batteries of mountain guns. The total force numbered some 10,000 troops plus 8,000 followers and 10,000 horses, mules, camels, and donkeys. Roberts led his column out of Kabul on 8 August and arrived outside Kandahar on 28 August, having completed 300-plus miles in 20 days – a feat which made 'Little Bobs' the hero of the hour with a public reeling from the shock of the Maiwand disaster.

To the new audience of newspaper readers it had all the drama of a rescue operation: the picked troops marching fifteen miles a day through a rough and restless country, exposed to blazing hot days and freezing nights, in constant danger of enemy attacks, led by a little general too ill to sit his horse but driving his men on by force of personality.

Finding a demoralised garrison at Kanadahar, who 'never even hoisted the Union Jack until the relieving force was close at hand,' Roberts defied his illness, mounted his horse, and on 1 September led an attack on the strongly-entrenched Afghan army. Under heavy fire the Highlanders and Gurkhas stormed the Afghan positions and drove them out of their entrenchments, capturing all their guns. The victory was complete, and it ended the Second Afghan War – a war which, in the words of one historian, Roberts had 'won virtually single-handed.'

General Roberts and his staff

A supply column forms up, ready to take food and ammunition to forward areas

Massacre at Majuba Hill

ON SATURDAY, 26 February 1881, one of of the most highly-regarded generals in the British army, Major-General Sir George Colley, led a party of about 500 British soldiers and sailors to the summit of Majuba Hill on the Transvaal border with Natal. By the following afternoon more than half of them had been killed, wounded or taken prisoner by the Boers, and he himself was among the dead. 'Dreadful news . . . Another fearful defeat,' the Queen noted in her journal. It was in fact General Colley's third defeat in what came to be called the First Boer War. How did it happen?

The First Boer War of 1880-81 arose out of long-continuing disputes between the British and Afrikaaner settlers in South Africa. Descended mainly from Dutch Calvinist immigrants in

Cape Colony, the Afrikaaners, alias Boers (meaning farmers), resented British control and criticism of the way in which freedom and equal rights were denied to Africans and coloured peoples. When all slaves were emancipated in the British Empire many Boers trekked north and founded two new republics across the Orange and Vaal rivers, the Transvaal and the Orange Free State. These territories were at first recognised by the British, but in 1877 they annexed the Transvaal as part of a move to form an all-South Africa federation under British control. The Boers naturally objected, and in 1880 proclaimed an independent Boer Republic.

In the war that followed they turned their apparent military weakness into strength. Lacking a conventionally trained and disciplined army, their 'farmers on horseback' were all good shots, armed with Mauser repeating rifles and trained as hunters to use every rock and hummock of the veldt as cover. Their irregular 'commandos' would suddenly appear from nowhere, destroy a British close-order column with deadly fire-power, and disappear again. Against only 3,500 British troops scattered in small garrisons throughout South Africa, the Boers could raise thousands of these well-armed mounted riflemen, all of whom knew every inch of the land they were fighting for.

The first British taste of Boer fighting tactics and the accuracy of their shooting was at Bronkhorstspruit a week before Christmas 1880. A column of about 264 officers and men of the 94th (Connaught Rangers), accompanied by a long line of supply wagons, was moving slowly to the support of the British garrison in Pretoria, about 35 miles away. They were marching along in light-hearted mood, with the band playing and the men singing, when suddenly they were challenged by a Boer horseman carrying a white flag. He handed a note to their Colonel, advising him to turn back. The Colonel ignored the warning. Minutes later he was dead, shot by concealed Boer riflemen, who went on to kill or

After capturing Majuba Hill, British troops were forced back by Boer snipers

124

Conventional tactics against the Boers cost General Colley his life, and the lives of many of his men

wound 155 of his officers and men before the rest of the column was forced to surrender.

The next 'fearful defeat' took place five weeks later. In another attempt to relieve the threatened British garrisons in the Transvaal, General Colley decided to attack the strong Boer defences at Laing's Nek in the Drakensberg Mountains on the Natal border. Having what a fellow officer called 'a dangerously high idea of what a few British soldiers can do,' he ordered the 58th (Northampton) and the 60th (King's Royal Rifles) to make a frontal attack in close order on the Boers, who were dug in on the brow of a hill near Laing's Nek. After climbing the hill, their red coats making them perfect targets for Boer riflemen, the troops who survived the enemy marksmanship fixed bayonets and charged, only to be mown down by deadly fire at point blank range. Most of the officers were killed and only a few of the men reached the Boer trenches. The British dead and wounded were over 180, the Boers lost only 41. This was the last occasion when British troops carried their regimental colours into battle.

Although aware that reinforcements led by General Sir Evelyn Wood VC were on their way, Colley was determined to defeat the Boers unaided. 'I mean to take the Nek myself,' he declared. His plan was to seize Majuba Hill and so force the Boers to withdraw from their entrenched position at Laing's Nek.

To climb and occupy the 2,500 foot hill he assembled a 'scratch lot' of troops: seven companies of infantry drawn from the 58th, 60th and 92nd (Gordon Highlanders) and a naval brigade. Among them was Lieutenant Ian Hamilton, later to win fame as a commander in the Second Boer War and at Gallipoli in 1917. He described the climb:

Up towards the flat top of that freak of an earthquake – that tall table-topped mountain – since ten o'clock on a dark night a party of British sailors and soldiers had been marching under a heavy equipment – full-sized picks and shovels, three days' rations, seventy rounds of ammunition, waterproof sheets and greatcoats. Every now and then a man would fall and there would be a clatter, curses and orders. 'Silence!' . . . until midnight was past, only the Commander and his Staff Officer had the remotest idea where we were marching or where we were . . . On hands and knees we hauled ourselves up by the tussocks of long grass . . . at last, about 4 am we began to trickle into the saucer-shaped table top of the extinct volcano, and found it empty! Not a shot, not a sound, and now we all knew that without one life dropped in the effort, we had captured the main bastion of the Boer fortress.

General Colley felt his position was so secure that he had brought no cannon and he gave no orders for the troops to dig themselves in or build earthworks. 'We could stay here forever,' he remarked confidently. Below, the Boers were at first alarmed when they saw British redcoats above them. But soon parties of volunteers started to climb the hill, while marksmen were posted to pick off any British troops who showed themselves on the skyline – the soldiers' scarlet tunics and sailors' blue jackets making them easy targets. By midday hundreds of Boers were swarming on to the summit. Lieutenant Hamilton asked General Colley for permission to attack, but was told: 'We will wait till the Boers advance on us, then give them a volley and charge.' By then it was too late. The British troops, some of them not fully awake, were taken by surprise and driven back. Many of them fled down the hill the way they had come. The general found himelf alone, and then he, too, fell to a Boer marksman. Some 280 of his men were killed, wounded or made prisoner.

'What can you expect for fighting on a Sunday?' said Ian Hamilton's Boer captor. Hamilton was so badly wounded that he was allowed to find his way back to the British camp – a typical example of chivalry displayed by the Boers.

After Majuba an agreement was reached under which Britain recognised Boer independence, subject to British 'suzerainty'. This term was so obviously open to dispute that another conflict became inevitable. So the war of 1880-81 came to be seen as little more than a dress rehearsal for the bloodier drama of the Second Boer War of 1899-1902.

HMS *Alexandra* was reckoned to be one of the more sluggish of Her Majesty's battleships, achieving a speed of no more than six knots under full canvas. She fired the first shot in the bombardment and was, in turn, hit about 60 times by the shore batteries

The Bombardment of Alexandria

WHEN IN SEPTEMBER 1881, an Egyptian-born officer, Colonel Arabi Pasha, rose up against the Khedive and demanded the dismissal of all his ministers, the condominium powers, France and Great Britain, could not decide what action, if any, they should take. About the only thing on which they were agreed was that Turkey should not be allowed to intervene – which was more than a little high-handed of them given that Egypt, nominally at least, was still part of the Ottoman Empire. But since the purchase of the Suez Canal shares in 1875, the Egyptian authorities had been obliged to pay far more attention to edicts from London and Paris than to those coming from Constantinople.

Arabi Pasha chose his time well. He had succeeded in rousing his countrymen against the power clique of Turks and Levantines who surrounded the now powerless Khedive. He had most of the Egyptian army behind him and, despite his anti-European attitudes, he had won the sympathy of many liberally-minded people in Britain and France who saw him as a national liberator, ready to throw off the Turkish yoke.

In January 1882 he struck again by engineering what was virtually a *coup d'état*. Single-handedly he imposed a new constitution, sacked the prime minister and awarded himself the post of minister of war. Once again Britain and France looked on helpless with indecision. A series of talks was hurriedly arranged in which all the powers played some part, but since no-one had any clear idea of what to do next they were doomed from the outset. Meanwhile, as the tempers of Arabi Pasha's followers rose with the summer heat, things got more and more out of hand.

In May 1882 it was decided to send an Anglo-French fleet to the great Mediterranean seaport of Alexandria as a precaution against disorder. A few weeks later severe rioting broke out in the city, in which 50 Europeans, including the British consul, were killed and many others wounded. Order was restored by troops loyal to the Khedive, but it was Arabi Pasha who remained in effective control. His men started to fortify Alexandria on a massive scale, building new earthworks and bringing new gun batteries into position aimed at the warships anchored offshore.

On 10 June the British admiral, Sir Beauchamp Seymour, threatened that if these new fortifications were not surrendered they would be destroyed by naval bombardment. The French thought otherwise, and promptly ordered the immediate withdrawal of all their ships. Paris, it seems, was still haunted by the defeat of 1870 inflicted by the Prussians and was determined 'to avoid risks outside Europe in order to meet those within it'.

Doubtless encouraged to see the French fleet disappearing over the horizon, Arabi Pasha rejected Seymour's ultimatum and awaited further developments. He did not have to wait long, for at 7 am the following morning a salvo from HMS *Alexandra* crashed into one of the new earthworks, sending clouds of smoke and dust into the clear morning air. This was the signal for the start of a general bombardment, and soon all the 60 and 80 ton guns of the eight British battleships were blazing away at the Egyptian shore positions. Their onslaught was supported by a flotilla of small gunboats, commanded by the dashing Lord Charles Beresford. They made for the shore under the muzzles of the enemy artillery to land naval brigades, whose small arms fire caused heavy casualties among Arabi Pasha's gunners.

The Egyptian shore batteries had smaller guns than those mounted on the battleships of the Royal Navy but the action took place at such close range (1,500 yards), that many direct hits were scored. HMS *Alexandra*, for example, was struck about 60 times but only four members of her crew were killed. A boatswain, Israel Harding, won the VC by seizing an unexploded enemy shell that had penetrated the side of the ship and plunging it into a tank of water – thus emulating in almost every respect the gallantry of Charles Lucas, who performed a similar act of valour on board HMS *Hecla* during the Crimean War to receive the first Victoria Cross to be awarded.

By an odd chance, another of the British ships at Alexandria was also an HMS *Hecla*, but she was a torpedo boat depot ship, launched in 1878, whose main function was to deliver ammunition to the gun vessels. HMS *Inflexible* also took part in the bombardment: by common consent she was one of the ugliest vessels afloat, with guns so powerful that their recoil and concussion severely damaged the upperworks and smashed her boats. After firing 88 of her huge shells she returned to Portsmouth for a refit before another spell of duty in the Mediterranean.

'Well Done, *Condor!*'

Foremost among the gunboats at Alexandria was the sloop *Condor*, commanded by Lord Charles Beresford. Their principal task was to pass on signals and not take part in the main engagement, but not content with so passive a role Beresford took his vessel close inshore and, with his single gun, started to engage the heavily-armed Fort Marabout at the southernmost point of the Egyptian defences.

In doing so he drew some of the enemy fire upon himself, away from the larger ships further out. Then, with great skill and daring, he sailed so near the shore that the Egyptians were unable to depress their guns sufficiently to get his vessel in their sights.

Meanwhile, he pressed home his attack and was joined by other gunboats whose commanders, inspired by his example, went to his assistance. Their combined fire silenced Fort Marabout, whereupon a great cheer went up from the British squadron, and Admiral Seymour hoisted his now-famous signal – 'Well done, *Condor!*'

Lord Charles Beresford was regarded as a hero by his crew not only for his dash and leadership in action, but also for his work as an advocate of naval reform. He was one of the first senior officers to realise the importance of the press in rallying public opinion to a cause. As a Sea Lord he used his considerable personal prestige to achieve a number of changes in the Navy that he saw were long overdue.

'Bluejackets to the Front!'
A Naval Brigade in action: 1884

Other British battleships were HMS *Monarch*, launched in 1868 with a displacement of 8,322 tons, which in many ways was a forerunner of the kind of battleship used in the First World War, with steam powered steering and rotating gun turrets. HMS *Sultan* and HMS *Superb* also went into action, together with HMS *Invincible*, HMS *Temeraire* and HMS *Penelope*. The frigate HMS *Inconstant* arrived on the scene too late to take part in the bombardment, as did the battleship HMS *Minotaur*, thus keeping intact her reputation for never firing a shot in anger. She was in commission for 18 years, went into reserve for a further six years and then became a laundry ship before she was broken up in 1922.

The bombardment continued throughout the morning, but shortly after midday return fire from the Egyptian positions ceased altogether, and a small force was landed to occupy the forts. No opposition was encountered, and the land-ing party was able to put out of action those enemy guns not already destroyed. British casualties were remarkably few: only 10 men had been killed by enemy fire, and 27 wounded. Some of the Royal Navy's ships sustained no losses at all, nor was there any loss of life among the gun-boat crews.

After the seamen returned to their ships to await further orders, looters and rioters rampaged through the city for two days, setting fire to buildings and murdering poeple out of hand. Landing parties had to be sent ashore once again to restore order, and found themselves engaged in fierce street fighting with a well-armed and determined enemy. One of the seamen, Thomas Holman, takes up the story:

After finishing the sailor's part of the business then, and giving Arabi's forts their quietus, we had to buckle on blankets and water bottles, and do what we could to prevent those skulking Arab thieves from looting the town. So, with a naval officer installed as head of police, we landed, and with machine-guns, rifles and bayonets, and even fisticuffs if required, we bullied those dogs into some sort of obedience and civility . . .

Meantime, other parties of British Blues are employed in other duties. Some mounted, some on foot: some in the fighting line of skirmishes that have constant brushes with the enemy; others with their nine-pounders form a field battery, mounted on shanks' pony alone, and dragging their guns through the sand in grand style, even keeping pace with the less encumbered infantry artillery as they swing along to the strains of martial music.

Others are employed with gun cotton and dynamite, destroying gun, fort and bridge, and assist-ing the engineers generally. Naval signalmen are to be found here, there, and everywhere, flashing their lights by night and swinging their flags by day, passing and receiving messages in Morse as quick or quicker than the Army signallers themselves.

Yes, my brothers, here are some of your Tars at work. Nearly all the groups are interchangeable, and can change duties at any moment without breaking the continuity of their work, and can, tomorrow, all assemble on board their ships again ready for instant battle. You surely get your money's worth out of these tarry souls, do you not?

Warming to his theme, and perhaps aware of the fact that he is in danger of upholding naval honour at the expense of his army comrades, this highly literate sailor – who these days would almost certainly find himself employed in naval public relations rather than on board ship – ends with this resounding peroration:

Sailors and soldiers know too much of each other nowadays and have fought side by side in too many of our recent little campaigns to allow the old jealousies between the two services to arise again . . . Our comradeship sealed by a thousand grogs between, a thousand divided fowls from a thousand forages, and tens of thousands of common dangers in as many thousands of places.

Gatling guns were used by men of the Naval Brigades to clear rioters and looters from the streets of Alexandria in 1882

The Hero of
Tel-el-Kebir

FROM THE ADMIRALTY'S point of view
the bombardment of Alexandria was a copybook operation. The forts were destroyed and
order restored to the city with minimum loss:
another lustrous chapter was added to the already
bright annals of the Queen's Navy. Politically,
however, the attack was a disaster. Sir Garnet
Wolseley later described it as 'silly and criminal',
for riots broke out in many parts of Egypt and
considerable impetus was added to the national
movement. The bombardment also marked the
start of a British entanglement in Egyptian affairs
that lasted more than seventy years.

When Arabi Pasha threatened to destroy the
Suez Canal 'in the defence of Egypt' and to burn
down Cairo 'rather than surrender', Gladstone
felt it necessary to intervene. Such were his
powers of persuasion that he was able to convince
his fellow Liberals that the only possible course
was the despatch of an expeditionary force to
'restore law and order' and safeguard the Canal.
France was invited to take part in a combined
operation, but after the ignominy of Alexandria
this was no more than an empty formality. The
French cabinet would go no further than a
commitment to defend Suez, but even this was
too much for the Chamber of Deputies, who
threw out the government and declined to have
anything more to do with the whole affair.

So the British decided to go it alone, which
immediately raised the question – who should
lead the expedition? Garnet Wolseley, now a
lieutenant-general and Adjutant-General of the
Army, was the obvious choice. But as a champion
of reform he had engaged in a long-running
quarrel with his C-in-C, the Duke of Cambridge,
who loved the Army with an equal passion and
did not want to see it changed in any way.
'Wolseley is a very pleasant man to deal with –
when he likes' the Duke told Queen Victoria.
'His great fault is that he is so *very ambitious . . .*'
The Queen naturally supported her kinsman.
Like the Duke, she saw no need for change in
her beloved army, and took the greatest excep-
tion to a remark, reportedly made by Wolseley,

Garnet Wolseley, who has been called
'the most brilliant general of the Victorian era, perhaps the most brilliant
general in British history', was born
in 1833 into an impoverished army
family. He was given a commission
when he was eighteen by the Duke of
Wellington in recognition of the services of his father and grandfather.

From the start he had a burning
desire for military glory, and 'longed
to hear the whistle of a bullet fired in
earnest.' His ability and his ambition
were soon noticed, and after being
wounded in a desperate charge in the
Burma War, he was promoted to
the rank of lieutenant. At the siege
of Sebastopol in 1855, which he
'thoroughly enjoyed', he made a point
of working with the Royal Engineers 'in
the post of greatest danger'. Wounded
by a bursting shell, he lost the sight of
his right eye.

During the Indian Mutiny he saw
action with the 90th Light Infantry at
Cawnpore and at Lucknow, and was
promoted Brevet Major. In 1861, he
was posted to Canada to become
quartermaster-general with the rank
of colonel. His first independent command was the Red River Campaign of
1869-70, in which the rebellion of
Louis Riel was suppressed without
bloodshed. It showed him to be a past
master of careful planning and preparation, giving rise to the Cockney
expression 'All Sir Garnet'.

The Ashanti campaign was another
outstanding example of the 'All Sir
Garnet' method, and it made Wolseley's claim for high command almost
irresistible. Although there were
frequent expeditions and minor campaigns, none gave him an opportunity
to put his talents to full use. He found
himself side-tracked into the post of
Lord High Commissioner in Cyprus,
and was not chosen for a command in
the Second Afghan War.

'I feel like an eagle that has had his
wings clipped,' he said. It was not
until the war in Egypt in 1882 that the
eagle was allowed to stretch his wings
and soar into full flight.

Wolseley's 'Gang'

While he was still a subaltern **Sir Baker Creed Russell** first saw action in Meerut, at the outbreak of the Indian Mutiny, and took part in many of the operations that followed. He was one of Wolseley's most able officers during the Ashanti War, and fought also in the Transvaal. In the teeth of fierce opposition from the Prince of Wales and others, Wolseley gave him the temporary rank of brigadier and put him in charge of a brigade of cavalry in preference to Sir Henry Ewart of the Life Guards, who had never seen a shot fired in anger. It was this appointment that upset the Establishment of the day, but Wolseley stuck to his decision. As he explained in a letter to his wife, Russell 'had entered the service and gone through his first campaign before Ewart had been gazetted into the Army at all.'

Sir Evelyn Wood was a member of Garnet Wolseley's original 'gang', but in later years relations between the two men had grown somewhat cool. Wolseley saw him as a potential rival, and was envious of his ability to get on well with the Queen. 'I am forced to leave Wood . . . in Alexandria,' he said. 'He will fume, but I cannot help it . . . he will miss the big coup here and I am very sorry for him.'

Another of Wolseley's close associates was **Redvers Buller**, whose reputation for bravery and endurance was well-deserved. He was, however, less renowned for his intellectual grasp or imaginative power. His appointment as chief of intelligence therefore came as a surprise to many on headquarters staff. Wolseley himself came to regret his choice, for Buller believed that the only way of assessing the enemy's strength was to visit the front line and see for himself. This was how he became directly involved in the battle of Tel-el-Kebir during which he fought, once again, with great courage and determination.

Redvers Buller was probably one of the officers **William Butler** had in mind when he wrote in his memoirs 'the thing that astonishes me is the entire absence of the thinking faculty in nine out of ten of the higher-grade officers with whom I was associated.' But he had the greatest admiration for Wolseley – 'the best and most brilliant brain . . . in the British army'. It was an admiration reciprocated by his commander, who gave Butler a place on his staff in Egypt, where he was appointed adjutant as well as assistant quartermaster-general.

Others called to Egypt, who had served with Garnet Wolseley on one or more of his earlier campaigns, included **Colonel Lanyon, Colonel Maurice, Hugh McCalmont, Archibald Alison, Herbert Stewart, John McNeill, Drury-Lowe, Gerald Graham, Bindon Blood** and **Sir John Ayde** who, despite protests from the Duke of Connaught and the fact that he was fourteen years older than Wolseley, was appointed chief of staff.

By no means all the officers alongside Wolseley enjoyed his confidence. Although he was able to avoid having the Prince of Wales on his staff, he did accept **Arthur, Duke of Connaught**, the Queen's third son, in an attempt to please Her Majesty. He took care, however, to keep him away from the front line, giving him command of the 1st Guards Brigade. Another royal was the **Duke of Teck**, the Queen's cousin, who had seen little active military service since his presence at the battle of Solferino. He complained constantly about the state of his quarters and the hardships of the campaign. 'Just like a spoiled child' said Wolseley firmly, who entrusted to his care a handful of foreign military observers to keep him, and them, out of harm's way.

An officer of his choice, but one who earned Wolseley's displeasure by telling him how to conduct the campaign, was **Sir Edward Bruce Hamley**, author of a widely-acclaimed book on strategy. 'An angry man with an exaggerated opinion of his own capacity as a commander' was how Wolseley later described him. He was put to work drawing up comprehensive operation plans for an attack at Aboukir Bay. News soon leaked out that this was where the major blow was to fall; everyone, including the Duke of Cambridge, the war correspondents, most of his own officers – not to mention the Egyptians – fell into Wolseley's trap, as he sailed off quietly in the opposite direction with the greater part of his army, to seize the Suez Canal. Thoughtfully he left a note explaining that the Aboukir Bay plan had always been 'a humbug'. But Sir Edward, who fought with distinction when the time came at Tel-el-Kebir, never forgave the man who had so shamelessly used him as a pawn in the pre-battle deception game.

that if the Prince Consort were alive there would have been Army reform long since.

Wolseley himself was fully aware of the situation; in a letter to his wife he bitterly observes:

I have done my best for my country, and if my country's sovereign does not appreciate my services, I cannot help it.

In the end it was the Duke himself who resolved the dilemma. For all his conservatism he was a fair-minded man of honest character who admired Wolseley's abilities as much as he disagreed with his views. When it became clear that his was the name most likely to go forward from the Secretary of War, the Duke sent a private and confidential letter to Her Majesty, in which he said:

. . . I do not think it would be advisable to oppose the selection, as I am satisfied that the public will be very pleased with the appointment, and I further think that Wolseley is very decidedly as able a man for the field as we have got. I therefore would suggest that you would graciously *accept* the submission if made.

Wolseley took up his command on 20 July 1882 and immediately started work on his campaign. It says much for his brilliant planning and characteristic vigour, and for the state of readiness of the British and Indian armies, that in

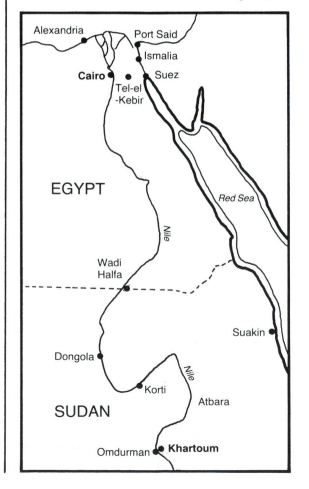

exactly a month he landed a force of 20,000 men in Egypt with huge quantities of equipment, supplies and ammunition. It was, as we should say today, a completely professional operation, that showed the British military machine at its best. The soldiers were well-armed and well-supplied, and their morale was of the highest. There could have been no greater vindication of Lord Cardwell's earlier reforms, or stronger evidence of Sir Garnet Wolseley's genius for leadership.

Convinced that the British attack would follow the classic Napoleonic route up the River Nile to Cairo, the Egyptians concentrated most of their forces in the delta and along the Mediterranean coast. When Wolseley outflanked them by seizing the Suez Canal and establishing his main base at Ismalia, Arabi Pasha sent the rebel army to the east and strengthened the defences at Tel-el-Kebir, a village about 25 miles away from the Suez Canal, situated between the railway line and the so-called Sweetwater Canal. Together, these represented a crucial strategic link between Ismalia and the Egyptian capital.

On high ground above the village had stood for many years an Egyptian army base and other military installations: a fairly steep escarpment bordered the high ground in the south, while to

the north it sloped away as table-land. In an otherwise flat and featureless landscape, consisting mainly of sandy and rocky soil, the heights of Tel-el-Kabir formed a natural barrier which Arabi Pasha decided to fortify with an elaborate and extensive network of trenches. There was no shortage of labour to carry out the work: what the Egyptians lacked was time. And although the ambitious plans were never completed, what was achieved was formidable enough: main trench lines to a minimum depth of 5ft, with breastworks as high as 6ft; salients at regular intervals commanding wide fields of fire across the open terrain; to the rear, shallower shelter trenches with well constructed rifle pits, and gun emplacements on the higher ground above.

These defences impressed Wolseley, who thought that they would prove 'a very hard nut to crack'. A frontal assault across open terrain against a well-armed and well-equipped enemy would lead to a bloodbath. Not only was it imperative to avoid heavy casualties on purely military grounds, but all Wolseley's instincts as a commander were to achieve his objectives with minimum loss.

He and his staff spent four days making a thorough reconnaissance of the position, during which it was discovered that the Egyptians did

1882

TEL-EL-KEBIR (Egypt)

Life Guards
Royal Horse Guards
4th Dragoon Guards
7th Dragoon Guards
19th Hussars
Grenadier Guards
Coldstream Guards
Scots Guards
Royal Irish
Duke of Cornwall's L.I.
Black Watch
King's Royal Rifle Corps
York and Lancaster
Highland L.I.
Seaforth Highlanders
Gordon Highlanders
Cameron Highlanders
Royal Irish Fusiliers

Dawn at Tel-el-Kebir. The Highland Brigade came face-to-face with some of Arabi Pasha's toughest warriors

Arabi Pasha was born in 1840 near Zagazig, not far from Tel-el-Kebir. The son of a desert sheik, he studied at the University of Cairo before being conscripted into the Egyptian army at the age of 14. He became a protégé of the then Viceroy, and rose rapidly in rank to become a lieutenant-colonel by his 21st birthday.

When Ismail came to power his privileges ceased, and for the next 20 years Arabi nursed a growing hatred of the ruling class.

His time came when Ismail was replaced by Tewfik, who appointed him Colonel of the Guard. This gave him the power base he needed to make his successful bid for leadership of the national movement and rebel forces.

not man their outposts after dark. This gave Wolseley the key he was looking for. Against all conventional military wisdom he decided on a night march against the enemy, to take him unawares and overrun his positions before he could rally an effective defence. It was an audacious and risky plan because soldiers in the dark, unable to see their officers or NCOs, can quickly lose their bearings and become confused. To carry out such a large and intricate manoeuvre in total silence requires a level of training and discipline of a very high order. One shout in the darkness, one rifle shot accidentally discharged, and the vital element of surprise is lost with unpredictable results. Wolseley knew all this, of course: on the eve of the battle he wrote to his wife –

I know that I am doing a dangerous thing, but I cannot wait for reinforcements; to do so would kill the spirit of my troops, which at present is all I could wish it to be . . . If they are steady in the dark – a very crucial trial – I must succeed. Otherwise I might fail altogether, or achieve very little. You can fancy that this responsibility tells a little upon me, but I don't think any soul here thinks so . . .

In the event, these fears were unfounded. The silent army moved forward in the darkest hours before dawn on the morning of 13 September 1882. As the tension mounted, one drunken Scotsman did let out a peal of laughter, but he was quickly suppressed and taken to the rear to sober up.

The Highlanders failed to get into their proper positions and had the misfortune of coming face-to-face with some of the toughest troops in Arabi's army – seasoned fighters from the Sudan who gave no quarter and expected none.

But after an intial setback the line held and was steadied by the arrival of a second wave of Highlanders. Meanwhile Drury-Lowes's cavalry had started their advance on the right flank, while the Indian brigade were moving towards the rear to cut off the Egyptian's line of retreat.

With artillery support the Highlanders broke through the heavily-defended forward positions, inflicting heavy casualties as they cleared the trenches. They encountered determined opposition, as Charles Royale later reported:

The Egyptian soldier displayed real courage. The black regiments, composed of Negroes from the Soudan, were especially notable for their pluck, fighting bravely hand-to-hand with their assailants.

Royale was quite clear that had the Egyptian officers shown 'more intelligence and less downright cowardice' they could have converted their men into 'a formidable army'.

As the British forces gained the upper hand so there began a general retreat, but many of the fleeing rebels were either cut down by the cavalry or found themselves running on to the guns and lances of the Indian brigade.

Within two hours it was all over. For the loss of 57 men killed, with 383 wounded and another 30 missing, Sir Garnet Wolseley had crushed

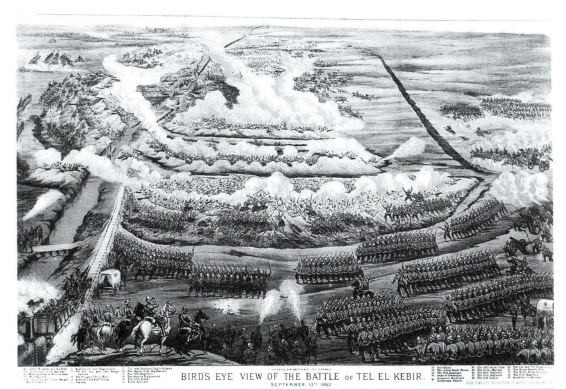

BIRD'S EYE VIEW OF THE BATTLE OF TEL EL-KEBIR.
SEPTEMBER 13TH 1882.

Arabi Pasha and scattered his rebel forces, bringing to an end in less than two months a war that the British government had been reluctant to fight.

The road to Cairo, fifty miles away, was now open, and with great daring the British cavalry raced ahead of the main force, persuaded the garrison commander not to offer any resistance and then proceeded to the Citadel to negotiate the final surrender of the city. Arabi Pasha was arrested, to be later banished to a comfortable exile in Ceylon. Meanwhile, on 15 September 1882 at 9.45am General Wolseley, with an escort provided by the Scots Guards, arrived in Cairo by special train. It was a novel and characteristically Victorian way of entering a city in triumph.

After Tel-El-Kebir – the 'most complete and decisive British victory during the whole of Victoria's reign', as one commentator describes it – spokesmen of the Liberal party said repeatedly that British forces should leave Egypt now that their military task had been accomplished. There is no reason to doubt their sincerity, and most certainly it was Gladstone's wish. But there were two important reasons why he was unable to follow his political instincts. The first, of course, was the fact that the Suez Canal could not be left undefended, and the second was that Egypt itself was still bankrupt and in turmoil.

The problems were so great that if the British had decided on an outright annexation of the country the other major powers would almost certainly have uttered a ritual squawk of protest and then turned a blind eye, each thankful that no part of the responsibility for clearing up the mess was theirs. As it was, Gladstone and his colleagues dithered and it was not until many months had passed that they filled the political vacuum in Cairo by appointing Major Evelyn Baring as British agent and consul-general. He had distinguished himself as finance member of the Viceroy's council in India: suddenly he was recalled to London, presented with a knighthood and sent to Egypt, where he served at the very centre of affairs for more than 23 years.

On his arrival, Sir Evelyn Baring found yet another major problem on the Egyptian plate. Even while Arabi Pasha's revolt was being dealt with, a new national leader calling himself El Mahdi (Messiah) had emerged in the southern province of the Sudan. By charismatic leadership, reinforced by a series of victories in minor skirmishes with the Egyptian army, he had managed to unite for the first time the warlike tribes in the north and the primitive tribes of the south. By the early part of 1883, virtually the whole of the Sudan to the west of the Nile was under the control of his followers – 'Dervishes' as they were called by the British.

The Egyptian authorities decided to take matters in hand by entrusting the command of

The eyes, painted with antimony, flashed extraordinary fires; the exquisite smile revealed, beneath the vigorous lips, white upper teeth with a V-shaped space between them – the certain sign of good fortune. His turban was folded with faultless art, his jibbeh, speckless, was perfumed with sandalwood, musk and attar of roses. He was at once all courtesy and all command. Thousands followed him, thousands prostrated themselves before him; thousands, when he lifted his voice in solemn worship, knew that the heavens were opened and that they had come near to God.

LYTTON STRACHEY

Mohammed Ahmed – the Mahdi

'Prophets are not uncommon in Muslim countries, but seldom do they arouse such hatred or such fanaticisim,' said one Western observer about the Mahdi – The Guided One of the Prophet – who inspired his followers with the belief that he had a mission to regenerate Islam and establish the faith across the whole of northern Africa.

The son of a carpenter, Mohammed Ahmed, was a young boy, apprentice to a boatbuilder on the banks of the Nile. But after receiving a severe beating one day he fled to Khartoum, where he entered a free school run by a dervish of 'great sanctity'. He completed his religious education at another school near Berber, and then settled in a village south of Kana, on the White Nile, where he became a disciple of the local mullah.

By assiduous fasting and prayer his own reputation for sanctity grew, and by the mid-1860s he had his own small group of followers. He had also had an established position in the local community, having married a number of wives – taking care always to choose daughters of influential sheiks.

The principles of his teaching were 'Universal equality, universal law and religion, with a community of goods.' All who refused to credit his mission, 'were to be destroyed, whether Christian, Mohammedan or pagan'. Like other Muslim leaders, before and since,

he took one of the most powerful passages in the Koran to convince his followers that from every field of battle a path leads to Paradise.

As a result of years of neglect and maladministration of the Sudan by the Egyptian authorities the whole vast territory was ripe for revolt. So when, during the feast of Ramadan in August 1881, the Mahdi proclaimed his coming, 'as has been foretold by the Prophet', thousands flocked to his standard. The first clash with the authorities came at the end of that year, when his men defeated, with heavy losses, a body of regular Egyptian soldiers who had been sent to suppress the revolt.

More success followed, and many thousands of fighters from different tribes joined the Mahdi's cause, so that he could claim – with justice – to be the first man to bring unity to the Sudan. Each victory brought more recruits and after the defeat of the Hicks and Baker expeditions the Mahdi had in his armoury not only Dervish spears, but also many modern rifles and other valuable weapons, including machine-guns and artillery pieces, captured from his enemies.

As his power and influence grew it seemed to many that nothing could halt his ambition to spread, by the sword, his own particular kind of Islamic belief throughout upper Egypt and beyond.

133

The Tarnished Hero

William Hicks was given his command partly on the recommendation of one of Victoria's most unlikely and – it has to be said – ineffective heroes. His name was Valentine Baker; born in Enfield in 1827, the son of a rich merchant, he went to Ceylon at the age of 21 with his elder brothers. He soon decided that he wanted to be a soldier, not a planter, and enlisted in the Ceylon Rifles as an ensign.

He transferred to the 13th Lancers and saw active service in the Kaffir War, attracting favourable attention from his superior officers, and was also present at the battle of Tchernaya in the Crimea. Promoted to field rank at the early age of 32, he exchanged to the 10th Hussars and took command of the regiment the following year.

Routine soldiering, however, did not satisfy his ambitions; he became an expert on military sciences, went to the Austro-Prussion and Franco-Prussian wars as an observer, and travelled widely in Russia and Persia. In 1874 there came an appointment as assistant quartermaster-general at the army headquarters in Aldershot.

Happily married, and well-placed for senior rank, Valentine Baker's career struck disaster in 1875 when he was charged with 'indecently assaulting a young lady in a railway carriage'.

He was found guilty, fined £500, sentenced to a year's imprisonment and cashiered.

After serving his prison term he fled to Turkey, where he was offered a senior command in the Turkish army with the rank of major-general. He distinguished himself in rearguard actions against the Russians and was promoted to the rank of lieutenant-general.

The British then offered him the job of rebuilding the Egyptian army after the defeat of Arabi Pasha, but when he reached Cairo he discovered that the offer had been withdrawn – presumably to spare junior British officers, also on attachment, the embarrassment of having to serve a commander with a criminal record.

As a way out of the dilemma Baker was then offered the gendarmerie – a quasi-military force. Desperately anxious to get himself reinstated in the British army, and believing that the new post offered some chance of seeing active service in the field, Baker reluctantly accepted his new command.

Six weeks later came the order to proceed at once to Suakin. As his force was small in number, and his men not at all well-trained, he was told to act with great caution and not to engage the enemy except under the most favourable circumstances.

As advice it went unheeded: as an order it was ignored. Valentine Baker had other ideas.

---

their army in the Sudan to a British officer. There was never any shortage of candidates for vacancies of this kind in Queen Victoria's time. The choice fell upon William Hicks: in his early fifties, this officer was about to retire with the rank of colonel and a not very distinguished career in India, broken only by a brief spell of service in Abyssinia under the command of Lord Napier of Magdala.

The British, anxious to maintain the pretence of an independent Egyptian government, made no objection to the appointment. Indeed, they provided Hicks Pasha – as he was now styled – with a small number of European officers to staff his headquarters. But otherwise they declined to be involved in any way with the Sudan, or with expeditions into the huge territory, one of the hottest, most barren and desolate places in the world.

Shortly after he took over, Hicks Pasha scored some successes in minor engagements with the Dervishes south of Khartoum. Suitably encouraged, he then gathered together his main force of about 10,000 men including survivors of Tel-el-Kebir, many of whom had to be shackled to prevent them from deserting. With such unpromising material General Hicks Pasha mounted an expedition into the desert to track down the Mahdi in his own country and destroy his army. After weeks of marching across the desert the exhausted and demoralised Egyptian army eventually found the Mahdi and his Dervishes waiting for them at Kashgil where, on 5 November 1883, they walked straight into an ambush and were slaughtered to a man.

News of this disaster was greeted with horror in London not only because British lives were lost, but also because the annihilation of Hicks Pasha and his army left dangerously exposed a number of isolated inland garrisons based in and around Khartoum. If the Mahdi's forces were to overrun these positions and then move on to control the Red Sea coast, this would post another threat to international – and especially, British – shipping using the Suez Canal. Furthermore, Upper Egypt would itself be in jeopardy if powerful and united forces were to occupy the whole of the Sudan. There was no alternative. Direct intervention in the territory was unavoidable if the vital lines of communication to India and the Far East were to be properly safeguarded. In such a way was the mesh of British entanglement in the affairs of Egypt and the Sudan drawn still tighter.

Rear Admiral Sir William Hewitt, the new C-in-C of the East Indies, received orders from the Admiralty to protect the Red Sea coast, and as soon as he heard of Hicks Pasha's defeat he sent the gun vessel *Ranger* to Suakin, the only Sudanese port of any consequence. Surrounded by coral reefs and small in size, Suakin was nevertheless of considerable strategic importance because, among other things, it provided quicker access to Khartoum than the long journey up the Nile from the base of Wadi Halfa, on the Egypt/Sudan border.

Ranger was to be joined as soon as possible by other vessels from the Mediterranean fleet. Meanwhile, the Egyptians decided to reinforce Suakin against attack by one of the Mahdi's most ardent supporters, Osman Digna, who had already laid siege to two garrisons in the interior, Tokar and Sinket. A force of 2,500 gendarmes was assembled for this purpose and placed under the command of an English-born officer in the Turkish Army, Valentine Baker.

As soon as he arrived at Suakin, Baker set about augmenting his force with local Sudanese troops and a handful of European volunteers, bringing the total number of men under his command to about 3,500. Then, against all his written instructions, he moved down the coast to Trinkitat before marching inland to relieve

Tokar, not more than 20 miles away. Soon the expedition encountered a small number of local tribesmen, the Hadendoa, who kept them under observation until, on 4 February 1884, they reached a village named El Teb. Here, led by the formidable Osman Digna, they launched their attack. The results were devastating, as Valentine Baker described:

On . . . being threatened by a small force of the enemy, certainly less than 1,000 strong, the Egyptian troops threw down their arms and ran, carrying away the Black troops with them, and allowing themselves to be killed without the slightest resistance. More than 2,000 were killed. They fled to Trinkitat. Unfortunately, the Europeans who stood suffered terribly.

This latest disaster caused consternation in Cairo and London. Although Baker's force was ill-trained, it was equipped with rifles and had two Gatling machine guns as well as four Krupps guns at its disposal. The dervishes, on the other hand, possessed nothing more than clubs and spears to take into battle, and yet they appeared to be invincible. Within days of El Teb came news that Sinkat had also been overrun.

Although Gladstone's hard-pressed cabinet had already decided to leave the defence of Suakin and the Red Sea coast to the Royal Navy, it was now agreed that Wolseley's plan to send regular British troops to relieve the Egyptian garrison at Tokar should be put into effect. This short-term measure drew a waspish reaction from Her Majesty:

I am glad that my government are prepared to act with energy at last. May it not be too late to save other lives!

Other measures included an order to Egypt to withdraw from the Sudan south of Wadi Halfa, and – a decision full of portents – the despatch of General Charles ['Chinese'] Gordon to the city of Khartoum to supervise the evacuation of the remaining Egyptian garrisons.

Meanwhile, military action in the Suakin sector continued. The detachment of British regulars, about 3,000 in all, landed on 28 February 1884 at Trinkikat under the command of General Gerald Graham VC, with Redvers Buller as his second-in-command and Herbert Stewart leading the cavalry.

On arrival Graham was told that Tokar had also fallen, but he decided to carry out his orders nevertheless. Once again at El Teb the dervishes were lying in wait and descended on his column in a furious charge, outnumbering the British force by about two to one. But on this occasion the outcome was very different. The regulars stood their ground, killing more than 2,000 of their assailants with devastatingly accurate fire.

1882-1884

EGYPT
Life Guards
Royal Horse Guards
4th Dragoon Guards
7th Dragoon Guards
19th Hussars
Grenadier Guards
Coldstream Guards
Scots Guards
Royal Irish
Duke of Cornwall's L.I.
Royal Sussex
South Staffordshire
Black Watch
Sherwood Foresters
Royal Berkshire
Royal West Kent
King's Shropshire L.I.
King's Royal Rifle Corps
Manchester
York and Lancaster
Highland L.I.
Seaforth Highlanders
Gordon Highlanders
Cameron Highlanders
Royal Irish Fusiliers

The harbour at Suakin

Graham reported in his dispatch that when the rebels found their retreat cut off they would 'charge out singly or in scattered groups to hurl their spears in defiance at the advancing lines of infantry, falling dead, failry riddled with bullets . . .' He went on to say that women of the tribe were present 'with hatchets to despatch our wounded.'

Among the few casualties suffered by the British force was Valentine Baker, who was badly hit in the face. His wounds, although severe, proved not to be fatal and he survived for another five years, dying in 1889 at the age of 62.

After his succes at El Teb, Graham went on to Tokar, which he found unoccupied, and then returned to base to plan the next move. He decided to track down Osman Digna's camp and set out from Suakin a month later with a force of 3,216 men and 116 officers in search of the Mahdi's cruel henchman, many of whose supporters came from the fierce Beja tribe. One of their characteristic features was tightly-frizzled hair, which is why they were called 'fuzzy-wuzzies' by the British soldiers, who had a very healthy respect for their fighting prowess.

Graham caught up with the dervishes at a place called Tamaii, where he determined to engage them in battle. He camped overnight on slightly sloping ground to ensure clear fields of fire, and then moved forward the next morning using two traditional British square formations, supported by cavalry and mounted infantry. Abyssinian Scouts were the first to draw enemy fire and as they withdrew to safety Graham ordered the Black Watch to counter-attack, which they did with considerable success. But at that moment, as Graham explained in his dispatch:

. . . a more formidable attack came from another direction, and a large body of natives, coming in one continuous stream, charged up to the edge of the ravine, charged with reckless determination, utterly regardless of all loss, on the righthand corner of the square formed by the 1st York and Lancaster. The Brigade fell back in disorder and the enemy captured the guns of the Naval Brigade, which, however, were locked by officers and men, who stood by them to the end.

Gradually the situation was restored, although not without the loss of more than 200 British officers and men either killed or wounded. The casualties among the dervishes were far greater, and steady fire from the British squares forced them back from ridge to ridge until they made off from the battlefield 'like men defeated but not routed'. When Graham's army entered Tamaii they found the village deserted, with huts piled high with ammunition, stores and other trophies captured in previous, more successful, engagements. Of Osman Digna there was no sign: he had fled and lived on to fight another day, as he had done so often in the past.

Graham's victories in the Sudan gave a much-needed boost to civilian morale at home. But the British pro-consul in Egypt, Lord Cromer, while expressing satisfaction that it had been shown once again that 'a small body of well-disciplined British troops could defeat a horde of courageous savages', recommended that no further military action should be taken in the Sudanese interior. This advice coincided with the views of Gladstone, who had already described the campaign as 'frightful slaughter of most gallant Arabs in two bloody battles.' So British troops were ordered to return to the base a Suakin, and by May 1884 most of the surrounding territory had fallen back under the control of Osman Digna. We are not told what General Graham thought of these proceedings; possibly he was too loyal, too patriotic, too much of a Victorian gentleman to express his feelings. One thing is certain, however; the decision to abandon the Sudan sealed the fate of General Gordon in Khartoum.

Lieutenant-General Sir Gerald Graham VC, KCB

General Gerald Graham was an impressive figure, over six feet tall and of powerful physique, who as a lieutenant in the Royal Engineers had fought gallantly in the Crimea, where he was twice wounded and had won his Victoria Cross. In 1860 he served in China with Wolseley, who described him as 'a man with the heart of a lion and the modesty of a young girl'. In the campaign against Arabi Pasha he added further laurels to his crown. In manner he was quiet and gentle, and numbered General Charles Gordon among his personal friends.

CHARLES GEORGE GORDON was born in 1833. His father was a Lieutenant-General, and his mother came from a much-travelled merchant family. Although he trained for the Royal Artillery, Gordon took his commission in the Royal Engineers. At his first posting, to Pembroke, he came under the influence of a 'very religious captain of the name of Drew'. When he was 21 the Crimean War broke out, and he managed to get himself sent out to Balaclava. His 'conspicuous gallantry' at Sebastopol singled him out for preferment. When the war came to an end a team of engineers and surveyors was needed to mark the exact border between Turkey and Russia, Gordon was among those chosen, spending nearly two years in Bessarabia on this special duty.

In 1860, shortly after his return home, came the outbreak of the war with China. Gordon arrived too late to take part in the capture of the Taku forts, but he was present when the Summer Palace in Peking was burned down. When the Governor of Shanghai, hard-pressed by the Taiping rebellion, asked the British for the loan of an officer to take command of the local army, Gordon's name was suggested. Which is how, at the age of thirty, he found himself a general in the service of the Emperor of China.

It was a brilliant appointment. By sheer force of character Gordon put his stamp on an ill-organised and ill-disciplined 'mass of ruffians'. By sudden attacks and surprises he cleared a vast tract of Yangtse delta territory of all rebel units. His enemies treated him with a god-like reverence; more than once their snipers were told not to aim at the brave foreign soldier, who led his men into battle with a gentle smile upon his face.

More military successes followed. When he laid siege to the important city of Soochow he gave a pledge to the rebel leaders that their lives would be spared if they agreed to an honourable surrender. When they did so, however, they were at once killed on the Governor's orders. Gordon was outraged and resigned his command on the spot; only with the greatest difficulty was he persuaded to complete his mission, and to accept a medal specially struck in his honour on the orders of the Emperor.

On his return to England he was made a Companion of the Bath, and then given the uncongenial task of strengthening defence works along the Thames estuary. During his six years at Gravesend he devoted all leisure time to religious studies and to charity. According to Lytton Strachey, the kind Colonel became a familiar and well-loved figure in this poverty-stricken district, 'chatting with the seamen, taking provisions to starving families, or visiting some bed-ridden old woman to light her fire.'

He also helped the local urchins and rough sailor lads; he found them jobs and kept in touch with them after they went out into the world.

Suddenly, and without warning, he was uprooted from this Dickensian setting, with an appointment to represent Great Britain at an international commission charged with the responsibility of improving navigation on the river Danube. At one of the meetings, in Constantinople, Gordon fell into conversation with Nuba Pasha, the Egyptian minister, who promptly offered him a post that was about to become vacant – the Governorship of the Equatorial Provinces of the Sudan.

'To be happy, a man must be like a well-broken horse, ready for anything,' Gordon wrote to his sister. 'Events will go as God likes.' He took up his new appointment in 1874, and there followed another six years of hard, un-remitting labour – this time in the most primitive of countries, full of disease, poverty, despair and corruption, baked for the greater part of the year by the harsh African sun. At the end of the third year he resigned but the Khedive, anxious to retain his services, offered Gordon the

After his brilliant career in China Gordon was posted to Gravesend, where he devoted all his leisure time to helping the poor. The contrast could not have been greater, but in both roles Gordon displayed those heroic qualities most admired by his Victorian contemporaries

137

governorship of the whole of the Sudan, with headquarters at Khartoum. It was during this second spell of duty that he met Sir Evelyn Baring in Cairo: both men took an instant dislike to each other.

In his efforts to stamp out the slave trade and to establish order throughout the Sudan, Gordon had acquired many enemies. So when his duties ended, and after he had embarked on a fruitless mission to Abyssinia, he found on his return to Cairo the whole of the official world ranged against him. Those who wielded power in Egypt had no further time for this forceful and eccentric Englishman, and they were glad to see the back of him.

He was ill and exhausted when he reached home early in 1880, but there followed three years of hectic activity in various parts of the world. First he went to India as Private Secretary to the Viceroy, only to resign three days after his arrival at Bombay. Then he visited China, soon to be ordered home by anxious authorities in Whitehall. He took command of a Royal Engineers unit in the remote island of Mauritius, where he stayed for a year. Early in 1882 he was asked by the Cape Government (who had ignored a previous offer from him) for help in their war against the Basutos. He went to South Africa, carried out his mission, and then quarrelled violently with the Cape authorities. The King of Belgium asked for his services in the Congo, but at a future date to be agreed. This gave Gordon an opportunity to visit Palestine to pursue his biblical studies.

It was while he was in this country that the summons came from Belgium, but on his arrival in Southampton he was interviewed by the editor of the *Pall Mall Gazette* about the latest crisis in Egypt and the Sudan. The interview was published in full next day, 9 January 1884, together with a demand that Gordon should immediately be sent to Khartoum with all necessary powers to deal with the situation. Many other newspapers took up the cry, and in three or four days a new national hero had emerged from relative obscurity. Few ordinary men and women had heard of Gordon, or knew much about him; now his name was on everyone's lips. He was obviously the man for the job: only he could prevent disaster in the Sudan.

A secret proposal had already been sent to Cairo as soon as the decision had been taken to withdraw from the Sudan, that Gordon should be sent to supervise the operation. The idea had, however, been firmly turned down by Sir Evelyn Baring. Now, with public clamour at its height, his name was put forward once more, only to be turned down as before.

Finally, pressure was applied. Sir Garnet Wolseley had a private meeting with his old army colleague to ask if he would be ready to serve. Gordon replied that he would be willing to do so if the Belgian authorities released him from his obligation. Baring, not prepared to raise an objection for a third time, agreed to Gordon's appointment 'provided there is a perfectly clear understanding with him as to what his position is to be and what line of policy he is to carry out. Otherwise not . . . Whoever goes should be distinctly warned that he will undertake a service of great difficulty and danger.'

With the principal players now in place, the curtain was ready to be raised on the last act of the drama.

□ □ □

ANYONE WHO imagined that Gordon would be content to pull out the Egyptian garrisons and merely 'report' on the situation under Baring's scrutiny, seriously under-estimated the man; just as Gordon under-estimated the growth of the Mahdi's influence during his four-years' absence from the Sudan. The wild fanatic had become the leader of a powerful national movement and a very dangerous man to deal with.

On 18 January 1884, Sir Garnet Wolseley, Lord Granville and the Duke of Cambridge gathered at Charing Cross station to see Gordon and his second-in-command, Colonel Stewart, on to the 8pm train for Dover. Just as they were about to leave, Gordon found that he had no money with him. Wolseley turned out his pockets and pressed into Gordon's hand whatever cash he could find, together with his watch and chain. He was not to see them again.

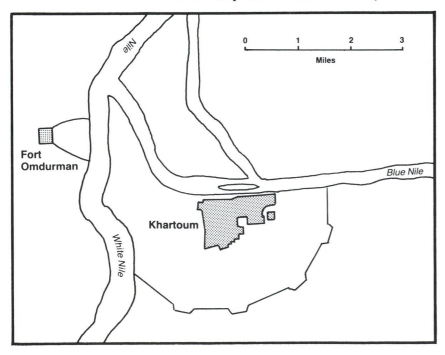

After the Channel crossing, the travellers eventually reached the southern Italian port of Brindisi, where the *SS Tanjore* waited to take them on to Egypt. Gordon spent the three days on board in a frenzy of planning. He decided to avoid Cairo and sail on to Suakin and thence by land to Khartoum in order to save time. He weighed up the pros and cons of granting to the sheikdoms of the Sudan their independence, at least nominally, rather like India's princely states. He would personally seek out the Mahdi to reach a settlement with him.

These and many other options raced through his mind. Some of them he wired to Baring, whose worst fears were thereby confirmed. He 'requested' Gordon not to go on to Suakin – the cross-desert route to Khartoum was already much too dangerous – but to travel direct from Port Said to Cairo. He also warned Gordon that any attempt to negotiate with the treacherous Mahdi would end in disaster.

Gordon did as he was told. He went to Cairo, made his peace with Tewfik, Khedive of Egypt, and was confirmed as Governor-General of the Sudan. He gave an assurance that he supported the policy of evacuation and that he would follow instructions from Baring and from the Egyptian government. A sum of £100,000 was put at his disposal, with a promise of more later should he need it. Arrangements were made for his journey south – first by train, and then up the Nile valley by boat and camel.

On reaching Berber, Gordon tried to secure the loyalty of local sheiks by revealing the evacuation plan and promising independence. He also said that nothing would be done to disrupt slave-trading. The sheiks were not impressed. They had no intention of being at the mercy of the Mahdi with the departure of the last Egyptian soldier, and as for slaves they knew that not even Great Britain had the power to stop their trafficking completely.

So Gordon's diplomatic initiative failed, but his entry into Khartoum on 18 February was a triumph. The whole city, it seemed, turned out to greet him, and amid scenes of great jubilation he was installed once more in the Palace. He immediately cancelled debts, released prisoners, offered peace terms to the Mahdi and declared that his followers were free to leave the city if they wished.

To these overtures there came no response. The desert sun burned more fiercely with each passing day and Gordon began to entertain doubts about the policies he had been entrusted to put into effect. Was it wise to evacuate the Sudan? Should not the Mahdi's power be broken first? If the whole of the Sudan fell into his hands, would not Egypt itself be threatened? Signal after signal landed on Baring's desk in Cairo

until 13 March 1884, when suddenly the deluge stopped. Tribes at Berber had risen up, declared their allegiance to the Mahdi, and had cut the telegraph line as well as blocking traffic on the Nile. Gordon was now encircled.

On 22 March the Mahdi turned down Gordon's peace offer, and invited him instead to become one of his followers. He also called for the surrender of the city and its garrison. Gordon, on his part, rallied the defenders of Khartoum who rejected unanimously the Mahdi's demands. Meanwhile, tribes loyal to the Mahdi started to gather on the southern and eastern flanks of the city, where Gordon ordered new trenches and earthworks to be prepared.

Baring was among the first to recognise the political dangers. 'The question now,' he wired to Granville at the Foreign Office, 'is how to get General Gordon and Colonel Stewart out of Khartoum.' The British press demanded action, and the Queen – always alert to the mood of her

General Gordon had for years been Governor-General of the Sudan; General Gordon alone had the knowledge, the courage, the virtue, which would save the situation; General Gordon must go to Khartoum.
Lytton Strachey
Eminent Victorians.

1884

EGYPT
10th Hussars

1884-1885

NILE (Sudan)
19th Hussars
Royal Irish
Duke of Cornwall's L.I.
Royal Sussex
South Staffordshire
Black Watch
Essex
Royal West Kent
Gordon Highlanders
Cameron Highlanders

subjects – started to press her ministers. In a letter to Lord Hartington, Secretary of State for War, she said: 'Gordon is in danger: you are bound to try and save him.' She told her private secretary that Gordon must not be abandoned, not only for humanity's sake, 'but for the honour of the Government and the nation.'

Meanwhile, under Gordon's firm and confident leadership, living conditions in Khartoum were very little affected by the siege. In eastern Sudan, however, vast tracts of desert were controlled once more by Osman Digna, the ally of the Mahdi, with Graham's return to Suakin after his victories at El Teb and Tamaii.

The crisis dragged on through May and June, with frequent assurances from Gladstone and others that Gordon was safe in Khartoum and able to leave the city at any time. But for General Gordon himself, of course, this was the sticking point: he was not prepared to desert 'his' soldiers. Either they came with him, or he stayed in

the city. His honour as a soldier and as a gentleman, and his sense of Christian duty led him inexorably to this position. Principles were at stake on which there could be no possible compromise.

In Britain, where public indignation mounted to fury as nothing was done, there came a breaking point in July when Lord Hartington threatened to resign. Gladstone knew this would bring down the Government, and he was forced to take action at last. On 8 August it was announced that a force of 7,000 men would be sent up the Nile and into the Sudan, commanded by Lord Wolseley.

The size of his task was formidable as were the risks involved. From the southern base at Wadi Halfa to Khartoum is over 400 miles as the crow flies – a distance more than doubled by the meanderings of the Nile. There were three major cataracts to overcome, and the constant threat of marauding attacks by enemy tribesmen on both banks of the river.

Wolseley gathered many of his gang around him and prepared for action with his usual vigour and ingenuity. To the fury of the Duke of Cambridge he chose some of his best men to form units of camel cavalry and camel-borne infantry. To the scorn of the Admiralty he ordered nearly 100 specially-built boats to negotiate the more hazardous stretches of the river. And to protests from the War Office (but to the Queen's warm approval) he decreed that liquor would not be included among the stores: extra quantities of jam and marmalade were laid on instead.

Gordon was unaware of these plans, and the Mahdi remained confident that he could starve his enemy into submission long before Wolesley and his column reached Khartoum. In this he was mistaken, for food supplies in the city were holding up well. But in other respects Gordon's situation was far less satisfactory. Early in September Mahdists launched a major attack on the perimeter, killing about 800 Egyptian soldiers. Morale, already much lower than at the start of the siege, started to crack altogether and Gordon knew his time was running out. He decided to send Col Stewart in the steamer *Abbas* back down the Nile, with dispatches calling for immediate help. It was a dangerous, but not impossible, mission that came to grief. The vessel struck a rock 60 miles below Abu Hamed, and in the belief that they had reached friendly territory Stewart and others went on shore, only to be massacred by warriors of the Monasir tribe.

By November, as he had foreseen, Gordon's position had become critcal. Food supplies had been cut and malnutrition was now rampant. With captured guns the Mahdi started to shell the city, and although the impact was minimal – the loss of the best of the remaining river

Colonel Burnaby meets a cruel death at the Battle of Abu Klea

steamers was far more serious than any damage to buildings – it did have a bad effect on morale. The Mahdi's forces had also surrounded Omdurman fort, cutting it off from the city and from the river.

Along the Nile, the progress of Wolseley's column was painfully slow. The whaling boats proved their worth, but inept administration and bad communications piled one delay upon another. Lord Wolseley rode up and down the banks of the Nile in a lather of frustration. On the other hand, an advance post had been set up under the command of a promising young officer, Major Kitchener, while at Korti a colourful and highly-experienced soldier, one Colonel Frederick Augustus Burnaby, turned up out of the blue, and promptly found a place on Lord Wolseley's staff.

It was at Korti that Wolseley intended to bypass a great loop in the Nile by sending a mobile column across the desert to Metemma, where some of Gordon's Nile steamers would be waiting. He had received strict orders not to lead this Desert Force in person, so he put Herbert Stewart in charge, with Burnaby as his second-in-command. The main party moved out on 6 January 1885 and was attacked, 11 days later, by 10,000 tribesmen near wells at Abu Klea, some 45 miles from Korti. In a wild charge, Arab horsemen briefly penetrated the British square, but it held firm as ranks closed. In an action lasting no more than five minutes, over 1,000 of the Mahdi's followers were either killed or wounded. British losses were much lighter, but among the nine officers killed was the valiant Colonel Burnaby.

After Abu Klea the rest of the Desert Column regrouped to march further south. At the same time it was clear that the Dervishes were preparing for a second attack. They kept the British column under fire, as a result of which Stewart was himself struck in the groin. Command now passed to Sir Charles Wilson – a good staff officer who had not previously led troops into battle. He was able, nevertheless, to hold off the second attack, at Gubat, and succeeded in leading his exhausted column to the banks of the Nile on 21 January 1885.

The steamers brought grim news of conditions inside Khartoum. By the end of December maize supplies had run out completely, and every living animal in the city had been killed for food. The streets were filled with those dying from starvation, and those already dead, while survivors went about their duties 'in a trance-like state, not really knowing what they were doing, or why.' On 5 January Omdurman fort had surrendered to the Arab forces, now closing in on every side as the bombardment of the city continued. Yet General Gordon still kept hope

alive, inspiring the defenders by his courage and leadership. And the Mahdi, unnerved by news of the British success at Abu Klea, still hesitated to strike a final blow.

Sir Charles Wilson, too, hesitated on the banks of the Nile, losing three precious days before sending his soldiers on the last lap of their rescue mission. He had no reason to believe, as he later claimed, that a few more days would make any substantial difference to the situation in Khartoum: he considered that his first duty was to his own men, taking care of the wounded and preparing adequate defences for those he would leave behind. It was not until 24 January that he embarked some of his more able-bodied men on two steamers and set off for the besieged city. When they arrived four days later, Wilson's flotilla came under heavy fire from both banks of the river, and it became clear that the defences had collapsed. After holding out for more than 317 days the city had fallen to the Mahdi and General Gordon had been speared on the steps of Government House, 48 hours before Wilson arrived on the scene.

'Too late!' was the cry that went up from an anguished nation. '. . . would you express to your other sisters and your elder Brother,' wrote Queen Victoria to Gordon's sister, 'my true sympathy, and what I do so keenly feel, the *stain* left upon England, for your Brother's cruel, though heroic fate!' In military and political circles recriminations and demands that heads should roll could be heard on all sides, and Gladstone's administration was saved only when public attention was suddenly diverted by a Russian attack on a village in Afghanistan – the so-called Penjdeh Incident.

From the roof of the Palace at Khartoum, Gordon kept a constant watch for the relief column that never came

The Road to Mandalay

BRITISH INVOLVEMENT in the remote and largely inaccessible kingdom of Burma, on the eastern shore of the Bay of Bengal, began well before the young Victoria came to the throne. It was during the 1820s, in the days of the East India Company, that a series of incursions across the border into India were made by fierce tribesmen, who ignored warnings to desist. This brought about the first Anglo-Burman War, as a result of which the large northern territory of Assam was occupied together with western Arakan and the entire Burmese coastline. Among the landmarks seized by the British was the pagoda at Moulmein, made famous much later in the century in Rudyard Kipling's poem.

A formal treaty was signed, and an uneasy peace prevailed for 20 years or more. But the geography of Burma makes it a difficult country to govern, and border bandits (or 'dacoits' as they were known to the British) were able to operate more or less at will, quite outside any centralised government control. Tension slowly increased once more until – as one history book rather quaintly puts it – 'outrages upon British subjects and insults to the British flag necessitated a fresh war with Burmah.'

On 12 March 1852, Lord Dalhousie, the Governor-General of India, sent an ultimatum to the King of Burma, followed by an expeditionary force under General Godwin. Five regiments of the Queen's Army and twelve East India Company regiments took part. On 14 April they assaulted and captured Rangoon, and then advanced inland to Prome. In January 1853 the province of Pegu (lower Burma) was annexed to British India. Although the Second Burmese War was over, Burmese guerrillas went on fighting. 'But the beasts don't give in,' grumbled Lord Dalhousie when the Burmese refused to recognise 'their actual inferiority to the British power.'

The wars in Burma showed once again that in pitched battles and formal assaults the numerical superiority of ill-trained and poorly armed 'native' armies was no match for the fire-power and artillery of highly-disciplined European troops. More men died of disease than from Burmese bullets and arrows. During the naval bombardment of Rangoon an English officer noted that many Burmese soldiers dived into the river to escape 'as if resolved on becoming targets for practice.' And in the heavy fighting around the Shwe Dagon Pagoda, 20,000 defending Burmese were driven out by British troops.

'It was amusing to see them,' noted another British officer, 'chevied through the bushes, across the plain, where the artillery was drawn up, by the European soldiers. Crack! Crack! Crack! – away they ran as if a legion of evil spirits were after them.' But as Lord Dalhousie complained, there was 'no symptom of submission', and sporadic fighting continued for many years. The war was 'generally inglorious', said *The Times*, and it cost 3,000 British lives and a million pounds.

The Queen's Army in Burma, and in other tropical parts of the Empire, may have been better disciplined and armed, but in their dress, like their enemies, they adhered to traditional ways, as Garnet Wolseley noted on arriving in Burma from India:

The Queen's Army took an idiotic pride in dressing in India as nearly as possible in the same clothing as they wore at home. Upon this occasion, the only difference was in the trousers, which were in ordinary Indian drill dyed blue, and that around our regulation forage cap we wore a few yards of puggaree of a similar colour. We wore our ordinary cloth shell jackets buttoned up to the chin, and the usual buckskin gloves. Could any costume short of steel be more absurd in such a latitude? The officers of the East India Company were sensibly dressed in good helmets with ample turbans around them, and in loose jackets of cotton drill. As a great relaxation of the Queen's regulations, our men were told they need not wear their great stiff leather stocks. This was a relief to the young recruits, but most of the old soldiers clung to theirs . . .

A generation later, in 1885, came the Third Burmese War. Under their anti-British King Thebaw, the Burmese ignored their treaty obligations with Britain, persecuted and insulted British traders and officials, and were foolhardy enough to start secret negotiations with the French. A British ultimatum was followed by a strong Field Force commanded by Major-General H.N.D. Prendergast VC. This included battalions of the Queen's Own, the King's (Liverpool), the Hampshire Regiment, and the Royal Welch Fusiliers, as well as six batteries of Indian artillery, six companies of sappers and miners, and a naval brigade.

The main objective was to take Mandalay, the capital, and capture King Thebaw. Carried by a fleet of steamers and flats, the Field Force moved steadily up the Irrawaddy from Rangoon, occupying forts and villages on the way. It came under heavy fire from Burmese troops hiding in the dense jungle, and as before the British troops suffered severely from the heat and humidity, malaria and dysentery. But Ava and Mandalay were quickly taken; the King was made prisoner and deported to India. The British thereupon annexed Upper Burma – but the Burmese still refused to recognise defeat, and their 'dacoits' continued to resist for years to come. The Field Force became an army of occupation, and sent columns to pursue the guerrillas and their leaders in most regions, including Shan States, the Arakan and Chin Hills, and the Chin Lushai territory. It was not until 1890 that the Field Force was disbanded.

A party of the 23rd Bombay Light Infantry captures a pagoda 'held by dacoits' near Phailingdan, 1887

The 2,120-ton corvette HMS *Turquoise* was one of six composite iron and timber vessels designed by the Admiralty. Built by the Earle shipyard at Hull and launched in 1876, she had a maximum speed of 12.3 knots and carried twelve 64-pounder MLR guns. Sent to the Pacific in 1877, she was found to be too slow as a colonial cruiser, and was cut down to a barque to carry out patrol duties in the Indian Ocean. On her return to Britain she was deemed unfit for further service or conversion, and was sold for scrap in 1892.

In 1885 Robert Woodward, captain of the corvette HMS *Turquoise*, was ordered to Rangoon to form a naval brigade to assist in the capture of Mandalay and the overthrow of King Thebaw. On arrival he soon converted a couple of river barges into gunboats, using two of the *Turquoise*'s 64-pounders, and assembled a flotilla of paddle steamers and launches.

With this improvised force he sailed up the Irrawaddy, destroyed a battery of eleven enemy guns near Pagan and went on to capture a fortified camp at Mingay. After successfully reaching the main objective, Mandalay, some of his crew sailed on to Bhamo, near the Chinese border. For these exploits Capt Woodward was awarded the CB.

The Pathan Revolt

IN AUGUST 1897, barely two months after Queen Victoria and her subjects had celebrated her Diamond Jubilee and all the glories of Empire, the Pathans on the North-West Frontier of India rose in revolt. From Swat to Baluchistan, British forts and garrisons fell to their onslaughts, and even the Khyber Pass – a powerful symbol as well as a strategic keypoint – was wrenched from the British grasp.

This Pathan Revolt, as it came to be known, was the most widespread of all the tribal uprisings that provided the Indian and British armies with combat experience for more than a century. Dramatic events at remote and romantic-sounding places such as Ambela, Chitral, Malakand and Tirah caught the attention of the Victorian public, but they were in fact little more than highlights in a savage and unremitting war. Almost every year a field force was despatched to quell the Pathans, the Afridis, the Mohmands, the Oraksais, the Waziris or some other troublesome tribe. For the tribes it was a holy war against the British as infidels and interlopers. For the British, it was all for the sake of law and order and preserving the security of a troublesome frontier. But as Byron Farwell said, 'it is difficult to escape the conclusion that . . . the struggle went on because both sides took a keen delight in martial exercise.'

What undoubtedly enraged the tribesmen of the area was the presence of British garrisons in the Malakand Pass controlling the route to Chitral. But the immediate cause of the 1897 uprising was a bearded holy man in Swat who called for a new *Jihad* against the British infidels. Today, he would be regarded as a fundamentalist, but to the less respectful Victorian soldier he was simply 'The Mad Mullah'. Proclaiming that the heavenly hosts were backing him, he declared that he would drive the British from their advanced posts at Chakdara and in the Malakand Pass, and sweep them completely out of the frontier.

British officers in the area were aware that trouble was brewing, but they found it difficult to take the rumours seriously. In the words of Lieutenant Winston Churchill of the 4th Hussars, who was with the Malakand Field Force as a correspondent:

. . . everybody doubted if there would be a rising, nor did anyone imagine that even should one occur, it would lead to more than a skirmish. The natives were friendly and respectful. However, on 26 July, (Churchill added) the tribesmen of the Swat Valley, irritated by the presence of the troops in what they had for generations regarded as their own country, had suddenly burst out in fury . . . They had attacked the garrisons holding the Malakand Pass and the little fort of Chakdara which, peeked up on a rock like a miniature Gibraltar, defended the long swinging bridge across the Swat River. The misguided tribesmen had killed quite a lot of people . . . There had been a moment of crisis in the defence of the Malakand Pass from a sudden and surprise attack. However, . . . in the morning light the Guides Cavalry and the 11th Bengal Lancers had chased those turbulent and forward natives from one end of the Swat Valley to the other.

But the trouble spread. Soon garrisons and forts were falling to Pathan attacks all along the frontier. On 25 August came the greatest blow

Colonel Warburton – 'Warden of the Khyber'

For the British to lose control of the Khyber Pass was to leave India open to attack by the wild tribes of the frontier – or even by a greater power. For generations the Khyber was patrolled, its forts manned, its tribes watched by British troops and political officers. Outstanding among the political officers was Colonel Robert Warburton (1842-1899), another forgotten hero for Victoria. For many years Warburton exercised such a powerful influence over the Afridis and other tribes of the North-West Frontier area that he came to be known as 'the warden of the Khyber' and even 'the king of the Khyber.' In effect, he kept the peace by sheer force of personality; where every man went armed Warburton carried only a walking-stick. The son of a British artillery officer who had married the niece of Dost Muhammad, the Amir of Afghanistan, he spoke fluent Pushtu and Persian, and the wildest tribesmen respected and listened to him because they knew he understood them as no ordinary British officer could or did. From among such men he had raised the Khyber Rifles, the force that kept the Frontier peaceful and under British control. In 1897 Warburton retired, and within a few months of his departure the British lost the Khyber.

Col. Adams. V.C.   Lieut Maclean. Lieut Greaves. Lord Fincastle, V.C.

of all to British prestige: the Khyber Pass fell to the tribesmen. By then the Malakand Field Force was in action against the Swats and Bunervals of the Swat Valley. Commanded by Brigadier-General Sir Bindon Blood KCB – 'a striking figure in these savage mountains and among these wild rifle-armed clansmen,' said Churchill – the Malakand Field Force had a strength of 6,400 bayonets, 700 lances or sabres, and 24 guns. The infantry consisted of battalions of the Royal West Kent Regiment, the Buffs, the Queen's (Royal West Surrey) Regiment, the 22nd, 24th and 31st Punjab Infantry, the 35th and 45th Sikhs, the 38th Dogras, the Garwhal Rifles, and the Guides Infantry. The cavalry consisted of seven squadrons of the Bengal Lancers and Corps of Guides, and Artillery support was provided by RFA field batteries and British and Bengal mountain batteries.

Reporting how Sir Bindon Blood then forced the passage into the Malakand and relieved Chakdara, Winston Churchill described the Malakand Pass as 'a great cup with jagged clefts in the rim'. Much of the 'rim' was held by the tribesmen, and the force had to fight its way along narrow roads through the 'clefts' which were commanded by the heights on either side. The relieving column could not deploy and was in danger of being trapped in the narrow roads.

Sir Bindon noted, as nobody else seems to have done, that one of the many rocky peaks dominated the others and could be used as a key to the whole position. Having established 300 men from the Sikhs and Dogras, with two mountain guns, to occupy this peak, Sir Bindon climbed to the top himself, and was happy to note that 'we not only had complete command of the spur along which the road ran, but also of the enemy's main bivouac, so we were able to interfere seriously with their attempts to assemble.' Winston Churchill again:

The enemy, utterly surprised and dumbfounded by this manoeuvre, were seen running to and fro in the greatest confusion: in the graphic words of Sir Bindon Blood's despatch, 'like ants in a disturbed ant-hill.' At length they seemed to realise the situation, and,

Winning the VC in the Tirah Campaign: Lt Lord Fincastle of the 16th Lancers, with two Guides officers, Col (later Maj-Gen) Robert Adams and Lt Hector Maclean, went under close fire to the rescue of a lieutenant of the Lancashire Fusiliers who was lying wounded and surrounded by enemy swordsmen. Lt Maclean was mortally wounded in this action.

(overleaf) Elephant-drawn artillery of the Indian army on the North West Frontier

Sir Bindon Blood

When they survived shot, shell, spear and assegai, Victoria's heroes tended to live on, be-medalled and be-ribboned, to a ripe old age. Longest-living of all was probably Sir Bindon Blood (1842-1940), who collected his last 'gong' – the GCVO – when he was ninety years old.

A descendant of the notorious Colonel Blood, who tried to steal the Crown jewels in 1673, Bindon Blood was one of many Irishmen who rose to the top of his profession fighting in British wars. He was born at Jedburgh in Scotland, educated at Eton and Addiscombe College, and commissioned as a lieutenant in the Royal Engineers in 1860. His name continued to appear in the Army List for eighty years.

The first officer to command a telegraph troop, Blood joined the Bengal Sappers and Miners in 1837 and spent most of the next 35 years in India.

Tough, hardened and adventurous, he was constantly in action. His enemies included the Afridis, the Afghans, the Zulus, the Boers, the Pathans and the Chitralis. For his services in the Chitral Expedition he was appointed KCB.

He was a natural choice to command the Malakand Field Force, in which one of his officers was Lt Winston Churchill. During the Boer War he was in charge of 'rounding up' operations in the Eastern Transvaal. On his return to India he was appointed to the key post of military commander in the Punjab, and finally retired with the rank of full general in 1907.

However, on the outbreak of the First World War in 1914 he was recalled and, aged 72, became Colonel Commandant of the Royal Engineers. When the Second World War broke out even he was thought to be too old for active service; he died a year later, in 1940, at the age of 97.

descending from the high ground . . . opened a heavy fire at close range (on the relieving column). But the troops were now deployed and able to bring their numbers to bear. Without wasting time in firing, they advanced with the bayonet . . . The enemy, thoroughly panic-stricken, began to fly, literally by thousands, along the heights to the right . . . The passage was forced. Chakdara was saved. A great and brilliant success had been obtained . . . In that moment the General, who watched the triumphant issue of his plans, must have experienced as fine an emotion as is given to man on earth.

Blood was ordered to lead a column of the Field Force to lay waste the Mohmand Valley as a punitive measure. When he reached Upper Swat, he reported, 'I went to the top of the Karakar Pass and had an excellent view of the Buner country, which had not been invaded since the Pathans took possession of it nine hundred years ago.' By 11 October, the tribal leaders acknowledged their defeat at a full Durbar with Sir Bindon Blood and his staff. Blood told them as they had already been severely punished, there would be no further fines. The next day he led his force out of the valley. Churchill described the scene:

The tribesmen gathered on the hills to watch the departure of their enemies, but whatever feelings of satisfaction they may have felt at the spectacle were dissipated when they turned their eyes towards their valley. Not a tower, not a fort was to be seen. The villages were destroyed. The crops trampled down. They had lost heavily in killed and wounded, and the winter was at hand. No defiant shots pursued the retiring column.

The British losses were not light: out of 1,200 men in that operation, 33 officers and 250 men were lost.

The Siege of Chitral

CHITRAL IN 1893 was a thinly populated country which had the misfortune to be situated in the northern extreme of the Frontier, where the borders of British India, Afghanistan, Russia, and China converged. About the size of Wales, Chitral, wrote Ian Hamilton, was 'a hot little valley just stuffed with olives, pomegranates, walnut trees and mulberries,' where the Himalayas 'shoot up sheer precipices in the most giddy and dramatic profusion.' Chitral was also the place where, according to Winston Churchill writing in 1898, 'the whole vast question of frontier policy is raised. We hold the Malakand Pass to keep the Chitral road open because we have retained Chitral. We retain Chitral because of the "Forward Policy".'

Fort Chitral stood at the end of the road from the railhead at Nowshera in British India. It passed through the territories of independent tribes, who maintained and protected it. But key points along the road, such as Malakand and Chakdara, were garrisoned by British Imperial forces. At Fort Chitral there was a British political agent. The Chitralis were at that time an independent people, variously described as light-hearted, charming, cruel, and treacherous. Their ruler, the Mehtar, had put his state under the 'protection' of his near neighbour, the Maharaja of Kashmir, who was himself under the 'protection' of British India.

The Chitralis and all other tribes on the North-West Frontier knew what this meant: before long the British would enter their country 'in order to restore law and order' and then annex it to their Indian Empire. What Winston Churchill referred to as the 'Forward Policy' required the Government of India to control, and if necessary occupy, the restless, independent tribal states whose territories straddled the recently agreed India-Afghan border (the 'Durand Line'), so as to ensure that no ruler in the area would fall under Russian influence. Chitral was a pawn in the Russo-British struggle for supremacy in Central Asia known as 'The Great Game'.

Surgeon-Major Robertson

As an army officer who was not a gentleman by birth, and a Political Agent who had been a medical officer, Surgeon-Major Sir George Robertson KCSI had a distinctly unusual career. Born in 1853, the son of a pawn-broker, he studied medicine at Westminster Hospital, and joined the Indian Medical Service in 1879. After serving with the Kabul Field Force in the Second Afghan War, he was appointed surgeon to Colonel Durand (who mapped the 'Durand line'), the Political Agent at Gilgit.

In 1890-91 he spent a year travelling in the Chitral area, studying the land and its people, and a few years later he succeeded Colonel Durand as Political Agent at Gilgit. The senior officer at Chitral, he made it clear that there would be no withdrawal, telling Captain Townshend that to leave the fort would bring certain death. Lacking a flag, he had one made, saying 'it seemed almost improper, not to say illegal, to fight without the Union Jack over our heads.'

To repel the besiegers as they moved ever closer to the walls, he designed fire-balls to throw down on them – bags filled with straw and pine chips and soaked in kerosene. As the weeks went by without news from the outside world, Robertson remained supremely confident that 'the long arm of the Government of India must be stretching itself forth to rescue us.' His confidence was well-founded: even as he spoke two relief forces were fighting their way to Chitral, bitterly opposed by thousands of Umra Khan's men.

Surgeon-Major Robertson seems to have been a modest man with few illusions. For the great British public, the siege of Chitral became high drama, full of romance and adventure: Robertson's book on the affair called it 'A Minor Siege', and after the rescue he said 'My mind was weary, and my life seemed fatigued also.' However, it is difficult to forget his vivid description of the country where 'All colour is purged away by the sun's glare; and no birds sing,' and of its people 'who have a wonderful capacity for cold-blooded cruelty, yet none are kinder to children.'

Captain Townshend

Captain C.V.F. Townshend (1861-1924) seems to have been one of the more unusual of Victoria's heroes. The heir of Lord Townshend, he was an able and ambitious officer who never seemed able to fit in or belong in any unit he joined, and his promotion was slow even for the period. He served in the Gordon Relief Expedition, and fought at Abu Klea and Gubat. Transferring to the Indian Army, he found himself commanding Kashmiri troops at a remote fort between Gilgit and Chitral, when he was ordered to join the force escorting Surgeon-Major Robertson. The siege of Chitral made his name, and he was appointed a CB, but somehow he never achieved the success he felt he merited. He fought in the Sudan campaign and in the Boer War, before obtaining a long series of posts and transfers in India, South Africa, France, and England. In the First World War, he was the Major-General in command at the siege of Kut in Mesopotamia. After 147 days, in April 1916, he surrendered to the Turks, with 10,000 troops, at that time the largest British force ever to surrender to an enemy. Townshend was never given another military appointment.

The Guides Cavalry and the 11th Bengal Lancers cross the Swat River during the advance on Chitral

1895

CHITRAL:
North West Frontier
  Buffs
  Bedfordshire and
    Hertfordshire
  King's Own Scottish
    Borderers
  East Lancashire
  King's Royal Rifle Corps
  Gordon Highlanders

When the Mehtar of Chitral died in 1892, there followed the usual prolonged and murderous struggle for the succession. Seizing his chance, Umra Khan, the powerful ruler of the neighbouring Pathan state of Jandol, invaded Chitral in support of his chosen candidate for the throne. The British ordered him to get out or be thrown out, and in January 1895 Surgeon-Major George Robertson, the Political Agent of the Gilgit area, arrived in Chitral with a force of 400 Sikh and Kasmiri troops. His mission was to restore stability in the territory and support the British choice for the throne. 'The country people were delighted with us,' he said, mistakenly, and he repeated the British ultimatum. Umra Khan's reply, supported by the Chitralis, was to besiege the fort.

The siege of Chitral lasted from 3 March to 19 April. The fort was about eighty yards square, with rough stone walls, about twenty-five feet high and eight feet thick, built on a framework of wooden beams. There was a twenty feet high tower at each corner, and a fifth tower which protected the covered way to the Chitral river, the only source of water, which was fifty yards away. Over 500 men were crammed into the fort, including 99 riflemen of the 14th Sikhs, 301 Kasmiri infantrymen, about 50 unreliable Chitralis, and a score or so of clerks, messengers, drivers and servants. There were six British officers, of whom the most senior was Captain

Colin Campbell. However, he was seriously wounded during a reconnaissance in force carried out before the siege began, and as a result Captain C.V.F. Townshend became the new commandant.

For more than six weeks the beleaguered force came under constant sniper fire by day, and stealthy assaults under cover of darkness. They repulsed a large number of full-scale attacks, inflicting heavy casualties on the marauding tribesmen. But ammunition supplies and food stocks ran low: the defenders were reduced to eating their own horses in order to survive. No news reached them from the outside world, so they had no means of knowing that deliverance was on its way.

The larger of the two relief forces set out from Peshawar on 1 April under the command of Major-General Sir Robert Low KCB, with Sir Bindon Blood as his chief staff officer. This force was designed to overpower any resistance, and consisted of two cavalry regiments, four infantry brigades, four batteries of artillery, three companies of sappers and miners, and a large number of field hospitals.

Some of the finest troops in India marched with Sir Robert Low's force, including the Buffs, the Gordon Highlanders, the Scottish Borderers, the King's Own Fusiliers, the King's Royal Rifle Corps, the Bedfordshires, the 4th Sikhs, the 4th Gurkhas, the Bengal Lancers and the Corps of

Guides, as well as several battalions of ordinary native infantry and pioneers. Powerful as it was, the force had to contest almost every mile of the route through heavily guarded, snow-covered passes. Everywhere the fighting was heavy, for the tribesmen fiercely defended the high ground, while the relieving forces had to advance over open ground to storm the heights 'under a burning sun and in the face of galling fire.'

However, Low and his men stormed their way through the Malakand Pass, crossed the Swat River, and finally captured Umra Khan's main fort, but not Umra Khan himself, for he had managed to escape with his army. When they at last arrived at Chitral they were naturally somewhat disappointed to find that the second and much smaller Relief Force had got there first.

This had set out from Gilgit on 27 March under the command of Lieutenant-Colonel J.G. Kelly, a middle-aged officer who had served thirty-two years and had taken twenty of them to reach the rank of major. His force consisted of nearly 400 of the 32nd Sikh Pioneers (troops who had never been under fire, being normally employed on road-mending and similar jobs), about two hundred Kashmiri infantrymen and sappers, and two old mountain guns. With him were seven young officers as brave and resolute as himself. Kelly marched this puny force for over 200 miles in 28 days, and fought and won two hard battles in narrow passes against well-posted enemies. Their route lay across the 12,000-feet high Shandar Pass, a mountain plateau deep in snow. The men were not prepared or equipped for the severe cold, and suffered terribly from snow-blindness and frostbite. Nevertheless, they marched triumphantly into Chitral on 20 April, and Captain Townshend noted in his diary:

The siege, which had lasted 46 days, was at an end . . . The Gilgit column accordingly arrived at 2pm on the 20th, the 32nd Pioneers looking in very good trim and good condition.

'There were no extravagant greetings,' noted Surgeon-Major Robertson, coolly, but when Major-General Low arrived on 16 May, a victory parade was drawn up, and there were congratulations all round, particularly from the Queen-Empress, always proud of the gallantry of her soldiers.

2nd Punjabis in action at Tirah

Terror in the Tirah

'Everything quiet here,' the British Commissioner at Peshawar signalled to the Viceroy on 17 August 1897, a few weeks after the attack on Malakand; 'reliable sources indicate that Afridis are unaffected'. This reassuring message had hardly reached Calcutta when reports came in that thousands of Afridi warriors, led by 1,500 mullahs, were overpowering British posts and forts in the Khyber, including the vital Landi Kotal with its garrison of nearly 400 men of the Khyber Rifles. Soon the flood of fanatics was pouring into the Kohat and the Kurram valleys. The loss of the Khyber on 25 August 1897 was an immense blow to British power and prestige. In response, the Government assembled a punitive force of nearly 50,000 troops with orders 'to march through the country of the Afridis and

On the Dargai heights Piper Findlater of the Gordon Highlanders continues to play despite his wounds. An act of bravery that won him the VC

Oraksais and to announce from the heart of the country the final terms which will be imposed. The advance is made to mark the power of the British Government to advance if and when they choose.' The heart of the country was the Tirah, the sacred stronghold of the Afridis, where no white man had ever been seen.

In command of the Tirah Field Force was Lieutenant-General Sir William Lockhart GCB, KCSI (1841-1900), another unremembered Victorian hero who had fought and won medals in the Indian Mutiny as well as in Bhutan (1864); Abyssinia (1867-68); the Hazara Black Mountain (1868); the Dutch East Indies (1875-77) while military attaché to the Dutch Army; the Second Afghan War (1879-80) and the Third Burma War (1885-87). He had held commands with field

forces on the North-West Frontier against the Miranzai (1891); the Isazai (1892) and the Waziris (1894-95), always serving with enough distinction to gain the approval of the Government, but not enough to win the heart of the late Victorian public.

The Tirah Field Force included battalions of the Gordon Highlanders, the Dorsets, the Sherwood Foresters, the Royal Scots Fusiliers, The Duke of Cornwall's Light Infantry, and the Royal Irish Rifles, as well as the Gurkhas, the Sikhs, the Bengal Lancers, the Punjab Frontier Force, and several batteries of mountain guns. To transport and supply this force required 60,000 mules, donkeys, camels, elephants, and bullocks. A young gunner officer described the scene on the road to Tirah:

The roads in every direction were full of gathering troops; Highland regiments, Gurkhas, Sikh corps, long lines of Indian cavalry, their lances standing high above the acrid dust that they stirred. By the side of the roads strings of laden camels padded on beside the troops, the jinkety-jink of the mountain guns, the skirling of the pipes . . . all contributed to the wild excitement and romance of the scene.

The tribesmen made the Force fight every mile of the way, and one of the greatest moments came on 20 October at the Dargai heights, a steep ridge which covered the approach to Tirah. The Gordon Highlanders, supported by mountain guns, drove the Oraksai defenders from the ridge early on the 18th, only to have it retaken later the same day. The Gordons and the Gurkhas, followed by the Dorsets and the Derbyshires, all then tried to recapture the position; but as the same gunner officer reported:

. . . the defenders awoke to what was in progress. The remainder of the Gurkhas . . . encountered a tremendous fire, chiefly of Martini bullets aimed by the best marksmen on the frontier. Every expert in the cleft above had two or three loaders. Hardly a shot missed its billet. The men, dribbling over, were hit time and again, and rolled down the slopes on either side or lay on the fairway . . .

Then came the inspiring operation of which so much was written at the time. Colonel Matthias (of the Gordons) ordered officers and pipers to the front. The swagger with which the pipe major threw his plaid and his drones well over his shoulder was magnificent. The Colonel strode out in front, and the pipes set up 'Cock o' the North'. And out on to that narrow ridge scrambled a mass of some six hundred cheering Highlanders. The artillery redoubled their supporting fire, and though many men fell, the mass, as the Colonel expected, got over, and in their train came Gurkhas, Sikhs and the men of Dorset and Derby. Piper Findlater, lying wounded . . . played his pipes as the men rushed on, a gallant incident that was to make him famous (and win him the VC).

'Dargai Day' is still celebrated by the Gordon Highlanders, who suffered heavy losses in this action, as did the Gurkhas, the Dorsets and Derbyshires. The Queen, as ever, was quick to send a message:

Please express my congratulations to all ranks, British and Native troops, on their gallant conduct in actions 18th and 20th. Deeply deplore loss of precious lives among officers and men of my army. Pray report condition of wounded and assure them of my true sympathy.

After Dargai the tribesmen fought the rest of the campaign in their own way 'appearing suddenly in threatening force at points where they are least expected and dispersing without necessarily losing tactical cohesion when they find themselves worsted,' as one officer put it. 'Such methods are bewildering to the commanders of disciplined troops opposing them.' But in spite of their continual sniping, their raids on foraging parties, and their attacks on the rear of marching columns, the Afridis could not prevent Lockhart's troops from advancing into the fertile and populous Maidan Valley in the heart of the Tirah, and destroying it by fire and sword. 'The camp,' said the Reuter correspondent, 'was ringed by a wall of fire – byres, outhouses, homesteads, and fortresses one mass of rolling flame.' Even grain fields and walnut groves were uprooted and destroyed, and the people of the valley were driven to find what food and shelter they could on the bleak hill tops.

Frightfulness of this kind was not new in Frontier warfare, though condemned by such heroes as Charles Napier, Colin Campbell, Neville Chamberlain and 'Bobs' Roberts – who told the House of Lords after Tirah: 'Burning houses and destroying crops, necessary and justifiable as such measures may be, unless followed up by some form of authority or jurisdiction, mean starvation for many of the women and children – and for us a rich harvest of hatred and revenge.' And in fact, although some of the tribes surrendered their weapons and paid their fines, most remained as fierce and implacable as ever in their attacks on the British interlopers in their land.

Her Majesty also had doubts:

The fighting on the frontier continues very severe, and causes the Queen much pain and anxiety, as the loss of life is so great and distressing and the loss of officers most serious . . . As we do not wish to retain any part of the country, is the continuation and indefinite prolongation of these punitive expeditions really justifiable at the cost of so many valuable lives? The Queen cannot help feeling that there was a want of preparation, of watchfulness, and of knowledge of what the wild tribes were planning, which ought not to have been.

VRI

Royal questions the politicians and generals failed to answer.

Lt-Gen Sir William Lockhart, GCB, KCSI, commander of the Tirah Field Force

The Army Ordnance Corps

For over four centuries the royal Ordnance had its headquarters in the Tower of London. Its duties included the provision of arms, notably artillery, when the king raised an army. In 1683 it became the civil Board of Ordnance charged with the responsibility of procuring, storing and issuing arms, ammunition and other military equipment.

Until 1855, when the Board moved from the Tower to Woolwich, it was also responsible for the Royal Artillery and the Royal Engineers, as well as for a body called the Field Train. In the middle of the reign, it consisted for some years of two departments – the Military Store Department (officers) and the Military Store Staff (soldiers), which were renamed the Ordnance Store Department (officers) and the Ordnance Store Branch (soldiers).

In 1896 these became the Army Ordnance Department (officers) and the Army Ordnance Corps (soldiers), and not until 1958 did it receive its current title of Royal Army Ordnance Corps.

The Royal Engineers

Under various identities – the Military Artificers, the Royal Sappers and Miners, the Corps of Engineers – there have been military engineers in the service of the Crown since the king's engineer landed with William the Conqueror in 1066, and set about building his fortifications. Under Queen Victoria in 1856 the Royal Sappers and Miners and the Corps of Engineers were merged to form a single Corps of Royal Engineers.

A remarkable number of Heroes for Victoria were drawn from their ranks. Notable among them was Sir John Burgoyne, who at 72 served as second-in-command to Lord Raglan in the Crimea; he it was who chose the army's invasion point, and showed how an attack on the Malakoff would ensure the fall of Sebastopol.

It was also his energy and foresight before the Crimean War that brought about the substantial increase in the total numbers of Royal Engineers and Royal Sappers and Miners that later were to prove so necessary during the actual campaign. Burgoyne was the first of five Royal Engineers to become Field-Marshal: the others were Lord Napier of Magdala, Sir John Simmons, Lord Nicholson and Lord Kitchener.

Sir George Everest, who carried out the great Ordnance Survey of India and after whom the highest mountain in the world is named, was trained as a Royal Engineer. So, too, were General Sir Harry Prendergast VC, who captured Mandalay; General Sir Gerald Graham VC, who won fame at Suakin; General Sir Charles Warren, who occupied Bechuanaland; General Gordon of Khartoum, and General Sir Bindon Blood, hero of the North-West Frontier.

Sappers, too, were Sir Colin Scott-Moncrieff, builder of the Nile Delta barrage, and Sir James 'Buster' Brown who, in a mere four years, built the great railway that runs from the Indus river to the passes beyond the city of Quetta. No fewer than 25 VCs were awarded to sappers during the reign of Queen Victoria. Of these, perhaps the most famous are Lt Home and Lt Salkeld, who blew up the Kashmir Gate at Delhi in 1857, and Lt Chard who led the defence of Rorke's Drift in 1879.

More peaceful tasks undertaken by sappers included field surveying and building roads, bridges and railways in Africa, India and many other parts of the Empire, excavating canals, constructing dams, irrigation systems and port installations, laying telegraph lines, and using balloons and heliographs for observation and communication.

The CRE has a very long tradition of heroism in the field, for many of the duties and the tasks it, and its many predecessors, fulfilled had to be carried out in exposed, dangerous positions well within sight of the enemy. Whether they were storming fortresses, as in Delhi in 1857, or the Taku forts in 1860, or building pontoon bridges under enemy fire as in the South African War, the Royal Engineers had to be there first to get the job done. They have served wherever British soldiers have fought, but the Corps itself boasts no battle honours. For sappers their motto *Ubique* [everywhere] is honour enough.

A Medal From Her Majesty

Queen Victoria always took a great personal interest in medals and orders, and whenever she could she presented them herself. In their turn, her troops – officers and men alike – greatly prized such awards. Typical was the remark of the private on his way to fight in the First Sikh War: 'all our talk and hope was: "Shall we be in time to get a *medal*?"'

Over thirty individual campaign medals were struck during the Queen's reign, with more than 140 bars or clasps bearing the name or date of a single battle or action, thus avoiding the need for scores of separate medals. Most campaign medals were accompanied by two or three clasps, but some 'General Service' medals carried many more: twenty-three were authorised for the East and West Africa Medal 1887-1900 and the India Medal 1895-1902, and twenty-six for the Queen's South Africa Medal 1899-1902.

So many a long-serving Victorian hero could legitimately sport a chestful of campaign medals and clasps. Oddly, these included survivors of the Napoleonic Wars, whose services went unrecognised (apart from the Waterloo Medal 1815) until some years after Victoria came to the throne. Over half a century after the campaigns they commemorated two medals were struck bearing the young Queen's head: in 1843 came the Military General Service Medal 1793-1815, with 29 bars, and in 1847 the Naval General Service Medal 1793-1840 with no fewer than 231 bars. Heroes for Victoria clearly included survivors of battles fought long before she was born.

Many a beribboned Victorian old campaigner was also entitled to wear medals recognising personal merit. Apart from the Victoria Cross (see page 73), the Queen introduced a number of new awards. The Distinguished Conduct Medal was instituted for the Crimean War only in 1854 and re-instituted in 1862. Like the Victoria Cross, this carried a cash award – £15 for sergeants, £10 for corporals, and £5 for privates. From 1845 outstanding bravery could earn

The Royal Regiment of Artillery

Until early in the 18th century army commanders found their guns and gunners as and when needed, and there was no regular force of trained artillery. The value of such a force was brought home to the government when no guns were available to cope with the Jacobite rebellion of 1715, and in 1722 the Royal Regiment of Artillery was formed.

For transporting its guns the RRA depended, as artillerymen always had, on commandering horses and cattle with their drivers, and they fought as adjuncts to the regiments of foot.

The need for a more mobile and independent force was recognised with the formation of the Royal Horse Artillery in 1793. A third force, the Royal Garrison Artillery, was responsible for coastal defence, siege operations and mountain batteries. These three branches of artillery existed alongside one another until 1899, when they were reorganised into the Royal Horse Artillery, and Royal Field Artillery, and the Royal Garrison Artillery.

The Victorian army's gun-power was formidable, particularly to the native armies who were its principal enemies. In 1859 it could muster 29 batteries of horse artillery, 73 batteries of field artillery, and 88 batteries of garrison artillery. The overwhelming power of these batteries often decided the issue in the small wars of the age. Even the indomitable tribesmen of the North-West Frontier could be shocked into sumbission by the range and accuracy of Victorian mountain guns.

Such was the importance and prestige attached to the guns, that 'saving the guns' became a matter of honour, for which men gave their lives. It was their heroic and mainly unsuccessful dash at Colseno on 15 December 1899 to save two batteries of guns trapped under a hail of Boer bullets, that won VCs for three gallant artillerymen – Corporal (later Lt Col) George Nurse,

Capt (later Lt Col) Harry Schofield, and Capt (later Maj Gen) Hamilton Lyster Reed. In all seven VCs were won in that desperate action, one of them being Lieutenant Frederick Roberts (only son of Field Marshal 'Bobs' Roberts), who was mortally wounded that day.

Some 38 VCs were won by artillerymen, eight of whom later rose to general rank. On one of the few occasions when the Victoria Cross was awarded by ballot, as the rules allowed, the Commander-in-Chief, Lord Roberts, found it impossible to decide between the individual members of 'Q' Battery of the RHA, all of whom had shown exceptional heroism under close small-arms fire at Korn Spruit, South Africa, in 1900. By the time the order to retire came, almost every man had been killed or wounded. Four VCs were awarded, and they went by ballot to Major Phipps-Hornby, Sergeant Charles Parker, Gunner Isaac Lodge, and Driver Harry Glasock.

Like the Royal Engineers, the Royal Regiment of Artillery holds no battle honours as such, and shares with the CRE the well-deserved and distinctive motto *Ubique*.

The Corps of Military Police

The Corps of Military Police has claims to being the oldest service in the British Army. The office of Provost Marshal, with powers to punish soldiers 'on the spot' for disobedience, desertion, plunder and outrage dates back to at least the fifteenth century, 'I do not know in what manner an army is to be commanded at all without the practice,' said Wellington.

From 1844 Provost Marshals were given the rank of captain, and from 1855 volunteer NCOs were selected from cavalry regiments to be mounted policemen. These were the origin of the Military Mounted Police formed about twenty years later. The Military Foot Police was formed in 1885, and the two bodies operated side by side for several decades.

In a number of the later small wars of the reign Corps of Military Police were especially raised, and it is said that the familiar red cap was designed by the wife of a Provost Marshal serving in the Egyptian campaign of 1882. The two corps did not become one Corps of Military Police until 1926 and were not 'Royal' until 1946.

The Corps of Army Schoolmasters

About the time of the Crimean War one in five of the Queen's beloved soldiers could not read or write, a further one in five could read but not write, and only one in a hundred could claim 'a superior degree of education.' The Corps of Army Schoolmasters had then been in existence since 1846.

Staffed by Warrant Officers and senior NCOs and aided by civilian teachers, it tackled the mammoth task of educating men who were probably the less intelligent representatives of an illiterate population, in the teeth of opposition from conservative army officers who firmly believed that education was bad for discipline.

By 1867, however, illiteracy had been halved. Encouraged but still strongly resisted by many officers, the War Office appointed a Director-General of Military Education in 1870 – perhaps converted to Sir Garnet Wolseley's belief that an educated soldier is a better soldier. But the Corps of Army Schoolmasters had to wait another fifty years before it became the Army Education Corps.

The Army Service Corps

Not until 1888 did the Army Service Corps come into independent existence. Until then its twin functions of supply and transport – keeping the army equipped and fed as well as mobile – were the responsibility of two separate bodies: the Commissariat and a transport corps whose identity and title seem to have changed from war to war.

The army's first organised transport corps was the Corps of Waggoners (1794-95), which later became the Royal Waggon Corps (1799-1802), the Royal Waggon Train (1802-33), the Land Transport Corps (1855-56), and the Military Train (1856-69). In 1869 Supply and Transport were combined in a new, fully combatant corps called the Army Service Corps. Notwithstanding the success of this first ASC in handling the very different transport and supply needs of the Red River Campaign in Canada (1869-70) and the second Ashanti War (1873-74),

both commanded by Sir Garnet Wolseley, it was abolished in 1881 and reorganised as the Commissariat and Transport Department.

When Sir Redvers Buller VC – who seems to have been a better administrator than he was a war commander – became Quartermaster-General, he set about creating a new professional corps, staffed by specialist officers, to handle the changing supply and transport needs of the late Victorian army. He succeeded brilliantly. The Army Service Corps which he formed in 1881 served the army well in the remaining campaigns of the reign.

Heroism was not perhaps the first obligation of men of an essentially supportive service, but heroes there were, and it seems unlikely that the VCs won by Commissary J. L. Dalton at Rorke's Drift in 1879 and by Farrier Michael Murphy and Private Samuel Morley (both of the Military Train) at Azimghar in India in 1858 were isolated examples of bravery in the chequered history of what became the Army Service Corps.

The Royal Army Medical Corps

Until 1855 the health of Victoria's troops was left to the tender mercies of regimental surgeons, who were not necessarily the most highly qualified members of their profession. The Crimean experience having revealed the inadequacies of provision for the sick and wounded, the War Office formed a Medical Staff Corps which was in effect a body of medical orderlies – 'men able to read and write, of regular steady habits and of a kindly disposition.' The body was later renamed the Army Hospital Corps and incorporated with the Medical Staff (Officers) to form the Royal Army Medical Corps.

The 'Poultice Wallopers' or 'Linseed Lancers' as they were variously nicknamed, although non-combatant, did not lack heroes. The need to give prompt help to the wounded exposed them to much the same dangers as the fighting men, and many were themselves killed or wounded. Seventeen of them were awarded the VC, and many more commended for their bravery under fire.

Notable of them was one of the two youngest winners of the VC – Hospital

senior NCOs the Conspicuous Gallantry Medal, and in 1849 sergeants in the Marines were made eligible for this award.

Officers, who were eligible for one or other of the Orders of Knighthood, as well, of course, for the Victoria Cross, had to wait until 1886 before outstanding – but perhaps rather less heroic – conduct was recognised by the issue of the Distinguished Service Order. This was awarded to officers who rendered meritorious or

distinguished service in war under fire or in conditions equivalent to service in actual combat with an enemy.

The Imperial forces were not overlooked. In 1837 two Indian Orders were instituted: the Indian Order of Merit conspicuous gallantry by officers and men of the Indian Army, and the Order of British India for long and faithful service by native officers. New Zealand's army and police forces were singled out by the institution of the New Zealand Cross in 1869, and a Military Medal was struck for all Colonial Forces in 1894. In 1883 the special worth of women in wartime was recognised, perhaps for the first time, by the introduction of the Royal Red Cross 'for women of whatever nationality who nurse the sick and wounded'.

Although no honour or award ranks higher than the Victoria Cross, 'VC' even taking precedence of 'KG' for Knights of the Garter, the most senior Order of Knighthood, it was the Queen's prerogative and pleasure to mark her appreciation of her most distinguished heroes by awarding them the insignia of one of the Orders of Knighthood. For military and naval commanders who had displayed outstanding courage and leadership, there would be the order of the Bath – Knight Grand Cross (GCB), Knight Commander (KCB) or Companion (CB). To those who rendered valuable service in her Colonies came the Order of St Michael and St George (G CMG, KCMG or CMG). For great services in India she instituted in 1861 the Most Exalted Order of the Star of India (GCSI and KCSI), and in 1877 the Order of the Indian Empire (GCIE, KCIE and CIE). That the Queen initiated and personally awarded so many medals and orders is a measure of her esteem for the men who were her heroes.

Apprentice Fitzgibbon, aged 15, who showed great coolness and courage while attending the wounded, though himself wounded, under intense fire at the capture of the Taku Forts, China, in 1860. Throughout the day-long Zulu attack on the mission hospital at Rorke's Drift in 1879 Surgeon-Major Reynolds calmly continued to attend to his patients in spite of very close-range fire. At Colenso in December 1899 Major Babtie (later Sir William Babtie KCB KCMG) braved the intense and accurate fire of Boer sharpshooters to bring in Lt Frederick Roberts who was lying wounded on the veldt.

The Royal Army Chaplains' Department

Although Anglican chaplains were first awarded commissions in 1662, the Royal Army Chaplains' Department of Victoria's day, which was formed in 1858 was not restricted to clergy of the Established Church. It consisted of 20 Staff Chaplains, 35 Assistant Chaplains, all Anglicans, together with 19 Roman Catholic priests, 5 Presbyterian ministers. Wesleyans were commissioned in 1881 and Jewish Rabbis in 1892. From 1860 army chaplains, though non-combatant by profession, wore uniforms and held ranks parallel to combatant officers, a fourth-class chaplain being equivalent to a captain and a first-class chaplain a major-general.

Non-combatant as they were, army chaplains often found themselves exposed to the same dangers as the fighting men, and were called upon to show equally great courage and devotion to duty – possibly greater, since they were unarmed and were probably looked to for an example.

Only one army chaplain in Victoria's armies was awarded the Victoria Cross, but it seems unlikely that the extreme bravery of the Rev J. W. Adams of the Indian Army (Bengal Ecclesiastical Department), who won his VC in the Afghan War of 1879, was exceptional. When some troopers of the 9th Lancers, closely beset by the enemy, fell into a deep and wide ditch and found themselves trapped beneath their horses, the Rev Adams rushed into the water, dragged the horses away and extricated the men. During all this time he was waist-deep in water and under heavy fire from the

enemy, who were only a few yards away. His prompt and gallant action undoubtedly saved the Lancers from being killed. Not surprisingly, the Queen later appointed the Rev Adams to be her honorary chaplain.

The Army Pay Corps

For centuries it seemed to be a soldier's lot to be paid badly and late, if at all. Regimental colonels, for whom their regiment was virtually a personal estate, engaged clerks and agents to handle regimental pay and finance. In 1878 the War Office assumed control of all army financial matters, and a Pay Department was formed, staffed by suitably qualified officers. This became the Army Pay Corps in 1893, but not till 1920 was it granted the 'Royal' prefix.

The Army Nursing Service

The sufferings of the troops in the Crimea and the achievements of Florence Nightingale undoubtedly opened the eyes of the Victorian public, and not least those of their Queen, to the urgent need for proper hospital care for sick and wounded soldiers. Nursing in the army was still almost entirely in the hands of male orderlies of the recently-formed Army Hospital Corps, but by the late sixties women nurses were working in most military hospitals.

The country's first general military hospital, the Royal Victoria Hospital at Netley, near Southampton, was opened by the Queen in 1856, but not till 1869 was it headed by a Matron. An Army Nursing Service was formed in 1881, and it was ruled that every military hospital with over 100 beds should have a staff of Nursing Sisters, all of whom must have been trained in a civil hospital.

In 1883 the Queen instituted the Royal Red Cross as a decoration for outstanding service by nurses, and the following year the Army Nursing Reserve was established. After the Boer War the Army Nursing Services were reorganised as Queen Alexandra's Imperial Military Nursing Service – forerunner of today's Queen Alexandra's Royal Army Nursing Corps.

The Yeomanry

In 1794 the likelihood of an invasion by the French Citizen Army prompted the government to authorise the formation of a Yeomanry and Volunteer Corps, using the large numbers of volunteer cavalry who had already shown themselves willing to serve. This new mounted force came to be known as the 'Gentlemen and Yeomanry Cavalry', a yeoman being traditionally a respectable freeholder. Yeomanry commissions were awarded by the Lords Lieutenant in the King's name. The officers were invariably drawn from the nobility and gentry, other ranks from the lesser landowners and tenant farmers.

Throughout Victoria's reign service in a Yeomanry regiment provided a socially acceptable alternative to the Militia, which was disliked and despised by 'the classes'. Their full dress uniform, particularly for the officers, tended to be colourful and flamboyant, and colonels or honorary colonels were drawn from 'great' county families – the Beauforts in Gloucestershire, the Gerards in Lancashire, the Williams Wynns in Montgomeryshire.

Many Yeomanry troops were named from the great landed estates where they were stationed – the Woodstock Troop, the Holkham Troop, the Chudleigh Troop, and so on; or from the names of their noble colonels – Compton's Horse and Lovat's Scouts. Yeomanry Reviews, Field Days, Parades and Competitions were great social occasions where the entertainment was on a lavish scale, even for the lower orders.

In the first three decades of the nineteenth century the authorities' failure to satisfy demands for radical social and political reform led to mass protest meetings and violent disturbances up and down the country. Lacking a strong police force, the magistrates often summoned the Yeomanry 'to aid and protect the Civil Power in the preservation of Peace and the protection of Property'. This inevitably made them unpopular with people whose political sympathies lay with the Radical and Chartist movements of the time. During the first five years of the young Queen's reign the Yeomanry were frequently called upon to quell Chartist riots in many of the big towns, but when an effective country-wide police force was established, their services were seldom needed. The last time Yeomanry were called to aid the Civil Power was when the Royal 1st Devon Yeomanry overawed food rioters in Exeter in 1867.

For national defence, however, the Yeomanry continued to be seen as an important source of light and auxiliary cavalry. When Napoleon III became Emperor of France, his very name evoked new invasion scares, and there were 'crises' in 1848, 1851 and 1859 which led to an influx of Volunteers, and a number of new corps of Yeomanry were formed. As rifles began to replace pistols and the old smooth-bore carbines, the new Yeoman volunteers tended to become mounted riflemen, but the sword remained the preferred weapon of the Yeoman Cavalry.

With the Cardwell Army Reforms came important changes in the organisation and training of the Yeomanry. They were brigaded in regimental districts in conjunction with the Regular Army. Their training was made more permanent and professional, and they became liable to periodic inspection by Regular Army officers. In the event of an invasion they were required to be available for service anywhere in the country.

But it was in the Boer War of 1899-1902 that the Yeomanry came into its own. The Regular Army suffered such losses, particularly during 'Black Week' in December 1899, that the government was forced to appeal for volunteers – who anyway were pressing to be used. The response was overwhelming. Many new volunteer units were raised and were combined with the existing Yeomanry regiments to form battalions of 'Imperial Yeomanry'. Within a few weeks many companies of Imperial Yeomanry were at sea on their way to South Africa. Most of them fought as mounted riflemen, armed with Enfield rifles, as well as Colt or Maxim guns.

Though relatively untrained, the Imperial Volunteers rapidly adapted themselves to the peculiar conditions of warfare on the South African veldt. There seems little doubt that their country skills and horsemanship helped them in fighting the elusive Boer commandos. During their two years of 'real war', many Yeoman were killed or wounded, many suffered from enteric fever, and all won the battle honour 'South Africa'.

The Gurkhas

THE GURKHAS come from Nepal, an independent kingdom wedged between the Himalayas and the northern border of India. With its capital at Kathmandu, 4,500 feet above sea level, Nepal is a land of nearly 54,000 square miles of mountainous country, just over 500 miles long and about 100 miles wide. Following attacks on British frontier posts by the Nepalese army, in 1814 the Indian government (then the East India Co.) sent a large force to pacify the area, but it took 50,000 British and Indian troops and several fiercely fought campaigns to defeat the Gurkhas, who showed themselves to be exceptionally stubborn, skilful and brave mountain fighters.

In the Convention signed at the end of the war, Nepal ceded its western province of Kumaon to the British, but continued to be a totally independent kingdom. In recognition of the Gurkhas' fighting spirit, their general and his troops were allowed to return to their country with full military honours. In spite of, or perhaps because of, the unyielding ferocity with which both sides fought and the huge casualties they suffered, the British and Gurkha troops came to respect one another, discovering that the fiercest of enemies could be friends. The military friendship formed in 1815 has lasted till this day.

The British lost no time in recruiting these formidable but friendly ex-enemies to their own

army, and a Gurkha Corps of four battalions was formed as early as 24 April 1815. From then on 'the Gurkha contingent became a regular feature of the British Indian army and distinguished itself in every campaign from the Mutiny onwards.' (Vincent Smith) Throughout the greater part of Victoria's reign there were nine Gurkha infantry regiments (a tenth being added in 1890), whose names were changed with remarkable frequency – the First Gurkha Regiment had eleven different names between 1815 and 1901. Gurkha battalions fought with almost all the many 'field forces' that campaigned year after year on the North West Frontier. They were intensely proud of their reputation as tough fighters: after one prolonged siege fighting side by side with British troops, they said of them: 'they were very nearly the equal of us.'

It was at the siege of Delhi in 1857, defending the keypoint of Hindu Rao's house outside the city walls, that the Gurkhas proved their fierce loyalty. Although they tended to jeer at the Mutineers, saying 'We obey the bugle call', British commanders still had some doubts about 'native troops'. When a Mutineer force attacked Hindu Rao's house, the Gurkhas, supported by their friends from the 60th Rifles, fought hand-to-hand for sixteen hours, doing terrible slaughter with their kukris, until the mutineers fled. The Gurkha's commandant, Major Charles Reid, rejoiced to see his superior officers share his own boundless confidence in his Gurkhas:

My little fellows behaved splendidly and were cheered by every European regiment. I may say every eye was upon us . . . The General was anxious to see what the Gurkhas could do and if we were to be trusted . . . but I think they are now satisfied.

Some thirty years later, during the Second Afghan War, the 5th Gurkhas played a memorable role in the assault on the main enemy position on the Peiwar Kotal. Followed by the less nimble Highlanders, they charged up a steep and heavily defended hillside, drew their kukris and leaped into the Afghan entrenchments. By the time the Highlanders caught up, they saw only bleeding corpses and the Gurkhas far ahead, pursuing the terrified Afghans. The Kotal was taken, and in that campaign five Gurkhas were awarded the Indian Order of Merit, which was at that time the Indian equivalent of the Victoria Cross.

To Indians in the 1990s it must seem curious to reflect that so many of their ancestors fought on the side of those who came to conquer and rule. The British had no difficulty in raising first-class fighting forces from the people they classed as 'the martial races' – particularly the Sikhs, Pathans, Baluchis, Garhwalis, Dogras, Punjabis and Marathas. The British-officered Indian Army of the Queen-Empress included nineteen regiments of the renowned Bengal Lancers, four of Punjab Cavalry, three of Madras Horse, seven of Bombay Lancers and Cavalry, and well over a hundred regiments of infantry, artillery, sappers and miners, recruited mainly from 'the martial races' numerous regiments of Bengal, Punjab, Sikh, Madras, and Bombay infantry and artillery.

A feature of the Indian Army, particularly before 1857, was its 'irregular' corps. These were usually light cavalry regiments raised and led by 'soldiers of fortune', many but not all of them Eurasians. Such were James Skinner of 'Skinner's Horse', James Hodson of Hodson's Horse, Captain Fane of Fane's Horse, and Colonel Harry Lumsden who formed the Corps of Guides Cavalry and Infantry in 1860 – perhaps the greatest of all the 'irregular' corps. All of them found their true glory in the hard and bloody Frontier campaigns.

The Militia

The Militia, the country's oldest military formation, numbered some 100,000 men in Victoria's day. It had its origin in Anglo-Saxon times when every adult male had a duty to defend his country (or county) and to bear arms according to his status and means. In the Middle Ages it was the duty of the sheriff to raise and train the Militia. The Tudors made the Lord Lieutenant of each county responsible for seeing that Militia men were regularly called to musters and adequately trained, and hence they came to be known as the 'trained bands'. The government fixed the number of Militia men for each county, and registers of available men were kept. Service was decided by ballot, and was generally unpopular, but it was often possible for a man to pay a substitute to do his militia service.

Although the Militia was the country's first line of reserve in time of war, it was not available for overseas service; when the monarch needed an army for a foreign war he and his lords and gentry had to raise it personally for each campaign. Apart from the Militia, which was in effect a citizens' reserve defence force, it was unlawful to maintain a standing army in time of peace, and the legitimacy of the regular British Army has always depended on the passing of the annual Army Act.

In 1794, when a French invasion seemed highly likely, the Militia was substantially increased and its training became much more rigorous. Cavalry units, known as the Yeomanry, were added, recruited mainly from country gentlemen and farmers. An Act of 1803 provided that all men aged 17-55 were to be listed, as well as all households with details of male and female members and non-combatants, but after 1816 the Militia reserves and auxiliary forces were disbanded. Under Victoria the Militia was only embodied in years of apparent national need – for the Crimean War (1854), the Indian Mutiny (1857), the French Invasion scare (1859), and the Egyptian War (1885). In 1881 Militia and Volunteer units were linked to county regiments of the Regular Army.

The fear of a French invasion in 1859 and after was probably unfounded but none the less seriously felt, and it coincided with the introduction of the rifle as a more accurate weapon than the smooth-bore 'Brown Bess' used by generations of British infantrymen. Rifle Volunteer Units and Rifle Clubs sprang up all over the country – an enthusiasm encouraged and patronised by the Queen and the Prince Consort. For some years volunteers flocked to enlist and rifle shooting competitions became extremely popular. It attracted the urban middle-classes, the artisans and office-workers, who did not care for the Yeomanry which was seen as the preserve of farmers and country-house folk. Both movements tended to lose ground when the invasion scare passed away. Precursors of the Territorial Army, they had their moments of usefulness and glory during the Second Boer War of 1899-1902.

Execution at Omdurman

AFTER THE fall of Khartoum and the murder of General Gordon in January 1885, the Mahdi took up residence in Omdurman and gave himself up to a life of great ease and luxury. But not for long, for within five months he had died; some say from smallpox while others say from over-indulgence. His place was taken not by one of his numerous progeny but by the Khalifa Abdullah – a born leader, as energetic as he was treacherous and as charming as he was cruel. He was not alone among Arab leaders to be astonished by Britain's withdrawal from the Sudan, after an abortive attempt to build a railway from the port of Suakin to the Nile. That a warrior nation had chosen not to avenge the death of a great hero was beyond their comprehension, and cut right across their own codes of conduct and of honour.

Because the Royal Navy continued to patrol the Red Sea to protect the Suez Canal and keep open crucial sea lanes to the Orient, Britain kept a force in Suakin. It was the scene of frequent skirmishes between friendly tribes – that is to say those who had been bribed by its resourceful Governor, Major Kitchener – and Osman Digna, who remained a thorn in the lion's foot for many years to come.

Tyrannical rule and force of character kept the Khalifa's grip firmly on the Sudan for some time. But then came a series of disasters that included drought and plagues of locusts and of mice, bringing misery and hardship to the people. In Omdurman there were outbreaks of cannibalism in which children were eaten by the starving inhabitants, while every day bodies were to be seen piled in the streets or floating down the Nile.

The Egyptian authorities found comfort in the weakening of their southern neighbours, and slowly British attitutdes towards the Sudan changed as well. In the grab for Africa the French were becoming increasingly active, and it was thought they now had the territory in their sights. On the other hand, Britain's allies – the Italians – had been defeated in Abyssinia and would welcome a diversion on the Nile. On the domestic front, with the departure of Gladstone and the subsequent defeat of the Liberals, signs of a renewal of imperialistic fervour were evident. There was increasing talk of revenge for the death of Gordon. The British public was mentally preparing itself, not unwillingly, for yet another military adventure.

By 1896 about 10,000 Egyptians and their British officers with Herbert Kitchener – now a General – in command, were poised on the Sudan border. They progressed down the Nile at a snail's pace – Wolseley's expedition was hasty and improvised by comparision – and it was not until April 1898 that there was an action of any real significance. This took place in Atbara, where one of the Khalifa's most warlike generals decided to confront the advancing column. He attacked in force but was soon repulsed, leaving more than 2,000 of his warriors dead upon the field of battle. As Kitchener 'rode along the line,' reported Churchill, 'the British brigades raising their helmets on dark, smeared bayonets cheered him in all the loud enthusiasm of war.' A more shameful episode followed a few days later in the nearby town of Berber, where Kitchener had Mahmoud, his defeated enemy, shackled and bound, and in a victory parade dragged him through the streets with a halter round his neck.

Encouraged by success, Kitchener continued his stately progress down the river. In early summer the column arrived at Metemma, where Wolseley's men had established their base 13 years earlier, and by 1 September the main objective, Omdurman itself, had been reached. Kitchener's force was extremely formidable. His army now included many British units and had increased in size to 20,000 men. There were 100 pieces of artillery, and Royal Navy gunboats on the Nile. And in support there stretched across the desert sands, as far as the eye could see, an endless supply column.

The Khalifa's army of 50,000 was larger but armed only with spears for the most part, and with captured guns now long obsolete. But he told his men that Allah had spoken, ordering them into battle. So at dawn on 2 September the Dervishes launched their attack, charging straight into the mouths of the British guns.

1898

ATBARA (Sudan)
Royal Warwickshire
Royal Lincolnshire
Cameron Highlanders
KHARTOUM (Sudan)
21st Lancers
Grenadier Guards
Royal Northumberland
Fusiliers
Royal Warwickshire
Royal Lincolnshire
Lancashire Fusiliers
Seaforth Highlanders
Cameron Highlanders
Rifle Brigade

Winston Churchill, of the 21st Lancers, gives this account:

. . . (The Dervishes) paused to rearrange their ranks and drew out a broad and solid parade along the crest. Then the cannonade turned upon them. Two or three batteries and all the gunboats, at least thirty guns, opened an intense fire. Their shells shrieked towards us and burst in scores over the heads and among the masses of the White Flagmen. We were so close, as we sat spellbound on our horses, that we almost shared their perils. I saw the full blast of Death strike this human wall. Down went their standards by dozens and their men by hundreds. Wide gaps and shapeless heaps appeared in their array.

The artillery bombardment was followed by withering rifle fire from the Anglo-Egyptian army. Kitchener, realising that the enemy's assault had been broken, turned his main force towards Omdurman using the river to guard his left flank. The Dervishes now flung their last reserves into the battle and for a time posed a serious threat to Kitchener's men, no longer fighting from prepared positions. But iron discipline and greatly superior fire-power won the day, and the surviving Dervishes melted away into the desert leaving many thousands of the fellow-warriors dead upon the sand. Among the survivors was the Khalifa, who made good his escape to El Obeid. But his doomed army was totally destroyed: 'it was an execution, not a battle' was how one war correspondent described the carnage.

One pointless episode remained. Churchill's cavalry squadron, commanded by Major Flinn, received orders to outflank a group of enemy soldiers concealed in a hollow depression. With parade ground precision the squadron wheeled into line, and with drawn swords and lances at the ready proceeded to charge. The Arabs waited for them with their spears: this was hand-to-hand fighting with a real foe – something they understood – not meaningless slaughter by shrapnel from the skies. In the brief and bloody action that followed the 21st Lancers lost a quarter of their strength. Churchill and his companions were not to know that they helped to make history on that day, by taking part in what proved to be the last true charge to be made by a British cavalry regiment.

Kitchener celebrated his victory by staging a memorial parade for General Gordon in front of the ruins of the Palace in Khartoum. From the Mahdi's tomb he had the body disinterred and flung into the Nile after the head was cut off. The skull was sent to Cairo, but when she heard about this act of barbarism the Queen was outraged and said that it 'savoured too much of the Middle Ages.' Sensible, level-headed Baring took charge of the affair and had the skull secretly buried by night in a Muslim cemetery at Wadi Halfa.

Kitchener had urgent matters to attend to other than macabre trophies, for he received orders from London to proceed further up the river to deal with a party of Frenchman who had established themselves at Fashoda, in the valley of the Upper Nile, after an heroic 3,000-mile march from the west coast of Africa. To his credit, Kitchener showed considerable diplomatic skill in his negotiations with the leader of the French expedition, and although the incident brought Britain and France to the brink of war the use of his overwhelming force was avoided. In November 1898, it was possible to announce in the House of Commons that the crisis was over.

One further item remained on Kitchener's agenda. More than a year after the battle of Omdurman, spies brought news that the Khalifa was in hiding at a camp deep in the desert, some 400 miles or more south of Khartoum. A force of 8,000 men was despatched, commanded by Wingate, and on reaching the area they intercepted and destroyed a caravan taking grain to the fugitives. Two days later, on 23 November 1899, scouts found their camp, and Wingate attacked at dawn the following day. The action was Omdurman on a smaller scale: a thousand Arabs, including Khalifa Abdullah and many of his allied chieftains, were slaughtered and over 10,000 prisoners taken.

'Mahdism is now a thing of the past,' wrote Kitchener in his report to London. 'I hope that a brighter era has now opened for the Sudan.' Britain's honour had been restored and General Gordon's murder avenged. Although whether he would have approved of the manner in which these things had been achieved is a question one may presume to ask, but not to answer.

A bird's-eye view of the battle of Omdurman. At top left can be seen Khartoum and the confluence of the Blue and White Nile

The Jameson Raid

The relations between the Uitlanders and the Boers of the Transvaal and between the British and the Boers were driven almost to breaking point by the almost farcical 'Raid' carried out by Dr Jameson. A former Scottish surgeon of great promise, Starr Jameson was a close friend of Cecil Rhodes, the immensely wealthy Prime Minister of Cape Colony. When Rhodes seized Mashonaland (now part of Zimbabwe, formerly Rhodesia), for the South African Company (usually known as 'the Chartered Company'), a mining and development company he had founded, he appointed Jameson as its administrator. In 1893 Jameson extended the Chartered Company's territory by seizing Matabeleland, and two years later a Royal charter bestowed the name 'Rhodesia' on all the Chartered Company's territory. 'To have a bit of country named after one is one of the things a man might be proud of,' said Rhodes. Convinced that the British had an almost divine right to rule South Africa, he found himself

□ □ □

Dr Jameson and the survivors of his ill-conceived and ill-fated raiding party were rounded up by the Boers at Doornkop on 2 January 1896. Detail from a painting by R. Caton Woodville.

Joseph Chamberlain

up against the Boers, who wanted to see South Africa ruled by Afrikaans-speaking people.

In the Transvaal the Uitlanders, who were denied political rights, seemed to be on the point of rebellion, and in 1895 Dr Jameson gathered a force of 500 mounted riflemen and rode into Boer territory, expecting that the Uitlanders would rise in his support. Instead, he and his men were rounded up by Boer commandos and handed over to the British government. They were duly tried and convicted, but the affair embittered relations with the Boers – who suspected with some reason that both Cecil Rhodes and the British Colonial Secretary, Joseph Chamberlain were parties to the Raid.

THE SECOND BOER WAR

WHAT THE BRITISH public thought of as 'the Boer War' or 'the South African War,' and the Boers as 'the English War' was quite different from other Victorian wars, in which British forces were pitted against ill-trained and ill-equipped 'native' armies. Like the Crimean War, it was a 'major' war by the scale of the times, and was waged against troops of European descent. But the Crimean War was still one which Wellington might have recognised. In all other Victorian wars, except significantly the First Boer War, the traditional British infantry tactics of the advancing 'thin red line', supported by artillery fire, led by gallant officers, and finishing with a bayonet charge, had usually overwhelmed the stoutest enemies.

But in the South African War the Boer commandos, armed with long-range repeating rifles, almost always fought under cover. They were an unseen enemy who usually avoided hand-to-hand fighting; a bayonet is little use if your enemy won't face it. Against the Boers the British officer who stood up to lead his men was a dead man, which is perhaps why it has been called 'the last of the gentleman's wars.' To fight the Boers the British army was forced to change its tactics, its formations, its weaponry and even its uniforms. As one military historian put it:

No more line of battle solid ranks, no more volley-firing and scarlet and gold. (It was) the end of an era when a commander could watch the progress of a battle with his own eyes.

The war was long in the making. By the mid-nineties the Boer republics of the Transvaal (the South African Republic) and the Orange Free State felt that their independence and way of life were once again threatened by the British. By Conventions made after the First Boer War they were precluded from making treaties with foreign powers without British approval, and British annexation of Zululand. Bechuanaland, Basutoland, and other territories surrounding the two republics had effectively hemmed them in and blocked their access to the sea. The discovery of diamonds along the Orange river in 1867 and of gold in Southern Transvaal in 1886 attracted

The Last of the Gentlemens' Wars

huge numbers of investors and foreign settlers (Uitlanders). A bitter struggle now began for the control of the government of what had become one of the world's richest countries.

Throughout 1899 the British and Boers prepared for war. When the grass had grown enough to feed the Boers' horses and cattle, Paul Kruger, President of the Transvaal Republic, issued an ultimatum demanding an end to British suzerainty, and on 11 October Boer troops invaded Cape Colony and Natal.

At the time the Boer commandos could call on as many as 80,000 tough fighting men to confront the 15,000 British troops scattered in garrisons throughout South Africa. But opposing forces in the field, for the Boers split their resources in order to lay siege simultanenously to Ladysmith, Mafeking, and Kimberley. Meanwhile British reinforcements were on their way to Natal from the Empire. Totalling some 10,000 men, they included such battle-scarred regiments as the 2nd King's Royal Rifles, the 1st Gloucesters and the 1st Devonshires from India, the 1st Border Regiment from Malta, the 1st Royal Irish from Alexandria, and the 2nd Rifle Brigade from Crete.

At the start of the war a British Army Corps of nearly 47,000 troops was mobilized and despatched to South Africa under the command of General Sir Redvers Buller VC. Sailing with Buller was a man sent to cover the war for the new Biograph film company, also a young Hussar officer and war correspondent of the *Morning Post* named Winston Churchill.

On landing at Cape Town at the end of October, Buller learned that the Boers had seized the initiative. Under Generals Joubert and Cronje two columns of mounted riflemen had moved swiftly across the borders of Cape Colony and northern Natal. The British garrisons in Kimberley and Mafeking in eastern Cape Colony were surrounded by Cronje's commandos, and Joubert had occupied the whole of Natal north of the Tugela river. A large part of the Natal Defence Force was bottled up in Ladysmith along with its commander, Sir George White.

Only two British battalions and local volunteer forces stood between Joubert and Durban, the capture of which would give the Boers their longed-for access to the sea.

The first battle of the war took place on 20 October at Talana, near Dundee, in northern Natal. Technically, this was a defeat for the invading Boers who were driven from their commanding position, and the hill captured,

A contemporary illustration showing the arrival of the New South Wales Lancers in Cape Town. They were one of many of the volunteer contingents to fight alongside the British in the Boer War.

The War of 1899-1902 was the longest of all the Victorian wars and the first which deeply stirred the emotions of the general public. New means of communication, including the new illustrated press and the first cinematograph films, brought the war home to the public, and civilians and civilian interests were affected as in no previous war. Great numbers of volunteers from all levels of society rushed to join the army. The Second Boer war could therefore be described as not only 'the last of the gentlemen's wars, but the first of the people's wars. Compared even with the Crimean War, very large armies were involved on both sides. For the first time the new growing nations of the old Queen's empire rallied to the support of the Mother Country, and troops from Australia, Canada, New Zealand, India, Ceylon and other colonies served in the veldt alongside the British.

General Sir Redvers Buller VC
1839-1908

The first Commander-in-Chief of the British forces in South Africa was a soldier of proved courage ('fighting Buller') who won his VC in the Zulu War. A stern, grim-faced commander who inspired great confidence, he was greatly loved by his men because he made it his business to see that they were well-fed, well-housed and well-cared for. 'He would never sleep under canvas, if his men had nothing but the sky above', said one historian, and the men said that under Buller 'we all live like fighting cocks.'

Redvers Buller was one of the Wolseley 'gang' and had seen service in India, the China war of 1860, the Red River Expedition in Canada, the Ashanti War, the Zulu War, the Arabi revolt in Egypt and the Gordon Relief expedition. He fought with Wolseley at the battle of Tel-el-Kebir and was appointed KCMG. In South Africa he found himself promoted beyond his abilities, and he became hesistant, confused, and demoralised, and at one point he even seems to have advised General Sir George White in Ladysmith to surrender, although he later denied that his message had that meaning. But this and his failures during 'Black Week' led to his replacement as Commander-in-Chief by 'Bobs' Roberts.

but the British casualties were heavy – 41 officers and men killed, 185 wounded. The British General, Sir W. Penn Symons VC, followed the traditional tactics: artillery bombardment followed by a frontal attack by the infantry and a cavalry charge. He paid for his conservatism with his life. The infantry in this costly action consisted of three battalions: the 2nd Dublin Fusiliers, the 1st Royal Irish Fusiliers, and the 60th Rifles – 'Dublins first line, Rifles second, Fusiliers third'.

Not one of them had ever faced the fire of accurate, smoke-free magazine rifles that was about to hit them. As they moved forward they were pinned down by a screen of Mauser bullets fired by invisible riflemen on the hillside. The General, accompanied by his red pennant, rose up to rally his men – and was at once shot in the stomach. Captain Nugent of the 60th described the scene as his men charged towards the hill:

The ground in front of me was literally rising in dust from the bullets, and the din between the hill and the wood below and among the rocks from the incessant fire of the Mauser seemed to blend with every other sound into a long drawn-out hideous roar. Half way over the terrace I looked round over my shoulder and I confess I was rather horrified at what I saw. I saw S--- was close behind me, and a few men here and there, but the whole ground we had already covered was strewn with bodies, and no more men were coming over the wall. At that moment I was hit the first time . . . I was hit through the knee. The actual shock was as if someone had hit me with their whole strength with a club. I spun round and fell, my pistol flying one way and helmet another . . . I was hit a second time by a shot from above; the bullet hit me on the back above my right hip and came out in front of my thigh . . .

Although Nugent was hit yet again, he managed to reach the top of the hill. To his horror he and a fellow officer then found themselves under fire from their own artillery. 'It seemed so hard, after escaping from the Boers, to be killed by your own people'.

After Talana hilltop had been taken by the British and their guns moved up into position, the Boers hoisted a white flag and retreated to safety. Meanwhile, the 18th Hussars and a party of mounted infantry had been ordered to move round the enemy's flank. The manoeuvre completely failed: the force was surrounded by an 'overwhelming' number of Boers. British casualties totalled 208 killed, wounded or taken prisoner.

Other engagements during this opening phase of the Boer War were to prove just as costly. The battle of Elandslaagte, fought in a raging thunderstorm and claimed as a victory by the British, inflicted further heavy losses on them. A grim lesson was being slowly and painfully learned – the Boers were far stronger and far better soldiers than anyone in the British army had supposed.

Churchill and 'The Armoured Train Disaster'

By the outbreak of the Boer War the young Winston Churchill had already established a reputation as an author as well as an adventurous man of action. His two books, and his despatches – some unsigned to the *Morning Post* on the battle of Omdurman – had yielded an income 'about five times as much as the Queen had paid me for three years of assiduous and sometimes dangerous work'. So he decided to resign his Army commission (but not until he had steered his regimental team to victory in the Polo tournament in India!) and devote time to his next book (on the Sudan campaign) and standing unsuccessfully as a Parliamentary candidate in a by-election.

No sooner had war been declared than Churchill found himself principal war-correspondent of the *Morning Post* on £250 a month, all expenses paid, and a roving commission to go where he wished and to report freely on what he saw. Of Sir Redvers Buller, his fellow-passenger on the *Dunottar Castle*, Churchill later wrote:

He had shown himself a brave and skilful officer in his youth, and for nearly twenty years he had filled important administrative posts of a sedentary character in Whitehall. As his political views were coloured with Liberalism, he was regarded as a very sensible soldier. . . . Certainly he was a man of a considerable scale. He plodded on from blunder to blunder and from one disaster to another, without losing either the regard of his country or the trust of his troops, to whose feeling as well as his own he paid serious attention.

Two weeks after his arrival in South Africa, Winston Churchill was invited to take a trip on an armoured train ('nothing looks more formidable and impressive; but nothing is in fact more vulnerable and helpless') on its daily reconnaissance run from Estcourt to Colenso in the province of Natal. After about 14 miles the train reached Chieveley station, where Boer activity on the line ahead was spotted. It was decided to retire immediately, but by this time the enemy had already cut off retreat by setting up an ambush and blocking the line with boulders.

A huge white ball of smoke sprang into being and tore out into a cone, only as it seemed a few feet above my head. It was shrapnel – the first I had seen in war, and very nearly the last! The steel sides of the truck tanged with a patter of bullets. There was a crash from the front of the train, and a series of sharp explosions . . . suddenly there was a tremendous shock and he (Haldane) and I and all the soldiers in the truck were pitched head over heels on to its floor. The armoured train travelling at not less than 40 miles an hour had been thrown off the metals by some obstruction, or by some injury to the line.

In the action that followed Churchill distinguished himself by organising, with great coolness and presence of mind under heavy enemy fire, a number of attempts to set the wagons back on the rails. But the Boers overran the position and took him prisoner, together with about 50 officers and men. Two British soldiers were killed in the attack and 20 seriously wounded.

Churchill was imprisoned in Pretoria from which he made a daring escape, finding his way back to British lines on foot and by coal truck. His story hit the headlines in Britain. 'My imprisonment and escape' he said afterwards, 'provided me with materials for lectures and a book which brought me in enough money to get into Parliament in 1900.'

The Making of a Victorian Hero

This graphic account is taken from Churchill's autobiography, 'My Early Life', published in 1930:

As I passed the engine another shrapnel burst immediately as it seemed overhead, hurling its contents with a rasping rush through the air. The driver at once sprang out of the cab and rushed to the shelter of the overturned trucks. His face cut open by a splinter streamed with blood, and he complained in bitter, futile indignation. 'He was a civilian. What did they think he was paid for? To be killed by a bombshell – not he!' . . . So I told him that no man was hit twice on the same day: that a wounded man who continued to do his duty was always rewarded for distinguished gallantry and that he might never have this chance again. On this he pulled himself together, wiped the blood off his face, climbed back into the cab of his engine, and thereafter obeyed every order I gave him.

More than 10 years were to pass before Churchill was able to keep his promise. By then he had become Home Secretary, one of whose duties was to advise the King upon awards of the Albert Medal. Through the Governor of Natal and the railway company, the train-driver and fireman were traced: they each received the highest reward for gallantry open to civilians.

Colonel Baden-Powell at
Mafeking

Mafeking, Kimberley and Ladysmith

AFTER THE INITIAL success of their invasions of Cape Colony and Natal, it is surprising that the Boers failed to seize the opportunity of pushing on to the sea. At a time when their forces were numerically superior to the scattered British, they chose to bottle up their troops in three fruitless sieges. The first of these was at Mafeking.

A little town in Bechuanaland, then in the extreme north of Cape Colony and on the border of Transvaal, Mafeking was threatened by General Piet Cronje with 8,000 men and ten guns, including a 94-pdr Creusot siege gun, known as 'Long Tom'. The defenders of Mafeking numbered barely 1,000, with four muzzle-loading cannon and a few machine and quick-firing guns.

Why Cronje's force did not simply storm and capture Mafeking, as it seemed so easy to do, is still a mystery, but undoubtedly one of the reasons was the determination and ability of Baden-Powell. Another was that Kruger had given Cronje strict orders to incur no more than fifty casualties in his attack. This played straight into the hands of the inspiring and ingenious commander of the besieged garrison.

Colonel Robert Stephenson Baden-Powell (known as 'B-P' for short) was then aged 42, a man of many extraordinary talents. A conventional army officer who had commanded the 5th Hussars in India, he was full of unconventional military ideas (such as the value of scouting) which were ridiculed by his fellow-officers. He loved amateur theatricals and carried his talent for acting a part into the serious business of defending Mafeking. Behind a mask of buffoonery he hid an iron will to win. At times he was the life-and-soul of the party ('one of the best fellows going', said one of his men, 'he sings comic songs . . .') keeping up the morale of his little force; at others he was the stern commanding officer, directing raids on the Boers, cutting down the food rations (usually at the expense of the Africans), and handing out death sentences.

facing page
Long Tom – the largest artillery piece available to General Cronje – was an impressive-looking weapon that did very little damage during the siege of Mafeking

Before modern signals, heliographs were widely used by the British in the Boer War and on the North-West Frontier in India

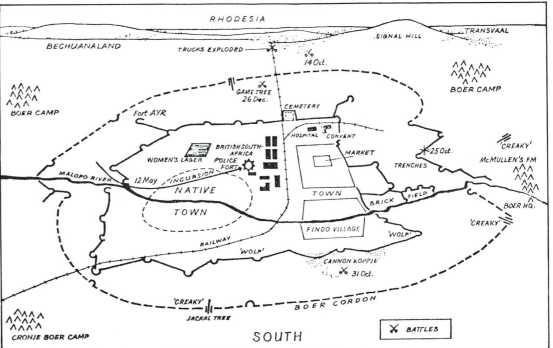

Baden-Powell's own sketch map showing enemy positions and the defences at Mafeking

164

He had starving Africans shot for stealing food, but he also took the unheard of step of *arming* Africans to increase the size of the garrison.

He devised a number of stratagems to persuade the Boers that Mafeking's defences were stronger than they really were. An example was his 'minefields'. He had notices posted up around the town, which read:

The inhabitants are warned that mines are being laid at various points outside the town in connection with the defences. Their position will be marked, in order to avoid accidents, by small red flags.

Cattle herds and others should be warned accordingly.

In fact, the mines were nothing more than wooden boxes filled with sand and connected by wires to his headquarters. But some of the boxes did contain dynamite, which could be detonated in well publicised trials to impress the Boers, whose spies in the town passed on the message.

Baden-Powell had been sent to the Bechuanaland Protectorate not long before the war started, charged with the task of raising a colonial force to threaten northern Transvaal and draw Boer troops away from Natal and Cape Colony. In the event he succeeded in drawing away General Cronje and almost a fifth of the Boer armies. The Bechuana Protectorate Regiment he had raised numbered 450 men. Together with the mounted Cape and British South African Police, and local volunteers, he had just under a thousand part-trained men, about a hundred railwaymen and a score of British regular officers, with which to hold back the cordon of Boer troops on the six-mile perimeter of Mafeking.

Before the siege began Baden-Powell ordered the construction of a circle of defensive earthworks and sent away as many as possible of the town's women and children: underground shell-proof shelters were built for those who stayed. He had the nearest Boer trenches cleared at bayonet point, and recruited the railwaymen to the garrison strength. He used them to produce armoured trains which were employed in a number of successful actions on unsuspecting Boer mounted riflemen.

'Old Creaky' and 'B-P'

Day in and day out, Mafeking was subjected to heavy bombardment, particularly from Long-Tom – nicknamed 'Old Creaky' by the garrison. Most, but by no means all, of the bombs did little damage. Early in the siege 'B-P' had posted a casualty list outside Dixon's Hotel, where he had his HQ. It read:

Killed: one hen
Wounded: one yellow dog
Smashed: one window

The British had no reply to 'Old Creaky' until an eighteenth-century 16-pdr ship's gun was found half-buried on a farm. Cleaned and refurbished clearly the letters B.P. were revealed on the breech. Standing for Bailey and Pegg, the name of the foundry, they were taken as an excellent omen. The old gun was christened 'Lord Nelson' and tested. To everyone's surprise, particularly the Boers, its roundshot bounced like a cricket ball into one of their laagers about 3,000 yards away. Another half-buried naval gun barrel was dug up, converted into a gun that could throw home-made 18-pdr shells 4,000 yards. These two makeshift pieces of artillery forced the Boers to move their laagers back three miles.

Lord Methuen
1845-1932

A great English landowner who knew all the right people, Lord Paul Methuen was fifty-four when General Buller gave him command of an 8,000-strong field force and told him to relieve Kimberley. He had served, without great distinction, in several African campaigns, but was not one of Wolseley's 'ring'. Indeed, Wolseley doubted if he was 'man enough . . . to "run the show" in the Cape', and Wolseley's doubts turned out to be well founded. Methuen had never been more than a painstaking staff officer of average ability, and he clung to the belief that frontal attack was the way to beat the Boers. However, despite his failures at the Modder River and Magersfontein, he survived Roberts' purge of the incompetent, although he was demoted. He was later wounded and taken prisoner when leading a column against the Boer guerrilla leader General Christiaan de Wet. His lack of success as a general did not prevent Lord Methuen from being promoted Field-Marshal, and in 1908 he became GOC-in-C South Africa.

Paul Kruger
1825-1904

In the years before and during the Second Boer War, the gloomy, whiskered face of Paul Kruger was familiar to millions of British newspaper readers as the man they loved to hate. Born in Cape Colony, in 1825, he travelled north with his *voortrekker* family in the Great Trek of 1835-37, settling first in Natal and later in the Transvaal. A farmer, fighter and hunter, who read nothing but the Bible, he became the leader and figurehead of the Boer nationalists, and cherished a dream of an all-South African confederation led by the Boers – just as Cecil Rhodes dreamed of a British-led South African confederation. Under the Boer commando system of military service, Kruger rose to be a Field Cornet when he was 27. He played a leading role in the humiliation of the British forces in the First Boer War, and became President of the Transvaal in 1881. When the second war came to an end Kruger was taken into exile aboard a Dutch cruiser, and he died in Switzerland in 1904.

Shortage of food was inevitably a problem, and as the weeks went by Baden-Powell's rationing grew stricter and stricter. Horses were shot and he described what happened then:

When a horse was killed, his mane and tail were cut off and sent to the hospital for stuffing mattresses and pillows. His shoes went to the foundry for making shells. His skin after having the hair scalded off, was boiled with his head and feet for many hours, chopped up small, and . . . served out as 'brawn'.

His flesh was taken from the bones and minced in a great mincing machine and from his inside were made skins into which the meat was crammed and each man received a sausage as his ration. The bones were then boiled into rich soup, which was dealt out at the different soup kitchens; and they were afterwards pounded into powder with which to adulterate the flour.

But the principal food came from the flour mill, a kind of porridge made from the husks of oats. Locusts were plentiful and enjoyed by the local tribesmen, and even by some Europeans. Lady Sarah Wilson, wife of one of Baden-Powell's officers and aunt of the dashing young Winston Churchill, sent a message home:

BREAKFAST TODAY HORSE SAUSAGE, LUNCH MINCED MULE CURRIED LOCUSTS. ALL WELL.

Stories from Mafeking fired the imagination of the British public as almost no other event, before or since. From the Queen came a message which showed that she was well aware of the exploits of this latest of her heroes:

I continue watching with confidence and admiration the patient and resolute defence which is so gallantly maintained under your ever resourceful command.
V.R.I.

On 17 May 1900 a relief column, composed mostly of South African mounted irregular troops, rode into Mafeking, and the 217-day siege was over. In London the crowds went mad with excitement, and the word 'mafficking' was added to the dictionary. But amid all the rejoicings, the congratulations and the awards, and the relief funds, no one gave a thought to the majority of the garrison and workers who had made it all possible – the Africans.

□ □ □

In Kimberley, close to the Orange Free State Border, there were two prime targets for the Boers: the De Beers diamond mines and the managing director of De Beers, the Boers' arch enemy Cecil Rhodes. As at Mafeking, the defences of the town, including the diamond mines, had been prepared shortly before the war broke out. A ring of earthworks and barbed wire fences had been built, strong-points established,

A forceful personality, Cecil Rhodes assumed the unofficial leadership of the British community in South Africa and thereby alienated the Dutch. During the siege of Kimberley he organised a soup kitchen (*left*) and tried to take over the defence of the town, much to the fury of Colonel Kekwich (*below*), who threatened to place him under arrest

searchlights installed, telephone cables laid, an observation tower erected and landmines placed.

All this was the work of the garrison commander, 45-year-old Colonel Robert Kekewich of the 1st Loyal North Lancashire Regiment. With him he had about 400 men of his regiment and their officers, and a company each of the Royal Artillery and the Royal Engineers. The remainder of the garrison of about 4,500 men consisted of detachments of Cape Police and over 3,000 mounted volunteers raised by De Beers, who also supplied their horses and weapons. The siege began on 15 October 1899 and kept some thousands of Boers tied down for the next four months – troops who might otherwise have advanced deeper into Cape Colony.

As at Mafeking and Ladysmith, the Boers made no serious attempt to take the town by storm, preferring to attempt to bombard or starve it into surrender. For Colonel Kekewich perhaps the biggest problem was Cecil Rhodes, who tended to act as though *he* were the garrison commander. Aware that it would hardly have been possible to defend Kimberley without the irregular troops provided by De Beers 'he behaved as though he had the town in his pocket.' He sent messages direct to General Buller in Cape Town, suggesting that the town was close to surrender. But when Lord Roberts took over supreme command he dealt with the situation by intimating to Kekewich that if necessary he

should use his powers of arrest. From time to time Rhodes stormed into the colonel's office demanding more aggressive action against the Boers. When the military facts were explained to him, he would become very abusive:

You damned soldiers . . . with your damned military situation! . . . You are afraid of a mere handful of farmers. You call yourselves soldiers of an Empire-making nation. I do believe you will next take fright at a pair of broomsticks dressed up in trousers . . .

On 23 November Kekewich received a delayed message from General Lord Methuen, commander of the field force charged with the task of relieving Kimberley: 'General leaves here with strong force on November 21st, and will arrive Kimberley November 26th, unless delayed at Modder River . . .' Buller had given into the pressure to relieve the towns under siege.

Methuen had 8,000 men with him; they included a Guards Brigade of one Grenadier, one Scots, and two Coldstream Guards battalions; and the 9th Infantry Brigade consisting of the King's Own Yorkshire Light Infantry, the Northumberland Fusiliers, the Northamptons, the Loyal North Lancashires, and the Munsters. His mounted troops included the 9th Lancers, a detachment of the New South Wales Lancers, and Rimington's Guides, a corps of Afrikaans-speaking scouts. Accompanying the column were two batteries of the Royal Field Artillery,

facing page
Corporal McKay of the
Argyll and Sutherland
Highlanders rallies his
comrades at the battle
of Magersfontein

four companies of Royal Engineers, a Naval Brigade and the Royal Marines, armed with 12-pounder guns. The Highland Brigade guarded his line of communications.

A painstaking but limited general, Lord Methuen had taken great care to prepare his troops for fighting the Boers. Khaki replaced colour, brass buttons and insignia were removed or painted khaki ('they will be making us dye our whiskers khaki next', growled one sergeant). Drill and formal dressing was abandoned in favour of 'very extended order, men getting quickly from rock to rock, irregularity of line being sought and regular dressing avoided.' Methuen took the lead in making himself inconspicuous: 'I look like a second-class conductor,' he wrote, 'in a khaki coat with no mark of rank on it and a Boer hat . . .' Even shaving was no longer compulsory – water was too scarce. On the march tents were left behind and the troops bivouacked, carrying with them the minimum kit – even greatcoats being left behind.

The Boers were waiting for them. In three minor battles, at Belmont on 23 October, at Graspan on 25 November and on the Modder river on 28 November, Methuen won costly and indecisive victories, and on each occasion the

Boers lost fewer men than their opponents, and their commandos escaped to fight again. At the Modder River Methuen's force walked into an ambush. Using an inaccurate map and ignoring warnings of Boer concentrations, he ordered the Guards to advance into apparently unoccupied land in front of the river. A report by the Guards commander, General Colville, takes up the story:

At 8 a.m. I found Lord Methuen and his Staff looking at a clump of trees some 1,500 yards to our front which he said was on the Modder River. It had been reported that this was held by the enemy, but he thought they had gone. He, however, ordered me to extend the attack . . . it seemed as if we should make short work of the enemy over this nice level ground . . . As we watched Arthur Paget and his Scots Guards moving ahead to the right, Lord Methuen said to me, 'They are not here.' 'They are sitting uncommonly tight if they are, sir,' I answered; then, as if they had heard him, the Boers answered with a roar of musketry. [sic]

The casualties were severe, and the battle for the river crossing lasted all day. Overnight the Boers withdrew, and Lord Methuen could claim a victory, but at a cost of nearly 500 killed, wounded and missing. And Kimberley was still under siege.

Beyond the Modder River the Boers were entrenched in front of Magersfontein Hill, blocking the British advance to Kimberley. Methuen decided on a dawn attack after a night march. However, a British bombardment the previous day had alerted the Boers, who fully manned their trenches. In spite of their experience at the Modder River, the British did not suspect that the enemy would be entrenched in front of the hill, but on top of it. Once again they were taken by surprise, and suffered a severe defeat with enormous casualties. The losses among the Highland Brigade were particularly heavy; fifteen officers, including the commanding officer, Lord Wauchope, and 173 men were killed, and 559 officers and men were wounded or missing, out of a total of 948 casualties that day. And once again Kimberley had to wait for a relieving force.

About a month after Roberts and Kitchener arrived in South Africa they established a base camp on the Modder River. Sir John French with his 5,000 strong cavalry division was then ordered to take up the challenge and relieve Kimberley. Everything depended on surprise, and so French and his flying column, with their gleaming sabres and lances, rode like the wind, charging through the centre of the Boer lines. At last the way was open, and on 15 February 1900 French rode into Kimberley, ending the first of the three sieges.

'B-P' Sir Robert Baden-Powell
1857-1941

'The Hero of Mafeking', founder of the Boy Scout Movement and later Lord Baden-Powell of Chigwell, was part conventional pig-sticking army officer, part overgrown schoolboy. Gazetted into the 5th Hussars straight from school, he commanded the 5th Hussars in India, and served in the Ashanti and Matabele campaigns. He wrote numerous articles and books on such subjects as cavalry instruction, reconnaissance, scouting and pig-sticking, and his 'Scouting for Boys' was a world best-seller. His reward for Mafeking was promotion to Major-General, the youngest in the British army, and his services to youth earned him a peerage.

Sir George White
1835-1912

'The Hero of Ladysmith' was one of many much-decorated Victorian generals whose battle experience included fighting hand-to-hand with the enemy. At Chasariah in the Second Afghan War he led an attack on a strongly fortified hill; taking a rifle from an infantryman, he went forward alone and shot the enemy leader. At Kandahar in the same war he led the final charge and personally captured a couple of guns.

Field-Marshal Sir George White VC, OM, GCSI, GCMG, GCIE, GCVO, was born in 1835 in County Antrim. Like so many of his countrymen, he was drawn to an army career, and he became a cadet at Sandhurst. He was gazetted Ensign in the 27th Inniskilling Fusiliers, and fought throughout the Indian Mutiny. He was promoted Captain in 1863 and Major ten years later – even for the most promising Victorian officers promotion was snail-like.

However, a well-deserved VC could open doors, and White won his at Charasiah, after which he became in turn Military Secretary to the Viceroy of India, Assistant Quartermaster-General in the Egyptian Campaign of 1884-85, and commander of the Zhob Valley expedition in 1889. Having pacified Baluchistan, he was appointed GCIE, and was Commander-in-Chief of the Indian Army during the Chitral and Tirah campaigns of 1895-97.

The Second Boer War saw White in command in Natal. He was much criticised for allowing his 10,000-strong force to be surrounded and rendered virtually ineffective in Lady-

smith, but he always maintained that this move had saved Natal from being over-run by the Boers. After the siege he fell ill with a fever and was invalided home. He spent the remainder of his life in such mainly decorative posts as Governor of Gibraltar and Governor of Chelsea Hospital. He died in 1912.

Under Siege at Ladysmith

Among eye-witness accounts of life under siege at Ladysmith are the following extracts from letters home sent by the officers in charge of the hospital:

'We are besieged by a large force of Boers, and although we have 10,000 men here we can't get out and so are waiting until we are relieved. We had about three very hot days in Ladysmith as the Boers shelled the town and the shells were screaming and bursting all over the place and considering the number of shells very few people were hit though there were many narrow escapes . . .

I have seen some of the Boers for as I am in charge of the hospital out here, I have several times met Boers under a flag of truce to discuss sundry matters. Those I have seen have all been very pleasant fellows indeed and very friendly. They have behaved *extremely* well to our wounded prisoners, attending to them and giving them everything they had themselves. All our prisoners speak highly of the kindness they have received at their hands . . .

The bullet the Boers use is an extraordinary missile: it is about one and a quarter inches long and as thin as a lead pencil. It incapacitates a man but it does not kill him like the old Martini and other bullets. I have seen men shot through the brain, matter oozing out of the hole in the skull and yet the man recovered very shortly too. Men shot through the lungs have very little trouble from the wounds . . .

I get about fifty-five sick a day into this hospital, and I am now in charge of no less than 1,270 sick and wounded, including sixty-five officers . . . about 500 cases of enteric fever, 180 of dysentery and 150 wounded . . . We have had about 90 deaths . . .

We are getting very short of food, at least of everything in the shape of luxuries. All we have now is meat (very tough) and bread, tea, sugar, and porridge made from Indian Cola meal. No milk, butter, vegetables, eggs or anything else; very little meat, not enough for a second helping, no matter how hungry you are . . .

Buller will have a very hard fight before he relieves us, for the country is all big steep hills very strongly fortified by the Boers . . . We know nothing of what is going on outside this place for we are very closely besieged and letters and newspapers cannot be got through except for a few [newspaper correspondents'] despatches . . . We are in heliographic communication with Buller, but he tells us very little . . .'

Some of the actions that took place during the course of the siege are described in these extracts taken from the diary of a gunner at Ladysmith:

Thur. Nov 2nd: . . . the siege has started. The Boers opened fire with their artillery into the town, but luckily they did no harm.

Thur. Nov 9th: Stood to arms till daybreak, at 5.20 am the Boers opened fire on us from heavy artillery all around us, shelling the camp and Town, firing very fast all the while. At 7.30 am the Boers attacked King's Hill in force; but met with a warm reception, being repulsed three times with loss, then they attacked Ceazers [Caesar's] Hill and met with the same result . . .

Sat. Nov. 11th: A few rounds from long Tom [the Boers' 94pdr Creusot fortress guns, which they could move rapidly from place to place].

Sat. Nov. 18th: Stood to arms as usual till daybreak. Johnny Dutchman still wasting his ammunition.

Sun. Nov. 19th: Stood to arms but all was quiet . . . church parade.

Mon. Nov. 20th: Boers' capture of an armoured train [at Frere] . . . with an escort of mounted Infantry who made good their escape. [This seems to refer to the train in which Winston Churchill was travelling]

Thur. Dec. 7th: Long Tom spoke to us again with the same old Talk.

The siege dragged on for 118 days, and more men died from disease than enemy action. The constant bombardment, the inactivity and the depressing news of 'Black Week' told on morale, and many officers chafed: 'I would have bothered the Boers constantly by night with small parties of say half companies,' said one, 'they could have stalked the Boer pickets . . . anyway they would have given the Boers no peace.'

The day after the battle of Talana, a squadron each of the 5th Dragoon Guards and the 5th Lancers, and several squadrons of the Imperial Light Horse (an irregular force of South African Colonial horsemen), together with detachments of the Manchesters, Devons and Gordon Highlanders attacked and routed a Boer force at Elandslaagte, near Ladysmith. Of the officers taking part in this engagement three were destined for high command: Major-General John French led the cavalry, with Major Douglas Haig as his chief staff officer, and the infantry were commanded by Colonel Ian Hamilton. Though small-scale, the victory hit the newspaper headlines in Britain, and undoubtedly made the reputations of the victors. Traditional British tactics of bayonet and cavalry charges seem for once to have unnerved the Boer riflemen.

But this success did not prevent the Boers from surrounding Ladysmith, the second largest town in Natal, where General Sir George White, Commander-in-Chief of Natal, with some 10,000 troops, virtually allowed himself to be bottled up. Why he did not try to keep his forces free for action by establishing a defensive position on the Tugela river has never been explained.

One major action was initiated by the Boer generals, Piet Joubert and Louis Botha. On 6 January 1900 they assembled an assault force of 5,000 men to attack the southern sector of the Ladysmith defences, where Ian Hamilton was in command. At one point 250 Boer riflemen, hidden among the rocks on a hillside, held off two thousand British infantrymen. Time and

After sixteen hours of desperate fighting in hot sun followed by a violent thunderstorm, the Boers abandoned the assault, having lost about 250 killed and wounded. In this action Lieutenant Masterson, a company commander of the Devons, crossed one hundred yards of open ground under heavy fire in order to ask the Imperial Light Horse for support in the attack on the Boer line. He was hit in both thighs but managed to crawl on to deliver the message – an act of bravery that won him the Victoria Cross.

After the battle on 27 February at Pieter's Hill, the last Boer strongpoint before Ladysmith, the way was open for General Buller's relief column. Winston Churchill rode in with two squadrons of the Imperial Light Horse and Carbineers:

. . . the two squadrons were allowed to brush through the crumbling rear-guard, and ride into Ladysmith. I rode with these two squadrons, and galloped across the scrub-dotted plain, fired at by only a couple of Boer guns. Suddenly from the brushwood up rose gaunt figures waving hands of welcome. On we pressed, and at the head of a battered street of tin-roofed houses met Sir George White on horseback, faultlessly attired. Then we all rode together into the long, almost starved-out Ladysmith . . .

Private Tucker saw it rather differently, but he was not writing for the *Morning Post*.

. . . Instead of being cheered by all as we had imagined, most of them [the troops of the garrison] seemed to say with their looks: 'Well, you have come at last, but you have taken your time over it.'

again a gallant infantry officer, still unaware of the power of the repeating rifle, would lead his men, bayonets fixed, across the few yards separated from two sides, only to be mown down instantly. Finally, Hamilton stopped such suicidal charges, and the Boers quietly disappeared.

top
A 'Spy' cartoon of Sir Ian Hamilton, who won his spurs at Elandlaagte

far left
Major-General Sir John French, one of a number of British commanders during the Boer War who were to play a leading part in the First World War

top left
A contemporary photograph showing the firing line of the 1st Devons at Elandslaagte

The advance guard of Buller's army enters Ladysmith after the raising of the siege

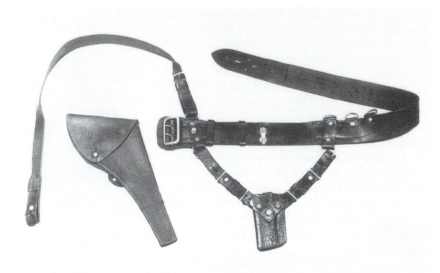

The familiar Sam Browne belt worn by army officers and warrant officers (1st class) was invented by General Sir Samuel Browne who, after losing an arm in battle, determined to design a new piece of equipment which would make it possible for him to draw his sword – and revolver – in as convenient a manner as possible. The belt came into use during the 1870s, and is now standard wear for most Western army officers.

General Sir Samuel Browne VC 1824-1901

'Black Week'

GENERAL SIR REDVERS BULLER, had been sent to South Africa with an agreed War Office plan for defeating the Boers quickly. His Army Corps was to land at three ports – Cape Town, Port Elizabeth, and East London – converge on the Orange River and then advance in strength to the enemy capitals at Bloemfontein and Pretoria. But by the time Buller landed at Cape Town, the Boers had occupied most of northern Natal and had surrounded Kimberley, Ladysmith and Mafeking. He considered that the loss of any or all of these places would be an unacceptable blow to Britain's military position and prestige, and so he made the fateful decision to divide his forces – just as the Boer commanders had divided theirs. The effect was much the same: the ability to deliver a knock-out blow was lost.

Buller divided the Army Corps into three parts. About half was despatched to Natal to be commanded by himself. General Lord Methuen was given a field force to relieve Kimberley, and the rest, commanded by Generals Clery and Gatacre, including most of the cavalry under General Sir John French, was to contain the threat of a Boer invasion of Cape Colony across the Orange River.

The immediate consequence of this change of plan was what the British public called 'Black Week'. Three times in the week of 10-16 December came news that British forces had suffered defeat at the hands of the Boers. Each part of the divided Army Corps suffered a disaster. Methuen was outwitted at Magersfontein on 10 December. Gatacre was 'misled' and in his own words 'met with serious reverse in attack' at Stormberg on the same day, and Buller himself was so badly beaten at Colenso on 15 December that he was relieved of his command. The casualty lists for the week filled several columns of the newspapers, but the general public, like the old Queen, was more defiant than depressed. 'There is no depression in this house,' she told visitors at Windsor. 'We are not interested in the possibilities of defeat. They do not exist.'

COLENSO

Between Buller and Ladysmith, with its trapped 10,000 British troops, was the Tugela River and one of the Boers' most able generals, Louis Botha. He had under his command about 6,000 men, compared with 21,000 on the British side – perhaps the biggest single force to be led by an English general since the time of the Crimean War.

Buller decided to cross the river in force at Colesno, but from the outset everything went wrong. No proper reconnaissance had been made and the maps Buller used seem to have been inaccurate. General Sir George White in Ladysmith had not been asked to create a diversion in Botha's rear. As at Magersfontein,

the British gave advance notice of the coming attack by bombarding the Boer positions heavily for two days. The Boers did not respond. Before the planned main attack on the bridge at Colenso, Major-General Hart was ordered to take the Irish Brigade and make a flanking attack across a drift on the left. Before leaving, he gave his men half an hour's drill ('the only way to keep the men in hand'). Then he led them in close order straight into a river loop where they presented an easy target for the Botha and his burghers. Private Fred Tucker of the Rifle Brigade was there and described the scene in his diary:

As soon as General Hart's Irish Brigade moved forward in quarter columns towards the banks of the Tugela, the Boers sent their first shell into his closed

'Black Week' brought a rush of volunteers eager to fight the Boers. A new corps, the Imperial Yeomanry, was formed and by January 1900, the first 10,000 of these mounted volunteers (who, unlike the existing Yeomanry, were subject to Regular Army discipline and paid at cavalry rates) were on their way to South Africa. A number of other volunteer service contingents were raised, and mounted troops poured in from Britain's overseas Colonies (as they were then called). Of the 448,725 troops who fought on the British side, about 30,000 came from overseas and nearly 60,000 from South Africa itself.

One of the 4.7-inch naval guns in action at Colenso. From a drawing by A. Forestier

173

'*My Brave Irish*'
The 2nd Royal Irish
Fusiliers on Pieter's Hill.
Painting by
R Caton Woodville

1899-1902

SOUTH AFRICA:
Second Boer War
Life Guards
Royal Horse Guards
King's Dragoon Guards
Queen's Bays
3rd Dragoon Guards
5th Dragoon Guards
6th Dragoon Guards
7th Dragoon Guards
Royal Dragoons
Royal Scots Greys
3rd Hussars
5th Lancers
Inniskilling Dragoons
7th Hussars
8th Hussars
9th Lancers
10th Hussars
12th Lancers
13th Lancers
14th Hussars
16th Lancers
17th Lancers
18th Hussars
19th Hussars
20th Hussars
Grenadier Guards
Coldstream Guards
Scots Guards

ranks and took twelve men off one section and then it seemed as if all hell had been let loose. Mauser, rifle, pom-pom, Maxim big guns and I don't know what else rang out until the air seemed alive with iron and lead. The Irish Brigade retired at the double but soon advanced again in open order with the intention of crossing the river at the ford but they could not find the right place to cross. The wily Boers had forseen this and dammed the river making it unfordable. Several men attempted to swim across but a shell fell amongst them and they all lost their lives, either by blast or they were drowned. The Boers had also laid barbed wire entanglements in the bed of the river. All the time there was terrific roar of musketry from both sides . . .

. . . we received orders to support the Irish Brigade . . . who we could see were falling fast. My regiment at once extended in one long line, each man six paces from the other, and advanced towards the firing line. I have never seen a regiment extend and move forward in such good order as ours did that day; if it had been doing the same movement at ordinary peace manoevures it could not have been done better. No-one seemed to take the least notice of the shot and shells that were falling amongst us, everyone was cracking jokes and making as much fun as they could. Luckily for us, few of the Boer shells exploded . . . Just at this time the Irish Brigade began to retire, which meant that we came in for all the shot and shell the Boers had to spare; which was considerable. Pretty soon we had the stretchers at work amongst us . . . [The shells] fell within a few feet, showering us with clouds of dirt and a shrapnel burst just over our heads, the pieces falling over our bodies like acorns from a tree. It was a very trying time and I think it is

impossible to write of one's feelings when under fire for the first time as we were. I lit my pipe and smoked almost the whole time I was there. My Captain, who was beside me, lit a cigarette and began to write. I did the same. Not one of my regiment was hit by shells, although several were hit by Mauser bullets.

On the right the mounted brigade was pinned down by a curtain of rifle and pom-pom fire from 800 concealed Boers, and their attack was halted. But the worst and most shaming disaster took place in the centre, where eleven guns were lost. Instead of using his artillery to support the infantry advance, the colonel in charge pushed far ahead of the main force and drew up his guns in a tidy parade-ground line. So intense was the Boer fire that the gunners had to be withdrawn, leaving twelve guns behind. Buller rode up and took personal charge, calling for volunteers with limber teams to bring back the guns. Two of them were rescued under a hail of bullets, but only after seven men and thirteen horses had been lost. 'No living man could have got more of those guns away,' said Buller, and he ordered them to be abandoned. Among the volunteers killed was Lieutenant Fred Roberts, son of the Field Marshal, who with four others was awarded the Victoria Cross after his death. At this point Buller seems to have lost his nerve, and he ordered a general withdrawal. Private Tucker described the retreat in these terms:
It is the general opinion that this loss of guns lost us the day, for it precipiated the order for a general

174

retirement. We held the ground while the remainder slowly fell back. When our turn came, we rose from the ground with keen bitterness in our hearts but comforted by the thought that our turn would come some day. As we stood up to retire the Boers caught sight of us once more and renewed their rifle fire, but they could not hurry us and we retired even better than in the advance, leisurely and without the slightest hurry. Indeed anyone meeting us would have thought that it had been a victory, instead of the reverse.

General Buller, who by this action soon came to be known as 'Sir *Reverse* Buller', struck a very defeatest note after Colenso. He wrote to the Government:

My view is that I ought to let Ladysmith go, and occupy good positions for the defence of south Natal, and let time help us . . .

To Sir George White in Ladysmith he sent a similar message by heliograph:

Can you last long? If not, how many days can you give me in which to take up a defensive position? After which I suggest your firing away as much ammunition as you can, and making the best terms you can.

Sir George rejected the very idea of giving in:

Things may get better. The loss of 12,000 men would be a heavy blow for England. We must not yet think of it.

Shocked into action by the idea of 'letting Ladysmith go,' the Cabinet in London decided to replace Buller and accepted the offer of 67-year old Field Marshal Lord Roberts to go at once to South Africa as Commander-in-Chief. With him they sent Major-General Lord Kitchener as his Chief of Staff. Both were successful field commanders as well as popular figures, much admired by the Queen.

□ □ □

In one of Buller's columns bogged down on its way to Spion Kop, two private soldiers were overheard by the war correspondent of the *Manchester Guardian*:
'What are we waiting 'ere for?'
'Don't yer know?'
'No.'
'To give the Boers time to build up their trenches and fetch up their guns. Fair – ain't it?'
The correspondent of *The Morning Post*, Winston Churchill was also at Spion Kop and his report revealed the reason why the private had to wait:

The vast amount of luggage this army takes with it on the march hampers its movements and utterly precludes all possibility of surprising the enemy. I have never before seen even officers accommodated with tents on service, though the Indian frontier and the Sudan lie under a hotter sun than South Africa. But here today, within striking distance of a mobile

enemy whom we wished to circumvent, every private soldier has canvas shelter, and the other arrangements are on an equally elaborate scale. The consequence is that the roads are crowded, drifts are blocked, marching troops are delayed, and all rapidity of movement is out of the question. Meanwhile the enemy completes the fortification of his positions and the cost of capturing them rises. It is poor economy to let a soldier live well for three days at the price of killing him on the fourth.

It was because Buller looked after his troops and made sure that they were well fed that he was so popular with his men, who overlooked his blunders and cheered him wherever he went. But it meant that his huge columns of infantry, cavalry and guns were followed by an almost endless trail of wagons, mules, oxen, not to mention clerks, orderlies, signallers, stretcher-

Canadian troops storm
a kopje

Royal Scots
Queen's
Buffs
King's Own
Royal Northumberland
    Fusiliers
Royal Warwickshire
Royal Fusiliers
King's
Royal Norfolk
Royal Lincolnshire
Devonshire
Suffolk
Somerset L.I.
West Yorkshire
East Yorkshire
Bedfordshire and
    Hertfordshire
Royal Leicestershire
Royal Irish
Green Howards
Lancashire Fusiliers
Royal Scots Fusiliers
Cheshire
Royal Welch Fusiliers
South Wales Borderers
King's Own Scottish
    Borderers
Cameronians
Royal Inniskilling Fusiliers
Gloucestershire
Worcestershire
East Lancashire
East Surrey
Duke of Cornwall's L.I.
Duke of Wellington's
Border
Royal Sussex
Royal Hampshire
South Staffordshire
Dorset
South Lancashire
Welch
Black Watch
Oxford and Bucks L.I.
Essex
Sherwood Foresters
Loyal North Lancashire
Northamptonshire
Royal Berkshire
Royal West Kent
King's Own Yorkshire L.I.
King's Shropshire L.I.
Middlesex
King's Royal Rifle Corps
Manchester
Wiltshire
North Staffordshire
York and Lancaster
Durham L.I.
Highland L.I.
Seaforth Highlanders
Gordon Highlanders
Cameron Highlanders
Royal Irish Rifles
(Royal Ulster Rifles)
Royal Irish Fusiliers
Connaught Rangers
Argyll and Sutherland
    Highlanders
Leinster
Royal Munster Fusiliers
Royal Dublin Fusiliers
Rifle Brigade

Field-Marshal Sir Evelyn Wood 1838-1919

Few heroes for Victoria fought in more battles, received more wounds, more decorations and more awards, and suffered more accidents and illnesses than Sir Evelyn Wood VC. By the age of eighteen he had been twice wounded, twice mentioned in despatches; awarded the Crimean medal with two clasps, as well as the French *Légion d'Honneur* and the Turkish Medjidie 5th Class; recommended for (but not awarded) the new Victoria Cross, and had nearly died of typhoid fever and a lung infection.

He actually won his VC in India when he was twenty-two. By then he had suffered frequently from malaria, dynsentry, sunstroke, toothache, neuralgia and an ear infection that left him partially deaf; had received severe facial injuries when trodden on by a giraffe he was trying to ride, and had broken his collar-bone and nose when his horse galloped into a tree.

The future Field-Marshal Sir Evelyn Wood joined the Royal Navy as a midshipman at the age of fourteen. Two years later he was in the Crimea with the Naval Brigade helping to work the guns at Balaclava in a fierce artillery duel with the Russians. In July 1855 he was one of a storming party at the assault on the Redan, where all his fellow-officers were killed or wounded before they had gone 300 yards. Wood was wounded in the hand and then in the elbow. The army doctors promised to 'have your arm off before you know where you are,' but Wood protested vigorously. His arm was saved when Lord Raglan, who foresaw a brilliant career for the brave and stubborn young officer, sent a carriage to take him on board HMS *Queen*, whose captain was Wood's uncle.

Finding life ashore more exciting than life at sea, Wood transferred to the army (helped again by Lord Raglan) and was commissioned into the 13th Light Dragoons, later exchanging into the 17th Lancers – for him appropriately nicknamed 'The Death or Glory Boys'. He fought as a cavalry officer, and was frequently wounded, in the Crimea, India, Ashantiland, Zululand, and Egypt. Although he had recently broken his ankle and been given an overdose of morphine, he was pronounced fit to serve with

Wolseley in the Ashanti War of 1873, where a piece of a nail fired from a musket became embedded in his chest and seems to have remained there for years. In the Zulu War of 1879, he commanded a column, and served with such distinction that he was appointed KCB. Two years later he was second in command to General Sir George Colley in the First Boer War and took over in Natal after Colley was killed at Majuba Hill. He was heavily criticised when he made no attempt to avenge that defeat, but he insisted that his duty was to obey his government's instructions to make peace with the Boers.

Evelyn Wood was one of the Wolseley 'gang', and in Egypt in 1882 he commanded the 4th Brigade under Wolseley. The Queen, who described him as 'an admirable General with plenty of *dash* as well as prudence . . . most agreeable as well as amusing, very lively yet *very discreet*,' went on board to say goodbye. 'She embraced my wife,' he said, 'and was very gracious to me.' This did not please Wolseley, who fumed with jealousy and left Wood behind in Alexandria. After the conquest of Egypt he was given the task of forming a new Egyptian army of which he was to be the first British *Sirdar* (Commander in-Chief). The officer he chose as his second in command was Major Herbert Kitchener, the future Sirdar and Field-Marshal Lord Kitchener of Khartoum. Back in England, Wood was appointed CO of Eastern Command in 1886. Lieutenant-General and in GCB, Adjutant-General, commander of the Second Army Corps in 1901 and Field-Marshal in 1903.

bearers, cooks, bakers, farriers, and auxiliaries of every kind. Small wonder that when Buller began to move his army of about 30,000 men towards the Tugela River in a renewed attempt to relieve Ladysmith, it took five days to cover a mere sixteen miles.

His strength had been increased by the arrival of the 5th Infantry Division under 59-year old Lieutenant-General Sir Charles Warren, to whom he gave an independent command to break through the Boer defences west of Spion Kop.

The reinforced army set out on 10 January 1900, the day Roberts and Kitchener landed in Cape Town, and a week later crossed the Tugela by two separate drifts. There followed, at Spion Kop, one of the most futile and bloody battles of the whole war. If captured, Spion Kop (meaning 'watchers hill') would have put Buller in a good position to turn the Boer defences and move on to Ladysmith. But, as at Majuba, British troops discovered that once on the summit they were exposed to Boer marksmen posted on nearby heights. The Lancashire Fusiliers' trenches, for example, were enfiladed with such accurate fire that seventy men were all hit by bullets on the right side of the head. General Woodgate, who was in command, was mortally wounded, and soon all was confusion. After five hours of such fire, some of the troops started to surrender – not realising that the Boers themselves felt close to defeat. At 8.15 pm Colonel Alec Thorneycroft, who had succeeded Woodgate on the summit ordered a withdrawal, saying 'better a withdrawal now than a mop-up in the morning,' and General Warren agreed. Winston Churchill had climbed to Spion Kop to see for himself:

Streams of wounded met us and obstructed our path. Men were staggering along alone, or supported by comrades, or crawling on hands and knees, or carried on stretchers. Corpses lay here and there. There was, moreover, a small but steady leakage of unwounded men of all corps. Some of these cursed and swore. Others were utterly exhausted, and fell on the hillside in a stupor. Others, again, seemed drunk, though they had no liquor. Scores were sleeping heavily . . . One thing was quite clear – unless good and efficient cover could be made during the night, and unless guns could be dragged to the summit of the hill to match the Boer artillery, the infantry could not, perhaps would not endure another day. The human machine will not stand certain strains for long.

But at the same time as the British were withdrawing on one side of Spion Kop the Boers were leaving on the other. When they came back at dawn to collect their dead, they found the summit deserted and immediately reoccupied it. A fortnight later Buller resolved on yet another attempt to cross the Tugela and fight his way through the hills to Ladysmith. This time he planned to seize two hills on the Boer side of the Tugela, Vaal Krantz and Doorn Kop, and march his army between them. Private Tucker was at the attack on Vaal Krantz:

We fell in at 6.30 am knowing we were to attack yet another of those hills which the Boers know how to fortify so well . . . My regiment and the Durhams were still advancing in skirmishing order, no shot or shell could stop us that day, and soon the foot of Vaal Krantz was reached, and with fixed swords, we charged up the hill in the face of deadly shot and shell fire . . . Very soon the whole of the regiment was on the hill and the men set to work at once building walls for protection as we were still under a very heavy cross fire from the left and the right . . . The Boers kept firing until it was quite dark, so it was not safe to move our casualties, which were very heavy – about eighty in the Rifle Brigade . . . At daybreak the Boers let us have it from all sides with their long range guns . . . A great many men were wounded during the day while we waited, fully expecting some movement from the other troops, but none came . . . and we were relieved at 7.00 pm under cover of darkness by another brigade led by Colonel Kitchener [brother of Lord Kitchener] . . . who told [our] Colonel Billy Norcott that we had been greatly praised by General Buller for the way we had taken the hill . . . During the night . . . the hill we had lost so many lives taking was evacuated. So all our hopes of relieving Ladysmith this way were scattered.

Several more days of hard fighting were needed before the Boers' resistance crumbled at Pieter's Hill on 27 February, and they began a general retreat. Private Tucker felt it a great honour that his regiment, the 1st Rifle Brigade, along with the East Surreys, was selected for the final do-or-die attack on the hill, especially as the Irish Brigade had failed three times:

About 3.00 pm we moved up to our advanced post near the railway, and there, once more, we came in for a heavy fire . . . We caught sight of the East Surrey just up a hill, on our flank; we all gave a good, hearty cheer and yell of 'Remember Majuba!' and we started off on the race for the top of the hill. Hardly had we left cover of the kopje before our men began to fall fast and how any of us survived all the bullets, pom-poms and pieces of shell with which we were greeted as we ran the gauntlet to Pieter's Hill, is a marvel to me . . . We kept rushing forward, stopping every now and then to fire as we saw a chance. We quickly reached the side of Pieter's Hill, where we lay down and pelted them in such a heavy manner that some Boers, who were able, thought it best to move. As they retired we rushed with the bayonet . . . When we reached the [Boer] trenches, Riflemen and East Surreys were all mixed up, so neither regiment could claim the honour of being first in the trenches. My company had, however, led the attack and really were first up Pieter's Hill.

The way was open to Ladysmith, but the victory had taken weeks of bitter fighting and had cost 5,000 men killed, wounded or missing – a sixth of Buller's army.

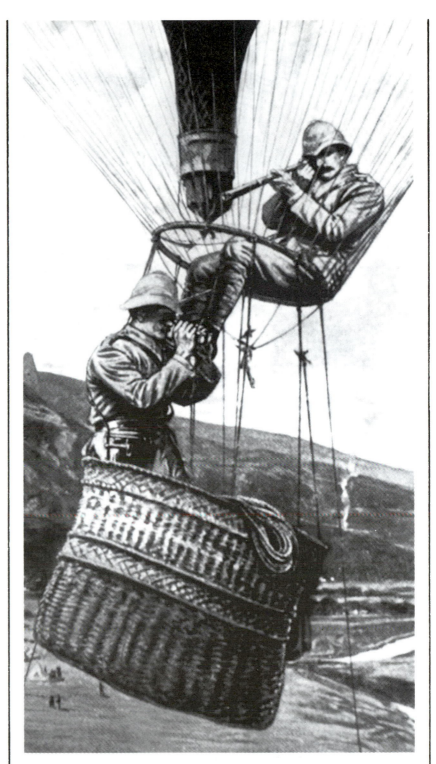

Balloons v. Boers

Observation balloons were a novelty during the Boer War, even though balloons had been used on and off for military reconnaissance and dropping bombs since the end of the eighteenth century. Twenty balloons were in service in South Africa. The wicker basket accommodated two observers and was connected by land line and telephone to a field HQ. Lord Methuen, for example, was informed by aerial reconnaissance that a perceived 1,500-yard gap in the Boer line at Magersfontein had been rapidly closed and no longer offered an opportunity for one of his brigades to slip through.

Chocolates for Victoria's Heroes

Queen Victoria sent every soldier at the front a red and gold tin box of chocolates, insisting that her gift was to go only to soldiers – any 'overs' were to be destroyed. Some soldiers sent theirs home unopened to be kept as mementoes, but Private Tucker ate his chocolate first:

[When] we received the Queen's gift of chocolate, which we had been anxiously awaiting . . . such a cheer went up that the Boers must have thought we had taken leave of our senses and gone mad. That night I had a meal of chocolate, biscuits and water. After the meal I slept soundly with the chocolate box forming part of my pillow . . . I carried it [the empty tin] during all the fighting my regiment was involved in until I had a chance to send it to England. I fear the box got a few knocks but it still remains the Queen's gift and much cherished.

Guerrilla Warfare

By July 1900 all formal resistance by the Boers had ended, and in September the Transvaal was annexed to the British Empire. But even so the war was by no means over; for the next eighteen months guerrilla forces led by Generals Louis Botha, Christiaan de Wet and John De La Rey conducted unceasing raids on British columns and lines of communication, and resisted

all efforts to capture them. Kitchener, who had taken over from Lord Roberts, adopted a series of extremely harsh measures – described by his and his government's opponents as 'methods of barbarism'. Hundreds of farms, on which the commandos depended, were burned to the ground, and the women and children living on them were gathered into refugee camps (which were given the ominous name of 'concentration camps') to save them from having to wander about the veld, exposed to all its dangers. A chain of 8,000 garrisoned blockhouses was built, linked by barbed wired fencing. The system covered about 4,000 miles and was designed to keep the commandos from crossing and recrossing the two former Boer republics. Finally, Kitchener ordered columns of mounted troops – some of them 50 miles long – to sweep the country, and mop up the Boer commandos. These ruthless measures drove the Boer leaders to capitulate, and on 31 May 1902 they signed the Treaty of Vereeniging by which they accepted British sovereignty. Eight years later the Union of South Africa was proclaimed in Cape Town.

Victory at Paardeberg

AFTER 'BLACK' WEEK Buller was replaced by Roberts as Commander-in-Chief, but remained in charge of the army in Natal. The immediate reason why he was replaced was his cable to the government saying 'My view is that I ought to let Ladysmith go.' So it seems extraordinary that the day after Colenso, and even before he left for Cape Town, Roberts advised the government that Kimberley, Mafeking and Ladysmith ought not to have been held, and though the first two 'being left to their fate now would be deeply regretted it seems unavoidable.' Meanwhile, in Natal, Buller 'should be ordered to act strictly on the defensive.'

Roberts and Kitchener arrived in Cape Town on 10 January 1900 with a completely new strategy, approved by the War Office, and backed by heavy reinforcements. These included three divisions of the Regular army, the newly raised Imperial Yeomanry, and fresh bodies of mounted troops from the colonies. In all, they had about 40,000 men, including a complete cavalry division and one hundred guns. The new plan of attack was to assemble an Army Corps on the Modder River, advance northwards, outflanking the Boer General Piet Cronje's commandos based at Magersfontein, and invade the two Boer republics with overwhelming force. General Buller was instructed to remain on the defensive in Natal, but when nevertheless he made a fresh attempt to relieve Ladysmith, he was told that speed was essential.

Meanwhile Roberts and Kitchener reorganised the British forces, replacing unsuccessful generals, ineffective brigadiers and incompetent colonels, removing army transport from regimental to central control (which, in the event, caused both confusion and resentment in the field), and reinforcing the artillery and cavalry arms.

Elaborate methods of deception were used to mislead the Boers waiting at Magersfontein as to the direction of the coming attack. Cables giving incorrect information were sent 'in clear' for the benefit of Boer informers. Phoney battle orders

were leaked to spies, and a newspaper correspondent was fed with a false news story, 'in strict confidence' – which, as intended, he promptly published in a London newspaper for the Boers to read. Only when British artillery was raining lyddite shells into his trenches at Magersfontein, and when French's cavalry had broken through his lines on their way to Kimberley, did Cronje realise that Roberts's huge army was between him and the Transvaal. At first stunned into inaction, he recovered himself and ordered a general withdrawal. On 17 February his forces arrived at Paardeberg Drift on the Modder River. Here the British caught up with them, and Kitchener – who was temporarily in command while Roberts was suffering from a chill – decided on an immediate frontal attack on Cronje's laager, which was entrenched in a sunken river bed.

The attack began at 7.00 am on 18 February. Kitchener looked at his watch and said to some of his officers: 'It is now seven o'clock. We shall be in the laager by half-past ten . . .', adding that he would then send Sir John French and his cavalry straight on to Bloemfontein. When night fell the Boers were still in the laager, and the British had lost 1,262 men killed and wounded. But Cronje and his men were trapped, with only twenty horses and no trek oxen left alive. The next day Roberts, having recovered from his chill, decided not to risk more losses, but to wait for Cronje to surrender. For ten more days the Boers suffered bombardment by shrapnel and lyddite shells, with no means of hitting back until on 27 February ('Majuba Day') Cronje sent a message with a white flag. With Cronje 4,000 of his men were made prisoners of war.

The Boer commandos were now, in the words of one of their generals, 'a disorderly crowd of terrified men flying before the enemy.' On 13 March Roberts entered Bloemfontein. In just over two months the British position in the war had been transformed from depression and defeat to triumph. Kimberley and Ladysmith had been relieved, Cronje and his army captured, the Orange Free State occupied, and the Boers chased out of Cape Colony. Two months later Mafeking was relieved (17 May), and at the same time Buller broke down the last Boer resistance in Natal. In May and June Roberts led his army into the Transvaal and captured Johannesberg (31 May), then Pretoria, capital of the Transvaal (5 June). All Boer resistance came to an end when Roberts and Buller joined forces at Vlakfontein on 5 June.

179

'Little Bobs'

Lord Roberts of Kandahar

Lord Roberts, with Lord Kitchener at his side, leads his men across the Vaal River

LIKE MANY another British military hero, from Wellington to Montgomery, Field-Marshal Earl Roberts of Kandahar VC, KG, CH etc, came from an Anglo-Irish family. The son of General Abraham Roberts of the Bengal army, he was born in Cawnpore in 1832. Educated at Eton and at the Addiscombe college of the East India Company, he returned to India in 1852 as a cadet in the Bengal Artillery and A.D.C. to his father. He spent the next forty-one years in India, ending a brilliant career as Commander-in-Chief, first of the Indian and later of the British Army. Probably the most consistently successful of all Victorian generals, he was certainly the most popular: all ranks loved 'Little Bobs'.

Small of stature, with delicate health and impaired vision in one eye, Frederick Sleigh Roberts would almost certainly have failed a modern army's medical examination, but what he lacked in inches and health he made up for in courage and dash. Like most Victorian officers, he had a great zest for action and excitement, and he never hesitated to face the most withering enemy fire or hand-to-hand combat against odds. An act of spectacular bravery won him the VC during the Indian Mutiny: while fighting a group of mutineers who had seized the regimental colours, he saved the life of a loyal *sowar*, pursued and cut down two of the mutineers, and recaptured the colours.

At the start of the Mutiny he had been appointed staff officer with the famous Movable Column, formed by such able officers as John Nicholson and Neville Chamberlain. He fought at the siege of Delhi, where he received his first wound, and at Cawnpore and Lucknow. Exhausted after the Mutiny, his never robust health broke down, and he was sent back to England to rest.

Roberts served with distinction in many of the colonial wars of the reign, slowly climbing the promotion ladder. In the Ambela Campaign of 1863, as an ADC to the C-in-C he was one of the two British officers present when the Bunervals undertook the destruction of the Hindustani Fanatics' village. The officers and their escort of Guides cavalry and Bunerval tribesmen, as he said, 'found themselves in the presence of strong tribes, certainly not over well pleased with their visitors, or the errand on which they had come.' On the way back after burning the village, they were surrounded and threatened by furious Pathans. They were saved by an old Bunerval chief, who called out to the angry tribesmen: 'You can, of course, murder these English and their escort; but if you do you must kill us Bunervals first, for we have sworn to protect them with our lives.'

Roberts served under Napier in Abyssinia, but to his disgust he found himself in charge of disembarking men and stores at the Red Sea invasion port, and saw no action. His well-publicised march from Kabul to Kandahar during the 2nd Afghan War made him a national

hero. After the disaster at Majuba Hill in 1881 the War Office sent him out to take charge of the Transvaal war, but by the time he reached Cape Town peace had been made, and he returned immediately.

The greatest moment in his life came when, at his own prompting, he was chosen to take command in South Africa. He found himself leading Britain's biggest-ever army, and he was successful almost immediately. Only a few weeks after landing in South Africa on 10 January 1900, he had relieved Kimberley. 'It is a great feat to have accomplished,' declared the *Daily Mail*, 'and the happiest omens for the future. There is no one like Bobs!' Two weeks later he marked the anniversary of Majuba Hill by capturing 4,000 Boers and their leader Piet Cronje, and on 10 March he led his troops into Bloemfontein, the capital of the Orange Free State. Pretoria fell to him on 5 June 1900.

In December of that year Lord Roberts was appointed Commander-in-Chief in succession to Lord Wolseley, a post he held until it was abolished in 1904. His interest in military affairs, however, and in the welfare of the serving soldier remained undimmed. After the outbreak of the First World War, he went to France where he inspected Indian troops on the Western Front. It was during this visit he caught a chill and died, at the age of 82.

The Boxer Rebellion

Events in China as well as in South Africa, cast a shadow over the last months of the Queen's reign. Bands of fanatical nationalists calling themselves Boxers, whose aim was to expel all foreigners, attacked and murdered many European residents, including diplomats, Christian missionaries and their converts. They were secretly backed by the Manchu dynasty and the government.

Early in June 1900 the Boxers seized Pekin, murdered the German Minister, and besieged the Legation Quarter, with its 11 foreign missions. Over 2,000 men, women and children of various nationalities were trapped in the area. A multi-national garrison of about 500 guards and volunteers, commanded by the British Minister, Sir Claude MacDonald, held out for 55 days against constant heavy fire.

It took an initial relief force of sailors and marines from the British, American, French, Russian, Austrian and Japanese navies, supported by international contingents of infantry, cavalry and artillery, several months of heavy fighting to force the Chinese to capitulate, and to rescue the besieged foreign missions.

A Final Tribute

On 2 January 1901 Roberts was invited to attend Her Majesty at Osborne. She gives this account of the visit in her Journal:

'I received him most warmly, and he knelt down and kissed my hand . . . Lord Roberts spoke of officers who had not done well, and of others who had done excellently; also of all the difficulties our army had had to contend with . . . I then gave [him] the Garter, which quite overcame him, and he said it was too much. I also told him I was going to confer an earldom on him, with the remainder to his daughter . . .'

Lord Roberts, in fact, was the last of a long line of heroes to be honoured by his sovereign, for three weeks later Queen Victoria was dead.

Appendix 1

Cavalry regiments, Corps and Infantry regiments, listed in order of precedence, show the composition of the British and Indian armies at the end of Queen Victoria's reign. Details of home depots (not available or relevant in some cases) refer to the year 1900/1901.

BRITISH ARMY

Cavalry

Raised		Depot
1660	1st Life Guards and 2nd Life Guards	Birdcage Walk, London
1661	Royal Horse Guards (The Blues)	Birdcage Walk, London
1685	1st (King's) Dragoon Guards	
	2nd Dragoon Guards (Queen's Bays)	Edinburgh, Scotland
	3rd (Prince of Wales's) Dragoon Guards	Shorncliffe
	4th (Royal Irish) Dragoon Guards	
	5th (Princess Charlotte of Wales's) Dragoon Guards	Canterbury
	6th Dragoon Guards (The Carbiniers)	
	7th (Princess Royal's) Dragoon Guards	Aldershot
1661	1st (Royal) Dragoons	
1678	2nd Dragoons (Royal Scots Greys)	Winchester
1685	3rd (King's Own) Hussars	
	4th (Queen's Own) Hussars	
1689	5th (Royal Irish) Lancers	
	6th (Inniskilling) Dragoons	
1690	7th (Queen's Own) Hussars	Aldershot
1693	8th (King's Royal Irish) Hussars	
1715	9th (Queen's Royal) Lancers	
	10th (Prince of Wales's Own Royal) Hussars	Woolwich
	11th (Prince Albert's Own) Hussars	Canterbury
	12th (Prince of Wales's Royal) Lancers	Colchester
	13th Hussars	Norwich
	14th (King's) Hussars	Curragh
1759	15th (The King's) Hussars	
	16th (The Queen's) Lancers	
	17th (Duke of Cambridge's Own) Lancers	
	18th (Queen Mary's Own) Hussars	Canterbury
1858	19th (Queen Alexandra's Own Royal) Hussars	Canterbury
	20th Hussars	Canterbury
	21st (Empress of India's) Lancers	

Corps

1793	Royal Horse Artillery	Woolwich
1716	Royal Field Artillery	Woolwich
	Royal Garrison Artillery	Woolwich
1717	Corps of Royal Engineers	Chatham
1888	Army Service Corps	Aldershot
1898	Army Medical Corps	Frimley
1877	Corps of Military Police	Chichester
1878	Army Pay Corps	
1881	Army Veterinary Corps	Victoria St, London SW1

Infantry

1660	Grenadier Guards 3rd Bn	Horse Guards, Whitehall
1650	Coldstream Guards	Horse Guards, Whitehall
1660	Scots Guards	Horse Guards, Whitehall
1900	Irish Guards	St George's Barracks, Charing X
1633	The Royal Scots 1st Foot	Glencorse, Scotland
1661	The Queen's (Royal West Surrey Regt) 2nd	Guildford
1665	The Buffs (East Kent Regt) 3rd (Raised 1572 The Holland Regt)	Canterbury
1680	The King's Own Royal Regt 4th (Raised 2nd Tangier Regt)	Lancaster

Raised		Depot
1674	The Royal Northumberland 5th Fusiliers (Raised 1673 The Holland Regt)	Newcastle-on-Tyne
1688	The Royal Warwickshire 6th Regt (Raised 1673 The Holland Regt)	Warwick
1685	The Royal Fusiliers 7th	Hounslow
	The King's Regt 8th	Warrington
	The Royal Norfolk Regt 9th	Norwich
	The Royal Lincolnshire 10th Regt	Lincoln
	The Devonshire Regt 11th	Exeter
	The Suffolk Regt 12th	Bury St Edmunds
	The Somerset Light Infantry 13th	Taunton
	The West Yorkshire Regt 14th	York
	The East Yorkshire Regt 15th	Beverley
	The Bedfordshire and 16th Hertfordshire Regt	Bedford
	The Royal Leicestershire 17th Regt	Leicester
1683	The Royal Irish Regt 18th	Clonmel, Ireland
1688	The Green Howards 19th	Richmond
	The Lancashire Fusiliers 20th	Bury
1678	Royal Scots Fusiliers 21st	Ayr, Scotland
1689	The Cheshire Regt 22nd	Chester
	Royal Welch Fusiliers 23rd	Wrexham, Wales
	The South Wales Borderers 24th	Brecon, Wales
	The King's Own Scottish Borderers 25th	Berwick-on-Tweed
1794	The Cameronians 26th (Scottish Rifles) 90th	Hamilton, Scotland
1689	Royal Inniskilling Fusiliers 27th	Omagh, Co Tyrone
1861	Royal Inniskilling Fusiliers 108th	
1694-28	The Gloucesterhire Regt 28th	Bristol
1758	The Gloucestershire Regt 61st	
1694	The Worcestershire Regt 29th	Worcester
1701	The Worcestershire Regt 36th	
1702	The East Lancashire Regt 30th	Preston
1755	The East Lancashire Regt 59th	
1702	The East Surrey Regt 31st	Kingston-on-Thames
1758	The East Surrey Regt 70th	
1702	The Duke of Cornwall's Light Infantry 32nd	Bodmin
1741	The Duke of Cornwall's Light Infantry 46th	
1702	The Duke of Wellington's Regt 33rd	Halifax
1787	The Duke of Wellington's Regt 76th	
1702	The Border Regt 34th	Carlisle
1755	The Border Regt 55th	
1701	The Royal Sussex Regt 35th	Chichester
1854	The Royal Sussex Regt 107th	
1702	The Royal Hampshire Regt 37th	Winchester
1758	The Royal Hampshire Regt 67th	
1702	The South Staffordshire Regt 38th	Lichfield, Staffordshire
1793	The South Staffordshire Regt 80th	
1702	The Dorset Regt 39th	Dorchester
1755	The Dorset Regt 54th	
1717	The South Lancashire Regt Prince of Wales Volunteers 40th	Warrington
1793	The South Lancashire Regt Prince of Wales Volunteers 82nd	
1719	The Welch Regt 41st	Cardiff, Wales
1758	The Welch Regt 69th	
1730	The Black Watch 42nd	Perth, Scotland
1780	The Black Watch 73rd	
1741	The Oxfordshire & Buckinghamshire Light Infantry 43rd	Oxford
1755	The Oxfordshire & Buckinghamshire Light Infantry 52nd	
1741	The Essex Regt 44th	Warley
1755	The Essex Regt 56th	
1741	The Sherwood Foresters 45th	Derby
1832	The Sherwood Foresters 95th	
1741	The Loyal Regt 47th	Preston
1793	The Loyal Regt 81st	
1741	The Northamptonshire Regt 48th	Northampton
1755	The Northamptonshire Regt 58th	
1743	The Royal Berkshire Regt 49th	Reading
1758	The Royal Berkshire Regt 66th	

Raised		Depot
1755	The Queen's Own Royal West Kent Regt 50th	Maidstone
1824	The Queen's Own Royal West Kent Regt 97th	
1755	The King's Own Yorkshire Light Infantry 51st	Pontefract
1839	The King's Own Yorkshire Light Infantry 105th	
1755	The King's Shropshire Light Infantry 53rd	Shrewsbury
1793	The King's Shropshire Light Infantry 85th	
1755	The Middlesex Regt 57th	Hounslow
1787	The Middlesex Regt 77th	
1755	The King's Royal Rifle Corps 60th	Gosport (temp) and Winchester
1758	The Wiltshire Regt 62nd	Devizes
1824	The Wiltshire Regt 99th	
1758	The Manchester Regt 63rd	Ashton-under-Lyne
1824	The Manchester Regt 96th	
1758	The North Staffordshire Regt 64th	Lichfield
1824	The North Staffordshire Regt 98th	
1758	The York and Lancaster Regt 65th	Pontefract, Yorkshire
1793	The York and Lancaster Regt 84th	
1758	The Durham Light Infantry 68th	Newcastle-upon-Tyne
1839	The Durham Light Infantry 106th	
1777	The Highland Light Infantry 71st	Hamilton, Scotland
1787	The Highland Light Infantry 74th	
1777	Seaforth Highlanders 72nd	Fort George, Inverness-shire
1793	Seaforth Highlanders 78th	
1787	The Gordon Highlanders 75th	Aberdeen, Scotland
1794	The Gordon Highlanders 92nd	
1793	The Queen's Own Cameron Highlanders 79th (2nd Bn 1897)	Inverness, Scotland
	The Royal Ulster Rifles (late Royal Irish Rifles) 83rd	Belfast, Ireland
	The Royal Ulster Rifles (late Royal Irish Rifles) 86th	
	Royal Irish Fusiliers 87th	Armagh, Ireland
	Royal irish Fusiliers 89th	
	The Connaught Rangers 88th	Galway, Ireland
1823	The Connaught Rangers 94th	
1794	The Argyll and Sutherland Highlanders 91st	Stirling, Scotland
1800	The Argyll and Sutherland Highlanders 93rd	
1858	The Leinster Regt 100th (Canada) disbanded 31/7/1922	Birr, Ireland
1853	The Leinster Regt 109th (India) disbanded 31/7/1922	
1756	The Royal Munster Fusiliers 101st disbanded 31/7/1922	Tralee, Ireland
1839	The Royal Munster Fusiliers 104th disbanded 31/7/1922	
1748	The Royal Dublin Fusiliers 102nd (India) disbanded 31/7/1922	Naas, Ireland
1661	The Royal Dublin Fusiliers 103rd (Bombay) disbanded 31/7/1922	
1800	The Rifle Bigade	Gosport (temp) and Winchester

INDIAN ARMY

Bengal

Raised		Depot
1773	Governor-General's Body Guard	Dehra Dun
1803	1st Regiment of Bengal Lancers	Lucknow
1809	2nd Regiment of Bengal Lancers	Jullundur
1814	3rd Regiment of Bengal Lancers	Meerut
1840	4th Regiment of Bengal Lancers	Saugor
1841	5th Regiment of Bengal Lancers	Cawnpore
1842	6th (Prince of Wales) Regiment of Bengal Cavalry	Nowgong
1846	7th Regiment of Bengal Cavalry	Fyzabad
	8th Regiment of Bengal Cavalry	Bareilly
1857	9th Regiment of Bengal Lancers	Mooltan
	10th Regiment of Bengal (The Duke of Cambridge's Own) Lancers	Nowshera
	11th (Prince of Wales's Own) Regiment of Bengal Lancers	Jhelum
	12th Regiment of Bengal Cavalry	Peshawar

Raised		Depot
1858	13th (The Duke of Connaught's) Regiment of Bengal Lancers	Rawalpindi
1857	14th Regiment of Bengal Lancers	Allahabad
1858	15th (Cureton's Multani) Regiment of Bengal Lancers	Ferozepore
1857	16th Regiment of Bengal Cavalry (disbanded 1882, re-formed 1885)	Jhelum
1858	17th Regiment of Bengal Cavalry (disbanded 1882, re-formed 1885)	Meean Meer
	18th Regiment of Bengal Lancers	Sialkot
1860	19th Regiment of Bengal Lancers	Loralai
1886	No 7 (Bengal) Mountain Battery	
	No 8 (Bengal) Mountain Battery	
1899	No 9 Native Mountain Battery	
1803	Corps of Bengal Sappers and Miners	Roorkee
1776	1st Regiment of Bengal Infantry	Jhansi
1798	2nd (The Queen's Own) Regiment of Bengal (Light) Infantry	Agra
	3rd Regiment of Bengal Infantry	Allahabad
	4th (Prince Albert Victor's) Regiment of Bengal Infantry	Agra
1803	5th Regiment of Bengal (Light) Infantry	Bareilly
	6th Regiment of Bengal (Light) Infantry	Fyzabad
1804	7th (The Duke of Connaught's Own) Regiment of Bengal Infantry	Lucknow
1814	8th Regiment of Bengal Infantry	Lucknow
1823	9th Gurkha (Rifle) Regiment of Bengal Infantry	Lansdowne
	10th Regiment of Bengal Infantry	Meerut
1825	11th Regiment of Bengal Infantry	Lucknow
1838	12th (The Kelta-i-Ghilzai) Regiment of Bengal Infantry	Bareilly
1835	13th (The Shekhawati) Regiment of Bengal Infantry	Meerut
1846	14th (The Ferozepore Sikh) Regiment of Bengal Infantry	Mooltan
	15th (The Ludhiana Sikh) Regiment of Bengal Infantry	Mooltan
1857	16th (The Lucknow) Regiment of Bengal Infantry	Agra
1858	17th (The Loyal Purbiya) Regiment of Bengal Infantry	Benares
1795	18th Regiment of Bengal Infantry	Benares
1857	19th (Punjab) Regiment of Bengal Infantry	Jhelum
	20th (Duke of Cambridge's Own Punjab) Regiment of Bengal Infantry	Meean Meer
	21st (Punjab) Regiment of Bengal Infantry	Meean Meer
	22nd (Punjab) Regiment of Bengal Infantry	Jhelum
	23rd (Punjab) Regiment of Bengal Infantry (Pioneers)	Umballa
	24th (Punjab) Regiment of Bengal Infantry	Rawalpindi
	25th (Punjab) Regiment of Bengal Infantry	Jhelum
	26th (Punjab) Regiment of Bengal Infantry	Meean Meer
	27th (Punjab) Regiment of Bengal Infantry	Ferozepore
	28th (Punjab) Regiment of Bengal Infantry	Ferozepore
	29th (Punjab) Regiment of Bengal Infantry	Peshawar
	30th (Punjab) Regiment of Bengal Infantry	Peshawar
	31st (Punjab) Regiment of Bengal Infantry	Peshawar
	32nd (Punjab) Regiment of Bengal Infantry (Pioneers)	Umballa
	33rd (Punjabi Mohomedan) Regiment of Bengal Infantry (became Punjabi Mohomedan in 1891)	Ferozepore
	34th (Punjab) Regiment of Bengal Infantry (Pioneers) (disbanded 1882, re-formed 1887)	Umballa
1858	35th (Sikh) Regiment of Bengal Infantry (disbanded 1882, re-formed 1887)	Rawalpindi
	36th (Sikh) Regiment of Bengal Infantry (disbanded 1882, re-formed 1887)	Rawalpindi

Raised	Regiment	Depot
	37th (Dogra) Regiment of Bengal Infantry (disbanded 1882, re-formed 1887)	Rawalpindi
	38th (Dogra) Regiment of Bengal Infantry (became 38 Dogras in 1891)	Rawalpindi
1887	39th (The Garwhal Rifle) Regiment of Bengal Infantry (retitled in 1891)	Lansdowne
1858	40th (Pathan) Regiment of Bengal Infantry (retitled in 1891)	Meean Meer
1835	43rd Gurkha (Rifle) Regiment of Bengal Infantry	Shillong
1824	44th Gurkha (Rifle) Regiment of Bengal Infantry	Shillong
1856	45th (Rattray's Sikh) Regiment of Bengal Infantry	Mooltan

Gurkhas

Raised	Regiment	Depot
1815/86	1st Gurkha (Rifle) Regiment	Dharmsala
1815/86	2nd (Prince of Wales' Own) Gurkha (Rifle) Regiment (The Sirmoor Rifles)	Dehra Dun
1815/91	3rd Gurkha (Rifle) Regiment	Almora/Lansdowne
1857/56	4th Gurkha (Rifle) Regiment	Bakloh
1858/86	5th Gurkha (Rifle) Regiment	Abbottabad
1817	42nd Gurkha (Rifle) Regiment	Abbottabad

Punjab Frontier Force

Raised	Regiment	Depot
1849	1st (Prince Albert Victor's Own) Regiment of Punjab Cavalry	Kohat
	2nd Regiment of Punjab Cavalry	Edwardesbad
	3rd Regiment of Punjab Cavalry	Kohat
	5th Regiment of Punjab Cavalry	Dera Ismail Khan
1846	(The Queen's Own) Corps of Guides (Cavalry and Infantry)	Mardan
1851	No 1 (Kohat) Mountain Battery	
	No 2 (Derajat) Mountain Battery	
	No 3 (Peshawar) Mountain Battery	
	No 4 (Hazara) Mountain Battery	
	The Punjab Garrison Battery	
1846	1st Regiment of Sikh Infantry	Kohat
	2nd (or Hill) Regiment of Sikh Infantry	Edwardesbad
1847	3rd Regiment of Sikh Infantry	Edwardesbad
	4th Regiment of Sikh Infantry	Edwardesbad
1849	1st Regiment of Punjab Infantry	Dera Ismail Khan
	2nd Regiment of Punjab Infantry	Kohat
	4th Regiment of Punjab Infantry	Dera Ismail Khan
	5th Regiment of Punjab Infantry	Dera Ismail Khan
	6th Regiment of Punjab Infantry	Kohat

Madras

Raised	Regiment	Depot
1897	Governor's Body Guard	Madras
1787	1st Regiment of Madras Lancers (as 5th Regiment)	Bellary
1784	2nd Regiment of Madras Lancers (as 3rd Regiment)	Bangalore
	3rd Regiment of Madras Lancers (as 2nd Regiment)	Secunderabad
1865	Queen's Own Madras Sappers and Miners	Bangalore
1758	1st Regiment of Madras Infantry (Pioneers)	Bangalore
1759	2nd Regiment of Madras Infantry	Secunderabad
	3rd (or Palamcottah) Regiment of Madras (Light) Infantry	Secunderabad
	4th Regiment of Madras Infantry (Pioneers)	Bangalore
	5th Regiment of Madras Infantry	Madras
1761	6th Regiment of Madras Infantry	Bellary
	7th Regiment of Madras Infantry	Belgaum
	8th Regiment of Madras Infantry	Bangalore
1765	9th Regiment of Madras Infantry	Madras
1766	10th Regiment (1st Burma-Gurkha Rifles) of Madras Infantry	
1767	11th Regiment of Madras Infantry	Madras
	12th Regiment (2nd Burma Battalion) of Madras Infantry	Mandalay (Burma)
1776	13th Regiment of Madras Infantry	St Thomas' Mount
	14th Regiment of Madras Infantry	Bellary
	15th Regiment of Madras Infantry	Secunderabad
	16th Regiment of Madras Infantry	Madras
1777	17th Regiment of Madras Infantry	Bangalore
	19th Regiment of Madras Infantry	Belgaum
	20th Regiment of Madras Infantry	St Thomas' Mount
1786	21st Regiment of Madras Infantry (Pioneers)	Bangalore
1794	22nd Regiment of Madras Infantry	St Thomas' Mount
	23rd (or Wallajahbad) Regiment of Madras Infantry	Trichinopoly
	24th Regiment of Madras Infantry	Belgaum
	25th Regiment of Madras Infantry	Bangalore
	26th Regiment of Madras Infantry	Secunderabad
1798	27th Regiment of Madras Infantry	Madras
	28th Regiment of Madras Infantry	Madras
	29th Regiment (7th Burma Battalion) of Madras Infantry	Meiktila (Burma)
1799	30th Regiment (5th Burma Battalion) of Madras Infantry	Meiktila
1800	31st Regiment (6th Burma Battalion) of Madras (Light) Infantry	Meiktila
	32nd Regiment (4th Burma Battalion) of Madras Infantry	Mandalay
	33rd Regiment (3rd Burma Battalion) of Madras Infantry	Mandalay

Bombay

Raised	Regiment	Depot
1865	Governor's Body Guard	Ganesh-Khind
1817	The 1st (Duke of Connaught's Own) Regiment of Bombay Lancers	Poona
	2nd Regiment of Bombay Lancers	Deesa
1820	3rd (Queen's Own) Regiment of Bombay Light Cavalry	Neemuch
1817	4th (Prince Albert Victor's Own) Regiment of Bombay Cavalry (Poona Horse)	Neemuch
1830	5th Regiment of Bombay Cavalry (Sindh Horse)	Jacobabad
1846	6th Regiment of Bombay Cavalry (Jacob's Horse)	Quetta
1885	7th Regiment of Bombay Lancers (Belooch Horse)	Jacobabad
1867	Aden Troop	
	No 5 (Bombay) Mountain Battery	
	No 6 (Bombay) Mountain Battery	
	Corps of Bombay Sappers and Miners	Kirkee
1779	1st Regiment of Bombay Infantry (Grenadiers)	Ahmednagar
1796	2nd (Prince of Wales' Own) Regiment of Bombay Infantry (Grenadiers)	Deesa
1768	3rd Regiment of Bombay (Light) Infantry	Satara
1788	4th Regiment of Bombay Infantry	Nasirabad
	5th Regiment of Bombay (Light) Infantry	Satara
	7th Regiment of Bombay Infantry	Mhow
1768	8th Regiment of Bombay Infantry	Ahmednagar
1788	9th Regiment of Bombay Infantry	Ahmednagar
1797	10th Regiment of Bombay (Light) Infantry	Satara
1798	12th Regiment of Bombay Infantry	Deesa
1800	13th Regiment of Bombay Infantry	Deesa
	14th Regiment of Bombay Infantry	Poona
	16th Regiment of Bombay Infantry	Poona
	17th Regiment of Bombay Infantry	Poona

Raised		Depot
1817	19th Regiment of Bombay Infantry	Mhow
	20th Regiment of Bombay Infantry	Mhow
1777	21st Regiment of Bombay Infantry (Marine Battalion)	Bombay
1818	22nd Regiment of Bombay Infantry	Mhow
1820	23rd Regiment of Bombay Infantry	Nasirabad
	24th (Baluchistan; Duchess of Connaught's Own) Regiment of Bombay Infantry	Quetta
	25th Regiment of Bombay Infantry	Nasirabad
1825	26th (Baluchistan) Regiment of Bombay Infantry	Quetta
1844	27th Regiment (1st Baluch Battalion) of Bombay (Light) Infantry	Karachi
1846	28th Regiment of Bombay Infantry (Pioneers)	Kirkee
	29th (The Duke of Connaught's Own) Regiment of Bombay Infantry (2nd Baluch Battalion)	Karachi

Raised		Depot
1858	30th Regiment of Bombay Infantry (3rd Baluch Battalion)	Karachi

Corps

Raised		Depot
1860	Central India Horse (1st and 2nd Regiments)	Goona
1840	Malwa Bhil Corps	Sindapore
1859	Bhopal Battalion	Sehore
1857	Deoli Irregular Force (Cavalry and Infantry)	Deoli
1860	Erinpura Irregular Force (Cavalry and Infantry)	Erinpura
1840	Meywar Bhil Corps	Kherwara
1822	Merwara Battalion	Ajmere

The Hyderabad Contingent, raised in 1792 and reorganised in 1853, also came under the orders of the Government of India. It comprised four Regiments of Lancers, four Field Batteries and six Regiments of Infantry.

Appendix 2

CAMPAIGN CHRONOLOGY

There was scarcely a year of Victoria's reign when her armed forces were not in action somewhere in the world, and the following list of wars, campaigns, expeditions and operations, large and small, does not claim to be complete. The spelling of place names follows contemporary usage.

*An asterisk indicates the award of a campaign medal, clasp or star.

1837	Uprising in Canara, India
	Coorg 1837*
1837-38	Rebellion in Toronto, Canada
	Operations in the Persian Gulf
	Campaign in Kurnool, India
	Capture of Aden
	Campaign in Jodhpur, India
1839-42	First Afghan War
1839	Storming of Ghuznee
1841-42	Candahar*, Ghuznee*, Cabul*
	Siege of Jellalabad*
1842	Defence of Kelat-I-Ghilzee*
1842	Retreat from Cabul
	Recapture of Cabul
1840	Defence of Aden*
	Bombardment of Acre
	Kohistan Expedition, India
	Marri War, Scinde, India
1840-41	Syrian Expedition
1840-42	First China War*
1841	Zurmat Expedition, Afghanistan
	Shahjehanpore Expedition, India
1842	Arakan Frontier Expedition, India
	Shinwari Expedition, India
	Pirara Expedition, Guiana
	Occupation of Natal, South Africa
1842-43	Saugor and Nerbudda Operations, India
1843	Conquest of Scinde, India*
	Battles of Meanee* and Hyderabad*
	Gwalior Campaign, India*
	Battles of Maharajpur and Punniar
	Malabar Uprising, India
	First Expedition against Borneo pirates
	Rebecca Riots in Wales
1844-45	Mahratta War, India

1845	First Orange Free State Expedition, South Africa
	Second Borneo Expedition
	Intervention in Argentina
1845-46	First Sikh War – Sutlej Campaign*
	Battles of Mudkee*, Ferozesuhur*. Aliwal*, Sobraon*
1845-48	Maori Wars, New Zealand
1846	Siege of Aden
1846-47	Seventh Kaffir War, South Africa*
1847	Bogue Forts, China
	Swat Valley Expedition, North-West Frontier, India
1848	Sherbo River Expedition, Sierra Leone
	Second Orange Free State Expedition, South Africa
	Gold Coast Expedition, West Africa
	Uprising in Ceylon
1848-49	Second Sikh War – Punjab Campaign*
	Battles of Mooltan*, Chilianwala*, Goojerat*
1849-50	Kohat Expedition, NWF
	Sanghao/Yusufzai Expedition, NWF
	Mutiny of 66th N.I. Regt, India
1850-53	Eighth Kaffir War, South Africa*
1851	First Umarzai Waziris Campaign, NWF
	Capture of Lagos, West Africa
1852	First and Second Mohmand Expeditions, NWF*
	Basuto War, South Africa
1851-53	Second Burma War*
	Pegu*
	Black Mountain/Waziris Expedition, NWF
	Hasanzai Expedition*, NWF India
1852	The loss of the Birkenhead
	Second Umarzai Campaign, NWF
	Ranizais Expedition, NWF*
	Third Afridi Campaign, NWF*
1853	Kasranis Expedition, NWF*
	Shiranis Expedition, NWF*
	Bori Afridis Expedition, NWF*
1854	Third Mohmand Expedition, NWF*
	Uprising in Bassein, Burma
	Operation at Christenborg, Gold Coast, West Africa
	Singapore Chinese Riots
	Eureka Stockade, Australia

1854-56	The Crimean War*
	Alma*, Azoff*, Balaklava*, Inkermann*, Sebastopol*
	The Baltic 1854-1855*
1855	Fourth Afridi Campaign, NWF
	Miranzai Expedition, NWF*
	Orakzais Expedition, NWF
1855-56	Sonthals Uprising, Central India
1856	Kareem Operations, Burma
1856-57	Bushire Expedition, Persia*
	Battle of Mohammerah
1857	Martaban Operations, Shans and Karens, Burma
	Beydur Expedition against Baluchis, India
	Rajamundry Expedition, India
	Yusafzai Expedition, NWF
	Occupation of Perim Is., Aden
1857-59	Indian Mutiny*
	Delhi*, Defence of Lucknow*, Relief of Lucknow*, Lucknow*, Central India*
1857-60	Second China War*
	Fatshan 1857*, Canton 1857*, Taku Forts 1858* and 1860*, Pekin 1860*
1858	Khudu Khel Expedition
	Sittana Expedition, NWF*
1858-59	Great Scarcies River Campaign, Sierra Leone
1859	Bundelcund Campaign, India
	Kabul Khel Waziris Expedition, NWF*
1859-62	Bengal ('White') Mutiny
1860	Mahsud Waziris Expedition, NWF*
1860-61	Baddiboo War, Gambia, West Africa
	Sikkim Expedition, India
	Quiah War, Sierra Leone
1860-66	Maori Uprisings, New Zealand*
1860-72	'The Pig War', British Columbia
1861	Honduras Uprising
	Dahomey Expedition, West Africa
1863	Ambela Campaign, NWF*
	Operations against Malayan pirates
1863-64	First Ashanti War, West Africa
1863-66	Third Maori War, New Zealand
1864	Rodin Operations, Japan
1864-66	Defence of Shabkadar Fort, NWF
	Bhootan Expedition, N.E. Frontier, India*
1865	Freed slaves uprising in Jamaica
	Haitian Operations
1865-66	Mohmands Expedition, NWF
1866	Fenian Raids, Canada*
1867	Honduras Expedition
	Black Mountain Expeditions, NWF
	Little Andaman Island Expedition
	Fenian Troubles, Ireland
1867-68	Abyssinian War*
1868	Bizoti/Black Mountain Expedition, NWF*
	Basuto War, South Africa
	Hazara Expedition, NWF
1869-70	Fenian Raid, Canada*
	Red River Expedition, Canada*
1871-72	Looshai Expedition, N.E. Frontier, India*
1873	Capture of Elmina Castle, Gold Coast
	Bombardment of Omoa, Spanish Honduras
1873-74	Second Ashantee War, West Africa*
	Coomassie*
1874-75	Daffla Expedition, NWF
1875	Naga Hills Expedition, Assam*
	Congo Operation, West Africa
	Griqualand Rebellion, South Africa
1875-76	Mombasa Rebellion, East Africa
	Perak Expedition, Malaya*
1877-78	Ninth Kaffir War
	Jawaki Afridis Expedition, NWF*

1879	Zulu and Basuto War*
	Galekas 1877-78*, Griquas 1878*, Sekukini*, Moirosi*, Zulus 1879*
	Battles of Isandhlwana and Ulundi
	Rorke's Drift
1878	Occupation of Cyprus
	Borneo Operations
	Zakha Khel Afridis Expedition, NWF
1878-79	Naga Expedition, Assam*
	Mohmand Expedition, NWF
1878-80	Second Afghan War*
	Ali Musjid*, Peiwar Kotal*, Charasia*, Kabul*, Ahmed Khel*, Kandahar*,
	Kabul to Kandahar*
	Battle of Maiwand
1879	Transvaal Operation
	Kandahar/Quetta route: Thal-Chotiali Field Force
1879-80	Naga Expedition*, Assam
1880	Marris Expedition
	Mohmand Expedition, NWF
	Malikshahi Waziris Expedition, NWF
1880-81	Transkei Operations, South Africa
	Fifth Basuto War, South Africa*
1881	First Boer War, Natal
	Battle of Majuba Hill
	Mahsud Waziris Expedition, NWF
1882-89	Egypt*
	Alexandria 1882*, Tel-el-Kebir 1882*, El-Teb 1884*, Tamaii 1884*, Suakin 1884*,
	The Nile 1884-85*, Abu Klea 1885*, Gubat 1885, Kirbekan 1884-85*,
	Suakin 1885*, Tofrek 1885*, Gemaizah 1888*, Toski 1889*
1883	Bikaneer Expedition, India
1883-84	Akha Khel Expedition, NWF
	Zhob Valley Expedition, NWF
1885	Bechuanaland Expedition
	General Gordon at Khartoum
	North-West Canada*
	Riel's Rebellion, Saskatchewan*
	Bhutan Expedition, N.E. Frontier, India
1885-87	Third Burma War*
1887-89	Operations against the Yonnie Tribes, West Africa*
	Suppression of banditry in Burma*
1888-89	Black Mountain Expedition: Hazara Field Force*
	Sikkim Expedition, N.E. Frontier, India*
1889	Sierra Leone Operations
1889-90	Chin-Lushai Campaign, Burma*
1889-92	Eleven punitive expeditions in Burma*
	Lushai Expedition, Burma*
1890	Malakand Campaign, NWF
	Mashonaland Expedition, South Africa*
	Expedition against Sultan of Witu, West Africa*
	Somaliland Punitive Expedition
1891	Manipur Expedition, N.E. Frontier, India*
	Hunza-Naga Expedition, NWF*
	Operations in Miranzai Valley and Samana Heights, NWF*
	Hazara Field Force* in the Black Mountains, NWF
1891-92	Isazai Expedition, NWF
	Expedition to Gambia, West Africa*
1892	Expedition against Tambi, Toniataba and the Jebus, West Africa*
1892-93	Operations in Chin Hills, Burma*
	Punitive Expeditions in the Kachin Hills, Burma*
1893	First Matabele War, South Africa*
	Second Expedition against Sultan of Witu*
	Volunteer force against Somalis on Juba River, East Africa*
	Lake Nyassa Expedition, East Africa*
1893-94	Third Ashanti War, West Africa
	Abor Hills Expedition, Assam
	Operations in Sierra Leone and Gambia*
1894	Benin River Expedition, West Africa*
	Naval Brigade in Gambia*

1894-95	Waziristan Expedition★, NWF
	Nikki Expedition, West Africa
1895	Defence of Chitral★, Relief of Chitral★, NWF
	Brass River Campaign★, West Africa
1895-96	Second Matabele War, South Africa
	Fourth Ashanti War, West Africa★
	Mwele Expedition, South Africa
1896	Jameson Raid, South Africa
	Zanzibar Operation
	Matabele and Mashona Revolts in Rhodesia★
1896-97	Re-conquest of the Sudan★
	The Atbara★, Khartoum★, Firket★, Hafir★, Abu Hamed★, Sudan 1897★, Gedaref★, Gedid★, Sudan 1899 etc.
	Battle of Omdurman
	Suppression of revolt in Bechuanaland
1896-98	Punitive expeditions, Northern Territories of the Gold Coast★
1897	Expedition to Western Provinces, Niger★
	Rebellion in Mashonaland, South Africa★
	Punitive column sent to Benin, West Africa★
	Defence of Dawkita, Gold Coast★
	Defence and relief of Chakdara and Malakand, NWF★
	Operations at Samana, NWF★
	Madda Khel/Tochi Valley Expedition, NWF

1897-98	Lagos Frontier Force expedition against Ebos★
	Mohmand and Tirah Forces on Punjab Frontier, NWF★
	Tirah Campaign, NWF★
	Operations in Uganda, East Africa★
1898	Uprising in Crete
1898-99	Expedition in Sierra Leone★
	Operations in Somaliland★
1899	Expeditions in Southern Nigeria★
	Bebejiya Expedition, NWF
	Operations in Uganda★
	Second Boer War★
	Cape Colony★, Natal★, Rhodesia★, Relief of Mafeking★, Defence of Kimberley★, Talana★, Elandslaagte★, Defence of Ladysmith★, Belmont★, Modder River, Tugela Heights★, Relief of Kimberley★, Paaderberg★, Orange Free State★, Relief of Ladysmith★, Driefontein★, Wepener★, Defence of Mafeking★, Transvaal★, Johannesburg★, Laing's Nek★, Diamond Hill★, Wittebergen★, Belfast★, South Africa 1901★, South Africa 1902★, The Mediterranean★
1900	Expedition to Kaduna, Northern Nigeria★
	Boxer Rebellion – Third China War★
	Taku Forts★, Defence of Legations★, Relief of Pekin★
	Operations at Aden
	Rebellion in Borneo
	Fifth Ashanti War, West Africa★
	Defence of Kumassi★

Appendix 3

VICTORIA'S ARMY AND NAVY

	1837/40	*1869/70*	*1900/1*
The Army★			
Strength	129,000	191,000	430,000
Cost	£3,400,000	£13,000,000	£61,500,000

★Until 1858 approx. 20% of the Army's strength and cost was a charge on the East India Company; thereafter the figures for the Army include the British Army in India.

The Militia			
Strength	6,144 (Staff)	129,000	139,000
Cost	n/a	£770,000	£2,288,000
The Yeomanry			
Strength	18,500	17,000	12,000
Cost	£103,000	£89,000	£144,000
Volunteers			
Strength	—	275,000	265,000
Cost	—	£413,000	£1,230,000
Royal Navy			
Ships in commission	239	241	425
Strength	34,000	61,000	119,000
Cost	£5,100,000	£9,551,500	£32,000,000

Figures are based on House of Commons Papers (Army and Navy Estimates and Accounts), and have been rounded.

Bibliography

Ascoli, David *A Companion to the British Army 1660-1983*. Harrap (London) 1983

Bancroft, James W. *Rorke's Drift*. Spellmount Ltd (Tunbridge Wells) 1988

Barnes, R.M. *A History of the Regiments & Uniforms of the British Army*. Seeley Service (London) 1950

Barnes, R.M. *Military Uniforms of Britain and the Empire*. Seeley Service (London) 1960

Barnett, Correlli *Britain and her Army, 1509-1970*. Penguin Books (London) 1970

Barthorp, Michael *The Anglo-Boer Wars*. Blandford (London) 1987

Barthorp, Michael *To face the daring Maoris*. Hodder and Stoughton (London) 1979

Baynham, H. *Before the Mast: Naval Ratings of the 19th Century*. Hutchinson (London) 1971

Beattie, O & Geiger J. *Frozen in Time: The Fate of the Franklin Expedition*. Grafton Books (London) 1989

Bentley, Nicholas (ed.) *Russell's Despatches from the Crimea, 1854-56*. Andre Deutsch (London) 1966

Bowie, John *The Empire at War*. Batsford (London) 1989

Churchill, W.S. *My Early Life*. Fontana/Collins (London) 1959

Churchill, W.S. *The Story of the Malakand Field Force*. Longmans 1898/Mandarin 1989

Clammer, David *The Zulu War*. David & Charles (Newton Abbot) 1973

Cockerill, A.W. *Sons of the Brave*. Leo Cooper (London) 1984

Cook, H.C.B. *Battle Honours of the British and Indian Armies, 1662-1982*. Leo Cooper (London) 1987

Crook, M.J. *The Evolution of the Victoria Cross*. Midas Books (Tunbridge Wells) 1975

Dixon, Conrad *Ships of the Victorian Navy*. Ashford Press (Southampton) 1987

Dupuy and Dupuy *Encyclopedia of Military History*. Jane's (London) 1986

Edwardes, Michael *Battles of the Indian Mutiny*. Batsford, (London) 1963

Ensor, Sir Robert *England 1870-1914*. OUP (Oxford) 1936

Farwell, Byron *Queen Victoria's Little Wars*. Allen Lane (London) 1973

Farwell, Byron *For Queen and Country*. Penguin Books (London) 1981

Farwell, Byron *The Gurkhas*. Allen Lane (London) 1984

Featherstone, Donald *Colonial Small Wars: 1837-1901*. David & Charles (Newton Abbot) 1988

Featherstone, Donald *Victoria's Enemies*. Blandford (London) 1989

Fleming, Peter *The Siege at Peking*. Rupert Hart-Davis (London) 1959

Gordon, L.L. *British Battles and Medals*. Gale and Polden Ltd (Aldershot) 1950

Gould, R.W. *British Campaign Medals*. Arms and Armour Press (London) 1984

Harfield, Alan *The Indian Army of the Empress, 1861-1903*. Spellmount Ltd (Tunbridge Wells) 1990

Heathcote, T.A. *The Afghan Wars 1839-1919*. Osprey (London) 1980

Hibbert, Christopher *The Destruction of Lord Raglan*. Longman Green (London) 1961

Hibbert, Christopher *The Great Mutiny: India 1857*. Penguin Books (London) 1980

Hibbert, Christopher *Queen Victoria in her Letters & Journals*. John Murray (London) 1982

Hopkirk, Peter *The Great Game*. John Murray (London) 1990

Holt, Edgar *The Boer War*. Putnam (London) 1958

Kemp, Peter *The British Sailor*. Dent (London) 1970

Kipling, Rudyard *Barrack-Room Ballads*. Methuen (London) 1892

Laffin, John *Boys in Battle*. Abelard Schumann (London) 1966

McGuffie, T.H. *Rank and File*. Hutchinson (London) 1964

Mileham, P.J.R. *The Yeomanry Regiments*. Spellmount Ltd (Tunbridge Wells) 1985

Markham, George *Guns of the Empire*. Arms & Armour Ltd (London) 1990

Mason, Philip *A Matter of Honour*. Jonathan Cape (London) 1974

Moorehead, Alan *The White Nile*. Hamish Hamilton/Penguin (London) 1963

Myatt, Frederick *The British Infantry, 1660-1945*. Blandford Press Dorset 1983

Nicholson, J.B.R. *The British Army in the Crimea*. Osprey Publishing Ltd (Reading) 1974

Padfield, Peter *Rule Britannia. The Victorian and Edwardian Navy*. Routledge & Kegan Paul (London) 1981

Pakenham, Thomas *The Boer War*. Weidenfeld & Nicholson (London) 1979

Pearman, Sergeant John *Memoirs*. Jonathan Cape (London) 1968

Pearson, Hesketh *The Hero of Delhi*. Penguin Books (London) 1939

Pemberton, W. Baring *Battles of the Boer War*. Batsford (London) 1964

Preston, A. and Major, J. *Send a Gunboat!* Longmans (London) 1967

Register of the Victoria Cross, (Revised Edition). Cheltenham, 1988

Ridley, Jasper *Lord Palmerston*. Constable (London) 1970

Rogers, H.C.B. *Troopships and their History*. Seeley Service (London) 1963

Selby, John *The Boer War*. Arthur Barker (London) 1969

Selby, John *The Thin Red Line of Balaclava*. Hamish Hamilton (London) 1970

Smith, George Loy *A Victorian RSM*. D. J. Costello (Publishers) Ltd (Tunbridge Wells) 1987

Smith, Peter C. *Victoria's Victories*. Spellmount Ltd (Tunbridge Wells) 1987

Smith, Peter C. & Oakley, Derek. *The Royal Marines*. Spellmount Ltd (Tunbridge Wells) 1988

Smyth, Sir John *The Story of the Victoria Cross*. Frederick Muller (London) 1963

Spiers, E.M. *The Army and Society*, 1815-1914. Longmans (London) 1980

Strachan, Hew *From Waterloo to Balaclava. Tactics, Technology and the British Army*. Cambridge U.P. 1985

Strachan, Hew *Wellington's Legacy. The Reform of the British Army, 1830-54*. Manchester University Press 1984

Strachey, Lytton *Eminent Victorians*. Chatto & Windus (London) 1918

Todd, Pamela *Private Tucker's Boer War Diary*. Elm Tree Books 1980

Swinson, Arthur *North-West Frontier*. Hutchinson of London 1967

Wilson, H.W. *With the Flag to Pretoria*. (2 vols) Harmsworth (London) 1901

Winton, J. *Hurrah for the life of a sailor!* Michael Joseph (London) 1977

Woodham-Smith, Cecil *The Reason Why*. Constable (London) 1953

Woodward, Sir Llewellyn *England: The Age of Reform, 1815-70*. 2nd ed OUP (Oxford) 1961

Index

Page numbers in italics refer to illustrations

190

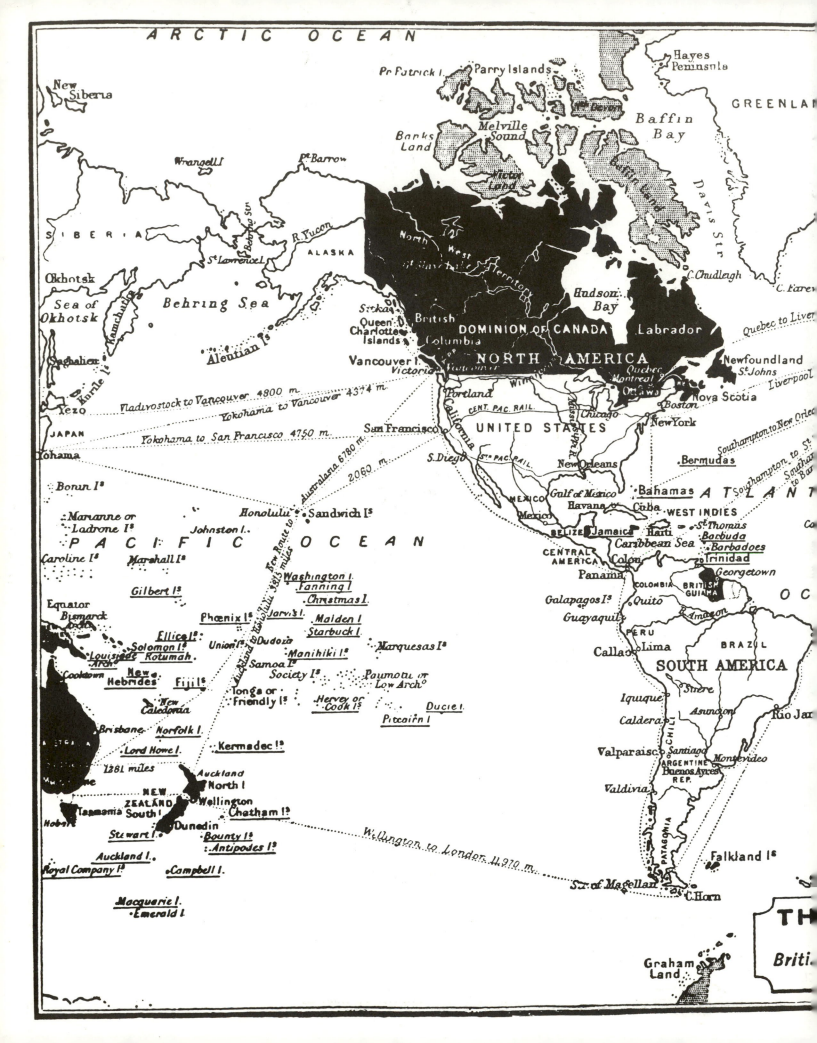